*The Canadian Pacific Railway and the
Development of Western Canada, 1896–1914*

The Canadian Pacific Railway and the Development of Western Canada, 1896–1914

JOHN A. EAGLE

McGill-Queen's University Press
Kingston, Montreal, London

Legal deposit first quarter 1989
Bibliothèque nationale du Québec

Printed in Canada on acid-free paper

This book has been published with the help of a grant
from the Social Science Federation of Canada, using
funds provided by the Social Sciences and Humanities
Research Council of Canada.

Canadian Cataloguing in Publication Data

Eagle, John A. (John Andrew), 1939–
    The Canadian Pacific Railway and the development
of Western Canada : 1896–1914
    Includes bibiographical references and an index.
    ISBN 0-7735-0674-8

    1. Canadian Pacific Railway Company—History.
2. Railroads—Canada, Western—History.   3. Canada,
Western—Economic conditions.   4. Northwest, Canadian—Economic conditions.   I. Title.

HE2810.C2E34   1989   385'.09712   c88-090453-4

But after all, our *great* gold mine is in the prairies
of the North West, and that has been worked this
year with results which are sure to tell on
immigration, for most of the farmers there have
got back from the grain crops and cattle of the
present year all that their lands cost them and all
that they have ever spent on them ...

W.C. Van Horne to Harry Moody,
9 November 1897.

Contents

Tables and Figures   ix

Preface   xi

Acknowledgments   xv

Abbreviations: Railway Titles   xvii

Illustrations   xviii

1 The Canadian Pacific Railway to 1896   3

2 Canadianizing the Kootenays: The Crow's
Nest Pass Agreement of 1897   23

3 Building the Crow's Nest Pass Railway,
1897–9   50

4 The CPR on the Prairies, 1897–1905:
The Start of Competition   69

5 More Competition: The Grand Trunk
Pacific Railway and the Canadian
Northern Railway, 1903–14   88

6 The CPR in British Columbia,
1898–1914   108

7 Serving the Traveller   148

8 Land and Settlement Policies in the Prairie
West   173

9 Urban Policies   213

10 Natural Resource Policies   232

11 The CPR West   258

Notes   265

Index   317

Tables and Figures

TABLES

1 Land Grants to the CPR in the Prairie
   West, 1881–1914   181

2 Location of CPR Main-Line Land Grant in
   1901   183

3 CPR Land Sales in Prairie West, 1896–1914
   (Excluding Townsites)   185

4 Sales of CPR Irrigated Lands,
   1908–14   204

5 Cancelled CPR Land Grants,
   1897–1913 209

6 Land Acquired by the CPR in BC,
   1886–1914   253

FIGURES

1 Railways in the Kootenays, 1900   26

2 Canadian Pacific, 1905   105

3 Canadian Pacific, 1914   106

4 Railways in the Kootenays, 1912 113

5 The Kettle Valley Railway   125

6 Canadian Pacific Land Grants   180

Preface

It is hard to imagine what Western Canada would have been like without the Canadian Pacific Railway (CPR). In 1897 CPR president William Van Horne described the prairie West as "our great gold mine."[1] His successor, Thomas Shaughnessy, adopted policies to develop both this region and British Columbia. The purpose of this book is to examine the manifold activities of the CPR in the prairie West and British Columbia in a critical period of their economic development, and to assess the impact of these policies on those regions. Its underlying theme is that CPR policies were designed to connect the West's economy as closely as possible with that of Central Canada in order to generate increased east-west traffic and to meet competition from the Canadian Northern and Grand Trunk Pacific enterprises. Some policies were intended to produce short-term profits, while others looked to the longer term for profitable results. The study begins in 1896 with the debut of negotiations between the CPR and the Laurier government that one year later produced the historic Crow's Nest Pass Agreement which lowered CPR freight rates in the prairie West, thus greatly assisting the expansion of prairie agriculture. It ends in 1914, with the close of the "wheat boom" period and the coming of the Great War, which severely restricted the raising of capital in the London market and so brought to an end the rapid expansion of railways in Western Canada.

There is a real need for extensive studies of the CPR which, since its inception in 1881, has greatly affected Canada's economic development. Most of the archival material is now at hand to facilitate such research. In 1973 the CPR gave the NAC permission to microfilm the letterbooks of W.C. Van Horne (president, 1888–99) and Thomas G. Shaughnessy (president, 1899–1918) and to retain copies for the use of researchers.[2] These are extremely valuable sources for studying the CPR, although the only author to have made use of them for a book-length study of the CPR has been Kaye Lamb, in his general history of the company published in 1977.[3] The CPR also now grants scholars access to the internal correspondence of these two presidents. However, I, like many others, have been unable to gain access to a crucial source, the minutes of the CPR's board of directors and executive committee. The CPR's policy on this matter was presented to me by Mr I.B. Scott, the company's vice-president administration and public affairs, in 1982. "Minute books of both the Board of Directors and the Executive Committee," Mr Scott stated, "are private records of the corporation and are available only to the Directors and the Auditors."[4] Another valuable source, which was opened to scholars in 1982, is the magnificent collection of James J. Hill Papers in St Paul, Minnesota.

Historians and economists have long emphasized the vital role that railways have played in overcoming the barriers of geography and linking the regions of Canada in an east-west transcontinental nation. In 1968 economist J. Lorne McDougall wrote a short company-sponsored general history of the CPR. Although he was often too sympathetic to the company's viewpoint, he did provide a succinct and accurate history for the general reader.[5] Equally sympathetic were Pierre Berton's two highly publicized volumes on the building of the CPR, which appeared in 1970 and 1971.[6] Berton is a superb narrative historian, and his vivid descriptions of major personalities, the drama and comedy of parliamentary debate, and the obstacles encountered by surveyors and contractors have given both volumes wide appeal to the general public. However, the major weakness of these works is their author's portrayal of the CPR as an instrument of national unity – of Canada's "national dream" – when it has been widely regarded in Western Canada as an instrument of Central Canadian imperialism. Robert Chodos' counter-company history appeared in 1973.[7] The author skilfully criticized Berton's glorification of the company as a force for national unity and effectively analyzed the development of the CPR into a conglomerate while concentrating on the skill of its officials in obtaining government assistance for company policies. Then in 1977 came Kaye Lamb's lively and detailed account of the company from its inception to the present. It was a more objective and analytical study than McDougall's, while the author's judgments were more moderate and balanced than those of Chodos. While critical of some CPR policies in Western Canada, on the whole Lamb regarded the CPR as a positive force in Canadian history.[8]

In 1983 the Glenbow Museum of Calgary commemorated the

centennial of the CPR's arrival in that city by sponsoring an important conference on the CPR and Western Canada at which Canadian scholars, including the author, came together to share their knowledge of the CPR. The papers, published the following year, present many new perspectives on the CPR and illustrate the importance of making use of the new sources available for the study of the company's history.[9]

This book was originally conceived as a biography of Thomas Shaughnessy. Two factors resulted in the shift to the present study. First, despite the diligent efforts of the present Lord Shaughnessy, very little personal correspondence of his grandfather was discovered. Second, during the 1970s I became increasingly interested in the history of Western Canada, influenced by my annual visits to the Western Canadian Studies Conference at the University of Calgary and by the views of my colleagues in the Department of History at the University of Alberta who worked in the field of Western Canadian history. It is my hope that this book will make a substantial contribution to our knowledge of the history of Western Canada.

Acknowledgments

I would like to express my great appreciation for the assistance of the Rt. Hon. Lord Shaughnessy. He supported my project over a long period, provided access to valuable documents in his possession, and gave freely of his time to discuss many aspects of his grandfather's career. As well, a number of colleagues furnished insights and information. David Hall provided useful suggestions for the chapters dealing with the prairie West, while Pat Roy shared her wide knowledge of British Columbia history. Other colleagues who were generous with their advice and encouragement were David Breen, David Dinwoodie, Ray Huel, Gordon Laxer, Rod Macleod, Ted Regehr, and the late Lewis H. Thomas. I would also like to thank Kaye Lamb and Paul Nanton for their assistance.

The staff of various archives were very helpful. In particular I should thank Chuck Mackinnon, Neil Forsyth, and Peter Rider of the National Archives of Canada, and Omer Lavallée and Jim Shields of Canadian Pacific Corporate Archives. I am indebted to Geoffrey Lester of the Cartographic Division of the Geography Department of the University of Alberta who prepared the maps. Shirley Ayer, Jim Braiden, Chris Leibich, Robert Neville, and George Richardson assisted in the research. Special thanks to Linda Clippingdale who did extensive newspaper research during 1978–79 academic year and to Lydia Dugbazah who typed the manuscript. And finally, I would like to thank my wife Margaret who has been very supportive of this project over a period of many years.

I wish to thank the Milwaukee County Historical Society for permission to use those parts of my article on Shaughnessy's Milwaukee years which appeared in the Spring 1983 issue of *Milwaukee History*. I am also grateful to Douglas and McIntyre Ltd and the Glenbow-Alberta Institute for permission to include portions of my article on

"Shaughnessy and Prairie Development, 1899–1914" from *The CPR West.*

Research for this study has been greatly assisted by grants from the Humanities and Social Sciences Research Council of Canada, and by grants from the University of Alberta for map preparation and course release, as well as for research.

This book has been published with the help of a grant from the Social Science Federation of Canada, using funds provided by the Social Sciences and Humanities Research Council of Canada.

I would like to acknowledge the excellent editorial assistance of Joan McGilvray of McGill-Queen's University Press and of copy editor Joan Irving. However, any errors or omissions must remain my responsibility.

Abbreviations: Railway Titles

AR&C CO	Alberta Railway and Coal Comany
AR&I CO	Alberta Railway and Irrigation Company
C&E	Calgary and Edmonton Railway
CPR	Canadian Pacific Railway
E&N	Esquimalt and Nanaimo Railway
GTPR	Grand Trunk Pacific Railway
GTR	Grand Trunk Railway of Canada
GN	Great Northern Railroad
ICR	Intercolonial Railway
KRVR	Kettle River Valley Railway
KVR	Kettle Valley Railway
NTR	National Transcontinental Railway
NK&S	Nicola, Kamloops and Similkameen Coal and Railway Company
NP	Northern Pacific Railroad
SF&N	Spokane Falls and Northern Railroad
VV&E	Vancouver, Victoria and Eastern Railway

Banff Springs Hotel, Banff, Alberta, c. 1890. In 1900 it was one of the top three mountain resorts in North America. (Courtesy Glenbow Archives, Calgary, Alberta)

Empress Hotel, Victoria, BC, 1908. This palatial hotel attracted many wealthy tourists to Victoria. (Provincial Archives of British Columbia, HP8207)

William C. Van Horne. Van Horne was president of the CPR from 1888 to 1899 and chairman from 1899 to 1910. (Courtesy National Archives of Canada, c-8549)

Thomas G. Shaughnessy, c. 1903. Shaughnessy was president of the CPR from 1899 to 1918 and chairman from 1918 to 1923. (Courtesy National Archives of Canada, c-6650)

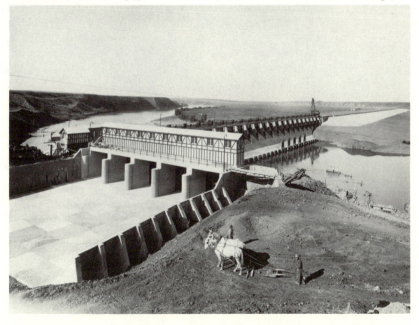

Irrigation dam, Bassano, Alberta, c. 1912–14. The dam was constructed between 1910 and 1914 by the CPR as part of its huge irrigation project in southern Alberta. (Courtesy Glenbow Archives, Calgary, Alberta)

Palliser Hotel, Calgary, Alberta, c. 1920. The nine-storey hotel, opened in 1914, was the tallest building in the city until the 1960s. (Courtesy Glenbow Archives, Calgary, Alberta)

Sir William Whyte, c. 1913, manager of CPR Western lines from 1886 to 1911. Whyte was a fervent believer in the economic potential of the West. (Western Canada Pictorial Index, University of Manitoba)

George Bury, c. 1913, dynamic and capable successor to William Whyte. (Western Canada Pictorial Index, University of Manitoba)

*The Canadian Pacific Railway and the
Development of Western Canada, 1896–1914*

CHAPTER ONE

The Canadian Pacific
Railway to 1896

The Canadian Pacific Railway Company (CPR) was incorporated by an Act of Parliament in 1881. Less than five years later the transcontinental line from Montreal to Port Moody, a distance of 2,893 miles, was completed. A special ceremony was held at Craigellachie in Eagle Pass in the Monashee Mountains of BC on 7 November 1885 to celebrate this important event in Canadian history. CPR director Sir Donald Smith drove in the last spike and the company's general manager, William C. Van Horne, tersely remarked, "All I can say is that the work has been done well in every way."[1] The first through passenger train left Dalhousie Square station in Montreal at 8:00 p.m. on Monday, 28 June 1886, and arrived in Port Moody sharp on time, at noon, on Sunday, 4 July. The running time was 139 hours and the average speed, including all stops, was 20.86 miles per hour. Van Horne later decided that the railway's western terminus should be Vancouver, which had an excellent harbour. In the spring of 1887, the main line was extended 12 miles west from Port Moody to Vancouver, and the first CPR train pulled into Vancouver on 23 May.[2]

In the decade from 1886 to 1896 the CPR expanded its mileage considerably. As of 31 December 1896 it operated 6,476 miles of railway: the Western Division, from Fort William, Ontario, to Donald, BC, operated 2,176 miles, and the Pacific Division in BC consisted of 626 miles. Thus, the CPR lines in Western Canada constituted 43.3 per cent of the CPR's total mileage.[3]

The CPR's financial position in 1896 had improved considerably over the period 1893–5, when the worldwide business depression had created serious financial problems for the company. The company's net earnings declined sharply, from $8,420,347 in 1892 to $6,423,309 in 1894. After fixed charges were deducted from 1894 earnings, there was a deficit of $526,731. The 1896 Canadian dollar had the buying power of about $8 in 1988.[4] The company had to use its special surplus account, which stood at $7,261,213, to pay this deficit and the dividends on the common and the new 4-per-cent stock; in all the surplus account was depleted by $4,521,420. In 1895, however, net earnings increased to $7,480,951. Dividends on preferred shares could now be paid out of net earnings rather than from the surplus account. The directors realized that the payment of a 2 1/2 per cent dividend on common stock in August 1894 had been a serious mistake, so the dividend had to be reduced in 1895 to 1 1/2 per cent, with the result that CPR shares fell to a low of $33. (Lord Mount Stephen, the company's first president, who had resigned from the CPR board in May 1893, had made the situation worse by advising his friends to sell their holdings while they were still worth something.) In 1896 net earnings increased again to $8,107,581, just a little lower than the 1892 level, and were sufficient to pay the preferred stock dividend and a 2 1/2 per cent dividend on common stock. By September 1896 Van Horne had become quite optimistic about the CPR's traffic prospects. The current prairie wheat crop was "about an average one in quantity and much above the average in quality." Wheat prices were "much better" than in 1895, so prairie farmers would be able to buy more manufactured goods from Eastern Canada, thus increasing the CPR's westbound traffic. He also observed that mining traffic in BC was increasing daily, so that the company would "soon have a very valuable business in that direction, and it is already helping us very much."[5]

In the late 1890's the CPR common stock was quite widely distributed. The available figures show this distribution as of 1 December 1900: Canadian holdings, 123,296; American holdings, 37,276; English and Foreign holdings, 489,428 for a total of 650,000 shares. Shaughnessy admitted privately in October 1900 that investment houses in London and Berlin had "large holdings" of CPR stock, but indicated that these shares were "rapidly going into the hands of investors."[6] From 1894 to 1900 the annual shareholders meeting was held on the first Wednesday in April. Then in 1901 the company's fiscal year was changed from 31 December to 30 June to bring CPR practice into harmony with that of most railways in North America. As a result shareholders meetings were held on the first Wednesday in October from 1901 to 1914.[7]

The CPR in the 1890s was the largest corporation in Canada as measured by the size of its work-force. In December 1891 the company had 23,050 men on its payrolls in Canada. It was slightly larger than the Grand Trunk Railway of Canada (GTR) which in 1896 had 20,000 employees, including those on GTR lines in the United States.[8]

The two most important officials in the CPR in 1896 were Sir William Van Horne, who had been president since August 1888, and Thomas G. Shaughnessy, who had been vice-president since June 1891. These two men, whose careers were so closely linked from their first association on the Chicago, Milwaukee and St Paul Railway in 1879 can be regarded as the "Siamese twins" of the CPR.

William Cornelius Van Horne was born on 3 February 1843, on a 360-acre farm near the town of Chelsea, Illinois. He was the eldest of five children of Cornelius Van Horne and his second wife, Mary Richards. Cornelius, of Dutch background, was educated at Union College, Schenectady and trained as a lawyer. He started a law practice in New York State, and in 1832 moved West with his wife and children, settling on a small farm near Chelsea, Illinois, and practising law. After the death of his first wife, he remarried in 1842 and bought a larger farm near Chelsea with financial help from a prosperous brother. He dabbled in farming and milling while building a clientele for his law firm. An active Democrat, he was appointed the first justice of the peace for the Chelsea district. In 1851 he sold the farm and moved to Joliet, a growing community of 2,000 people, 50 kilometres southwest of Chicago. He soon became a prominent figure in the town. When it received its city charter in 1852, Cornelius Van Horne was elected as the city's first mayor.[9]

William was educated at public schools in Chelsea and Joliet. Although he was a rather lazy student, he had a lively intelligence, an active imagination, and a phenomenal memory. He developed a passion for geology. On one occasion he borrowed a 262-page book on the subject from a friend and in five weeks laboriously copied it, including the illustrations. He later recalled what a valuable experience this had been. "The copying of that book did great things for me. It taught me how much could be accomplished by application; it improved my handwriting; it taught me the construction of English sentences; and it helped my drawing materially. And I never had to refer to the book again."[10]

In 1854 tragedy struck the family when William's father died of cholera, leaving a pile of debts and very little money. The family was forced to sell its spacious house and move to a small cottage in Joliet. In the spring of 1857 William left school to work as a telegrapher with the Illinois Central Railway in the company's Chicago office; his income was needed to support his family. Dismissed from this job for playing a practical joke on his superintendent, he was able to find a job as freight-checker and messenger for a 40-mile section of the Michigan Central Railway. His wage was $15 a month and he was now able to stay in Joliet. In 1858 he persuaded his superintendent to have the company install an independent telegraph line and was appointed the telegraph operator in Joliet. He soon became an expert telegrapher, who could discard the tape and receive his messages by sound alone. Since his duties as telegraph operator did not keep him fully occupied, he began to understudy the duties of the cashier, timekeeper, accountant, and others in the office.

A decisive event in Van Horne's life took place in 1861, when the railway's general superintendent made a rare visit to the Joliet office. "I found myself wondering," he informed his grandson many years later, "if even I might not somehow become a General Superintendent and travel in a private car. The glories of it, the pride of it, the salary pertaining to it, and all that moved me deeply, and I made up my mind then and there that I would reach it. And I did ten years later, at the age of twenty-eight."[11] From then on Van Horne had a definite goal; he pursued it with all his willpower, skills, and intellect.

In 1862 Van Horne took a position with the Chicago and Alton Railroad in Joliet, as operator and ticket agent. He was now earning a larger salary and was under the direct observation of the railway's top officials. Six years later, in 1868, he married Lucy Adeline Hurd, the daughter of a Joliet civil engineer. (The couple had three children – Adeline (1868), William (1871), who died at age five, and Richard Benedict (1877), known as "Bennie.") Also in 1868, Van Horne was promoted to superintendent of telegraphs and moved with his family to Alton. So well regarded was his work that two years later he was put in charge of transportation over the entire Chicago and Alton system. He now worked from the company's headquarters in Chicago. Early in 1872, he was appointed general manager of the St Louis, Kansas City and Northern Railroad, a Chicago and Alton subsidiary. At the young age of twenty-nine, he had achieved his goal of becoming a general manager. Van Horne did much to modernize this railway through improving its equipment and purchasing steel instead of iron rails.[12]

In 1874 internal divisions among the directors of the St Louis, Kansas City and Northern resulted in the resignation of two influential directors of the Chicago and Alton, John J. Mitchell and Timothy Blackstone. Some of Mitchell's associates were the New York bondholders of the Southern Minnesota Railroad, a small pioneer line which was bankrupt and in very poor condition. Mitchell persuaded these bondholders that Van Horne could make this railway a profitable line, and convinced Van Horne to become its president and general manager, effective 1 October 1874. From his office in La Crosse, Wisconsin, Van Horne directed all his abilities into transforming the Southern Minnesota into a paying property. In the first year of his management the railway's gross earnings exceeded that of any previous year, and operating expenses dropped from 72 to 56 per cent of earnings. By 1877 the railway was out of the receiver's hands, allowing Van Horne to turn his attention to construction; not only would extension of the line bring more traffic, but it would enable the railway to earn its Minnesota land grant of 315,000 acres. His goal achieved, Van Horne returned to the Chicago and Alton as general superintendent in 1878.[13]

During this period S.S. Merrill, general manager of the Chicago, Milwaukee and St Paul Railway (the Milwaukee Road), a fierce competitor with the Chicago and Alton, had developed a strong admiration for Van Horne's abilities. He and Jason Easton, a Minnesota capitalist who was a director of the Milwaukee Road, offered Van Horne the task of coordinating the various railways acquired by the Milwaukee Road and operating them as a unified system. Van Horne accepted and in January 1880 he became general superintendent of the Milwaukee Road. Despite his title, he was given the duties and powers of a general manager.[14]

This did not stop him from implementing many changes in the Milwaukee Road: trackage was substantially increased, the various lines were effectively coordinated, the storekeeping and accounting systems were overhauled and reorganized, and employees were taught new techniques for loading railway cars to their fullest capacity.

By this time Van Horne was meeting many influential businessmen in the Midwest. One of these was James J. Hill of St Paul, Minnesota, who owned a fleet of steamers on the Red River which carried substantial traffic to and from Winnipeg, Manitoba, in the young dominion of Canada. In June 1879 Hill and three associates (George Stephen, Donald Smith, and Norman Kittson) acquired control of the St Paul, Minneapolis and Manitoba Railroad (the Manitoba Road) which connected St Paul with the province of Manitoba. Hill was also a founding director of the Canadian Pacific Railway which, in 1881, would start construction of a railway from Montreal, west through the Canadian prairies, to the Pacific coast. When Hill, who had a great deal of admiration for Van Horne's abilities as a railway manager, learned that Van Horne was planning to extend the Milwaukee Road north to Manitoba (in which case it would compete directly with the Manitoba Road), he realized that the Manitoba

Road and the CPR would benefit greatly if Van Horne could be persuaded to become general manager of the fledgling CPR. It would acquire a dynamic manager while the Milwaukee Road might not carry out Van Horne's planned extension to the Canadian West.[15]

When George Stephen, president of the CPR, asked Hill to recommend a person for the post of general manager, Hill enthusiastically endorsed Van Horne. In September or October 1881 Stephen met Van Horne in Chicago and offered him the position, which Van Horne accepted by letter in October. Hill was delighted with Van Horne's decision and wrote enthusiastically to Stephen:

I am fully satisfied that we could not have made a better selection than Mr. Van Horne. His railway experience ... has been with good roads and has been in good positions. I have never met anyone who is better informed in the various departments: Machinery, Cars, Operations, Train Service, Construction and general policy which with untiring energy and a good vigorous body should give us good results.

He [Van Horne] remarked that the Canadian Pacific with its prospect of being a successful thru (sic) line with a heavy local business should take all the advantages of the experience of the successful roads up to the present time and in adopting standards try and get such patterns as experience had shown were the simplest cheapest and best having in view the work for which they are intended.[16]

The CPR had hired not only an experienced railway manager but also a practical innovator who would use the experience of the most successful American railways to the CPR's benefit.

Van Horne stepped off the train in Winnipeg on 31 December 1881 ready to assume – the next day – his new position as general manager of the CPR at the handsome salary of $15,000 a year. He was a large, powerful man, with a big chest, massive shoulders, and a huge head dominated by a bushy beard and moustache, and piercing ice-blue eyes. He spoke bluntly and directly and was accustomed to having his orders obeyed. His friend Jason Easton of the Milwaukee Road aptly described him as "the ablest railroad general in the world." Early on 2 January 1882, Van Horne was at work setting up offices on the second floor of the Bank of Montreal building.[17]

His most important task was to construct as rapidly as possible the prairie section of the CPR, from Winnipeg to the foothills of the Rockies. Pierre Berton presents an excellent account of Van Horne's managerial techniques, which resulted in the laying of the 418 miles of track in the 10-month period from April 1882 to January 1883. By 20 August 1883 the whistle of a construction engine was announcing that the rail line had been completed from Winnipeg to Calgary. The importance of this event was exemplified by the passenger list on the first train – it included George Stephen, the company's president, and Donald Smith, one of its most important directors. Construction pushed on and rails reached the summit of the Rockies by the end of the 1883 construction season.[18]

Stephen and the other CPR directors soon demonstrated their approval of Van Horne's performance. At the annual shareholders meeting on 14 May 1884, Van Horne was elected to the board of directors, replacing Duncan McIntyre, who declined re-election. Right after this meeting, a special meeting of the board of directors was held during which Van Horne was elected vice-president and appointed to the board's inner circle, the executive committee. The other members of this powerful committee were Stephen, R.B. Angus, and Donald Smith.[19]

Stephen's financial skills had been essential in the formative period of the CPR, when the company faced formidable difficulties raising capital. But by 1888 Stephen felt, as his biographer remarks, "That someone more experienced in railway administration should take his place." He had no doubts as to who his successor should be. In a letter to the company's shareholders explaining his decision to resign he confidently asserted that "it is, to me, a matter of the greatest possible satisfaction to be able to say that, in my successor, Mr. Van Horne, the Company has a man of proved fitness for the office, in the prime of life, possessed of great energy and rare ability, having a long and thoroughly practical railway experience and above all an entire devotion to the interests of the Company." Accordingly, Stephen submitted his resignation to the board on 7 August 1888 and Van Horne was elected as the new president. In August 1889 Van Horne's presidential salary was raised from $30,000 to $50,000 a year, retroactive to 1 January 1889. Clearly the directors had full confidence in his management of the company. Their confidence was not misplaced, for Van Horne had a deep loyalty to the CPR and a firm devotion to its interests. As he informed a close friend in 1898, "I have more regard for the CPR than for anything else in the world aside from my wife and children."[20]

The other "Siamese twin" of the CPR, Thomas George Shaughnessy, was born in Milwaukee, Wisconsin, on 6 October 1853. His parents, Thomas Shaughnessy, Sr and Mary Kennedy, were poor Irish immigrants who had emigrated to the US and settled in the little town of Milwaukee on the western shore of Lake Michigan, in 1835 and 1844 respectively. They married in 1846 and took up residence in the city's Third Ward, the Irish ghetto characterized by a large number of saloons and very poor housing conditions. There were six children in the family, with Thomas being the eldest. Thomas Sr joined the Milwaukee police force in 1856 and served 26 years before retiring. One Milwaukee newspaper described him as "perhaps the best detective in the west, [who] seems to know a rogue by instinct whenever he lays eyes upon him." His son Thomas seems to have inherited his father's drive and energy.[21]

Considering the family's tight financial circumstances, Thomas Jr received a good education. He attended the Milwaukee public schools, and then spent some time studying at a local Jesuit Academy which taught both classical and commercial subjects. Thomas was evidently an excellent student, especially in languages, for by the age of fourteen he had read the sixth *Book of Caesar* in Latin. In 1869 he studied for several months at a business college in Milwaukee. The college, founded by Robert C. Spencer, offered a wide variety of courses in such subjects as commercial arithmetic, bookkeeping, German, and political economy. Shaughnessy must have found the training very useful, for he later remarked to Spencer that "every young man, and woman too, who expects to succeed in business or commercial life should first take a course in your college, or some kindred institution." In July, 1869 Shaughnessy began his career, as a clerk in the purchasing department of the Milwaukee and St Paul Railway.[22]

The Milwaukee and St Paul Railway was formed in 1863 with headquarters in Milwaukee. Under the dynamic leadership of Alexander Mitchell, who became president in 1865, the company by the end of 1869 "controlled every through route leading from the Wisconsin shore of Lake Michigan to the Mississippi River." Having built a line into Chicago in 1873, in February, 1874 its name was officially changed to the Chicago, Milwaukee and St Paul Railway Company (Milwaukee Road).[23]

Shaughnessy did not advance rapidly in the company's service, for he was only a bookkeeper in the supply department after 10 years of service. This rather lacklustre performance may have been partly the result of his extensive activities outside the railway office. For some time he had been privately studying law. Then from 1875 to 1882 Shaughnessy carried on an active career in Milwaukee politics. In a by-election on 27 July 1875 he was elected to city council. An active Democrat like his father, he was returned unopposed in the Third Ward to a 3-year term in the regular civic elections held the following spring. Shaughnessy was, at this time, a "tall, slim, angular youth" whose appearance was so "youthful ... that it was necessary to produce the church register, showing the date of his birth, to convince his fellow aldermen he was old enough to be eligible to sit with them." He was 5 feet 10 inches tall with reddish hair which prompted a newspaper's description of him as the "pumpkin-haired alderman from the solid Third."[24] He won a second 3-year term in 1879, and was generally a reform-minded politician. He proposed that the board of school commissioners investigate the establishment of kindergartens in the public schools, and a year later the city council authorized the setting up of a kindergarten in one school on a trial basis. Shaughnessy also proposed the hiring of paid experts to investigate the adequacy of the city's water reservoirs. Two years later council adopted his proposal that the city hire qualified consulting engineers to report on the best and most economical method of solving the problems of the city's sewer and water works. When he presented his candidacy for a third term, in April 1882, he had no difficulty in being re-elected. His prominence in Milwaukee civic politics was further evidenced by his election as president of the city council in 1882.[25]

The year 1880 was important to Shaughnessy for on 12 January he married Elizabeth Bridget Nagle, the Irish-born daughter of another Milwaukee family, in the Third Ward Catholic church. The bride was 3 years the bridegroom's senior. For their honeymoon they travelled to Philadelphia and other eastern points. The couple's first child, Alice, was born 28 October 1880 in Milwaukee.[26]

An even more decisive event in Shaughnessy's life occurred in January, 1880, when William C. Van Horne, the brilliant and dynamic general superintendent of the Chicago and Alton Railroad, became general superintendent of the Milwaukee Road. Van Horne soon noticed his young clerk and, feeling that Shaughnessy had more to offer, promoted him to the position of purchasing agent in 1880. Van Horne became convinced that the company needed "a comprehensive store and accounting system." In October 1880 he appointed a three-member committee to study and report on the systems used by other large railroads. Shaughnessy, one of the members of this committee, "returned with an excellent report and recommendations, of which he almost wholly approved." In a short time Van Horne established "a complete and coordinated system of railway stores and accounting" which Shaughnessy carried successfully into effect in a new position as storekeeper, effective 1 January 1881.[27] The storekeeper was an important official, for he was in charge of all materials and supplies for the locomotive and car departments, and kept accounts for them including making up the payrolls.

By 1881 Van Horne and Shaughnessy were close friends; Shaughnessy was also clearly a protégé of Van Horne's, his senior by 10 years. Van Horne learned that Shaughnessy was an omnivorous reader and encouraged the young administrator to use his excellent personal library. As well as a comprehensive collection of books on geology, Van Horne had a cabinet of fossils, and the two men spent "many hours off duty" discussing and studying these specimens. From this period Shaughnessy's railway career was very closely linked with that of Van Horne, until Shaughnessy succeeded the latter as president of the CPR.[28]

When William C. Van Horne left the Milwaukee Road in December 1881 to become general manager of the CPR, he eagerly anticipated persuading Shaughnessy to make the move with him. Early in February 1882, he visited Shaughnessy in Milwaukee to offer him the position of purchasing agent of the entire CPR system. The Milwaukee *Sentinel* commented that while the offer was "a tempting one [it] was declined owing to the desire of management of the St Paul Railway that Mr. Shaughnessy remain in his present position." Shaughnessy's reluctance to accept Van Horne's offer may have been due in part to the CPR's low standing in US railway and financial circles at the time. The attacks of the Northern Pacific Railroad on the CPR had seriously damaged its credibility on Wall Street. However, Shaughnessy was able to use Van Horne's offer to increase his salary on the Milwaukee Road. But when Van Horne made another trip to Milwaukee later in 1882 and renewed his offer of the CPR position, "over a glass of Milwaukee beer, Shaughnessy agreed to come."[29]

Shaughnessy tendered his resignation as president of the city council and alderman of the Third Ward at the council's meeting on 30 October 1882. The following evening, 40 council members and civic officials gave Shaughnessy a farewell banquet at a large downtown hotel. Municipal Judge James A. Mallory, who presided, paid tribute to Shaughnessy's abilities, saying that while he regretted that such a promising young man should leave the city, he was aware that Canada was the gainer. If other promising young Irishmen would emigrate to Canada, he remarked, that country would soon be independent of Great Britain. Shaughnessy acknowledged his mixed feelings about his departure and that the decision had been a difficult one: "Born in this city," he declared, "I was during my youth, social and business life always surrounded by friends like you are, and it seems impossible that the betterment in business prospects should compensate for the sacrifice of tearing myself away from these associations. But professional railroad men must follow wherever their prospects lead them. I shall never cease to care for Milwaukee, and shall always be anxious to see the interests of Milwaukee furthered."[30]

The Milwaukee period was thus a formative one for Shaughnessy.

The son of poor Irish immigrants, he was an extremely ambitious young man, eager for success in business or politics. After his election to city council at the age of twenty-two and much success in politics, he abandoned politics upon joining the CPR in 1882 and channelled all his ambition into advancing to the top of that organization. In 1884 he advised a friend to accept "a position of any kind with a reliable firm or railroad" and to remain "with the firm until you have attained success. Continued changes work irreparable injury to the young businessman."³¹ Shaughnessy had also developed a close friendship with Van Horne while the latter was general superintendent of the Milwaukee Road. Van Horne used this relationship to persuade a reluctant Shaughnessy to leave his native city and join him in Montreal. Shaughnessy retained a strong affection for his birthplace and for the many close friends he had made there. In 1903 he was still subscribing to the Milwaukee *Sentinel*.³²

Shaughnessy and his wife Elizabeth arrived in Montreal on the morning of 2 November 1882 and took a room in the St Lawrence Hall. Soon after they and their daughter took up residence at 52 St Famille in the St Lawrence Ward.³³ Shaughnessy lost no time in reporting for work at the CPR's head office in the financial district. D.C. Coleman has presented a vivid picture of Shaughnessy's arrival: "On a dull, overcast morning in November, 1882 Bender [one of the clerks in the office] looked up to see a young man of striking appearance enter the room. He had clean-cut features, sharp Irish eyes and, according to the fashion of the Western United States in those days, his face was adorned with a moustache and an Imperial. He wore a black felt hat, a soft-flowing black tie, a morning coat and light striped trousers ... He announced in a few words that he was T.G. Shaughnessy, that Mr. Van Horne had appointed him Chief Purchasing Agent, and ten minutes later he was at work." Shaughnessy had soon sent for invoices and price lists and begun interviewing prominent manufacturers and their agents. As Coleman remarks, "They learned that the only factors which would be considered in Canadian Pacific purchases would be price, quality and rapidity of delivery."³⁴

Fourteen months after assuming his post, Shaughnessy was appointed Van Horne's assistant, in January 1884. During that and the following year, years of severe financial crisis for the CPR, Shaughnessy played a crucial role in keeping CPR costs down. After intense negotiations John A. Macdonald's Conservative government agreed, in early 1884, to provide the CPR with a loan of $22.5 million, of which $7.5 million would be made available immediately, while the remaining $15 million "would be calculated upon the proportion of the work done to that which remained to be done."[35] In March 1884 Shaughnessy advised Archer Baker, the general superintendent of the Eastern Division, that he wanted the men on his division paid "the lowest wage at which they could be obtained and [to make sure that the men] were charged an amount for their board corresponding to what they would have to pay in other places." He observed that some CPR section labourers received from $1.20 to $1.40 per day while the Grand Trunk Railway only paid $1 per day for section men on the entire line from Montreal to Sarnia. He criticized the manager of construction at Sudbury for ordering supplies from retailers rather than from wholesalers, who often gave the company rebates. Shaughnessy believed that it was "most unbusiness-like ... to demand these deductions [rebates] after purchases have been made." In November 1884 he soundly reprimanded William Whyte, general superintendent at Toronto, for granting his men too much overtime. "The overtime on your Parkdale shop pay rolls," he remarked, "is something terrible! There are painters who draw pay from 37 to 39 days; boiler makers and helpers from 37 to 40; and station enginemen 46 days in the month. It may be accepted that two-thirds of the overtime paid for is absolutely thrown away ... such overtime as that appearing on your October pay rolls would not be tolerated in any first class shop in the Country." Whyte again drew Shaughnessy's ire in December for paying "outrageous" prices on lamps. Shaughnessy withdrew authority from Whyte to make purchases of supplies in Toronto, except in emergencies. "Hereafter," he requested, "please have all requisitions for material to be purchased sent to me here [in Montreal], and no invoice for goods purchased outside the regular channel will be passed for payment, unless that they bear your certificate to the effect that circumstances prevented the requisition from going through the ordinary channels."[36]

By the beginning of 1885 the CPR's financial plight was so serious that Shaughnessy was compelled to ask suppliers for 3- to 4-months' credit. A letter to the Toronto wholesale grocer, Senator Frank Smith, is typical. Shaughnessy informed Smith that the company could not yet pay anything on his account because it had sent large quantities of material to Lake Superior and the Rocky Mountains to allow construction to continue. This situation, Shaughnessy remarked in a characteristic understatement, "naturally cramps us a little financially." He asked Smith to take a CPR note for four months "with interest at 6% from the time the account was due." Shaughnessy was also reluctant to pay a contractor's accounts until a final estimate had been submitted. "In a word, we don't want to pay any more on Contractors' accounts before the completion of the work than will be absolutely necessary to keep the men satisfied and insure rapid progress." Shaughnessy was already proving to be a valuable asset to the CPR. "That he served it [the CPR] well in the financial crisis of 1884–85 is beyond doubt," Berton asserts. "He never appeared to show the slightest tremor of panic as he kited cheques, kept creditors at bay, denied funds, made partial payments, and generally held the company together." The present Lord Shaughnessy tells an amusing story of the lengths to which his grandfather would go to keep the CPR solvent. An American railway supply company had tried to do business with the CPR, but without success. On several occasions in 1884–5 this company made out large cheques to Thomas Shaughnessy. The company finally reported this situation to the CPR board; it appeared that Shaughnessy had been taking money under the counter for favours rendered. Stephen summoned Shaughnessy before the board to explain this matter. Shaughnessy excused himself, went to his office and returned with a sheaf of deposit slips from the Bank of Montreal, all endorsed by him to the account of the CPR. Stephen asked if these were bribes. "Of course," came the cool reply, "but, by God, we needed the money, didn't we?"[37]

Shaughnessy's efforts at keeping CPR costs down earned him another promotion – to the post of assistant general manager (September 1885). During the period 1885–91 Van Horne substantially increased Shaughnessy's responsibilities to the point that, in October 1890, Shaughnessy informed a friend who was inquiring about mineral deposits on the CPR main line, "I have been so very much occupied during the past five or six years that I have really had no opportunity to give [the subject] any attention." But Van Horne and the directors must have been quite satisfied with his performance, since they appointed Shaughnessy assistant president on 9 September 1889.[38]

In the 1891 federal election Shaughnessy strongly supported Van Horne's direct intervention in the campaign. The Liberal party under Wilfrid Laurier campaigned on a policy of "unrestricted reciprocity" – free trade with the United States. On 24 February the Montreal *Gazette* published a letter from Van Horne to Senator George Drummond, a prominent Montreal businessman and a staunch Conservative, denouncing unrestricted reciprocity. "I am well enough acquainted with the trade and industries of Canada," Van Horne emphatically asserted, "to know that unrestricted reciprocity would bring prostration or ruin. I realize," he continued, "that for saying this I may be accused of meddling in politics, but with me this is a business question and not a political one, and it so vitally affects the interests that have been entrusted to me that I feel justified in expressing my opinion plainly." The CPR president made it clear that he believed unrestricted reciprocity would seriously harm *both* the country and the company. He asserted that the CPR "has built up or been instrumental in building up hundreds of new industries in the country, and it is the chief support of many of them." He was convinced that the Liberal trade policy "would make New York the chief distributing point for the Dominion, instead of Montreal and Toronto ... would ruin three fourths of our manufactories ... [and] would make Eastern Canada the dumping ground for the grain and flour of the Western States, to the injury of our Northwest." All these developments, he concluded, "would be bad for the Canadian Pacific Railway, as well as for the country at large." Van Horne did not change his views on free trade with the United States. During the 1911 federal general election he publicly denounced the Laurier government's Reciprocity Agreement with the United States, declaring, "I am out to do all I can to bust the damn thing." As his biographer Walter Vaughan remarked, "He [Van Horne] saw in dire peril his own splendid achievements and those of his associates in the building of the Canadian Pacific Railway, with its numerous spurs and far-flung branches, and in the development of the whole country tributary to it."[39]

On the February morning in 1891 that Van Horne's letter appeared in the *Gazette*, Shaughnessy arrived at his office in Windsor Station to find the company president waiting for him. Van Horne had, according to Shaughnessy, written the letter "on impulse without consultation with any of his colleagues." He now realized that he had made a "serious blunder" and was "in great distress." He asked Shaughnessy if it would be "wise to write another letter." Shaughnessy strongly opposed such action on the grounds "that nothing could now be done to modify the intense animosity of the Liberal Party who, if they came to power, would leave nothing undone to hamper and harrass the Company." He advised, rather, that the CPR should "come into the open and render all the assistance we could to the Conservatives." Van Horne agreed and the CPR, Shaughnessy related, "organized a most far-reaching and effective bit of election machinery, to which, in my mind, Sir John Macdonald owed his success in that campaign. This was the only occasion on which the Company or its Officers ever resorted to such measures, and for the sake of my successors I hope that it will never be necessary again." (Shaughnessy was to hold fast to this position even during the 1911 federal election. Though privately he regarded Reciprocity as "a deathblow to the best interests of Canada," he refused to make his position public or to use the CPR organization to work against the Liberals.[40])

The CPR had to organize its forces quickly, since polling day was 5 March, 1891, only nine days away. On 28 February Van Horne wrote Macdonald, "Our canvass is nearly complete and the C.P.R. vote will be practically unanimous." The outraged Toronto *Globe* (Liberal) castigated the CPR as "the Tory Government on wheels." However, the Conservatives were re-elected with a majority of only twenty-seven seats.[41]

Shaughnessy's excellent performance of his duties as assistant president and his firm support for Van Horne in the 1891 election were rewarded in June 1891, a month which proved to be very eventful for Shaughnessy. On 6 June, Prime Minister Sir John A. Macdonald passed away. Pending the resolution of differences in the party, the Conservatives chose a temporary leader, Senator Sir John Abbott, and on 16 June his administration was sworn into office. In view of his new position, Abbott, who had been a CPR director since 1888, submitted his resignation from the board of directors. It was accepted on 18 June and Shaughnessy was elected to fill the vacancy. At the same time, his promotion to the position of vice-president was approved. A family event culminated the busy month – on 23 June the Shaughnessy's fourth child, Marguerite, was born.[42]

From 1891 to 1896, Van Horne and Shaughnessy continued their close cooperation in managing the company. The president often gave his vice-president additional important tasks. For example, Shaughnessy was sent to the Orient to establish a CPR agency in Hong Kong that would look after all matters relating to traffic between China, Japan, and Vancouver. Travelling on one of the company's luxurious new Pacific steamships, the *Empress of Japan*, he left Vancouver on 19 November 1891 and arrived at Yokohama, Japan, on the morning of 2 December. He later continued on to Tokyo and Hong Kong. He was much impressed with Japan which he described as "the most charming country in the world." On his return trip on the *Empress of Japan*, he had a daunting experience one night. After he had retired to bed in his stateroom, "the berth and the chest of drawers under it, became loose, tipped over, and were thrown back and forth in the cabin. "Fortunately," he remarked, "I succeeded in getting out of the way. I then took the adjoining cabin, and within half an hour, had precisely the same experience." He later wrote a stern letter to the British company that had constructed the *Empresses*, remarking that the workman who had fastened the berths "cannot possibly have known much about ship's work." Shaughnessy reached

Vancouver safely on 26 January 1892. Later that year a CPR agency was established in Hong Kong.[43]

As we shall see in chapter two, Shaughnessy played a prominent role in the negotiations with the Laurier government in 1896–7 for a federal cash subsidy for the construction of a CPR line through the Crow's Nest Pass into the Kootenay mining district of BC.

The effective policy-making body for the CPR was the executive committee of the board of directors, although major decisions and agreements had to be ratified by the full board, which held its regular monthly meetings in the boardroom in Windsor Station in Montreal on the second Monday of each month at 2:15 p.m. In 1896 the executive committee had four members: Van Horne, Shaughnessy, Sir Donald Smith, and Richard B. Angus. (Shaughnessy had been appointed to this committee on 13 June 1892.[44])

Smith, the son of a tradesman, was born in Scotland in 1820. He joined the Hudson's Bay Company (HBC) in 1838 as an apprentice clerk, and worked his way through the ranks, becoming chief commissioner in 1871. By 1883 he was a director of the HBC and its largest shareholder. In 1889 he was chosen governor – chief executive officer – of the company, a position which he held until his death in January 1914. It was Smith who first directed Stephen's attention to the Manitoba Road in 1873 or 1874. The two men, along with Hill and Norman Kittson, acquired control of this railway in 1879. Smith was appointed to the CPR board on 14 March 1881. It is not yet clear how active Smith was on the executive committee from 1881 to 1896: it must be kept in mind that not only did he have extensive duties as HBC governor, but he was also president of the Bank of Montreal from 1887 to 1905. And in April 1896 Prime Minister Mackenzie Bowell had appointed Smith high commissioner for Canada in the United Kingdom, a post which he held until his death. His duties kept him in Britain for much of the year, so that he was unable to attend many meetings of the CPR executive committee. In 1897 he was elevated to the peerage as Lord Strathcona.[45]

The fourth member of the executive committee, Richard B. Angus, was particularly valuable for his wide knowledge of financial matters, derived from extensive experience in the banking field. Born in Scotland in 1831, Angus received his initial training in the Manchester office of the Manchester and Liverpool Bank. At the age of twenty-six he emigrated to the Province of Canada and entered the service of the Bank of Montreal. He advanced rapidly: put in charge of the bank's Chicago agency for a few years, he then became joint agent of the bank's New York agency, and, after several years, was appointed manager of the bank's Montreal office. In

November 1869 Angus was appointed general manager of the Bank of Montreal, at a salary of £2,000 a year. He worked very closely with George Stephen who became vice-president of the bank in 1871 and president in January 1876. Angus resigned as general manager in August 1879 to become vice-president of the St Paul, Minneapolis and Manitoba Railroad (the Manitoba Road) which Stephen and three associates had taken over in June 1879. James J. Hill, general manager of the Manitoba Road, was in charge of its daily operations. Two months after Hill resigned from the CPR board of directors, in May 1883, Angus ended his active role in the operation of the Manitoba Road. He had, however, been appointed one of the original directors of the CPR and subsequently joined the executive committee. He was an important link with the Bank of Montreal, particularly after his appointment to the bank's board of directors in 1891, a position he retained until his death in 1922. His stature in the bank is further indicated by his term as president from 1910 until 1913.[46]

In 1899 the executive committee was expanded to five members by the appointment of Toronto financier Edmund Boyd Osler, who had been elected to the CPR board of directors on 13 June 1885. Osler was born in Simcoe County, Ontario, the son of an Anglican clergyman. Educated at Dundas grammar school, he then worked 4 years as a clerk with the Bank of Upper Canada. In 1867, at age twenty-two, he and Henry M. Pellatt formed a partnership as money brokers and financial agents. In 1872 he married Annie Cochran, a native of Aberdeen, Scotland. He later travelled to Aberdeen and used his wife's family connections to persuade some of the city's bankers to invest in Ontario farmland with Osler managing the investments. In 1882 he and H.C. Hammond founded the Toronto firm of Osler and Hammond, financiers and stockbrokers, which, over the next three decades, became a very profitable company. The year before, he had been instrumental in forming the Ontario and Quebec Railway along with Hammond and George Stephen, the president of the newly formed CPR. This company, with Osler as president, built a railway from Smiths Falls to Toronto and acquired a number of railways in southern Ontario in the period 1881–4. Then, in January 1884, the CPR leased the Ontario and Quebec Railway for 999 years. Thus Osler had played an important role in developing a railway system for the CPR in southern Ontario; for this he was elected to the CPR board in 1885. Correspondence in the Shaughnessy letterbooks indicates that Osler and Shaughnessy became personal friends as well as close business associates. Shaughnessy frequently sought Osler's advice on financial matters. When elected to the executive committee, Osler seems to have played a very active role – certainly he travelled frequently from Toronto to attend its meetings and regular board meetings. The Toronto financier was also an important figure in the Conservative party in Ontario, and served as MP for Toronto West from 1896 to 1917.[47]

A sixth member joined the CPR executive committee in 1907, with the appointment of David McNicoll. At this time, McNicoll was the CPR's first vice-president and general manager – the railway's senior operating official under the president. Born in Scotland in 1852, he received a basic education in the local school of a small town, then took a job as clerk in a small Scottish railway at the age of fourteen. After 8 years as a railway clerk, he emigrated to Canada and became chief clerk in the general manager's office of the Toronto, Grey and Bruce Railway. He held this post until 1881, when he became the railway's general freight and passenger agent. His views regarding employment on small railways in Scotland and Canada were expressed in 1905. "The small corporation can't do anything. It can't borrow money. It can't branch out. It can't make a name for itself. It keeps you in poverty. You feel small, and you will remain small, so long as you belong to it." But his situation had changed in 1883 when he obtained the position of general passenger agent for the Eastern and Ontario divisions of the CPR. Capable and hard-working, he soon became an indispensable figure in the passenger department. Promotion came in 1889, when he was appointed general passenger agent for all CPR lines. He then served as manager of the passenger department from 1896 to 1899. A year later he was appointed the CPR's second vice-president and general manager. In December 1903, McNicoll was appointed first vice-president. Recognizing his effectiveness as general manager, Shaughnessy supported his election to the board of directors on 10 August 1903.[48]

In 1907, then, the executive committee consisted of six men: Shaughnessy, Van Horne, Angus, Lord Strathcona, Osler, and McNicoll. No changes were made to the committee until 1914, with the appointment of Herbert Holt, a Montreal financier and president of the Royal Bank of Canada, to replace Strathcona, who died in January 1914.[49]

The secretary of the CPR was present at all meetings of the board and the executive committee to take the minutes. From 1881 to 1908, Charles Drinkwater occupied this position. Born in the town of Ashton-under-Lyne in Lancashire, England, in 1843 and educated there, he started work at age sixteen as a clerk on the Manchester, Sheffield and Lincolnshire Railway. From 1860 to 1863 he was employed with the Great Northern Railway at its London headquarters. He secured the post of private secretary to John A. Macdonald in 1864 and served in that capacity for 10 years. Then he returned to railway service – in Canada now – as chief assistant to the managing director of the Grand Trunk Railway. In February 1881 he was chosen secretary of the newly organized CPR. Not only did Drinkwater perform his secretarial duties efficiently, he often acted as the liaison between the CPR president and federal politicians. In effect, he became the company's chief lobbyist in Ottawa, where he often met with cabinet ministers to argue the CPR's interests in proposed legislation. In May 1901 Drinkwater was given additional responsibilites as assistant to the president "in connection with all matters relating to legislation affecting the Company's affairs and the carrying out of the Company's policy with reference to subsidiary or controlled lines." Drinkwater's association with Macdonald gave him excellent contacts in the federal Conservative party, but he was also able to develop close links with members of the Laurier administration. In March 1908 he was promoted to the position of senior assistant to then president Shaughnessy. He served only briefly in this post, for he died suddenly on 23 April 1908. W.S. Fielding, Laurier's minister of finance, requested CPR chief solicitor, A.R. Creelman, for a railway pass for a friend in May 1908. He explained that he was troubling Creelman with this matter because, "With Sir Thomas Shaughnessy in London and Mr. Drinkwater in Heaven, my usual channels of communication with the CPR are cut off."[50]

Drinkwater's successor as secretary was Walter R. Baker, who began his duties on 1 March 1908. He was born in Yorkshire, England, in 1852 and was educated privately. In 1873 he emigrated to Canada and worked in Ottawa as the local freight and passenger agent for the Canada Central Railway. He was then fortunate to obtain the position of private secretary to the Governor General, the Marquis of Lorne. When Lorne's term of office ended in 1878, Baker became assistant secretary to the Treasury Board. From 1881 to 1883 he worked in the CPR office in Winnipeg. In 1883 he obtained the position of general superintendent on the Manitoba and North Western Railway, a small line which the Allans of Montreal were attempting to build through the northern prairies. Baker, whose office was in Winnipeg, was promoted to general manager of this line in 1892. When the CPR took over the railway in 1900 (see chapter four), Baker was appointed CPR executive agent in Winnipeg. Shaughnessy became impressed with his ability, and transferred him to Montreal to serve as assistant to general manager David McNicoll. Then, in 1905 Shaughnessy moved him to the president's office as his assistant, a title he retained when he was appointed company secretary in March 1908. Baker also performed the function of CPR lobbyist in Ottawa, following in Drinkwater's footsteps.[51]

The CPR's administrative structure in the 1890s was patterned on the system pioneered by the Pennsylvania Railroad and widely used in North America. Since the CPR spanned such a vast geographical area, a structure of regional divisions, each headed by a general superintendent, was essential. While power rested with the executive committee, each regional general superintendent was, according to Shaughnessy, "a king in his own territory." Two men important to the development of the CPR in the west were William Whyte, superintendent of the Western Division, and Richard Marpole, superintendent of the Pacific Division, whose careers will be discussed in later chapters.[52]

In 1896 the CPR, led by Van Horne and Shaughnessy, was faced with an important challenge in Western Canada – the building of a railway through the Crow's Nest Pass into the Kootenay region of southeastern British Columbia.

CHAPTER TWO

Canadianizing the Kootenays: The Crow's Nest Pass Agreement of 1897

The CPR's descision to build the Crow's Nest Pass Railway was a response to mining developments in the Kootenay region of south-eastern British Columbia in the late 1880s and 1890s, and to the efforts of American railways to divert this mining traffic to the United States. The CPR wanted to secure the rapidly increasing mining traffic of this region. The Crow's Nest Pass Railway would link the Kootenay mining region with Central Canada via the CPR's main line, providing a market for the industrial goods of Ontario and Quebec and for grain and cattle from the prairies.

Mining in the Kootenays had started in the 1860s, when American prospectors began moving into the district. In the early years the lake and river routes – the Columbia River, Kootenay Lake and the Kootenay River – made the transport of American goods into the Kootenays and ores to smelters in the US, mainly in Montana, fairly easy. But ore production soon increased. The first major find occurred in 1886, when the Hall brothers discovered rich silver and copper deposits on Toad Mountain, 5 miles from Nelson, BC. This discovery led to the establishment of the productive Silver King and other mines on Toad Mountain. The next major discovery was made at Red Mountain near Trail Creek in 1890, where rich deposits of silver and copper ore were uncovered. These were among the richest claims in BC. By 1890 five major claims had been staked – the Centre Star, the War Eagle, the Idaho, the Virginia, and the Le Roi. Finally, rich deposits of silver-lead ores were uncovered in the Slocan district north of Nelson in 1891. Now a host of prospectors and miners – mostly American – poured into the Kootenays. Many of the mine promoters were businessmen from Spokane Falls (later renamed Spokane) in Washington Territory.[1]

It soon became clear that better facilities were required to transport the ores to smelters in Montana. The Northern Pacific Railroad had completed its main line from St Paul, Minnesota, to Portland, Oregon, via Helena, Montana, Sand Point, Idaho and Spokane, Washington, in 1883. The CPR main line to Port Moody, BC, had been completed in November 1885, and in 1887 it was extended 12 miles to Vancouver. The two railways used steamboats and rail ferries to reach the Kootenay district: the CPR used the Arrow Lakes and the Columbia River to make a connection at Revelstoke on the main line, while the Northern Pacific utilized the Columbia River south of the Arrow Lakes. From the mid-1880s numerous navigation companies were offering regular service on these routes.[2]

Spokane began to emerge as the centre of the Kootenay trade. Located on the Northern Pacific main line, the town became the seat of Spokane County in 1886. Two years later it had the substantial population of 7,000 and controlled the transportation of ore from the Coeur d'Alene mines in Idaho through a railroad built by a skilful Spokane railway promoter, Daniel C. Corbin.[3] In 1888 Corbin became involved with a scheme to build a railway north from Spokane, through the rich agricultural region around Colville in Washington Territory, to connect with the CPR at Revelstoke. The Spokane Falls and Northern Railroad (SF&N) was incorporated in Washington Territory in April 1888. Its leading backers were wealthy Spokane businessmen, "most with mining or banking connections or both, and several had been associated with the Northern Pacific." Corbin supplied the expertise in railway construction, for he was the only director who had built a railway.[4] The following year Corbin took over management of the railway, and financial control shifted to New York City, where Corbin had a number of important business connections.

Corbin's first contract with the SF&N covered its construction from Spokane to Colville, in the new state of Washington, a distance of 88 miles. After completing this section in October 1889, he then planned to extend the SF&N across the international boundary and westward through southern BC to the Pacific coast. The Spokane railway promoter received support for his scheme from many British Columbians who felt that by encouraging his railway they would force the CPR to build through southern BC, and from "thousands of American citizens who had invaded British Columbia pursuing their fortunes in the mines."[5] But Corbin encountered stiff opposition in Central Canada to his plans to cross the international border. His strongest opponent was W.C. Van Horne, president of the CPR.

Nevertheless by June 1890, Corbin had extended the SF&N north along the Columbia River from Colville to Little Dalles, a distance of 22 miles. Early in 1890 the BC legislature incorporated the Columbia and Kootenay Railway and Navigation Company (Columbia and Kootenay), which was authorized to build a railway from the outlet of Kootenay Lake west to the junction of the Kootenay and Columbia rivers and to operate steamboats on the Kootenay and Arrow Lakes. The company was closely associated with the CPR; one of its chief promoters was Harry Abbott, the general superintendent of the CPR's Pacific Division. The Columbia and Kootenay was granted a land subsidy of 200,000 acres by the BC legislature and a cash subsidy of $3,200 per mile by the federal Parliament, which declared it to be a work "for the general advantage of Canada." On 20 August 1890 the Cabinet authorized the CPR to lease the Columbia and Kootenay for 999 years. That same month the SF&N and CPR signed an agreement with the Columbia and Kootenay for a tri-weekly steamboat service between Spokane and Revelstoke. It was clear that cooperation between Corbin and the CPR would be possible, if the Spokane promoter abandoned his plans to expand his railway into BC.[6] And, in fact, the CPR used the charter of the Columbia and Kootenay to build a 28-mile line from the mining town of Nelson on Kootenay Lake, southwest, to Robson on the Columbia River. It began operating in mid-June 1891, thus opening up a rail and water link from Nelson to Revelstoke via the Kootenay and Columbia rivers and the Arrow Lakes.[7] (See figure 1.)

However, Corbin did not abandon his plans to expand into Canada. In August and September 1892 the SF&N was extended 7 miles to Northport, just south of the international boundary. He also took over the charter of the Nelson and Fort Sheppard Railway in 1892 and persuaded the BC legislature to grant it a land subsidy of 10,240 acres per mile. The following year Corbin obtained a federal charter for the line which made it eligible for a federal subsidy of $3,200 per mile and allowed it to make connections with an extra-provincial railway. He then extended the SF&N to the international boundary and built the Nelson and Fort Sheppard from just outside Nelson to link up with it. This connection represented the first invasion of the Kootenays by an American railway. Ores from the Slocan mining district could be shipped by boat from Kaslo, in the Slocan, to Nelson, and thence by rail over Corbin's railways and the Northern Pacific to smelters at Tacoma, Washington. Trail Creek's ores could be barged down the Columbia to Northport on the SF&N. Corbin was gaining control of the principal mining camps in the Kootenays.[8]

The CPR had been actively considering the building of the Crow's Nest Pass Railway at least as early as 1890. Prime Minister Macdonald had recognized the necessity of such a line in order to prevent "the

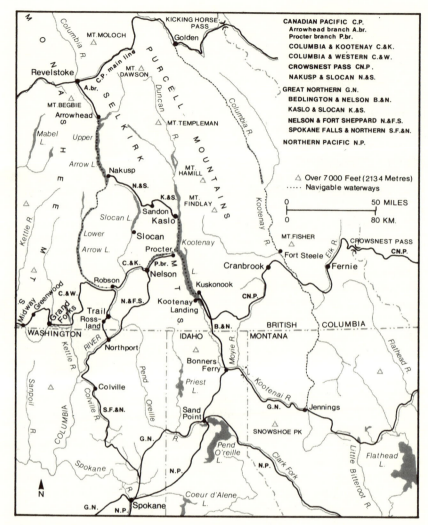

Figure 1 Railways in the Kootenays, 1900

permanent diversion southwards of the greater part of the ores of
the Kootenay and adjacent districts." As Van Horne explained to
J.S. Willison, editor of the Toronto *Globe*, "Sir John Macdonald realized the importance of this, and urged on by him we built the
Columbia and Kootenay Railway, and bought the Galt Road extending from Dunmore to Lethbridge; surveyed the line from Lethbridge to Kootenay Lake, and did some grading between Lethbridge
and Crow's Nest. But after his death, the Government seemed to

lose interest in the matter, and we were left to digest a large and useless expenditure of money."[9] The most important action taken by the CPR at this time in regard to the Crow's Nest Pass Railway was its lease in 1893 of the Alberta Railway and Coal Company's (AR&C CO) narrow-gauge railway from Lethbridge to Dunmore, on the CPR main line, east of Calgary. Sir Alexander Galt, backed by British investors, had built the AR&C CO into a substantial coal-mining operation at Lethbridge in the period 1882–90. After 1890 Galt's health rapidly deteriorated, and the AR&C CO's concerns were managed almost entirely by his son Elliot Galt. In 1890 the company built a railway from Lethbridge into Montana and signed a contract with J.J. Hill for the daily delivery of 200 tons of coal to the Great Northern Railroad.[10] However, expanded coal sales in the American market did not develop, while the domestic market was too small to support the Galt collieries. Galt needed to negotiate a contract with the CPR selling it a substantial amount of coal on a regular basis. He negotiated with Shaughnessy, playing off the Great Northern against the CPR, and reached an important agreement in July 1893. The CPR contracted to operate the Dunmore-Lethbridge railway, provided that the AR&C CO converted it from narrow to standard gauge. The CPR would provide all the rolling stock, pay the AR&C CO 40 per cent of gross revenues collected on the line, and purchase 200 tons of coal per day in Lethbridge, at $2.50 per ton. The agreement also gave the CPR the option to purchase the Dunmore-Lethbridge line. In compensation, the CPR gave the AR&C CO the option to extend the railway fom Lethbridge to Fort Macleod and lease it out under the same conditions. The widening of the Dunmore-Lethbridge line was carried out in the summer and autumn of 1893, and on 28 November the first CPR train steamed into Lethbridge.[11]

The CPR agreement with the AR&C CO was a clear indication of the former's serious interest in building a railway from Lethbridge through the Crow's Nest Pass to the Kootenay mining districts, since the Dunmore-Lethbridge line would connect it with the CPR main line. And, in 1894, the CPR board strongly endorsed this plan. Van Horne informed a businessman (November 1894) that "our Directors feel strongly that if any railway between the Crow's Nest Pass and the Kootenay District is to receive a subsidy from the Dominion Government, their Company should have it; and they feel bound to use every means in their power to prevent any subsidy being given to any other company proposing to occupy that ground." The CPR president approached Prime Minister Sir John Thompson in 1894 and told him of the "impossibility of getting the necessary money [to build the Crow's Nest Pass Railway] without overstraining the credit of the Company." The CPR president then asked for a $5,000 per mile federal subsidy for the line and a 20-year, $20,000 per mile loan. However, the Thompson administration was facing severe financial difficulties, "and were disinclined to issue bonds for such an amount, and nothing was done about it." Van Horne later concluded that the "disorganized state of affairs which has prevailed at Ottawa for some time back [i.e. since Thompson's death in December 1894] has prevented our making a new effort in this direction."[12]

A more serious rival for the trade of the Kootenays emerged in the period 1893–95, James J. Hill's Great Northern Railroad. Its transcontinental line through the Pacific Northwest, completed in 1893, ran north of the Northern Pacific main line, through Jennings, Montana, and Bonner's Ferry, Idaho, to Everett, Washington. (See figure 1.) Since the Great Northern was closer to the international boundary than the Northern Pacific, it was to have "considerably more effect on the Kootenays than its earlier rival."[13] The presidents of the CPR and Great Northern had known one another for over a decade; it was Hill who had recommended the hiring of Van Horne as CPR general manager in 1881. Both men were extremely competitive, and deeply distrusted each other's motives.[14] An initial conflict occurred in the Slocan mining district, where a discovery of silver-lead ore in August 1891 produced a stampede of prospectors in 1892. Soon about 40 tons of ore a day were being hauled by wagon over trails to Kaslo, on Kootenay Lake. From there the ore was transported by boat to the terminus of Corbin's Nelson and Fort Sheppard Railway.[15] The CPR president was impressed with the potential of the Slocan. An official of a large American refinery looked over the mines in the summer of 1894 and informed Van Horne "that there was more in sight in the Slocan District as the result of two years prospecting and development than in any district in the United States which has been opened for 25 years."[16] However, much of the ore was being shipped to the US via the Northern Pacific and Great Northern railways. Van Horne reported in November 1894 that "part of the ores [from the Slocan] are packed across the divide to Kaslo, on Kootenay Lake, whence they find their way out by way of Bonner's Ferry [on the Great Northern Railroad]; part find their way down to the Nelson and Fort Shep[pard] Road to Nelson; and part come to us at the end of our spur line below Revelstoke. The movement of ores by our line this year has very largely increased."[17] In 1895 the CPR and the Great Northern built railways to the mining camp at Sandon, in the heart of the Slocan district. The CPR took over the unfinished Nakusp and Slocan Railway in January 1895 and completed the 37-mile line from Nakusp, on Upper Arrow Lake, to Sandon. From Nakusp the ore was carried by steamboat via the lake and the Columbia River to Revelstoke. The Great Northern countered by financing and constructing the Kaslo and Slocan Railway, completed in 1895, from Kaslo on Kootenay Lake west to Sandon. This railway served as a link, via Kootenay Lake and the Kootenay River to the Great Northern at Bonner's Ferry.[18] The building of this line, Van Horne reported, "has brought upon us the necessity of building at once a spur from the end of the Nakusp and Slocan Line, to secure ourselves against the loss of some of our most important mining traffic."[19] In September 1895 the CPR started construction on the partially completed Arrowhead Branch, a 28-mile line from Revelstoke to Arrowhead at the head of Upper Arrow Lake; once completed, it reduced the water distance between the CPR and such points as Nakusp and Robson. Although the line was intended to facilitate the transporting of ores to a smelter in Revelstoke, "the mines continued to ship southward and the smelter closed."[20]

The CPR's financial difficulties in 1894–5 severely restricted any expansion of company lines in the Kootenays. Van Horne informed Mount Stephen in August 1895 that earnings for the first seven months of 1895 indicated that total earnings for that calendar year would be lower than the figures for 1892. In addition, the Columbia and Kootenay Railway had not earned its operating expenses for 1894 and for the first three months of 1895.[21]

Van Horne decided that his right-hand man, vice-president Shaughnessy, should visit the Kootenays and obtain a first-hand impression of the mining potential of the region, in view of the CPR's completion of the Nakusp and Slocan Railway into the Slocan. Shaughnessy and Harry Abbott, the general superintendent of the Pacific Division, made an extensive tour through the Kootenay district in July 1895, paying particular attention to the mines in the Slocan district. Shaughnessy was very impressed with the mining potential of the Kootenays in particular and British Columbia in general. "I believe," he reported to his old Milwaukee railway associate F.D. Underwood, "that British Columbia furnishes the best opening in the world to-day for people with a practical knowledge of mining. I look for enormous development North and South of the [Canadian Pacific] railway within the next five years."[22] He recommended to Van Horne that the CPR hire someone whose technical knowledge and general experience could keep the company informed of mining development in districts tributary to the CPR, and who could advise on the extension of lines "to secure the maximum volume of this mineral traffic." This recommendation was accepted and the company hired the American mining engineer, J.H. Susman, whom Shaughnessy had met during his visit to the Kootenays. Susman, an employee of the Kansas City Smelting and Refining Company, joined the CPR in September 1895 at the substantial salary of $3,000 a year. Shaughnessy had Susman make a report on mines in the West Kootenay region and then visit Vancouver and Nanaimo to investigate "the coke question, which will be one of vital importance in connection with the smelting industries in British Columbia."[23]

During his visit to the Kootenays, Shaughnessy was disturbed that many American goods were entering the region duty-free. As he informed N. Clarke Wallace, the federal controller of customs, "When I was in Rossland [in July 1895] ... I found that every waggon, piece of furniture, and nearly everything in the ways of groceries, provisions, and dry goods, come from the United States, and I am pretty confident that most of them contribute nothing to the revenue of Canada."[24] Shaughnessy's observations show clearly that Americans dominated the import trade into the Kootenays. He asked Wallace to instruct his customs officers to enforce strictly the payment of duties on American goods coming into the Kootenays. He asserted that the CPR was "doing everything we can" to ensure that Canadian businessmen benefited from the Kootenay trade, "but we shall utterly fail unless the Customs law be enforced." Shaughnessy was struck by the American character of the Kootenay towns. He noted that Rossland's population of 1,500 was made up "almost entirely" of miners from the United States, so that it was "to all intents and purposes a United States town."[25]

By building a line from Lethbridge through the Crow's Nest Pass to the mining centres of East and West Kootenays, the CPR could redirect the region's traffic from American to Canadian channels. This measure would effectively "Canadianize" the Kootenays. As Aitken has demonstrated, one of the main functions of the Canadian state has been "defensive expansionism" – the granting of federal aid to private enterprise to halt American economic and political domination of Canada. Federal aid to the CPR for building the Crow's Nest Pass Railway could be justified on these grounds.[26] It was also clear that the CPR would require federal aid to build what was going to be an expensive line.[27] Shaughnessy outlined the American threat more fully in April 1897: "The advantages arising from partial development of their [British Columbia's] mines [in the Kootenay region] have hitherto been enjoyed to [a] great extent by the people of the United States. The agricultural state of Washington has furnished a large portion of the food consumed ... A large proportion of the tools and machinery used in the mines and smelters is furnished by American manufacturers. At present, all the silver lead ores and a considerable portion of the gold ores produced in the Province are being transported to smelting centres in the United States."[28]

President Van Horne shared his vice-president's sense of urgency. He informed J.S. Willison in April 1896 that the Crow's Nest Pass Railway "should be built ... without delay if the *permanent* diversion southwards of the greater part of the ores of the Kootenay and adjacent districts is to be prevented." The problem was that the Conservative administrations that followed the death of Sir John A. Macdonald seemed, in Van Horne's words, "to lose interest in the matter." Van Horne caustically remarked later that month, "as soon as there is something like a Government to deal with, we will press as vigorously as possible ... for some decided steps towards the building of the Crow's Nest Pass line."[29] Of course, the economic recession of 1893–5 was also a major factor in preventing the construction of the Crow's Nest line.

The confused political situation in Ottawa in the first 6 months of 1896, Shaughnessy lamented, made it "quite impossible to do anything at Ottawa ... the Session of Parliament, changes in the Ministry, and the election, absorbing the attention of the Ministers."[30] However, Shaughnessy and Van Horne had to face the possibility that the Conservatives might be returned in the looming federal general election. Therefore, on 15 April Shaughnessy submitted to Railways Minister John Haggart a proposal for federal aid to the CPR to enable it to build the Crow's Nest Pass line. Shaughnessy had previously discussed his ideas with Haggart and other members of the Bowell government, stressing his view that the Crow's Nest Pass Railway was "the most important railway work if not indeed the most important work of any kind requiring the attention of Government." The purpose of the project was to preserve for Canada the mining traffic of the Kootenays and to promte the establishment of smelters in the region. The railway, an estimated 300 miles in length, would run from Lethbridge through the Crow's Nest Pass to Nelson, on Kootenay Lake, where it would connect with the CPR's Columbia and Kootenay Railway, which ran to Robson on the Columbia River. (See figure 1.) The company requested a cash subsidy of $5,000 per mile and a 20-year federal loan at 3 per cent for "an amount equivalent to twenty thousand dollars per mile of railway actually constructed." This request was not an official one, although Haggart was probably not made aware of this fact, since it "was not formally considered by our Board but was rather in the nature of a suggestion that would probably prove satisfactory."[31]

On 22 April, the day before the session ended, Haggart announced that a motion on the order paper for a federal loan to the CPR to build the Crow's Nest Pass Railway was being dropped. It appears that the Bowell government was unwilling to grant the company's request for a loan for $20,000 per mile. Haggart offered no explanation for his action; the Ottawa *Citizen* thought that the decision was "dictated probably by a desire to conserve the time of the House for other business." Shaughnessy had no idea that the Crow's Nest Pass Railway resolution was going to be brought down and did not know why the resolution had been withdrawn. When Sir Charles Tupper became prime minister on 1 May, he indicated his willingness to authorize a cash subsidy of $5,000 per mile as well as the loan.[32]

For several years Van Horne had been conducting, as David Hall observes, "an active programme of building bridges to the Liberal party."[33] The CPR had been regarded by the Liberals as a Conservative enterprise since its inception in 1881, and the company's massive intervention in favour of the Conservatives in the 1891 general election had strongly reinforced this attitude. As Richard Clippingdale notes, after the 1891 contest the CPR was regarded by Liberals "only slightly more favourably than Satan."[34]

Van Horne focused his attention on two prominent Ontario Liberals, James D. Edgar and John S. Willison. Edgar was a shrewd and powerful politician who had risen to prominence in the federal Liberal party during the leadership of Edward Blake (1880–7). When he was elected to the House of Commons in a by-election in 1884, as Robert Stamp observes, he "immediately assumed a position within the Liberal party that seemed to be second only to Blake himself." At the start of the 1885 session of Parliament he was named chief railway critic for the Opposition, a post for which he was qualified since he had once been a railway promoter. Edgar "was essentially a party organizer, a behind-the-scenes politician" who supervised the party's affairs in Ontario. When the *Globe* was reorganized in 1882 and brought under stricter party control, Edgar was one of the Liberal politicians appointed to its board of directors, a position he held for 7 years. In 1889 he helped start a move to drop John Cameron as the *Globe's* editor, and befriended J.S. Willison, who had been appointed editor in 1890. He strongly supported the selection of Wilfrid Laurier as Blake's successor, and was one of the new leader's closest advisors. Under Laurier's leadership, he once again assumed the role of chief Liberal railway critic. Although his influence in the party began to decline after 1893, his views were still respected by Laurier in 1896. But, as far back as the early 1890s,

Edgar had developed "a warm personal friendship with W.C. Van Horne, a friendship that helped keep the c.p.r. out of the Conservative camp in the 1896 campaign."[35] During a long, amicable discussion with Van Horne in Montreal in January 1896, the two men "discussed politics and found no divergence in our views." As Edgar reported to Willison, "V.H. directs the *policy* of the railway – no doubt of that. He believes firmly that we are going to win, and he does not lack ability to draw a few conclusions." Upon hearing a report of Edgar's conversation with Van Horne, Laurier was delighted. Edgar informed Willison, Laurier "agrees with me that it is impossible there can be any danger of the c.p.r. actively interfering against us [in the 1896 general election]."[36] Subsequently Van Horne did take several actions to emphasize his company's neutrality in the 1896 contest. (Undoubtedly though it was Shaughnessy who insisted on this policy as a result of his strong distaste for the CPR's activities on behalf of the Conservatives in the 1891 contest.) Railway passes were issued for both Liberal and Conservative organizers in Ontario. On 5 June Van Horne informed Edgar that his company "do[es] not intend to issue any free transportation to the voters of either party, both will stand exactly on the same footing in that regard."[37]

J.S. Willison's friendship with Van Horne developed from a trip he had made to Western Canada in the autumn of 1895. Reporting on this trip in the *Globe*, the editor strongly criticized the CPR's high freight rates in the West, and argued forcefully for regulation of the CPR and all other railways in Canada. He also strongly supported the building of a railway into the Kootenay mining region to counteract the Great Northern Railroad, which was busy establishing rail connections for the area with Spokane and other US centres. Willison was certain that the CPR wanted to build a line into the region. He favoured providing federal aid if the company surrendered its freedom from rate control and agreed to have it rates regulated by a federal railway commission. He also insisted that the CPR fix fair maximum rates on the carriage of coal, ore, grain, cattle, and other staple exports of the West. "From that time," he was to recall, "Van Horne was my friend and I had many evidences of his regard and good-will."[38]

Under Laurier's dynamic leadership, the Liberals won a resounding victory in the 23 June general election and the famous "Ministry of the Talents" was sworn into office on 13 July.[39] The important portfolio of railways and canals went to Andrew G. Blair, a powerful New Brunswick politician who had been premier of the province since 1883. A journalist who knew Blair well described him as "affable, genial, a man of broad vision and a capable administrator, ...

[and] also a democrat to the hilt." He was, in addition, a strong proponent of New Brunswick's interests in Cabinet. Van Horne was disappointed that Edgar had not obtained the railways portfolio and had been excluded from the Cabinet.[40]

Almost immediately the CPR began negotiations with the Laurier administration for federal aid to construct a railway into the Kootenay mining region. Early in September Shaughnessy travelled to Ottawa to discuss the question with the prime minister. He furnished Laurier and Blair with copies of the memorandum which he had submitted to Haggart in April.[41] The company, he informed them, was determined to construct the line immediately if sufficient federal aid could be obtained.[42] Van Horne was very optimistic about reaching an agreement with the Laurier government on the matter. He believed there was an "extraordinary amount of unanimity of sentiment [in favour of building the Crow's Nest Pass line] throughout the country ... and apparently the same unanimity in Parlament [sic] and in the Government." Therefore, the CPR president observed, "I do not think any special effort is necessary to move the Government in the matter of the Crow's Nest Pass line."[43] He did, however, impress on Edgar that, since 1891, the company had done considerable preparatory work for a Crow's Nest Pass line and should therefore have control of it. The CPR had, it will be recalled, taken over the operation of the AR&C CO's railway from Dunmore on the CPR main line to Lethbridge, made expensive surveys between Lethbridge and Kootenay Lake, and done some grading between Fort Macleod and the Crow's Nest Pass. The total cost of this work amounted to about $1,150,000.[44] Nonetheless, Van Horne was concerned about Blair's attitude to a subsidy for the Crow's Nest Pass line. Evidently the railways minister believed that the CPR wanted the federal government to cover the total expense of building the line. Van Horne had to assure Edgar that the company only wanted an "equitable" subsidy.[45]

Van Horne was on close terms with both BC premier John H. Turner and Colonel James Baker, the provincial secretary and minister of mines. Baker had extensive land holdings around Cranbrook in the East Kootenays, which the Crow's Nest Pass line would probably pass through. While Turner was absent in Vancouver, the BC cabinet held a meeting on 19 August 1896. The Cabinet, no doubt influenced by Baker's views, proposed sending a telegram to Laurier endorsing a vote in favour of financial aid to the Crow's Nest Pass line during the autumn 1896 session of Parliament, and urging that "it is of the utmost importance to the mining interests to get the line completed as soon as possible." Turner agreed with this proposal and on 20 August wired Laurier requesting a federal subsidy for the Crow's Nest Pass Railway be granted in the upcoming session. "The mining interests here," Turner asserted, "will so greatly benefit by the Line that undoubtedly the Dominion Revenues will be largely increased thereby."[46]

In October 1896 Van Horne made his regular annual inspection trip of CPR lines in Western Canada. While in Vancouver he gave a lengthy interview on the subject of rail facilities for the Kootenays. The coastal cities of Victoria, Vancouver, and New Westminster wanted the federal government to aid the construction of a railway from the Pacific coast to the Kootenays so that their merchants could sell their goods in the Kootenay region. The Vancouver Board of Trade had passed a resolution in favour of this proposal in October, but stated it was willing to see the Crow's Nest Pass Railway built at the same time. At this time the CPR was quite unpopular in British Columbia for many reasons, such as high freight rates, a "general sentiment against monopoly as in Manitoba," and a feeling that the company was too active in BC politics. Some BC politicians favoured government ownership of new railway lines in the province, among them the Liberal MP's W.W.B. McInnes and Hewitt Bostock.[47]

In his Vancouver interview Van Horne made it very clear that the CPR's first priority was to build the Crow's Nest Pass Railway from Lethbridge, through the Crow's Nest Pass, to Nelson, BC. Only the early construction of this line would "secure Canadian interests in the [Kootenay] trade already developed." If the building of this railway were "long delayed, the trade will become permanently established southwards and will be permanently lost to British Columbia and to the whole Dominion." His second priority was construction of local lines from the Crow's Nest Pass Railway to the mining camps. After its completion the CPR would build a line from Nelson to Revelstoke in order to establish an all-rail route between the Kootenays and the Pacific coast. Van Horne also endorsed the early building of a direct line from the Kootenays to the Fraser Valley. "That will follow the completion of the Crow's Nest Pass Line as certainly as one sunrise follows another," he asserted. The CPR president was opposed to government ownership of the Crow's Nest Pass Railway since he believed that his company could build the line more efficiently and cheaply. Besides, Van Horne doubted that the federal government would want to incur the large expense of building the many local lines to the mines.[48]

The Vancouver *News-Advertiser* devoted a long editorial to Van Horne's interview. The critical issue, in its view, was the timing of the construction of the coast-to-Kootenay railway. If this line were built some years after the Crow's Nest Pass Railway, the editorialist asserted, the result would be "detrimental ... to the commercial, industrial and agricultural interests of the Coast districts of the Province." This was a shrewd analysis, for the Crow's Nest Pass Railway was designed to provide a cheaper, shorter, and more direct transportation link between the Kootenays and Central Canada, thus enabling Ontario and Quebec business interests to dominate the Kootenay trade. The editorialist also suggested that the Crow's Nest line would enable the agriculture of the Western Territories to capture the Kootenay market.[49]

On 14 November, after returning from his western tour, Van Horne submitted a formal CPR request for federal assistance to build the Crow's Nest Pass line to Railways Minister Blair. The CPR was prepared to build a line from Lethbridge through the Crow's Nest Pass to Nelson, British Columbia, for a cash subsidy of $5,000 per mile and a 20-year federal government loan of $20,000 per mile. These were the same terms that Shaughnessy had outlined to Haggart in April 1896. However, the company had now located the approximate route of the proposed line and estimated the cost of construction. The line would be 327-miles long and would cost $8,013,280. Van Horne's terms would thus cover the entire cost of building the line, although the government would eventually be repaid for its loan of $6,540,000. The president stressed that the line would initiate the mining of "excellent coking coal" in the East Kootenay district, coal which could be used to supply existing smelters at Nelson and Trail, as well as new smelters in the East Kootenay region. This development would stimulate the mining of lower grade ores; at that time high transportation costs to US smelters had "made it impossible to profitably ship anything except high grade ores and concentrates." The building of the Crow's Nest Pass line, Van Horne asserted, "would naturally have the effect of building up in British Columbia smelting points that would rival in importance Butte, Helena or Great Falls."[50]

Van Horne did not receive an immediate response to his proposal from Blair. The railways minister left Ottawa for British Columbia on 25 November. He visited the Rossland and Slocan mining districts, as well as Victoria and Nanaimo. It seems likely that Cabinet had endorsed this trip, which would enable Blair to observe at first hand conditions in the Kootenay mining camps, and to gauge opinion in the province, especially in the two major urban centres, Vancouver and Victoria, on the question of the Crow's Nest Pass Railway. Suspecting that he would have to wait for a decision on his application for federal assistance until Blair returned to Ottawa, Van Horne, nevertheless, continued to campaign on the company's behalf. He wrote Colonel Baker and asked him to see Blair in Victoria and "fully impress him with the importance of immediate action" on the Crow's Nest Pass line.[51]

In November 1896 premier Turner wrote Van Horne explaining his government's position on railway matters in southern BC. Turner, the head of a large Victoria mercantile house, who had been premier since March 1895, also held the finance portfolio. He stressed that there was "a very strong feeling" in BC in favour of a "Coast to Kootenay" railway – a line from Vancouver direct to the Kootenay district. Turner indicated that his government would strongly support the CPR undertaking this line if it would build the railway at the same time as the Crow's Nest Pass Railway. He proposed some concessions that the CPR would be required to make to gain his government's support, such as "a common rate of freight to all Coast points," and a CPR ferry-and-passenger service between Vancouver and Victoria. He also suggested that the BC government would provide aid for both railways above and beyond federal assistance, although he made no definite proposal. Replying to the premier, Van Horne emphasized that the CPR could complete a line from Lethbridge through the Crow's Nest Pass to Nelson, British Columbia, in less than 2 years. He was aware that businessmen in Vancouver and Victoria wanted a direct line from the Fraser Valley to the Kootenay district. He also pointed out that such a line would have to follow a circuitous route and would be very expensive to build. It could not be used as a substitute for the CPR main line for through traffic, since it would be longer than the existing main line and it would have "more numerous and much more widely distributed gradients" than this line. But he recognized a problem – that Victoria and Vancouver businessmen would have to use the CPR main line to ship their goods to Revelstoke. From there these goods would be transported via the CPR branch to Arrowhead and then by lake steamers south to Nelson. Goods from Victoria and Vancouver could be transported more efficiently to the West Kootenay by shipping them in bond over the Great Northern line, the SF&N and the Nelson and Fort Sheppard to Nelson. So the CPR president promised to build a branch connecting the Columbia and Kootenay Railway and the Nakusp and Slocan Railway, in order to improve transportation between the West Kootenay mining districts and Revelstoke on the main line. The CPR, he concluded, "is earnest in its desire to do anything and everything it can within reason to avoid causes of complaint on the part of any of the Coast cities or any community in your Province."[52]

Then, in December, Blair visited the main mining towns in the

West Kootenay – Nelson, Trail, Robson, Sandon, Kaslo, and Rossland – before travelling to the Pacific coast via Spokane. At Nelson, the federal railways minister spoke strongly in favour of the Crow's Nest Pass Railway and "threw cold water on the [proposal for a] through road from the coast to Kootenay." This speech angered people in Vancouver, with the result that Blair declined an invitation to a banquet there. In Victoria he met with city council and with prominent businessmen. The railways minister "expressed himself as perfectly surprised at the wonderful mineral resources of British Columbia." He announced that as a result of his visit to the Rossland and Slocan mining districts he would recommend the Crow's Nest Pass Railway to Cabinet, but he did not commit himself on the matter of federal aid to the project.[53]

After a short trip to Nanaimo, Blair returned to Vancouver where he had a number of important meetings. The promoters of the Vancouver, Victoria and Eastern Railway (vv&e) had an interview with the railways minister. This project, promoted by prominent citizens of Victoria, Vancouver, and New Westminster, envisaged a railway through the southern section of the Fraser Valley and the Hope Mountains by the most direct route to Rossland. The Vancouver City Council presented a prepared speech to Blair which strongly emphasized the immediate need of a more direct rail link between the coast cities and the Kootenay mining districts. The council advocated the extension of the proposed Crow's Nest Pass Railway to the coast "with as little delay as possible ... so that the business community might reap those benefits to which the opening up of the interior fairly entitles them." Blair met the Vancouver Board of Trade, which also pressed strongly for the immediate construction of a coast-to-Kootenay railway. The railways minister observed that he and his cabinet colleagues had not been aware of the "importance of securing railway communication from the coast to the Kootenay." He promised that he would inform Cabinet of the strong support in BC for such a railway, but stressed that he could not predict what cabinet's decision would be on this matter. Finally, Blair spoke to a public meeting sponsored by the Vancouver Young Men's Liberal Club. He observed that the economic growth of BC would greatly benefit Manitoba and the North-West, which would find "the best market" for their agricultural products in BC.[54] Blair then left for Ottawa about 20 December.

The negotiations between the CPR and the Laurier government for a federal subsidy to the Crow's Nest Pass Railway began in earnest in January 1897. Van Horne had "a very satisfactory interview" in Ottawa on 15 January with Clifford Sifton, who had been appointed to the Laurier cabinet on 17 November as minister of the interior. This was the most important cabinet portfolio for the affairs of Western Canada. Sifton had been an influential member of the Greenway Liberal government of Manitoba for over 5 years. Van Horne informed Sifton that "nothing for a great while has given me such real pleasure as seeing you at the head of the Department of the Interior."[55] About this time Van Horne and Shaughnessy met with Blair in Ottawa to discuss the Crow's Nest Pass Railway. Blair was "very strongly of the opinion that the Crow's Nest Pass line should be built by the Dominion Government." The railways minister asserted that only this policy "would, in his opinion, satisfy the people of Southern British Columbia." However, he favoured leasing the railway to the CPR after it was constructed. The two CPR officials pointed out that if public opinion were strong enough to force the government to own the line, it would be "vastly more potent in preventing the lease of the line to the Canadian Pacific after it should be built." Van Horne and Shaughnessy had fully informed the Cabinet of their views, stressing that "many prominent people" were involved in this issue. Thus Van Horne was confident that Blair would soon realize that his policy was "impracticable."[56]

Van Horne then prepared a new CPR proposal which he outlined in a letter of 4 February to the railways minister. In it the president, who had the formal endorsement of the company's directors, requested a federal subsidy of $10,000 per mile instead of a federal loan. The company would raise the remainder of the funds for construction by issuing bonds on its own credit. The proposal made it clear that the CPR would raise some of the money for the line on its own, thus meeting Blair's objection that the company wanted the federal government to cover all costs of building the line. Van Horne adopted a conciliatory approach by expressing the confidence of the directors that "a satisfactory arrangement" could be reached with the government about "maximum through and local tolls" on the Crow's Nest line. This was a significant comment, for it was the first indication that government rate regulation was to be a major part of any agreement between the government and the CPR. Van Horne also promised that the line would be extended from Nelson, west to the Boundary Creek district, "in the near future."[57]

On 12 February Van Horne discussed the subject of federal aid to the Crow's Nest Pass Railway with Clifford Sifton. The minister of the interior set out five conditions on which federal aid should be based. First, maximum through and local rates on the Crow's Nest line should be agreed upon and supervised by the federal government. Second, the government should have the right to grant running powers to other railways "over any section of the line in the Crow's Nest Pass where the construction of a second line may be impracticable." (This condition was rather unrealistic, for it was unlikely that another railway would be needed in southern BC. The government was to use the condition to refute any claims that a CPR monopoly was being established in southern BC. The running-rights condition had an essentially political purpose. Similar provisions had been required in the Northern Pacific and Manitoba agreement in Manitoba; they held out the elusive hope that real competition might some day be provided.) Third, the CPR's grain rates in the Canadian North-West should be reduced by 3 cents per 100 pounds, with the reductions to become effective when the Crow's Nest Pass line was completed to Nelson. Fourth, the CPR should sell to the federal government all its lands east of the third meridian, amounting to 2,617,000 acres, at $2 per acre. This proposal originated with Sifton, who was critical of the alternate-section land policy and was determined "to use the [Crow's Nest Pass Agreement] as a lever to pry loose the railway lands east of the ... [third] meridian." Finally, Sifton wanted the CPR to turn over the 4-million-acre land grant of the British Columbia Southern Railway to the federal government. Evidently Van Horne, whose company was in the process of acquiring its charter, "almost jumped to the ceiling" when these conditions were presented to him.[58]

He, nonetheless, discussed Sifton's terms with his executive committee the following day and then wrote to the minister of the interior. He was willing to accept the first two conditions without modification. Regarding the rate reductions on grain, Van Horne suggested equalizing such rates throughout the prairie West, so that, for example, the freight rates on grain from Calgary to the Lakehead would be about the same as those from Winnipeg. As far as he was concerned the real sticking point was the *price* of CPR lands. The lands east of the third meridian, he informed Sifton, "form the cream of our grant." He was certain that the lowest price the directors would accept was $2.50 per acre. And finally, Van Horne wanted the CPR to retain the BC Southern lands "unless we can get adequate compensation for them."[59]

In a lengthy letter to Sir Donald Smith, Canadian high commissioner in London, Van Horne discussed the state of the CPR negotiations with the Laurier government as of 16 February. He was convinced that Sifton was the leading figure in these negotiations. Laurier had indicated that he would be "guided largely by Mr. Sifton's views, he being best acquainted with the situation in the West." Sifton was "very friendly" to the company and had "rather moderate

views" on grain rate reductions in the North-West. Sifton was willing
to settle for a reduction of 1.8 cents per bushel (3 cents per 100
pounds) on grain from points in the North-West to Fort William, to
come into effect when the Crow's Nest Pass Railway was completed.
Van Horne and Shaughnessy were convinced that such a reduction
"will be forced upon us by other causes by that time." The president
was willing to sell CPR lands at $2.50 per acre, but he did not believe
that Sifton could win Cabinet approval for such a price. He judged
that William Mulock and Louis Davies were the only cabinet ministers
who supported Blair's policy of government construction of the line.
He was nevertheless concerned that Blair "may block any other plan
and that nothing will be done."[60]

On 18 February a cabinet committee, appointed "to grapple with
the question of the construction of the Crow's Nest Railway," held
its first meeting in the office of Clifford Sifton. The three members
of this committee were Sifton, Blair, and Sir Oliver Mowat, the minister of justice.[61] Although Blair remained a strong advocate of government construction of the line, it soon became clear that Laurier
was firmly opposed to such a policy. The prime minister informed
a Liberal MP from Hamilton on 26 February that he strongly favoured CPR construction, provided the company made some important concessions. He saw the situation as an opportunity to "rid"
Western Canada of CPR "monopolies." Laurier was undoubtedly
thinking of the CPR's large land grant in the West and its effective
freedom from rate regulation. If the CPR gave up such "monopolies,"
the prime minister was convinced, Western Canada's economy would
develop rapidly, thus stimulating the economic development of the
entire country.[62] These were views that Sifton shared; indeed, the
minister of the interior probably played a large role in shaping them.

The 1897 session of Parliament opened on 25 March. By mid-
April the CPR officials still had no clear idea what the government's
policy on the Crow's Nest Pass Railway would be. The *Globe's* Ottawa
correspondent, Stewart Lyon, reported to J.S. Willison in Toronto
that Blair was "one of the dominant forces here ... and would probably have no objection to forcing upon the C.P.R. terms so stringent
that it must refuse in self defence." The railway minister's policy of
government construction was being supported by the four Liberal
MPs from British Columbia, as well as by some members from Manitoba and the North-West, notably Frank Oliver from Edmonton.[63]

While the CPR-government negotiations continued, two western
railway promoters, William Mackenzie and Donald Mann, lobbied
strongly to obtain the Crow's Nest Pass Railway contract with the
prospective government assistance for themselves or for a partner-

ship with Senator George Cox and other Central Canadian businessmen. The Laurier government was, as Regehr asserts, "unwilling to offer substantial subsidies unless firm freight-rate concessions to the Lakehead were promised." Only the CPR could guarantee rate reductions from the Lakehead; an independent company could only offer concessions from Lethbridge to Nelson. Thus, the federal government gave the entire project to the CPR to get rate reductions from the Lakehead to the Kootenays.[64]

Shaughnessy endeavoured to influence the cabinet committee's deliberations by sending a lengthy memorandum on 15 April to Sir Oliver Mowat, one of the committee members. The memorandum contained a strong dose of economic nationalism. Shaughnessy stressed that mining development in BC in the last few years had demonstrated that "Canada possesses in British Columbia a country of vast mineral resources." However, he was convinced that the United States had so far obtained most of the benefits of mining development in southern British Columbia. "The agricultural state of Washington has furnished a large proportion of the food consumed," he asserted. "A large proportion of the tools and machinery used in the mines and smelters is furnished by American manufacturers. At present, all the silver lead ores and a considerable portion of the gold ores produced in the Province are being transported to smelting centres in the United States." CPR construction of the Crow's Nest Pass Railway would enable Canadian agriculture, ranching, and industry to supply most of the requirements of the mining districts of southern British Columbia and would enable much of the ore to be smelted in British Columbia. The vice-president then explained that the CPR's poor financial performance in the years 1894 to 1896 had prevented the company from building the line without government aid. The Tupper administration had been prepared to grant the CPR substantial assistance to build the Crow's Nest Pass line, but the life of Parliament had expired before it could introduce the necessary legislation. Shaughnessy emphasized that if the government accepted the company's most recent proposal, the CPR would need to raise about $5 million on its own credit, "besides an additional very large sum for branch lines." Finally, he strongly denied press rumours that the CPR intended to gain a monopoly over coal production in the Elk River district of the East Kootenays.[65] There is no evidence that this was the CPR's intention, and subsequent events show that these rumours were untrue.

Despite Shaughnessy's efforts at persuasion, the cabinet committee was still deadlocked, with Blair insisting on government construction and ownership of the line. On 19 April Sifton gave Laurier his views on the conditions for federal aid to the CPR. He recommended that the government should have the power to grant running rights to other railways over sections of the Crow's Nest Pass Railway. He then discussed the vital question of freight-rate reductions in the prairie West. The minister had been receiving advice on this subject from the Winnipeg Board of Trade and from prominent Winnipeg merchant J.H. Ashdown. Sifton respected Ashdown's views but found them "a little extreme." He advised Laurier that there should be a reduction of 3 cents per 100 pounds on grain rates in Manitoba and the North-West Territories. He also wanted maximum rates on all traffic on the Crow's Nest Pass line connecting to any point on the CPR main line, and was particularly concerned about rates on coke and coal. No mention was made of rate reductions on westbound manufactured goods. And, showing some concern for CPR interests, Sifton rejected the proposal for abrogation of the 10 per cent clause in the CPR contract, which prevented government regulation of CPR rates, until the company had earned a 10 per cent dividend on its common stock. He pointed out that the 10 per cent clause was "one of the things that has been held out to foreign investors in C.P.R. stocks and bonds," enabling the company to raise capital in the US, Britain, and Europe. He wanted a clause in the agreement "which would prevent the [Crow's Nest] traffic being diverted to American lines." Sifton also proposed the government purchase of all CPR lands east of the third meridian – a total of 2,600,000 acres – at $2.80 per acre, a price which he felt the CPR directors would accept. Finally, the contract should require the CPR to complete the line by 1 January 1899. The minister of the interior urged that the legislation be introduced in the House as soon as debate on the tariff was finished: "It is absolutely necessary that the work should be proceeded with immediately," Sifton noted, advancing two reasons for this. In his last talk with CPR officials, "I thought they had begun to feel that there is a chance that the transaction may not be consummated this Session. Their stock is going down and they feel much discouraged." The more compelling reason was that construction of the line would involve a monthly expenditure of $500,000 which would immediately counteract "the disturbance of trade incident to the introduction of the tariff."[66]

While Cabinet debated the Crow's Nest Pass Railway in April and May, the CPR completed negotiations for the acquisition of the charter of the British Columbia Southern Railway. Van Horne informed J.D. Edgar on 21 April that the company "have secured practical control of the BC Southern land grant."[67] The Crow's Nest and Kootenay Lake Railway Company, originally chartered by the BC legislature in 1888, was empowered to build from the Crow's Nest Pass, by way of Cranbrook and the Moyie Pass, to the Lower Kootenay River. Its chief promoters, all British Columbians, were Colonel James Baker, then a member of the BC legislature, the prospector William Fernie, Edward Bray, and J.W. Humphreys. Each of them had claims on coal lands in the East Kootenay region. In 1891 the BC legislature incorporated the British Columbia Southern Railway Company, which took over the charter of the Crow's Nest Company. It was given additional powers to build west from the Lower Kootenay River to Nelson, Hope, New Westminster, and Burrard Inlet. Thus the company had authority to build a railway from the Pacific coast through southern BC to the Crow's Nest Pass. Then in 1893 the BC government awarded it a 20,000-acre-per-mile land grant, which would give it 3,755,733 acres of land if it completed the entire line from the coast to the Crow's Nest Pass. But no construction was undertaken. The CPR intended to use the BC Southern's charter as its authority to build westward from the Crow's Nest Pass into the Kootenays and to collect the large land subsidy, which would be especially valuable in the Crow's Nest Pass coal fields.[68]

On 17 May the prime minister called Van Horne and Shaughnessy to Ottawa to discuss the Crow's Nest Pass Railway with the cabinet committee. The meeting took place the following day. Intensive negotiations continued until 3 June, when the CPR and the government reached a final agreement. Van Horne outlined its basic terms in a letter to Sir Donald Smith and remarked, "All of us here feel well satisfied with the bargain."[69]

Railways Minister Blair introduced the Crow's Nest Pass Railway subsidy resolutions in the House on 11 June. The resolutions were approved on 18 June, and the next day Bill 146, "An Act to authorize a Subsidy for a Railway through the Crow's Nest Pass," received first reading. The provisions of this bill bear close examination, for it became the historic Crow's Nest Pass Agreement. The bill provided a cash subsidy of $11,000 per mile, to a maximum of $3,630,000, to the CPR for the construction of a railway from Lethbridge through the Crow's Nest Pass to Nelson in the West Kootenay region of British Columbia. The cash subsidy would meet about 45 per cent of the estimated cost of constructing the Crow's Nest Pass Railway, and the CPR undertook to operate this railway "for ever." The bill did not specify the exact route of the railway (the government and the CPR were to sign an agreement covering this matter), but it did require the CPR to build the railway through the town of Macleod and to establish a station there, unless Cabinet decided there were "good reasons" for building it outside the town limits. Cabinet approval was required not only for local and through rates on the Crow's Nest Pass Railway, but also for rates on any CPR line in BC south of the company's main line, and for rates on CPR steamers in southern British Columbia.

Then there were the famous rate-reduction clauses. The CPR undertook to reduce rates on certain merchandise shipped westbound from Fort William, effective 1 January 1898. The largest reductions were one-third on all green and fresh fruits and 20 per cent on coal oil. There was also a 10 per cent reduction on a variety of goods essential for the prairie farmer, most notably agricultural implements, but also such items as binder twine, paints, and household furniture. The company also agreed to make a reduction of 3 cents per hundredweight upon grain and flour shipped from the prairie West to Fort William. This reduction would come into effect in two stages: 1 1/2 cents on 1 September 1898 and the other 1 1/2 cents on 1 September 1899. These rate reductions constituted an important modification of clause 20 in the CPR contract of 1881, which exempted the company from government rate regulation until it earned a profit of 10 per cent on its capital stock. These rates were soon to acquire the status of a sacred charter – Holy Crow – among prairie farmers.

The bill also gave the Railway Committee of the Privy Council the authority to grant running rights over the Crow's Nest Pass Railway and its branches to other railway companies. Finally, there were the complex clauses relating to the British Columbia Southern Railway. A separate bill, also passed late in the 1897 session of Parliament, permitted this company to lease its works to the CPR, provided that the lease was authorized by the Cabinet and by a two-thirds vote of the CPR shareholders at a special general meeting. In effect, the CPR could acquire the BC Southern's provincial land subsidy of 20,000 acres per mile. The Crow's Nest Pass Subsidy Bill gave Cabinet the authority to set regulations for the sale of such lands (including the establishment of land prices), with the exception of coal-bearing lands. In addition, it required the CPR to transfer to the federal government 50,000 acres of coal-bearing lands in the East Kootenay region, in order to prevent it or any other company from obtaining a monopoly over these lands, and to keep coal prices in the Kootenays at a "reasonable" level.[70]

An important item in the negotiations which was missing from the bill was the sale of CPR prairie lands to the federal government. Why did the parties fail to reach an agreement on this important matter? Hall concludes that the Cabinet rejected the proposition. "The cabinet," he remarks, "was not prepared to accept an expenditure of

$7 million for lands on top of a subsidy for the railway which would exceed $3 million." In a recent study of the Crow's Nest Pass Agreement, economist Gillian Wogin has argued very persuasively that "it was in the Railway's self-interest to have government constrain its freight rates to raise the value of the [prairie] lands which it owned." In effect, she maintains that the CPR directors expected the low Crow's Nest rates to attract many settlers into the prairie West, thus increasing the value of its lands. Her view is supported by the fact that the CPR directors anticipated in February 1897 that the price of the company's prairie lands would increase in the near future.[71] This issue is fully discussed in chapter 8.

In defending the Crow's Nest legislation in the House of Commons, Blair emphasized two major themes: Canadian economic nationalism and prairie freight-rate reductions. He noted that the value of mineral production in BC had increased from $2,600,000 in 1890 to $7,146,000 in 1896. The railways minister then asserted that most of the economic benefits of mining development in the Kootenay region had gone to Americans, particularly the businessmen of Spokane. Spokane business interests used the Spokane Falls and Northern Railway to supply most of the mining equipment and consumer goods in the Kootenay mining camps, while Washington farmers provided much of the food supplies for these camps. Such trends would continue unless the Kootenays were linked to the Canadian railway system – in this case, the CPR. The Crow's Nest Pass Railway, Blair declared, "will open up large resources of great value, the development of which will stimulate all other industries in the country and greatly add to its wealth." He was convinced that such a railway would not have been built for many years, unless the government constructed it or gave aid to a private company to undertake the project. The government, he stressed, was providing "reasonable aid" to the CPR to construct the railway.[72] He also noted that the government had obtained "very substantial reductions" on existing CPR freight rates in the prairie West on "a considerable list of articles which go into very large consumption among the people of the western provinces." Blair then asserted that the government had made a better bargain with the CPR than the Conservatives had been prepared to make in 1896 when they were in power. The Conservatives had offered the CPR a cash subsidy of $5,000 per mile and a federal loan of $20,000 per mile, but had not demanded any rate concessions from the company.

Blair was strongly supported in the debate by Sir Richard Cartwright, the minister of trade and commerce, who also sounded a strong note of economic nationalism. "I believe," he asserted, "that the construction of a railway into that country [the Kootenays] will ... lead to bringing there a population of many thousands of consumers, who will afford a very valuable market to the inhabitants of the North-West portion of Canada and also to our manufacturers in the east." Ontario Liberal MP James Lister praised the rate reductions, especially those on grain and flour. He estimated that the people of the prairie West "will undoubtedly save ... from $500,000 to $750,000 a year in freight charges" as a result of the lower rates.[73]

The Commons debate on the bill was quite sedate because the Conservatives supported the legislation. Sir Charles Tupper, the leader of the opposition, gave "warm approval" to the bill. It was difficult for him to do otherwise in view of the fact that he had offered more generous financial aid to the CPR while he was prime minister, and had not required the company to make rate reductions. He felt the $11,000-per-mile subsidy was necessary because his London financial contacts had advised him that the Crow's Nest Pass Railway could not be built by the CPR without "large and substantial" aid from the Canadian government. He was also pleased that the government wanted the railway extended from Nelson to Penticton as soon as possible. Tupper raised the issue of government ownership in an attempt to divide the government, for he was aware that Blair and some Liberal backbenchers were privately in favour of government construction of the line. "I learned with infinite pleasure," he remarked, "that the Government had abandoned the idea ... of building this railway as a Government work." He then proceeded to develop the theme that "Governments cannot construct railways in an economic manner."[74] John Ross Robertson, the outspoken publisher of the Toronto *Telegram*, and an independent Conservative, criticized Tupper's views. He strongly supported government ownership and operation of the Crow's Nest Pass Railway, because people in Western Canada were "almost unanimously" in favour of this policy, and because the railway "is bound to be a dividend paying enterprise from the start." Robertson, who had been a stern critic of the CPR since its inception, was particularly critical of the BC land subsidy which the CPR would obtain under the bill. His views were not supported by other Conservatives, although Ontario Tory MP David Henderson did consider the cash subsidy too extravagant.[75]

However, a number of western Liberal MPs broke party ranks and opposed the government's legislation. The strongest of these critics were W.W.B. McInnes, a Vancouver lawyer, and Frank Oliver, the outspoken publisher of the Edmonton *Bulletin*. McInnes was a strong advocate of public ownership of railways; he regarded the Crow's Nest Pass Railway as "a case in which Government ownership could be put into practice with very great advantage." McInnes also wanted the federal government to disallow the lavish land grant to the BC Southern Railway. He represented the concern of the coastal cities – notably Vancouver and Victoria – that the Crow's Nest Pass Railway would give the trade of the BC interior to Central Canada, not to them. Frank Oliver advocated a policy of "competition in railway transportation" in the West, by means of government ownership of railways or federal aid to a railway company which would compete with the CPR. He was convinced that such a policy would, in the long run, result in more substantial rate reductions in the West than those obtained under the Crow's Nest Pass Railway Subsidy Bill. He also attacked the bill on the grounds that it would give the CPR an effective monopoly over the traffic of southern British Columbia.[76]

On the morning of 29 June, the last day of the session, Bill 146 received third reading in the House, without a recorded vote. It was then rushed through three readings in the Senate that same day, where R.W. Scott, the secretary of state, had charge of the bill. He made a very effective presentation, stressing the themes of Canadian economic nationalism and western rate reduction. It was also given Royal Assent that day.[77]

The complex arrangements provided for in the Crow's Nest Pass Railway Subsidy Act regarding the BC Southern's land grant are discussed fully in chapter 6. Essentially, the Crow's Nest Pass Coal Company obtained about 250,000 acres of coal-bearing lands in the East Kootenays.

The decision to build the Crow's Nest Pass Railway led the CPR to tighten its control over the AR&C CO. In September 1897 the CPR purchased the Dunmore-Lethbridge line for $976,950. As den Otter observes, the CPR "could not permit another company to control a vital part of its alternate route to British Columbia."[78]

Some writers who have studied the Crow's Nest Pass Agreement have accepted the public statement made by Sir Clifford Sifton in 1929 that the CPR was "on the verge of bankruptcy" when it requested aid for the Crow's Nest Pass Railway in 1896, and that the Laurier government had granted the CPR a cash subsidy "against the public sentiment of two-thirds of the people of Canada."[79] These remarks were made 32 years after the event; Sifton was clearly dramatizing the situation of the CPR in 1896. It was not in a strong financial position, but, as Lamb correctly observes, the CPR "was in no danger of bankruptcy."[80] The company wanted to build the Crow's Nest Pass Railway as soon as possible to counter American dominance in the Kootenay region. The CPR's credit rating in London was such that it could not raise funds to cover the entire cost of building the railway.

Also, Sifton's remarks obscure the fact that the Laurier government was eager to reach an amicable settlement with the CPR. It is difficult to assess public attitudes in the period before opinion polls, but the government's economic nationalist arguments may have won support for the agreement, although there was some opposition in the prairie West and particularly in British Columbia.

The Liberals, who had been severe critics of the "Tory" CPR since its inception, had now reversed themselves by granting the company a substantial cash subsidy to build a line into the Kootenay mining districts of British Columbia. At the same time, the federal government for the first time established some control over CPR freight rates – in the prairie West. Van Horne and Shaughnessy were pleased with the arrangement since it enabled the CPR to counter American control over the Kootenays and to hinder the efforts of D.C. Corbin and J.J. Hill of the Great Northern to enter the region. However, they were well aware that rapid construction of the Crow's Nest Pass Railway was now essential.

CHAPTER THREE

Building the Crow's Nest Pass Railway, 1897–9

Gigantic bodies of low-grade copper ore were discovered in 1891 in the Boundary district of BC, which lies some 50 miles west of Rossland, along the Canada-US border, between the valleys of the North Fork of the Kettle River and Boundary Creek. The problem was that the nearest railway was in Washington State, 75 miles to the south; there were no wagon roads in the region and freight charges were prohibitive. The decline of metal prices on the world market in 1893 caused the Boundary district to become almost deserted. But the CPR's decision to construct the Crow's Nest Pass Railway as far west as the West Kootenays revived interest in the copper deposits of the district, since the railway would transport the copper ore at reasonable rates. As a result, a mining boom developed in the Boundary district in 1897–8.[1] The CPR constructed the BC section of the Crow's Nest Pass Railway under the charter of the British Columbia Southern Railway, which had authority to build a railway from the summit of the Crow's Nest Pass to Nelson, Hope, and New Westminster. The company had acquired the charter in order to qualify for the BC Southern land subsidy of 20,000 acres per mile. In 1897 Parliament passed legislation which authorized the CPR to lease the BC Southern Railway. A cabinet Order-in-Council approved the lease of the eastern section of this company from the Crow's Nest Pass to Nelson on 18 August 1898. The CPR had authority under the 1897 subsidy legislation to build a line from Lethbridge to the Crow's Nest Pass.[2]

Van Horne was determined to push construction of the Crow's Nest Pass Railway as rapidly as possible, in order to counter the plans of D.C. Corbin, J.J. Hill, and a newcomer, Augustus Heinze. In June 1897 he informed a correspondent that he hoped to have the section from Lethbridge to Kootenay Landing, at the south end of Kootenay

Lake, "ready for business" by the end of November 1898. Since it would take some time to set up a construction organization, he thought that the line would reach the summit of Crow's Nest Pass "by the time Winter sets in." Hugh Lumsden was appointed chief engineer of the Crow's Nest Pass Railway. The Scottish-born Lumsden was a very capable civil engineer who had 29 years' experience locating railway lines in Canada, mainly in Ontario. In March 1897 he put engineers to work locating the permanent line of the railway east of the Crow's Nest Pass. The CPR was not able to send engineers west of the pass until the first week in July, "owing to snow in the passes."[3]

Van Horne decided to appoint Michael J. Haney as manager of construction of the Crow's Nest Pass Railway. Born in 1854 in Galway, Ireland, to Catholic parents, Haney emigrated to the United States with his family when he was four years of age. The family settled on a farm near Watertown, New York. A brilliant student, Haney attended high school in Watertown, where he did especially well in mathematics, studying algebra, calculus, and trigonometry. He intended to go on to become a lawyer, but his parents needed his financial support, and at age seventeen Haney started as an axeman with a company which was building the Kingston and Pembroke Railway. Within a year he had become the divisional engineer on this construction project. He then became a private contractor and obtained a number of other railway construction contracts. Using his connections with J.J. Hill and his Liberal political affiliation, he took over the federal government contract for the Pembina Branch (Winnipeg to the US border) after the original contractor had abandoned it for lack of funds, and completed it with impressive speed and efficiency. Having proved his abilities as a railway contractor, he was then hired to do extensive work on the CPR main line from 1882 to 1885. He was superintendent of the Rat Portage (Kenora) division of the CPR from 1882 to 1883. Having made a reputation on this section as a cost-cutter, he was hired by Andrew Onderdonk to manage construction of the section in BC from Port Moody to Savona's Ferry (the government contract), which was completed in 1885. He then moved on to projects with the Red River Valley Railway in Manitoba and the Michigan Central Railway's river tunnel from Windsor to Detroit, before his appointment on the Crow's Nest Pass Railway.[4]

Haney, whose flamboyant personality was emphasized by his flowing moustache, had full control over the construction of the Crow's Nest Pass line, from the hiring of sub-contractors to the appointment of doctors to serve the medical needs of the work-force.[5] When Sir Charles Tupper, the leader of the Conservative party, attempted to get a job for a friend on the Crow's Nest Pass project, Van Horne referred him to Haney. The president remarked that Haney was "held entirely responsible for time and cost and everything else" on the railway, and that the CPR "can't afford to give him a ground for defense in that any man was pressed upon him."[6] Shaughnessy was thinking along the same lines. As he informed Clifford Sifton, regarding a contract to supply beef for the Crow's Nest Pass railway workers, "Haney is a long way from head quarters, and in order to enable him to push the work with the expedition demanded he must be clothed with rather plenary power ... I know enough about Haney to feel confident that neither personal friendship nor any other consideration will induce him to sacrifice an unnecessary penny." Both Van Horne and Shaughnessy were impressed with Haney's reputation as a cost-cutter, and expected him to keep firm control over costs. The CPR vice-president was however a little concerned about Haney's managerial skills, noting that he was "a bit difficult to get along with some times on account of his temperament."[7]

The Laurier government approved a draft contract with the CPR for the construction of the Crow's Nest Pass Railway on 21 July 1897. This was signed on 6 October by Railways Minister Blair, who had recently returned from Europe, and CPR officials. It stipulated completion of the line from Lethbridge to the south end of Kootenay Lake by 31 December 1898, and the remaining section, to Nelson, by 31 December 1900. Until the latter section to Nelson was completed, the CPR undertook to provide barges and transfer boats to move freight from the south end of Kootenay Lake to Nelson. (See figure 1.) The cash subsidy of $11,000 per mile was to be paid in instalments on the completion of 10 miles of railway. Local rates on the Crow's Nest Pass Railway and any other CPR line (south of the company's mainline) that was operated in connection with the railway were subject to Cabinet approval.[8]

Under Lumsden's direction, the location survey was completed to Kootenay Landing at the south end of Kootenay Lake by November 1897, but the survey of the west shore of the lake was not finished until April 1898. It was necessary to construct a wagon road in order to bring in construction equipment, tools, supplies, and men. In July 1897 contractors started work on this road west from the summit of Crow's Nest Pass (there was already a wagon road from Macleod to the summit). In September work on a wagon road east from Kootenay Landing was begun. The two roads came together in November 1897 at Moyie Lake. At the western end, headquarters was at a point on the Goat River 20 miles east of Kootenay Landing. Supplies could be brought there from Nelson, south by boat on Kootenay Lake to

Kootenay Landing, and north from Bonner's Ferry, Idaho, on the Great Northern line via the Kootenay River.[9]

The eastern headquarters of construction was located at Macleod. Superintendent Sam Steele, in charge of the North-West Mounted Police (NWMP) post in Macleod, was very impressed by the speed with which the contractors, under Haney's direction, moved men and materials into the country. Grading began on 14 July, just 15 days after the Crow's Nest Pass Subsidy Act had become law. At the end of July about 5,000 men and 1,000 teams of horses were employed. By December the line from Lethbridge had been completed to within 12 miles of Crow's Nest Pass.[10] The CPR did the laying and ballasting of track on the entire line. In addition, the company also built all bridges on the first 100 miles west of Lethbridge. The clearing and grading, with the attendant blasting and collective pick and shovel work, was generally let to contractors in sections of one to ten miles.[11] The completed section from Lethbridge to Macleod was turned over to William Whyte, head of the Western Division of the CPR, for operation starting 15 June 1898.[12] By mid-June 1898 grading had reached Kootenay Landing, while track had been laid 118 miles west of Lethbridge (12 miles west of the Crow's Nest Pass) to Sparwood, BC. Tracklaying, which pushed ahead rapidly, was complete to Kootenay Landing on 6 October 1898. On the flats of the Kootenay River, where the river enters Kootenay Lake through a broad delta, 4 1/4 miles of trestles, as well as a steel bridge, were required to facilitate river traffic.[13] The remainder of the line, from Macleod to Kootenay Landing, was taken over as a branch of the CPR's Western Division on 14 November 1898. Lumsden's work was then complete. Malcolm Macleod was appointed superintendent of the Crow's Nest branch, with an office in Macleod.[14]

Van Horne took a party of friends and business associates on an inspection tour of the entire line in the latter part of October 1898. This party included two prominent CPR directors, R.B. Angus and E.B. Osler, as well as W.W. Ogilvie of the Ogilvie Milling Company of Montreal, Dr W. Peterson, principal of McGill University, and William Whyte, manager of the CPR's Western Division. Van Horne reported on this journey to Colonel Baker: "[I] was much impressed with what I saw between Kootenay Lake and the [Crow's Nest] pass. All that you have told me about that district seems quite within the mark. It contains vastly more potential wealth than I imagined. I was particularly struck by the magnificent forests and their extent and by the agricultural possibilities of the country."[15]

Construction of the Crow's Nest Pass Railway from Lethbridge to Kootenay Landing had taken 15 months and averaged nearly 3 miles every 5 days, including tunnels and bridges. Between Kootenay Landing and Nelson, passengers were transported by steamer, while freight cars were carried on large barges that were towed or pushed back and forth along Kootenay Lake by tugs. Because it was difficult in winter for Canadian Pacific steamers and car ferries to use the Kootenay River, the CPR later built an 18-mile section from Nelson, east to Procter. It was opened on 15 June 1902. However, the expensive 33-mile section from Kootenay Landing to Procter was postponed indefinitely and was not built until 1930. Mcdougall estimates the cost of construction of the Crow's Nest Pass Railway, excluding the section from Kootenay Landing to Procter, at $9,898,392. The CPR received a total cash subsidy of $3,404,720, about one-third of the initial cost of the line.[16]

Since the area was very sparsely settled, there was little controversy over the location of the line between the Crow's Nest Pass and Kootenay Landing – with one major exception. This was the issue of whether or not the line should pass through the town of Fort Steele, on the Kootenay River. Fort Steele was the first town in the southeast Kootenay region and the district's seat of government. The NWMP had built a fort there in 1887 – the first of its posts in British Columbia – and had wintered there in 1887–8. Samuel Steele was the superintendent of the NWMP detachment, and the town therefore adopted the name Fort Steele. During the period 1895–1900, the town experienced what Fred Smyth, a pioneer in the district, described as a "real western boom ... large hotels and business houses were erected and hundreds of prospectors' tents could be seen on the outskirts of the town and along the river bank. Livery stables did a big business; freighting was done with four-horse teams, and people travelled by stage, in hacks, buckboards and buggies or on horseback. Much freight and many passengers were also carried on the several boats plying between Jennings, Montana, and Fort Steele." So the townspeople probably expected the railway to pass through their town. R.L. Galbraith, who ran a general store in the town, also owned the townsite. He was confident that the CPR would run its line through Fort Steele if he gave the company an interest in the townsite.[17]

But Galbraith's optimism was misplaced. The CPR was closely allied with Colonel James Baker, who owned the townsite of Cranbrook, some 10 miles southwest of Fort Steele. Baker was determined to have the Crow's Nest Pass line bypass Fort Steele and run through Cranbrook, which he planned to develop as the major town in the East Kootenay region. Baker was the chief promoter of the BC Southern Railway, the charter of which the CPR used to construct the

Crow's Nest Pass Railway in southern British Columbia. He was also provincial secretary and minister of mines in the provincial government. Baker was born in London, England, in 1830, and had a distinguished career in the British army before emigrating to the East Kootenay district in 1884. He established a successful agricultural operation near Fort Steele and developed a townsite which he named Cranbrook. In Cranbrook he conducted a general store. Using his money and influence, Baker had won the provincial seat of Kootenay West in May 1887, only 4 years after his arrival in the area. He retained this seat in subsequent elections and was appointed to the Turner administration of March 1895. In addition to his other properties, he had a substantial interest in the rich coal lands in the East Kootenay and was president of the Crow's Nest Pass Coal Company, which was formed in Victoria in 1886. (This company had received most of the coal lands in the BC Southern's land subsidy.) Beyond using simply his influence to gain the Crow's Nest Pass line, Baker gave the CPR a half interest (alternate lots) in his Cranbrook townsite.[18]

BC Liberal MP Hewitt Bostock informed Laurier of Baker's activities. Although he was a strong supporter of Fort Steele, Bostock admitted that Colonel Baker might succeed in persuading the CPR to run its line through Cranbrook. "Col. Baker as you are no doubt aware," Bostock informed prime minister Laurier, "is Provincial Secretary and it is quite possible for him to use this power to build up Cranbrook at the expense of Fort Steele. The people here [in Fort Steele] therefore look to the Dominion government to help them at this juncture." Laurier intervened on Fort Steele's behalf by asking Shaughnessy to build a branch line from the Crow's Nest Pass Railway to the town in the summer of 1898. The prime minister increased the pressure by observing that Haney had promised the people of Fort Steele that a CPR branch line would be built to their town in 1898. Shaughnessy informed Laurier that according to his sources Haney had told the residents of Fort Steele that he had instructions to survey the branch line, but did not promise that it would be constructed in 1898. "It is our intention," the CPR vice-president remarked, "to build a branch from the Crow's Nest Line to Fort Steele, but we may not be able to do it this year." Shortly after, the controversy was resolved in favour of Cranbrook, which was made a divisional point on the Crow's Nest line. Construction of railway workshops was started there in the autumn of 1898. The provincial government offices were moved from Fort Steele to Cranbrook in May 1904. Shaughnessy did not honour his promise to Laurier until 1913, when a 23-mile line was completed from Colvalli, on the Crow's Nest branch, north to Fort Steele, under charter of the CPR-owned Kootenay Central Railway.[19]

In 1897 the Laurier government passed the Alien Labour Act, which made it illegal "for any person, company, partnership or corporation ... to assist or solicit the importation or immigration of any alien or foreigner into Canada under contract or agreement ... to perform labour or service of any kind in Canada." The building of the Crow's Nest Pass Railway was to be the first test for this legislation, which prevented the CPR from importing labourers from the large pool available in the American Pacific Northwest. The Laurier government, asserts Hall, "was determined that the line should be built only by Canadians or by immigrants intending to settle in Canada. It was equally determined that as far as possible Canadian contractors should be employed." The Crow's Nest Pass Agreement was popular not only in Western Canada but also in the East, because it was expected that construction of the line would employ thousands of Canadian labourers. Sifton was one of the strongest advocates in Cabinet of a Canadian preference policy for the Crow's Nest Pass Railway. The minister of the interior was convinced that the Macdonald Conservative administration had made no attempt to give employment to Canadians in the construction of the CPR main line. With a Canadian preference policy, the Laurier government could, Sifton observed, "claim the credit of having been the first Government which made an attempt to protect Canadian labourers and Canadian contractors." On 17 July 1897 Cabinet passed an Order-in-Council expressly prohibiting the CPR from letting or sub-letting the construction of the Crow's Nest Pass Railway to "any foreigner, or any corporation composed wholly or in part of foreigners." The CPR was also forbidden from employing anyone on the project who was not a British subject, a resident of Canada, or an immigrant intending to settle in Canada. The minister of railways could waive the labour clause only if he were "satisfied that there is not available sufficient Canadian labour to enable the Company to complete the work within the time limited therefor."[20]

Shaughnessy was not pleased with the government's Canadian preference policy, but he instructed Haney to carry out its provisions. "You can rest assured," Haney informed the CPR president in July 1897, "I will not in any way give the Government an opportunity to shew that either in act or in deed we have broken faith with them, and it would be well to advise them not to act on idle rumours circulated by disappointed contractors or disgruntled Americans, but rather reserve judgement until they have heard the whole evidence." Haney established $1.50 per day as the rate of pay for labourers on the Crow's Nest Pass line, and a charge of $4 per week for board. Initially controversy developed as a result of the hiring of British immigrants as labourers. This action had been initiated by immigration officials in Canada who were attempting to find work on the Crow's Nest Pass line for about 1,000 Welsh farmers and farm labourers who wanted to settle in Western Canada. The CPR was immediately interested in the scheme, since it would get a large pool of unskilled labour for the Crow's Nest line, while the immigrants would be able to supplement their income. However, as Avery comments, "the arrangement was not a success, largely because the Welsh workers were not prepared to tolerate the low wages or the camp conditions." The Welsh immigrant-workers were quite vocal in their criticisms, which the newspapers reported, causing embarrassment to both the CPR and the Laurier government. James Smart, the deputy minister of the interior, warned Shaughnessy that if the situation was not corrected, immigration to Canada "could be very materially checked." The CPR president bluntly informed Smart that "it would be a huge mistake" to send more immigrants from Britain for work on the Crow's Nest line. He observed that in Canada men who worked as railway labourers were "as a rule, a class accustomed to roughing it." But British farmers and farm labourers were not used to the rough conditions of railway construction. "We can get, in our country," he observed, "plenty of navvies accustomed to railway construction, and it is only prejudicial to the cause of immigration to import men who come here expecting to get high wages, a feather bed, and a bath tub." Donald Avery points out that Shaughnessy's views were shared by many Canadian businessmen who wanted workers who were physically strong, non-unionized, and "who could not use the English-Canadian language press to focus public attention on their grievances." The CPR president also expressed the bias held by many Canadian employers and Western Canadians that "the British labourer was not suited either physically or psychologically to the conditions on the frontier." Canadian immigration officials made no further efforts to recruit British immigrants for work on the Crow's Nest line.[21]

The CPR was also faced with widespread public criticism of its treatment of Canadian workers on the Crow's Nest Pass line. (Some months later a royal commission was appointed to investigate the charges.) The workers involved were mainly those who worked for the private contractors; workers employed by the CPR were treated much better. The men employed by the contractors did the hard pick-and-shovel work. Haney had assisted the contractors in hiring labourers by appointing agents at Montreal, Ottawa, and Winnipeg.

These agents had little trouble hiring workers, for work was scarce, especially in Eastern Canada. Also, some of the men wanted to settle in the West, and some were attracted by the Klondike gold rush, believing that they would be "within accessible reach of the Klondyke" when they were in the Crow's Nest Pass area. Most of those attracted by the Klondike were "physically unfit" for the hard labour involved – lawyers, actors, barbers, clerks, cooks, and others. Many of the men hired by agents were under the mistaken impression that their fare to the work site would be paid either by the CPR or by the contractor. It was not until they arrived at Macleod that they discovered that their fare would be deducted from their wages by the contractors. The CPR set a low fare of 1 cent per mile, which resulted in a fare of $22.50 for the trip from Ottawa to Macleod. This was a substantial sum for workers earning only $1.50 a day. In contrast, those who were employed by the CPR were only charged transportation from Macleod to their place of work. The company charged each contractor full transportation (at 1 cent per mile) from Ottawa, Montreal, or Winnipeg to Macleod, and the contractors had little choice but to deduct this charge from their workers' wages.[22] The North-West Mounted Police acted as the police authority along the Crow's Nest line in the district of Alberta; this mandate was extended to BC in November 1897 by the provincial government. Superintendent Sam Steele reported in November 1897 that the trouble between labourers and contractors "was caused principally by the agents in the East, who made promises to the men which they had no right to do." Inspector Cuthbert reported to Steele in September 1897 that the agent in Ottawa hired many French-Canadians and others with skills as axe men as "choppers for bush work." Only one-tenth of the French-Canadians could read English and understand the contract (written in English) which they signed. These men were put to work with a pick and shovel, but, Cuthbert remarked, "very few have ever handled a pick, shovel and scraper. They naturally get into trouble and in a great many cases refuse to do work they did not engage to do and cannot do, and then we are called upon to compel them or send them to jail. They are completely discouraged and do not much care what happens to them." Cuthbert was unhappy with his role as a justice of the peace in fining these men or sentencing them to short jail terms, and had informed contractors "that I will not deal with any more like cases, unless there is special reason, such as a new and well understood engagement." Many of the labourers were also complaining about poor living conditions. Some were forced to sleep in the open, often without blankets on the ground, or in "cold and filthy houses, box cars or boarding cars."

There were many complaints about the lack of proper washing facilities, charging of mail fees, overcharging for supplies by some of
the contractors, and other grievances.[23]

One of the most serious grievances was the inadequacy of medical
care, for which the workers were charged 50 cents per month. Many
of the men had to sleep in unheated tents during the winter and
had no way to dry their clothes. As a result they often suffered from
colds and rheumatism. Other prevalent diseases were cough, mountain fever, and some cases of diphtheria. The complaints from the
men were "universal" regarding the poor quality of medical care.
As the royal commissioners reported: "The men complained bitterly
of the length of time which elapsed between the different visits of
the doctors in the camps, and when in some instances attendance
was needed in the case of broken limbs, fever, and attacks of diphtheria, the medical assistance could not be obtained within a considerable time." In one case, it took over two days to get two men with
diphtheria to Pincher Creek where a private practitioner was sent
for but arrived "only in time to see them die." It was clear that a
chief of medical staff and four assistant doctors was insufficient for
the entire project.[24]

These problems could not be ignored by the Laurier government,
since they were reported by superintendents Steele and Deane (Lethbridge District) to Commissioner L.W. Herchmer in Regina, who
then summarized the reports in letters to Fred White, the NWMP
comptroller in Ottawa. White communicated the information to Clifford Sifton, the minister of the interior, and to the prime minister.
A Macleod lawyer named Harris had taken up the cases of some of
the French-Canadian workers and had sent a telegram to Laurier
outlining the situation as he saw it. Laurier raised the matter with
Shaughnessy in the latter part of November. The CPR vice-president
attempted to dismiss most of the complaints of the workers. He
informed the prime minister that the mayor of Macleod "seems to
have no information about the complaints that are being made, but ...
a designing Lawyer seems to have got hold of the men and is en-
deavoring to play upon the feelings of yourself and other members
of the Government. I think we may feel sure that Haney will not
permit the men to be unjustly treated."[25]

The labour situation on the Crow's Nest line was reported in
newspapers in November and December 1897. Winnipeg Liberal MP
R.W. Jamieson wrote Laurier in December denouncing the "White
Slavery" tactics of the CPR. That same month the Executive Com-
mittee of the Winnipeg Trades and Labour Council requested that
Laurier appoint a commission of three "independent men" to in-

vestigate the treatment of labour on the Crow's Nest Pass Railway. On 15 January 1898 the government acted by appointing a three-man royal commission. Reporting on 30 April, the commissioners substantiated many of the workers' grievances. They concluded that the charging of transportation from Eastern Canada to Macleod was the major source of unrest. Many of the workers who stayed, enduring the rough living conditions for 2 to 4 months, became discouraged when they found that they had not been able to save anything – mainly because of the deduction of the fare to Macleod (and from Macleod to the work site) from their wages. Compounding the problem was the CPR policy of charging ordinary fare for workers returning to their homes in Eastern Canada. This was a large sum – $64.40 from Macleod to Ottawa – and many did not have enough money to pay it. Moreover, if a worker left his job before his contract expired, he was "liable to arrest for desertion of his employment. Under such conditions," the commissioners observed, "he felt like a prisoner in a strange land." (Some workers did quit and made their way back to Eastern Canada on foot.) The commissioners also substantiated the "well-founded universal complaint concerning medical attendance." They were pleased that on 1 February 1898 the CPR had raised the daily wage to $1.75, but strongly urged that daily wages be raised to between $2 and $2.50 so that the men could build up some savings. They also strongly recommended that men who had worked for 3 months should be reimbursed for their fare to the Crow's Nest, while those working 6 months should receive either free return fare or a reduced fare.[26]

Shaughnessy was extremely upset by the report of what he described as "the commission of labour agitators." He was convinced that the commissioners' findings "have aroused a feeling of bitter animosity against the company in almost every section of the country ... The report is about as one-sided and unfair as it could be," he informed Haney, "because no attempt seems to have been made by the commissioners to explain in the report the conditions which must necessarily attach to frontier railway work, and they make no reference ... to the difficulties resulting from the unwillingness to work on the part of a good many of those who were carried West a distance of two thousand miles." He made no "official statement" on the report because he felt it "would only prolong the newspaper discussion on the subject." The CPR refused to implement the report's major recommendations other than to make an investigation to determine "as accurately as possible" if there were any wages owed to workers on the Crow's Nest Pass Railway. A year later Shaughnessy informed Sir Richard Cartwright that most of the high costs of the

Crow's Nest Pass Railway had resulted from the Laurier govnment's Canadian-preference policy for labour. The government forced the CPR to bring "inexperienced and incompetent labour" from Eastern Canada rather than allowing the company to hire "experienced railway navvies" wherever these were available. "The transaction with the Government," he continued, "was a most unsatisfactory one from every standpoint, and I frequently wish that we had built the line without any aid."[27] The Crow's Nest Pass Agreement had greatly improved relations between the CPR and the Laurier government, but subsequently the company's treatment of some of the workers building the railway had severely damaged this relationship.

While the Crow's Nest Pass Railway was under construction, the CPR was faced with competition from F. Augustus Heinze as well as D.C. Corbin for establishing rail connections between Nelson and the Boundary district. Heinze's activities are discussed fully in chapter 10; they are only briefly summarized here. A mining entrepreneur from Butte, Montana, Heinze built a copper smelter at Trail on the Columbia River in 1895–6. He obtained a valuable contract with the Le Roi Mining Company to smelter copper ore from its rich Le Roi mine at Rossland. Ore for the smelter was hauled from the mine to the Trail smelter in large horse-drawn freight wagons, a rudimentary system at best. Heinze decided to improve the transportation facilities, and in 1896 the BC government incorporated the Columbia and Western Railway, which was controlled by Heinze and a few business associates. It was authorized to build a narrow-gauge railway from Trail to the mines at Rossland, for a land subsidy of 10,240 acres per mile. Early in 1896 Frederick P. Gutelius, a thirty-one-year-old American engineer, arrived in Trail to superintend construction of the 13-mile line, which was ready for operation in June 1896. One of the difficulties he had had to overcome was the difference in altitude between Rossland and Trail of over 2,000 feet. Lamb observes that "as the little 13-mile railway squirmed up the mountainside, its steep grades, sharp curves, trestles and switchbacks made it an operational nightmare. Indeed, operation was possible only because the heavy ore traffic was carried on the downhill run."[28] However, the railway enabled the Trail smelter to treat larger quantities of ore from the Le Roi each day.

Heinze then wanted to direct the ores from the mines opening in the Boundary district, to the west, to his smelter at Trail. The Columbia and Western was authorized under its 1896 charter to build a standard-gauge line from Rossland west to Midway in the Boundary country, and then to Penticton, for a land subsidy of 20,000 acres per mile. However, Corbin out-manoeuvred Heinze by establishing a smelter at Northport, Washington, and persuading most of the American-controlled mines at Rossland to ship their ores to it. Corbin then proceeded to build the Columbia and Red Mountain Railway from Northport to Rossland; it reached Rossland in December 1896. Heinze responded by building a 19-mile, standard-gauge line from Trail north to Robson in 1897. But he could not afford to extend this line west to the Boundary district because he had too much capital tied up in his Montana mining properties. He therefore sold his smelter and his two railway lines to the CPR in February 1898.[29] Later that year the CPR changed the Trail-Rossland line to standard gauge, at a cost of $66,000. This work was also superintended by Gutelius, who was appointed superintendent of the Columbia and Western Railway. The charter of this railway provided a land subsidy of 20,000 acres per mile (for a standard-gauge line) which the CPR persuaded the Turner government to convert into a cash subsidy of $4,000 per mile. On 3 August 1898 the CPR leased the Columbia and Western, as authorized by federal legislation passed at the 1898 session of Parliament.[30]

The CPR now took vigorous action to nullify a threat from Corbin who was seeking a federal charter to build a railway from his SF&N line into the Boundary district. Van Horne informed Lord Mount Stephen early in February 1898, "we must push forward [the Crow's Nest Pass Railway] to the Boundary Creek district during the coming summer – 100 miles – or Corbin will certainly occupy the ground."[31] On 18 February 1898 Liberal MP Hewitt Bostock (Yale – Cariboo) introduced a private member's bill – Bill 26 – to incorporate the Kettle River Valley Railway (KRVR). Seeking incorporation were D.C. Corbin, his brother Austin, and business associate Charles Dupont. The route of the KRVR was rather complex: the line would commence at Cascade City in the West Kootenay district of BC, follow the course of the Kettle River to Carson City (where it would connect with the American section of the railway) and then continue to follow the Kettle River until it reached the international boundary just south of Midway in the Boundary district. Under its charter the KRVR was authorized to build a line from the boundary to Midway (see figure 1), and, on 19 March, the Kettle Valley Railway was incorporated in Washington State to build the American section of the railway. A federal charter was necessary for the KRVR in Canada because it would cross the international boundary at two points.[32]

Hewitt Bostock, whose constituency covered almost all of southern British Columbia, including the Kootenay and the Boundary districts, worked hard to secure passage of Bill 26. The thirty-three-year-old English-born MP had come to BC in 1893 and become a rancher and fruit grower near Kamloops in the Okanagan district. "Should the Government decide to oppose this measure," he informed Laurier, "I consider it my duty to my constituents and the people of British Columbia as a whole to go on with the Bill as a Private Member and make the best fight I can." Bostock was firmly convinced that the bill was "in the immediate interests of the people of the Boundary Creek country" because it would prevent a CPR railway monopoly in the region and give its residents the benefits of competition.[33] He was assisted by Ernest V. Bodwell, a prominent Victoria Liberal who met with Laurier in February in an attempt to persuade the government to support the KRVR Bill.[34] Resolutions from towns in West Kootenay (Nelson) and Boundary Creek (Grand Forks and Greenwood) strongly supported the KRVR charter, as did those from the South Kootenay Board of Trade, the Grand Forks Board of Trade, the Boundary Creek Mining and Commercial Association, the West Kootenay Mining Protective Association, and the Rossland Liberal Association. All these resolutions stressed that the KRVR would provide competitive rates in the region, especially low freight rates on ores.[35]

However, the Liberal cabinet and caucus were seriously divided on the issue. One of the main opponents of the bill in the House was the Liberal MP for Vancouver, W.W.B. McInnes, who declared that "if the charter is granted to three American promoters ... the trade [of the Boundary district] will go to the United States and cannot be retained for our people."[36] Van Horne used his influence in an attempt to defeat Bill 26 in the House of Commons Railway Committee in March. He anticipated a serious fight, because that "smooth talker" D.C. Corbin was also in Ottawa lobbying strenuously in favour of the bill. The two railway executives testified before the railway committee on 17 March. The CPR president asserted that "the Corbin proposal would, if carried out, divert trade southward into the United States." The *Globe* reporter thought that Corbin had presented his case more effectively than Van Horne, so that the members of the committee "seemed very much disposed to grant the [Corbin] application." However, an adjournment on the issue was granted.[37]

On 18 March the *Globe* published a lead editorial strongly supporting the KRVR Bill. It endorsed the bill because the promoters of the railway were proposing to build, without public assistance, a line into a district which was "badly in need of a railway." The editorial accepted Corbin's assertion that 90 per cent of the goods which his railway, the SF&N, carried into Rossland were of Canadian origin. The issue of whether ores would be smelted in Canada or the US would be settled by "the economics of the situation."[38] Van Horne immediately sent a forceful reply, which was delivered to the *Globe*'s offices on Sunday, 20 March, by the CPR superintendent in Toronto (J.W. Leonard) and published the next day. The CPR president stressed that Corbin's proposed railway would divert Canadian trade in the Boundary district to Spokane, where it would be handed over to the Great Northern and Northern Pacific railways. He estimated that over a 10-year period these American lines would tap $100 million worth of Canadian trade. Corbin's evidence on the amount of Canadian trade the SF&N carried into Rossland was, Van Horne asserted, "only somebody's estimate which we know to be very wide of the truth." He also pointed out that freight rates on ore on Corbin's Canadian line favoured the American smelter at Northport over the Canadian smelter at Trail. He then reminded the *Globe* that the CPR was built to develop Western Canada for Canadians. "To be potent, it must be kept strong," Van Horne asserted. "Every line permitted to enter Canadian territory from the south is a weapon in the hands of the competitors of the Canadian Pacific."[39]

The opponents of Bill 26 were pleased when on 24 March the BC legislature adopted a resolution, by a vote of 20 to 10, urging Ottawa to refuse a charter for the railway. The merchants and mine owners of Rossland immediately met and passed a resolution asking Parliament to disregard the provincial legislature's resolution on the grounds that "such resolutions are simple echoes of Victoria and Vancouver boards of trade. Southern British Columbia are [sic] unit for Kettle River Valley Railway as the mining interests are paramount to all other local interests."[40] Then the Vancouver and Victoria boards of trade sent petitions to the railway committee opposing the bill. Van Horne claimed that railways minister Blair withheld these petitions from the committee. The CPR president was successful in persuading the Montreal and Toronto boards of trade to adopt resolutions opposing Bill 26 on 28 March. On his advice, these resolutions were sent to James Sutherland, the chairman of the railway committee, who transmitted them to his committee. William Wainwright, assistant general manager of the Grand Trunk Railway, urged Laurier to disregard these resolutions, suggesting they were prompted by powerful interests, though he did not mention the CPR specifically.[41] The Winnipeg Board of Trade also opposed the bill. Despite these efforts, on 31 March the railway committee approved the bill by a vote of 54 to 48.[42]

The struggle now shifted to the House of Commons. Laurier had decided on 20 March to allow a free vote on the bill, because his

Cabinet was seriously divided on the issue. He had informed Shaughnessy of this decision on 21 March. Shaughnessy sent "a brief memorandum" to each MP explaining the CPR's position on the KRVR Bill. Cabinet ministers Andrew Blair, Clifford Sifton, W.S. Fielding, Sir Richard Cartwright, Richard Dobell, Charles Fitzpatrick, and William Paterson all voted for the bill, as did some prominent Conservatives such as Sir Adolphe Caron and Sir Charles Hibbert Tupper. Three Cabinet ministers voted against the bill: Israel Tarte, David Mills, and Sir Henri Joly de Lotbinière.[43] Tarte had long been a staunch defender of the CPR in Cabinet; on 13 April he made a vigorous speech in the House attacking the measure. In reply to a member's suggestion that the defeat of the bill would result in a CPR monopoly in southern British Columbia, Tarte responded: "Will my hon. friend say that it would be a monopoly to have a Canadian line on Canadian soil, to have Canadian smelters on Canadian soil? It cannot be a monopoly, it is simply national protection to national industries."[44] Tarte persuaded many French-Canadian Liberal MPs from Quebec to vote against it. And on 15 April the bill was defeated by a vote of 64 to 44. The following day Van Horne expressed his appreciation of Tarte's key role in defeating the bill. "I feel," he observed, "that the defeat of the Kettle River Ry bill is mainly due to you." Corbin simply remarked that the CPR had "used all its resources to defeat me."[45]

The CPR had blocked Corbin's efforts to extend his railway into the Boundary district and so divert the mining traffic of this area to American smelters. It was now imperative that the company build a line from Robson into the Boundary district as soon as possible, since Corbin might again attempt to charter a line into that territory.

The company constructed a line from Robson to Midway in the Boundary district under the charter of the Columbia and Western Railway. Tenders for construction of this line were called for May 1898, and in June the contract was awarded to Mann, Foley and Larsen of St Paul, Minnesota. The hiring of an American firm indicated that, if necessary, the CPR was prepared to hire American as well as Canadian workers. In June William F. Tye was appointed chief engineer of construction; he was to superintend "all matters connected with the engineering and construction work." The burly, six-foot-four native of Ontario had studied engineering at Ottawa College and the University of Toronto. After graduation in 1881 he had gained extensive experience locating and supervising the construction of railway lines in the Canadian prairie West, the American Northwest, and Mexico. In 1895 he was chief engineer for the construction of Hill's Kaslo and Slocan Railway. The next year he was hired by Heinze as chief engineer for the Columbia and Western Railway, under the direction of Gutelius.[46]

The CPR vice-president informed the contractors that he wanted the line from Robson to Midway completed "as quickly as possible, and it is understood that you will push it with the utmost vigor." The major reason for haste was Shaughnessy's conviction that "the Kettle River people" would make "another determined effort" in the 1899 session of Parliament to secure a charter for the KRVR. Shaughnessy learned in November 1898 that the GN had acquired Corbin's railways. He was certain that Hill would make an effort to have Parliament approve the KRVR charter in 1899.[47] The construction of the Crow's Nest Pass line between Kootenay Landing and Procter, which would be quite expensive, had been delayed so that the CPR could devote all its funds to building the line into the Boundary district. Construction costs of the Robson-Midway line were high because it passed through rugged, mountainous terrain. It was necessary to build a 3,000-foot tunnel east of the summit of the Midway Mountains, and many bridges to cross the numerous creeks and gulleys. The largest bridge, which spanned the Kettle River near Cascade City, was 1,000 feet long and 180 feet high. Shaughnessy kept a very close watch over expenses. In November 1898 chief engineer Peterson inspected the line and reported to Shaughnessy that contractors were classifying large quantities of earth as "loose rock and hard pan." The CPR president strongly advised Tye to go over the line, correct any "improper and unwarranted classification" and dismiss any of the engineers who were to blame. "I want this to be the cleanest and most economic piece of railway work that we have ever done," he informed Tye, "the contractors receiving every penny that they are entitled to but not one penny more."[48]

The Columbia and Western line reached Greenwood, about 15 miles east of Midway, in November 1899. Early the following month a large excursion party of businessmen and officials travelled over the new road from Robson to Greenwood. "At Greenwood they were met by a brass band and driven by hack to a celebration banquet. They lustily toasted the Queen, the Board of Trade and the CPR and were loud in their praise of the railway company for completing the gigantic project. It had cost fifty thousand dollars per mile but everyone thought it was well worth it."[49] The line reached Midway early in 1900. The length of the Robson-Midway line was 100 miles, 20 more than estimated in June 1898. Spurs were built to the mines at Deadwood and Phoenix. These and other mines in the Boundary district could now have their ores treated in smelters close at hand in Grand Forks and Greenwood.[50]

However, the CPR's dominant position in southern BC was now challenged by a formidable rival – James J. Hill and the Great Northern Railroad. In June 1898 Corbin obtained a substantial majority of the shares of the SF&N with the assistance of the New York banking firm of J.P. Morgan and Company. Corbin then sold these shares to Morgan on the understanding that they would then be sold to the Northern Pacific. On 1 July 1898 the Northern Pacific signed an agreement with the Great Northern transferring all its holdings of SF&N stock to Hill's company. This agreement gave the GN control of the SF&N and all its subsidiaries: the Columbia and Red Mountain Railway, the Red Mountain Railway, and the Nelson and Fort Sheppard Railway. Hill then used the charter of his Bedlington and Nelson Railway Company to build a line from Bonner's Ferry, on the Great Northern, to Kuskonook at the south end of Kootenay Lake, where it connected by lake steamer with the Kaslo and Slocan Railway. (See figure 1.) Now Hill could divert some of the ores of the Slocan to his line and to American smelters.[51]

Conflict between the CPR and the Great Northern developed in 1898 over a seemingly insignificant measure, the Nakusp and Slocan Railway Company Bill. This private member's bill, sponsored by Liberal MP T.H. Macpherson (Hamilton), received third reading in the House on 20 April 1898 with almost no discussion. The bill authorized the CPR-controlled Nakusp and Slocan Railway to build a branch from Nakusp on Upper Arrow Lake, for 10 miles parallel to Hill's Kaslo and Slocan Railway. It was a move by the CPR to prevent the Great Northern from controlling the traffic of the Slocan mining district. In the Senate, the bill was sponsored by Conservative Donald MacInnes, a prominent Hamilton businessman and a director of the CPR. The bill, however, encountered substantial opposition on third reading. Van Horne was convinced that this opposition was inspired by J.J. Hill.[52] The chief opponents of the bill in the Senate were Conservative Charles A. Boulton, a Manitoba farmer, and Liberals William Templeman, the publisher of the Victoria *Times*, and Lawrence Power, a Halifax lawyer. Boulton charged that the purpose of the bill was "to kill the competition" which the CPR faced in the Slocan district. He opposed the bill because he wanted "to keep down monopoly as much as you can in the interior of that country." Templeman and Power stressed that the people of the Slocan were opposed to the bill and public opinion in BC was against it. Boulton, seconded by Templeman, moved 3 months' hoist, a motion which was defeated on 12 May by a vote of 43 to 11. The bill then received third reading.[53] This was only a foretaste of the bitter rivalry which developed between the CPR and the GN in southern BC from 1898 to 1914, a subject which is discussed in chapter 6. The Canadianization of the Kootenays was by no means firmly established in 1898.

The CPR was also soon faced with a serious competitor in the prairie West – Mackenzie and Mann's Canadian Northern Railway. When Shaughnessy assumed the presidency in June 1899, one of his first tasks was to devise policies to meet this new challenge.

CHAPTER FOUR

The CPR on the Prairies, 1897–1905: The Start of Competition

In November 1897 president Van Horne was enthusing over the mining traffic that the Crow's Nest Pass Railway would soon bring to the CPR. "But after all," he informed Harry Moody, the company's agent in London, "our *great* gold mine is in the prairies of the North West, and that has been worked this year with [excellent] results ... for most of the farmers there have got back from the grain crops and cattle of the present year all that their lands cost them and all that they have ever spent on them."[1] Both Van Horne and Shaughnessy realized that the CPR's profits in Western Canada were largely derived from agriculture and ranching: the company moved grain and cattle over its lines to markets in Eastern Canada, Britain, and Europe, transported goods from Eastern Canada to prairie settlers and ranchers, and sold its vast prairie landholdings.

However, the CPR's policies for developing its "great gold mine" had made the company unpopular in Manitoba and the Territories since the early 1880s. One of the most contentious provisions in the CPR charter was the monopoly clause (clause 15) which was designed to give the company a monopoly of through traffic on the prairies and to prevent rival American enterprises such as the Northern Pacific Railroad from diverting some of that traffic to their own lines. From 1881 to 1887 the Macdonald government had protected this monopoly by disallowing Manitoba legislation chartering railways extending to the American border. Initially these railways were chartered by the Conservative administration of John Norquay to provide badly needed branch-line facilities for settlers in southern Manitoba. Another major grievance was the CPR's exemption from federal rate regulation until the company earned a 10 per cent dividend on its common stock. When the CPR raised its freight rates very substantially in 1883, a groundswell of protest developed in Manitoba, with farmers, merchants, and politicians of both parties demanding that the provincial government establish competing lines in order to break the CPR monopoly and reduce the costs of transportation. Another grievance was the exemption of CPR lands in Manitoba and the Territories from taxation for a period of 20 years.

In the 1886 general election the Norquay government of Manitoba was re-elected by a narrow majority. When the federal government disallowed Norquay's 1887 legislation chartering a railway from Winnipeg to the US border, the premier promised to build the line as a provincial public work. However, the Manitoba government could not raise the necessary funds when it attempted to sell provincial government bonds on the New York and London money markets. Defections in his party forced Norquay to resign in December 1887, and after a short period the Liberals under Thomas Greenway came to power in January 1888. The Liberals were also very hostile to the CPR monopoly clause. Greenway approached the Northern Pacific Railroad, which agreed to build a railway from Winnipeg to the US border to connect with the Northern Pacific system. The CPR attempted to block construction of this line, but was ordered by the Supreme Court of Canada to refrain from such activities. The CPR, realizing that the unfavourable publicity generated by its high-handed actions to preserve its monopoly in the prairie West were driving down the price of its shares in London, surrendered the monopoly clause in 1888 and the federal government abandoned its policy of disallowance against Manitoba. The following year the Northern Pacific lir e from Winnipeg to the American border was completed. The Northern Pacific built and acquired about 300 miles of branch lines in southwestern Manitoba in the 1890s with aid from the Greenway government. However, the company cooperated with the CPR in setting freight rates in southern Manitoba, in order to avoid a rate war with the CPR-controlled Soo line, which had lines in Minnesota and North Dakota. As a result the CPR faced no real competition in Manitoba in the 1890s.[2]

Relations between the CPR and the Greenway government improved in 1891 when president Van Horne reached an agreement with Greenway whereby the Manitoba government would subsidize the construction of a CPR line into the Souris coal fields, and in return the CPR would substantially reduce freight rates for soft coal in southern Manitoba. Then, in the 1892 provincial election, the CPR strongly supported Greenway and the Liberals. The company also completed work on its Glenboro branch. Greenway was looking forward to additional CPR branch lines for Manitoba in the near future. However, the financial panic of 1893 and the growing depression led

Van Horne to discontinue further branch line construction in Manitoba and to abandon any notion of rate reductions. Farmers in the province soon became very critical of the CPR for maintaining high freight rates in the face of the lowest international grain prices in years.[3]

The Greenway government responded by throwing its support to the railway projects of Mackenzie and Mann in Manitoba. William Mackenzie and Donald Mann, the architects of the Canadian Northern Railway, had been enterprising and energetic railway contractors on the CPR main line. They had then formed a business partnership as railway contractors and constructed a number of railways in the prairie West in the period 1886–92. Their partnership was revived in January 1896 when they purchased the charter of the Lake Manitoba Railway and Canal Company. (In 1902 this partnership was incorporated as a joint stock company, Mackenzie Mann and Company, with headquarters in Toronto. Since the two men were no longer "contractors personally" it was legal for them to become officers of the Canadian Northern Railway. Mackenzie, who served as the company's president, was a financial wizard who adeptly handled the company's finances; he frequently visited London to obtain information on the state of the London money market and to superintend the floating of Canadian Northern bonds there. Mann, a heavy-set, taciturn fellow, looked after most of the Canadian Northern's construction contracts and negotiated with the governments of the four western provinces. The third major figure in the company was Zebulon A. Lash, the railway's general counsel. A member of the prestigious Toronto law firm of Blake, Lash and Cassels, Lash had an extensive knowledge of company law and a brilliant capacity for drafting clear and precise documents that provided maximum benefits for the Canadian Northern.)[4]

In 1896, with the Greenway government's guarantee of the interest and principal on Mackenzie and Mann's railway company bonds, the two able contractors began building railway lines in the province. In exchange, they agreed to submit their freight rates to the provincial government for approval. By 1898 Mackenzie and Mann operated 161 miles of railway in Manitoba, made up of two short and separate local lines. In December that year their two railway companies were amalgamated to form the Canadian Northern Railway Company. This company received a federal charter with rights to build extensive mileage in Manitoba and the North-West Territories in July 1899. The federal legislation prohibited an amalgamation with the CPR, the sale or lease of any Canadian Northern lines to the CPR, and the pooling of earnings between the two companies

– clauses which were clearly designed by the Laurier government to promote competition between the two railways, especially in the prairie West. Laurier was now using the Canadian Northern rather than the CPR as an instrument of national economic policy. Mackenzie and Mann began to make serious plans to connect their two Manitoba railways and to extend them eastward to the Lakehead.[5]

In June 1899 an important change occurred in the management of the CPR: Van Horne was succeeded as president by his able lieutenant, Thomas Shaughnessy. Van Horne had thought of retiring as early as 1895, but, according to his biographer, "had been persuaded by Shaughnessy to remain until the position of the company was completely reestablished."[6] Poor health was one of the factors that led to Van Horne's resignation. For some time Van Horne had suffered from bronchitis. In April 1899 he informed Sir Charles Tupper, "my bronchitis has compelled me to run away and seek a place hot enough to burn it out and I am now en route to Southern California and will be gone for three or four weeks." For some time Van Horne had been grooming Shaughnessy as his successor. He told a correspondent in 1898 that "Mr. Shaughnessy can speak for this Company just as well as I can." But the CPR president was very concerned about the heavy work load that both he and Shaughnessy were carrying. He elaborated on this situation to Lord Strathcona in February 1899. "The business of the Company has clearly outgrown its organization," Van Horne asserted, "and we cannot go on longer without danger to the Company's interest. The Company has but two officers who are familiar with its general affairs and its working machinery. The brunt of the work has fallen more and more upon Mr. Shaughnessy, who has been all that could be wished; but he ... has his physical limitations. He cannot continue long under his present high pressure without breaking down and that would be a great calamity to the Company."[7] A solution would be to adopt the practice of major American railways and appoint several vice-presidents to be put in charge of the main departments of the railway. Once Shaughnessy became president, this plan was carried out gradually, as qualified individuals were found. David McNicoll, who had been with the CPR since 1883, was appointed general manager and second vice-president in 1900, with general supervision over railway operations. Then in December 1901 Isaac G. Ogden, who had started with the company at its inception in 1881 and had become comptroller in 1887, was appointed third vice-president in charge of finance. In the same month, George M. Bosworth, who had joined the CPR in 1882 and held a number of posts dealing with freight traffic, was named fourth vice-president in charge of traffic.[8]

On Monday 12 June 1899, at its regular monthly meeting in Windsor Station, the CPR board of directors accepted the resignation of Sir William Van Horne. He had been president for 11 years. The directors then proceeded to elect Thomas G. Shaughnessy in his place. Sir William paid Shaughnessy a handsome tribute in a press statement, remarking that "one of my chief reasons for asking our directors to permit me to relinquish the duties of the office of president was to secure the well earned promotion of Mr. Shaughnessy, whose services to the company have been beyond estimation, and whom I look upon as all that could be wished for as the chief executive officer of a great corporation – honourable, capable, energetic and fair-dealing." Van Horne retained his directorship and was appointed to the newly created office of chairman of the board. The chairman was an *ex officio* member of the CPR executive committee, so Van Horne could continue to play an important policy making role in the company in the future.[9] The Montreal *Star* presented an excellent portrait of Shaughnessy which captured something of his controlled intensity and nervous energy. "While he is walking about in his office," the *Star* reported, "he is ruminating upon a scheme which will at once enhance dividends and the glory of the company, which is his lode star. He has a mind for details and a love of order."[10] Shaughnessy was deluged with letters of congratulations. He was particularly touched by those from old friends in Milwaukee, who were evidently extremely proud of "their" man. One local businessman wrote: "It was a day of universal rejoicing here in Milwaukee when the news arrived of your election. Every man and woman of mature years seemed to claim you for a son and all the rest of the people as a near relative."[11]

A great deal of Shaughnessy's attention during his presidency was devoted to Western matters. At the time he became president, the vigorous immigration policies of Clifford Sifton were beginning to bear fruit, and large numbers of agricultural settlers were moving into the Canadian prairie West from Britain, the US, continental Europe, and Eastern Canada. In 1900 Shaughnessy informed a CPR official in Winnipeg that in the previous 10 years the company had spent over $40 million in providing additional and improved railway facilities between the Lakehead and the Pacific coast, and such expenditures would continue on a yearly basis as the region was settled. He noted that there was still "a vast area" of Manitoba to be provided with railway facilities, and asserted that the province had "everything to gain" by having the CPR retain its financial strength so that it could build branch lines in Manitoba "at a minimum of cost to the province."[12]

The manager of the CPR's lines in the West, and Shaughnessy's chief advisor on prairie policy, was William Whyte. Scottish-born Whyte, who emigrated to Canada in 1863 at the age of twenty, had served a short time as station agent on a Scottish railway. In Toronto he started as a brakeman with the Grand Trunk Railway, gradually rising through the ranks until his appointment as divisional superintendent at Toronto in 1882. The following year he became general superintendent of the Ontario and Quebec Railway. The CPR leased this railway in January 1884, and the following year Whyte was appointed general superintendent of the CPR's Eastern and Ontario divisions, with an office in Montreal. He was transferred from Montreal to Winnipeg in 1886 to become general superintendent of the Western Division; in 1897 this position was raised to that of manager, western lines. Whyte was well-regarded by most of the men on the Western Division. "Mr. Whyte's door was always on the swing, and a wiper from the roundhouse could see him just as readily as a captain of industry." This approachability and his determination to be fair to the men on his division "gave him enormous personal influence with all of them." In 1901 Augustus Nanton, the manager of the Winnipeg branch of Osler and Hammond, reported that on a trip to BC "I came in contact with many C.P.R. men and was greatly struck with their loyalty to Whyte ... With five out of six men against the C.P.R., as they are up here," he informed E.B. Osler, "it is no small advantage to the Company to have a man at the head of affairs who is personally liked as Whyte is, not only by his men but liked and respected by the public." And most important, he had a fervent belief in the economic potential of the West, "and when other men were in despair over bad years and slow settlement, he never lost 'the knack of hoping'." He vigorously supported expansionist policies for the CPR in the prairie region while Shaughnessy was president.[13]

When Shaughnessy assumed the presidency, one of his goals was to improve relations between the company and the Liberal Greenway government of Manitoba, in order to secure provincial aid for an extensive CPR branch-line construction program in Manitoba, and to prevent freight-rate reductions in the province by either the Northern Pacific Railroad or the Canadian Northern Railway. "If he [Greenway] acts fairly with us," Shaughnessy remarked, "he can expect fairness from us."[14] Negotiations between Greenway and the CPR were conducted through W.R. Baker, general manager of the Manitoba and North Western Railway, which the CPR was in the process of acquiring. Baker arranged for Greenway to discuss Manitoba issues with Shaughnessy in Montreal. The premier pushed strongly for the construction of a CPR branch line 20 miles west from Hamiota and the building of a CPR hotel in Winnipeg. Shaughnessy informed Whyte that "The twenty miles must be built now, if that will satisfy the Manitoba Government and prevent the construction of the line from Portage la Prairie by the Government, or by any Company with their assistance, this year." As a result of these discussions, Shaughnessy chose a site for the Winnipeg hotel next to the CPR station, and in June 1899 the company hired an architect to work on the plans.[15] Then late in July the CPR signed an agreement with the Greenway government to build the Snowflake and Wascada extensions, about 40 miles in total, in 1899. It appears that the Greenway government promised subsidies for these two lines, which were to be granted after the provincial election expected to be held later in the year.[16]

Greenway attempted to get support from the Northern Pacific in the 7 December 1899 election by offering this company government aid to construct a branch line west of Portage la Prairie. C.S. Mellen, president of the Northern Pacific, came to Winnipeg in July 1899 to discuss this proposal. The price of provincial aid, he learned, was a substantial reduction in Northern Pacific freight rates on wheat in Manitoba, but because he did not wish to provoke a rate war with the CPR, Mellen refused. Shaughnessy's conciliatory policy towards the Greenway government in 1899 makes it difficult to accept Joseph Hilts's claim that the CPR actively opposed the Liberals in the 1899 provincial election. The decisive factor in Greenway's defeat, as Hall observes, was the fact that Conservatives who had supported the Liberals on the railway monopoly issue and the Manitoba School Question had almost all gone back to the provincial Conservative party.[17]

The new Conservative administration in Manitoba was headed by Hugh John Macdonald, the son of Sir John A. Macdonald. In the 1880s he had supported cancellation of the CPR monopoly clause because he believed that cancellation would permit more railway construction in Manitoba and provide the competition which the West needed. But after doing a good deal of legal work for the CPR in the 1890s Macdonald became a strong supporter of the company. In 1892 he informed Shaughnessy, "I am anxious on Public and Party grounds to do everything I can to advance its [the CPR's] interests." He won a seat in Winnipeg in the 1896 federal general election but was later unseated for corrupt practices. The Tories then found a political refuge for him in the leadership of the Manitoba Conservative party, which he accepted in March 1897. Macdonald was particularly concerned about railway expansion, with the result that the 1899 Conservative platform endorsed "Adoption of principle of Government ownership of railways wherever practicable, and Government control of rates over all newly bonused lines, together with right of purchase." Macdonald was probably not wholly devoted to the principle of government ownership, but rather saw it as a policy that would attract many farmer votes. Shaughnessy was not happy with this "insane" policy of government ownership and was certain the Macdonald government would not adopt it. If the Manitoba Conservatives wanted such a railway system, "the sooner they try the experiment the better," he remarked.[18]

In March 1900 the CPR leased in perpetuity the Great North West Central Railway, which ran from Brandon, Manitoba, for 50 miles in a northwesterly direction.[19] Two months later, in May, the CPR took over the Manitoba and North Western Railway, which extended 225 miles from Portage la Prairie, Manitoba, to Yorkton in the Territories, and had 28 miles of branch lines. This was a valuable acquisition, for not only did this company have charter rights to build to Prince Albert, it also had accumulated a large land grant of 1,800,000 acres. The railway's general manager since 1883, W.R. Baker, was appointed CPR executive agent in Winnipeg, effective 15 May 1900.[20] In 1900–1 Baker acted as the CPR's representative in negotiations with the Manitoba government.

Shaughnessy was particularly concerned about the expansion of the Northern Pacific in Manitoba. But by February 1900 the Northern Pacific and the CPR had reached an understanding that each company would not build lines in the other's territory. Shaughnessy undertook to have the Soo line and the South Shore line cooperate in this policy. "I am pleased to note," he remarked to Northern Pacific president Mellen, "your statement that you are not committed at present to any extensions in Manitoba ... Personally, I have no desire to see a single mile added to our system [in the US] within the next two or three years, excepting such short branches as may be necessary to serve newly developed districts in our own territory."[21]

The CPR's relations with the Macdonald administration were poor almost from the time it took office. The CPR refused to undertake any new construction work in Manitoba in 1900 unless the Manitoba government granted it subsidies for the Wascada, Snowflake, and Hamiota extensions. Politically, such subsidies were impossible for the Macdonald government to accept. Shaughnessy realized the strength of public opposition to the CPR in Manitoba, but he was convinced that most of this hostility "may be traced to the misrepresentations of scheming politicians, who thought that the anti-railway cry would help them in their elections, and the unreliable newspaper men who want something."[22]

In its first session, the Macdonald government introduced railway taxation legislation which Shaughnessy vigorously opposed. The tax, which applied only to the CPR, was set at $150 per mile on the company's lines in Manitoba. Shaughnessy denounced it as "so onerous ... as to be without predecent anywhere on this Continent." As he affirmed to W.R. Baker, who was negotiating with the government to modify the tax, "we protest against taxation that is within the shadow of confiscation, or that in any manner will bear more severely on us than on other tax payers." Later Shaughnessy was very pleased with changes which Baker secured in this legislation, remarking that "the imposition of any tax is a sort of breach of faith, but, if it had to come, I think that we have got it in [the] best shape possible. The fact that these taxes are in lieu of others may mean a good deal to us in the course of ten years."[23] Shaughnessy also had Baker "keeping an eye" on the negotiations between the Northern Pacific and the Macdonald government for Manitoba's acquisition of some or all of the company's lines in Manitoba.[24] There was a real danger that the provincial government, once it acquired these lines, might lease them to Mackenzie and Mann of the Canadian Northern Railway, who in 1900 were making arrangements to finance a line from Winnipeg to Port Arthur. Then the CPR would be faced with serious competition in Manitoba.

In October 1900 Macdonald resigned as premier and entered the federal election campaign. He was succeeded by Rodmond Roblin, a farmer, grain merchant, and railway promoter. Roblin had an excellent understanding of the CPR's unpopularity in Manitoba, especially in the rural areas, and as Ted Regehr observes, "was not the man to preside over the re-establishment of a CPR monopoly."[25] The negotiations between the Manitoba government and the Northern Pacific intensified soon after Roblin became premier. Shaughnessy attempted to pressure president Mellen to retain the Northern Pacific lines in Manitoba, and asked James J. Hill, president of the Great Northern, to apply similar pressure.[26]

Shaughnessy then made a special trip to Winnipeg, where he had a lengthy meeting with Premier Roblin and his cabinet colleagues on the afternoon of 22 January 1901. The CPR president made a determined effort to acquire the Northern Pacific lines. (Provincial agreement was required since an 1899 agreement between the Northern Pacific and Manitoba Railway and the provincial government prohibited sale of the line to the CPR.) He offered the province a bonus of $500,000 which would go directly into provincial coffers. He proposed rate reductions over a period of 5 years, that would bring CPR freight rates on grain and flour from all points in Manitoba to the Lakehead to 10 cents per hundredweight by September 1906.

But there were several conditions attached to this offer. The CPR wanted the Roblin government to grant no aid to any railways in southwestern Manitoba for a 10-year period and to reduce CPR taxes to the level paid by the Canadian Northern. These two conditions were later withdrawn.[27]

Nevertheless the CPR could not match Mackenzie and Mann's proposals. The Canadian Northern agreed to Roblin's demand to set a rate of 10 cents per hundredweight on wheat moving from Winnipeg to the Lakehead, effective 1 July 1903. This figure was 4 cents lower than the Crow's Nest Pass rate. The Canadian Northern also agreed to reductions of between 15 and 25 per cent on a variety of other commodities shipped from the Lakehead to points in Manitoba and to provincial control over the rates on any of its lines subsidized by the Manitoba government. Mackenzie and Mann stressed throughout the negotiations that the 350-mile Northern Pacific network would fit well into their developing system, so that the Canadian Northern would soon become "the long-awaited competitor for the CPR." Mackenzie and Mann won their case and on 15 January 1901 the Canadian Northern leased the Northern Pacific lines from the Manitoba government (which had acquired them from the Northern Pacific); the Roblin government also provided additional aid to the Canadian Northern – guarantees on construction bonds of $20,000 per mile on the entire Ontario section of the Winnipeg to Lakehead line, and $8,000 per mile on the Minnesota section. Mackenzie and Mann used this funding to complete the Canadian Northern main line from Winnipeg to Port Arthur by January 1902.[28]

Shaughnessy was extremely upset by the outcome, although it is difficult to see how the CPR could have won its case, in view of the long tradition of public animosity to the corporation in Manitoba. Recognizing this fact, he informed CPR director W.D. Matthews that no CPR proposition would have been accepted by the people of Manitoba "who have gone wild on the subject of railway competition. It is unnecessary for me to say," he continued, "that I am disgusted with the result, but I suppose there is nothing for me but to grin and bear it." Shaughnessy was however pleased that by late February 1901, "a good many Conservatives seem to be pronouncing against the [Manitoba] arrangement." Privately, he informed Matthews that "in our newspaper work, [we] have confined ourselves to the weaknesses of the present arrangement with the Canadian Northern. Now that the subject has been taken up very generally by the public and by the press in Manitoba, I have told our people there that we should drop into the back ground and let others do the talking and writing.

It would not strengthen the opposition to the Bill if the impression got abroad that we had some motive in defeating it."[29]

Federal enabling legislation was required, since both the Canadian Northern and the Northern Pacific and Manitoba railways had federal charters; this legislation was introduced into Parliament in April 1901. It was hotly debated at the committee stage. Finally the government brought in an amendment making it clear that the federal government had the power to control inter-provincial freight rates.[30] It does not appear that Shaughnessy made a serious effort to defeat this legislation, though the president did have the company's lobbyist, Charles Drinkwater, spend most of his time in Ottawa during the 1901 session, ostensibly to deal with the many "pretty grievances" of Western MPS regarding the CPR. The president still resented the Manitoba agreement, which he described in mid-February as "the most scandalous that has been contemplated in this country, or any other." One of the western MPS opposed to the enabling legislation, R.L Richardson, did make a special trip to Montreal to discuss the issue with Shaughnessy. A strong supporter of government ownership of railways, Richardson criticized the Conservative government of Manitoba for its failure to live up to the plank of government ownership that had been in the party's 1899 platform. But Shaughnessy probably realized that opposition was pointless – that the enabling legislation had strong support on both sides of the House. The measure passed there on 13 May by an overwhelming majority of both parties.[31]

Despite his initial opposition, by April 1901, when the CPR and the Canadian Northern signed a traffic agreement, Shaughnessy emphasized the benefits of the Manitoba agreement: the CPR would now receive both Canadian Northern and former Northern Pacific traffic between the Canadian West and Eastern Canada. Previously, the Northern Pacific had sent all its Manitoba traffic over its own lines in the United States. Shaughnessy called the Canadian Northern Railway "a weak competitor" despite the fact that in October 1903 the CPR was compelled to lower its rates on grain and other commodities to the levels fixed in the 1901 agreement between the Canadian Northern and the Manitoba government. The company also cut its rates by 7 1/2 per cent to points in the districts of Assiniboia and Saskatchewan which were not then served by the Canadian Northern.[32] The CPR president knew that Mackenzie and Mann intended to extend their line to the Pacific coast, but he did not believe they could secure the government aid necessary to accomplish this. Shaughnessy clearly underestimated the political skills and driving ambition of Mackenzie and Mann and their determination to provide effective competition for the CPR in Western Canada. He remarked to a friend in England that "I do not think that you or I will live to see a line constructed through the Coast north of our line, although its construction would, no doubt, be an advantage rather than an injury to the Canadian Pacific."[33]

In May 1901 Shaughnessy made some major changes in senior staff positions, several of which affected operations in the prairie West. William Whyte was appointed assistant to the president, but he would continue to reside in Winnipeg. Whyte now became an important policy advisor on "all matters connected with colonization, proposed extensions of the company's railway system, the development of industry along the company's lines, the establishment of new business connections and the administration of the Company's lands, townsites and other properties of that description."[34] His replacement as general superintendent of the Western Division was James W. Leonard. Born in Ontario in 1858, he had worked for various railways in that province from age fourteen until he joined the CPR in 1884. He had been general superintendent of the Ontario and Quebec Division since 1893. Shaughnessy was impressed with Leonard's abilities. "He was selected for the important post at Winnipeg," he remarked, "because of the energy, ability and devotion to duty displayed by him in every position that he has occupied in the Company's service." Shaughnessy arranged for Leonard to discuss Western affairs with Clifford Sifton. Then, after a Toronto banquet in his honour on 12 June, Leonard left for Winnipeg. He began his new job without the valuable assistance and support of his predecessor, Whyte, who was touring the Russian railway system from June to October. Neither could he seek advice from W.R. Baker, who had extensive railway experience in Manitoba, since Baker was fully involved with making arrangements for the Royal Tour of the Duke and Duchess of Cornwall and York in September and October, and would be transferred permanently to Montreal in November.[35] Thus Leonard had to face the "grain blockage" crisis all alone. In the autumn of 1901 there developed serious problems in moving the prairie wheat crop to markets in Eastern Canada and Europe. This grain blockage was the result of the largest grain crop yet experienced in the prairie West. The CPR was severely criticized, particularly in the West, for not having enough box cars to handle the crop. Conditions were so severe in Eastern Assiniboia that farmers built 120 temporary grain sheds at Indian Head.[36] Though the criticisms were unfair, since the huge harvest was unexpected, the ultimate responsibility rested with Shaughnessy. On 17 June trackmen on the entire CPR system had begun a strike which was not settled until early September. Shaughnessy was extremely angry at "this infernal strike" which made it very difficult for the company to secure replacements in the West. He was also at this time deeply involved in the question of whether the company should develop its own fleet of Atlantic steamships. All these factors prevented him from paying sufficient attention to Western needs, especially more rolling stock.[37]

Nonetheless he had to respond to charges that the 1901 grain blockage indicated that the rolling stock of the CPR was inadequate. The problem was compounded by the fact that the 1900 grain crop in the West had been a poor one. "A year ago," Shaughnessy remarked to the secretary of the Indian Head Board of Trade, "owing to the short crop, we handled only about 4,500 carloads of grain before the close of navigation, while this year [1901] we handled four times as many." Therefore the CPR had little incentive to order additional rolling stock until it could make "some reasonable forecast of the crop prospect" in 1901. "We took some chances, however, and expended a large sum of money in securing cars and locomotives wherever they could be had."[38]

Privately, Shaughnessy was very critical of prairie farmers' practice of rushing "their grain to market in large quantities, within a very limited period in the fall." In his view, this practice enabled grain buyers to set their own prices at the farmers' expense. Farmers needed to provide granaries of their own. "Of course," he concluded, "we can say nothing on this subject, publicly, without arousing the antagonism of all the grain-buyers."[39] Shaughnessy did not have a very realistic understanding of conditions facing prairie farmers at this time. Problems of cash flow were vital; few farmers could afford the additional debt of constructing granaries to store their grain.

Amidst the controversies over the grain blockade and the CPR trackmen's strike, a pleasant event took place. In September 1901 the Duke of Cornwall and York, the heir to the British throne, and his wife made a cross-Canada tour on the CPR. On Saturday 21 September Shaughnessy, accompanied by his wife, attended a ceremony at Rideau Hall at which the Duke conferred upon him the honour of knighthood (KCMG). Telegrams of congratulation flooded in from all parts of Canada, Britain, and the United States. His old friend S.M. Green of Milwaukee remarked that "King Edward evidently knows a good thing when he sees it." His close friend, the Montreal businessman John Cassils, observed "that the appointment will afford genuine pleasure to your many friends, and to none of them in a greater degree than to myself." Israel Tarte was delighted at the honour which was "a fitting reward of a life full of activity and energy." "All Hail Sir Thomas" his New York friend G.B. Hopkins telegraphed.[40]

Soon after the Royal Tour ended, Shaughnessy responded to the need for more rolling stock and grain facilities in the prairie West. He met Prime Minister Laurier on 12 November and requested an increase of $20 million (par value) in the company's common stock. Although he did not want conditions imposed by the government on the use of these funds, he promised that "a very large amount [of the stock] will be required to increase the rolling stock of the company." On 17 December Shaughnessy sent Laurier the stock-increase bylaw, and discussed in some detail the company's planned expenditures. However, with the support of Clifford Sifton and others, the government did impose certain conditions on the disposition of the stock proceeds: that $8 million be spent on locomotives and cars for Western trade, and $5 million for improving and doubling trackage west of the Lakehead and increasing terminal elevator facilities. On 27 March 1902 the CPR shareholders ratified an increase in the common stock of $19,500,000 and authorized the transfer of $3 million from the surplus earnings fund into the capital fund. The Minister of Justice, Charles Fitzpatrick, introduced the necessary legislation on 17 April and it passed Parliament quickly. In a personal letter to a German investor in CPR stock, the president made it clear that much of the money would be spent on rolling stock. "The development of our traffic," he remarked, "particularly in North-Western Canada, is beyond our expectations ... our land sales indicate that settlers and land-seekers have their eyes on North-Western Canada, and that they are moving there in larger numbers than at any time heretofore ... We have been deplorably short of cars during the past six months, and, satisfactory as our earnings were, we could have increased them were it possible to obtain additional rolling stock from any source."[41]

The inability of prairie farmers to dispose of much of the large 1901 grain crop led to the formation of the Territorial Grain Growers' Association at Indian Head, Assiniboia, on 18 December 1901. The prime movers in this development were two Assiniboia grain farmers, W.R. Motherwell and Peter Dayman. The first Grain Growers' convention was held at Indian Head on 12 February 1901, at which Motherwell was elected president of the organization. The farmers at the meeting were extremely dissatisfied with several provisions of the Manitoba Grain Act of 1900, particularly the section that dealt with the allotment of railway boxcars. Farmers had complained during the 1901 blockade that CPR officials gave the elevator companies the preference in the allotment of any cars that were locally available. The convention therefore passed this resolution: "That the [Manitoba] Grain Act be amended making it the duty of the railway agent, when there is a shortage of cars, to apportion the available cars in the order in which they are applied for, and that in case such cars are misappropriated by applicants not entitled to them, the penalties of the act be enforced against such parties." This and other resolutions were taken to Ottawa, where the western grain blockade was being debated in the House of Commons in March 1902. The Laurier government was impressed with the complaints of the grain growers; their resolutions were incorporated in amendments to the shipping clauses of the Manitoba Grain Act and passed in the 1902 session of Parliament. The amendments required local railway agents to keep an order book and to supply cars in the order in which applications were made and to restrict block bookings by elevators.[42]

Shaughnessy gave CPR officials "positive instructions" to carry out the terms of the 1902 Manitoba Grain Act, and the company records showed that were doing so. However, many CPR officicals did not observe the car-distribution clauses of the new grain act. Motherwell and Dayman, acting for the Territorial Grain Growers' Association, travelled to Winnipeg in the autumn of 1902 and informed CPR officials that unless the car-distribution clauses were properly carried out, the association would take legal action to ensure their fulfilment. Though the officials at Winnipeg promised to give this matter careful attention, their assurances did not bring about observation of the car-distribution clauses by local CPR agents. The association then laid a formal complaint before Warehouse Commissioner C.C. Castle, the federal official responsible for administering the Manitoba Grain Act, charging that the CPR agent at Sintaluta (in Assiniboia), A.V. Benoit, had been guilty of infractions of the grain act in his allotment of cars at that town. Commissioner Castle and an official from the federal department of justice visited Sintaluta on 28 November 1902 to investigate and decided that legal proceedings should be taken against Benoit on behalf of the Crown. The case was tried in Sintaluta in December 1902 before magistrate H.O. Partridge, who was assisted by two local magistrates. The evidence presented regarding infractions of the act was so conclusive that CPR counsel J.A.M. Aikins admitted the facts and restricted his argument to the legal construction of the act. The magistrates found the defendant guilty of violating the priority clause in the act and levied a fine of $50 and costs. This decision was later upheld in an appeal before the Supreme Court. This was an important victory for prairie farmers. The CPR paid the fine and gave firm instructions to its agents to distribute cars strictly in order of application in the car-order book.[43]

Winnipeg merchants were also dissatisfied at the CPR's handling of the 1902 prairie grain crop, for as of 18 December almost 28 million bushels remained to be forwarded to terminal points. On 19 December the Winnipeg Board of Trade passed a resolution that "the conditions in regard to grain transportation during the present shipping season are as bad as, if not worse, than those which prevailed in 1901." William Whyte spoke briefly at this meeting, explaining that a strike at the Kingston Locomotive Works had delayed CPR orders for new engines. He informed the Winnipeg merchants that the CPR had ordered 92 new engines for 1903 and that freight cars "were being ordered wherever they can be built."[44]

Shaughnessy made an inspection trip over the CPR Western lines in June 1902. He was very concerned about the condition of the line between Fort William and Winnipeg, which, he informed David McNicoll, the CPR's general manager, "has been allowed to get into bad order, and, unless the work is pushed very vigorously, it will be late in the season before the track will be up to the proper standard. This is a section of the line that must not, under any circumstances, be permitted to run down, because ... it is, for many reasons, the most important section of our system." The president had begun to suspect that Leonard was not competent to manage the Western Division. "Evidently", Shaughnessy remarked, "he requires somebody on this section [Fort William to Winnipeg] who is very thoroughly up in maintenance."[45] West of Winnipeg the situation was not much better. The president observed that "the greater portion of the branch lines that I have travelled over to-day are absolutely disreputable ... I am satisfied," he concluded, "that our track work on this division is not getting the intelligent supervision that it should have." He was also "disgusted" with "the filthy conditions" of CPR locomotives on the Western Division. McNicoll was instructed to have F.P. Gutelius, one of the company's engineers in Montreal, report on the condition of the section from Fort William to Winnipeg at the end of June. It was these conditions which prompted the Winnipeg Board of Trade's criticism in December 1902 and which led the NWT Legislative Assembly to pass a resolution in April 1903 declaring that for the past 10 years the CPR had "absolutely failed to provide adequate facilities for the transportation" of Territorial grain and cattle. Shaughnessy was also aware of criticisms of the CPR from Western MPs.[46]

Early in May 1903, the president sent Leonard a strong letter expressing his anger at "the stony indifference with which your people up there [at Winnipeg] seem to view our abominable record in handling of merchandise traffic ... Every merchant in Winnipeg is complaining about our treatment of his shipments, and many of them are taking their business away from us as a consequence." A trip to Victoria later that month confirmed Shaughnessy's worst fears. Much of the track between Fort William and the Rocky Mountains was still in "an abominable condition." He had a "plain talk" with Leonard in Winnipeg, ordering him to "put these things right immediately." He also instructed McNicoll to take chief engineer McHenry and "to practically live on the Western Lines" for the summer, supervising track improvements. Their activities were successful, for there were no major problems in moving the 1903 crop, although Shaughnessy was privately critical of the Manitoba Grain Act, "because it makes it nearly impossible, however large our equipment, to handle the grain with anything like satisfaction." On 23 December 1903 the CPR board made some major changes: Leonard was removed from the Western Division, while William Whyte was elected second vice-president and put in charge of Western lines.[47]

It is clear that by 1903 Shaughnessy had developed as strong a belief in the economic potential of the West as that of Mackenzie and Mann. He was contemptuous of disparaging remarks made by James J. Hill, president of the Great Northern Railroad, that the Canadian West was cold, inhospitable, and unsuited to agriculture. "Year by year," he declared, "for any term of years, the Canadian West will produce better crops per acre than any corresponding area on the line of either the Great Northern or the Northern Pacific." In that year the CPR was spending "vast sums of money" to improve the Western Divison. At Winnipeg the company was building another yard with 30 miles of track and new shops which, when equipped, would cost $1.2 million. "All of our division points west of Winnipeg are being extended and enlarged at great expense." The company was making grade improvements and line changes across the prairies, and installing 80-pound rails to replace the original 56- and 60-pound rails.[48]

In 1903 the Laurier government passed legislation which sanctioned the development of two new transcontinental railways, the Canadian Northern Railway and the Grand Trunk Pacific Railway (GTPR). The assistance granted to the latter project is discussed in the next chapter. The Canadian Northern legislation represented the first *federal* bond guarantee for that company. The Laurier government guaranteed the principal and interest on first mortgage Canadian Northern bonds to a maximum of $13,000 per mile for 620 miles of railway from Grandview, Manitoba, to Edmonton, NWT, and for an additional 100 miles to connect the Canadian Northern line in Manitoba to Prince Albert, NWT. The face value of the guaranteed bonds amounted to $9,360,000. The legislation also placed the rates of the Canadian Northern Railway and its subsidiaries under the jurisdiction of the federal Cabinet. However, later that year, Cabinet's jurisdiction was passed on to the Board of Railway Commissioners, the tribunal established by the Laurier government to regulate the company's rates. The Canadian Northern legislation passed the House of Commons on 2 July 1903. The building of the main line to Edmonton "went into high gear" in the spring of 1905. The railway was built from Kamsack to Edmonton by 17 December 1905 – 546 miles of railway had been constructed in a single year.[49]

The CPR now began a rapid expansion of its branch lines on the prairies to meet the competition from the Canadian Northern Railway. One of Shaughnessy's first moves was to acquire ownership of the Calgary and Edmonton Railway (C&E) which the CPR had been operating on a short-term-lease basis since its inception in 1891. This 295-mile railway ran from Macleod through Calgary and north to Strathcona, the city on the south side of the North Saskatchewan River opposite Edmonton. After a visit to Calgary in April 1901, Augustus Nanton reported to E.B. Osler that "the prospects for business on the C.&E. were never better ... It is only a question of a short time when the C.P.R., in its own interest, will have to get hold of the railway." Shaughnessy observed that by 1902 this line was "showing fair net earnings." Mackenzie and Mann were very eager to purchase the line. Shaughnessy reported that in February 1903 the CPR directors "were met with a threat that, unless we took the bonds and stock, they would be transferred to some other Company with whom there were negotiations."[50] The CPR's purchase of the railway was completed by the end of July 1903, and on 8 January 1904 Cabinet approved an agreement by which it leased the C&E for 99 years. The CPR proceeded to make substantial improvements on the line. The CPR had access to Edmonton via a Canadian Northern-controlled line (the Edmonton, Yukon and Pacific) from Strathcona station across the North Saskatchewan River to the city centre, but passenger and freight destined for Edmonton had to transfer to this line at Strathcona.[51]

The CPR now wished to expand its lines in Saskatchewan. The company considered the purchase of the province's major north-south line, the Qu'Appelle, Long Lake and Saskatchewan Railway, which ran from Regina to Prince Albert via Saskatoon. The CPR had operated this line under a leasing arrangement since its construction in 1890. Operations had not been very profitable, and in 1904 the line had recorded a loss of over $50,000. Whyte had the earning capacity of this line carefully assessed by two of his officials in 1904. On the basis of these reports he advised against the purchase of the railway, at least for the present. Shaughnessy agreed with this assessment and observed that the extension of the Canadian Northern and the GTPR into this railway's territory would produce a serious decline in its earning power. In 1906 the owners of the Qu'Appelle line gave the CPR first opportunity to purchase, provided the owners could retain the lands earned from building the railway. Whyte advised Shaughnessy by telegram: "Long Lake Road expensive to operate on account of its grades but has some advantage over new road owing to established business. However, price asked is more than it is worth and would not recommend purchase."[52] The president agreed with Whyte's views, noting that if the CPR met this price and spent money on necessary improvements, the Qu'Appelle line would have fixed charges of "nearly $200,000 per annum, and ... the Qu'Appelle road cannot earn one-half that sum ... We could spend $5,000,000 to infinitely better advantage." The Canadian Northern then proceeded to purchase the line in July 1906. Regehr maintains that Mackenzie and Mann acquired the Qu'Appelle Railway because the CPR "lacked vision." The evidence indicates that Shaughnessy and Whyte decided, after careful consideration, that the railway was over-priced and that the CPR would gain more for its money by building branch lines in several districts in Saskatchewan.[53]

The CPR had been an instrument of national economic policy under the Macdonald Conservatives, and the Laurier Liberals had continued this approach by assisting the construction of the company's Crow's Nest Branch in 1897–8. But after 1899 Laurier gradually shifted his support to the Canadian Northern Railway and then to the Grand Trunk Pacific Railway, so that by 1902 the CPR was facing serious competition on the prairies. The start of construction of the GTPR in 1905 marked an intensification of this competition.

More Competition: The Grand Trunk Pacific Railway and the Canadian Northern Railway, 1903–14

The CPR was soon faced with a second competitor in Western Canada – the Grand Trunk Pacific Railway – which was constructed from Winnipeg to Prince Rupert between 1905 and 1914. The joint Grand Trunk Pacific (GTPR) and National Transcontinental Railway (NTR) project was launched in July 1903 as a partnership between the Laurier administration and the Grand Trunk Railway. The GTPR was a wholly-owned subsidiary of the Grand Trunk, which made all the major decisions regarding the development of the company. From 1903 until the defeat of the federal Liberals in the 1911 general election, the Grand Trunk and its subsidiary, rather than the CPR, were the Laurier government's instrument of national economic policy. Both partners shared the responsibility for financing the GTPR–NTR project. The Grand Trunk superintended the construction and operation of the GTPR main line from Winnipeg to the port of Prince Rupert on BC's Pacific coast, while the government constructed the National Transcontinental line from Winnipeg to Moncton, New Brunswick.

Since its inception in 1854, the Grand Trunk's head office had been located in London, England. Almost all the company's shareholders were residents of Great Britain, and shareholders' meetings were held semi-annually at Dashwood House, the company's offices on Broad Street in London. These were presided over by the president, who was also resident in England. The operating headquarters of the Grand Trunk were located in Montreal where the general manager resided. In 1894 the Grand Trunk incurred its first deficit in 9 years. The following year a group of rebellious shareholders instigated a major reorganization of the company's London board; they wanted the company to curtail expansion of its lines and concentrate on the earning of dividends for the shareholders. A new president was appointed: Sir Charles Rivers Wilson, a civil servant with almost no experience or knowledge of railway affairs, who had made his reputation as controller of the Egyptian National Debt. Soon after, the board replaced the company's English-trained general manager with Charles Melville Hays, a forty-year-old American who had 23 years' experience of every aspect of railway work in the United States. Hays was given a mandate to introduce American railway practices and techniques into the operation of the Grand Trunk because, as Rivers Wilson remarked, "the administration [of the company] had become sluggish and unfit to compete on equal terms with the go-ahead methods of its American and Canadian rivals."[1]

Hays dominated the Grand Trunk and the GTPR until April 1912 when he was drowned on the sinking of the *Titanic*. A.W. Currie describes him as "an indefatigable worker and an artful manipulator of politicians" who "introduced American operating methods, practically rebuilt the Railway, and extended it to the Pacific Coast." Under Hays's management, the Grand Trunk's earnings increased rapidly. In 1898 the company paid dividends on its guaranteed stock for the first time in 5 years, and in 1900 it declared a full dividend on its first preference stock for the first time in 13 years.[2] Hays was particularly astute in his dealings with prominent politicians, and established a very close relationship with Laurier. He appointed William Wainwright, an experienced Grand Trunk official, as his chief assistant and employed him as the company's lobbyist in Ottawa.[3] Some politicians and civil servants found Hays extremely ruthless and unscrupulous in negotiations. J.L. Englehart, head of the Ontario government's Temiskaming and Northern Ontario Railway, remarked that "Mr. Hays extracts, if not a pound, then nine-tenths of it" in railway negotiations. Clifford Sifton, a tough negotiator in his own right, described the Grand Trunk's general manager as the most "cold-blooded a raider of the treasury" that he had encountered.[4] The Grand Trunk's main line extended from Sarnia to Toronto and Montreal, and it had an extensive network of branch lines in the heavily populated sections of Ontario. It also operated a substantial system in the US, including a main line from Sarnia to Chicago, another from Montreal to the Atlantic port of Portland, Maine, and branch lines which were valuable as feeders for the company's lines in Canada.[5]

On 24 November 1902 Hays announced that the Grand Trunk would give its full support to a railway from North Bay, Ontario, the company's western terminus in Canada, to the Pacific coast, which would be incorporated as the Grand Trunk Pacific Railway Company. He stated that the railway would be built through northern Ontario, the northerly part of the prairie West, and the Peace River or Pine River Pass to Port Simpson on the Pacific coast. The Grand Trunk general manager was convinced that his company would reap large benefits by thus gaining access to the rapidly developing Canadian West. A month earlier he had privately asked Laurier for federal subsidies of $6,400 and 5,000 acres per mile for the proposed GTPR.[6] But Hays's request for federal subsidies created serious dissension in the Laurier cabinet, and the government was not able to agree on a policy toward the GTPR until July 1903.

At this time the CPR lacked a strong advocate in Cabinet, since Israel Tarte had been dismissed by the prime minister in October 1902 for publicly advocating increases in the Canadian tariff structure. Tarte confided to the Governor General, Lord Minto, that "the chief point of difference [between himself and other cabinet ministers] has been on railway policy, he himself having been a strong supporter of the c.p.r."[7] The Canadian Northern Railway had considerable support in cabinet. As Hays reported to Rivers Wilson, "they [the Laurier cabinet] feel to a certain degree committed to giving the Canadian Northern aid at least as far as Edmonton ... and hesitate to do what looks like forming a parallel line in helping us through practically the same country."[8] Hays was therefore strongly committed to a Grand Trunk takeover of the Canadian Northern.[9] Clifford Sifton was "the principal supporter" of the Canadian Northern in the Laurier cabinet. However he was absent during the crucial period of negotiations from late March to the end of June 1903, because he was in London defending Canadian interests in the Alaska boundary dispute. But Sifton was powerful enough to have Cabinet promise to pass a large bond guarantee for 720 miles of Canadian Northern lines to Prince Albert and Edmonton. This put Mackenzie and Mann in a strong position to resist a Grand Trunk takeover. When the Grand Trunk-Canadian Northern negotiations collapsed in late March 1903, the Canadian Northern bond guarantee legislation was then passed by Parliament in July.[10]

The government's negotiations with the Grand Trunk were further complicated by the position of Andrew Blair, the minister of railways, who strongly favoured a government-owned line from Montreal to the Pacific coast. Such a line would provide substantial traffic for the government-owned Intercolonial Railway (ICR) in the Maritimes. The prime minister therefore excluded Blair from the discussions with Hays and other Grand Trunk officials, and took charge of them himself. Blair was extremely upset at being bypassed in the negotiations, and resigned from Cabinet on 13 July just before the GTPR-NTR bill was introduced in the House of Commons. In a strong speech in the House he vigorously defended his policy of public ownership.[11]

Laurier overcame the divisions on railway policy by using his authority to dictate policy. As R.M. Coutts demonstrates, Laurier "literally forced his plan for the Grand Trunk Pacific on his Cabinet and browbeat his Ministers into acquiescence."[12] The Grand Trunk Pacific Incorporation Bill was introduced in the House as a private member's bill on 13 March 1903. It specified North Bay as the GTPR's eastern terminus. Laurier persuaded Hays to modify the GTPR project by extending it eastward, first to Quebec City and then to Moncton, New Brunswick. Hays informed Rivers Wilson in mid-March that the GTPR had been extended to Quebec. "This move has strengthened us very much with the Quebec Members of the Government who, as you know, constitute the element upon which the Premier relies for his majority in the House."[13] In hearings in the Commons Committee on Railways and Canals in May, strong pressure from Maritime MPs, both Liberal and Conservative, who wanted to protect the interests of the ports of Saint John and Halifax, resulted in a further extension eastward of the GTPR to Moncton, New Brunswick. W.S. Fielding, the minister of finance, strongly supported this change, and informed Laurier that Moncton was chosen as a neutral point between the two rival Maritime ports of Halifax and Saint John.[14] On 29 July 1903 Hays, Rivers Wilson, and four Grand Trunk directors signed a contract with the Laurier government setting down the basic terms for the GTPR-NTR project. The next day Laurier introduced the National Transcontinental Railway Bill[15] into the House and proclaimed that a railway from the Atlantic to the Pacific, "every inch of it on Canadian soil," was "a national and commercial necessity" for Canada. This bill provoked a heated 2-month debate in the House, and did not receive third reading until 30 September.[16] Rivers Wilson and the Grand Trunk board, who were critical of several aspects of the 1903 contract, succeeded in securing a number of modifications that were embodied in a supplementary contract signed on 18 February 1904.[17] The amended agreement was submitted to a large Grand Trunk shareholders meeting in London on 8 March. Both Rivers Wilson and Hays strongly endorsed the GTPR-NTR project, but a long and stormy debate preceded ratification of the amended contract by the shareholders. On 8 April Laurier introduced a bill to amend the National Transcontinental Railway Act of 1903. This bill also encountered strong criticism from the Conservatives, finally passing the House at 5:25 A.M. on the morning of 27 May 1904.[18]

The 1903–4 legislation and contracts constituted the foundations of the GTPR-NTR project. Under them, the GTPR was incorporated as a wholly-owned subsidiary of the Grand Trunk Railway, and was authorized to construct a railway from Winnipeg to Prince Rupert, BC, which was to be completed no later than 1 December 1911. The Pacific terminus had been shifted somewhat to the south because the Alaska Boundary Award of 20 October 1903 had placed Port Simpson in American territory.[19] For purposes of construction, the GTPR was divided into two sections: the Prairie section from Winnipeg to Wolf Creek, a point 122 miles west of Edmonton, and the Mountain section from Wolf Creek via the Yellowhead Pass to Prince Rupert. Government assistance for the construction of the GTPR consisted of guarantees of principal and interest on company first mortgage 3 per cent bonds. On the Prairie section the government undertook to guarantee principal and interest on these bonds to a maximum of $13,000 per mile, while on the Mountain section the guarantee extended to a maximum of 75 per cent of construction costs. The government also promised to pay the interest on Mountain section guaranteed bonds for 7 years from the date of issue. The balance of GTPR construction costs were to be raised by the sale of bonds guaranteed by the Grand Trunk Railway, which acquired in return all the GTPR's common stock.

The other part of the project was the government-financed NTR from Winnipeg to Moncton.[20] The government pledged to build this line "with all reasonable despatch" but no time limit was fixed for its completion. Construction of the NTR could not begin until the GTPR had approved the specifications. After the company's chief engineer had inspected and approved the completed line, the GTPR agreed to lease it for a 50-year period, at an annual rental of 3 per cent of the cost of construction. In the first 7 years of this lease there would be no rental fee, and the GTPR would only be required to cover the operating expenses of the line. The GTPR was obligated, by clauses 42 and 43 of the 1903 contract, to carry all traffic "not specifically routed otherwise by the shipper" to Canadian ocean ports and to promote "the development of trade through Canadian channels." In effect, the GTPR was obligated to send its traffic from the Canadian West via the NTR to Quebec City and Canadian ports in the Maritimes. However, it was permitted to build a branch line from the NTR to the Lakehead, which enabled it to divert Western export traffic via the Great Lakes and American lines to American ports.

Publicly, Shaughnessy welcomed the GTPR project. In a statement published on 25 November 1902 he noted that although the CPR operated 6,000 miles of railway in Western Canada, "there was plenty of room for more lines." However, he indicated that government aid for the GTPR was no longer "absolutely essential" as it had been for the CPR in the 1880s. Rivers Wilson commented caustically to Hays, "[Shaughnessy] is reported as having spoken in a friendly way respecting the proposed new Road, stating, however, that of course no Government subsidy or assistance would be given it! an impudent assumption which belies the pretended friendliness."[21] Privately, Shaughnessy was critical and suspicious of the project. He suspected that the Grand Trunk was attempting to put Mackenzie and Mann "into a tight place" so that the GTR could purchase the Canadian Northern properties "at a low figure." He did not think that the GTR would use an all-Canadian route at this time, but would link the Western portion of the GTPR with their connection at Chicago. Shaughnessy expected that if the GTPR scheme were carried out, the CPR would need to build extensively in GTR territory in Ontario, since the company would no longer obtain westbound traffic from its competitor. And finally, he suggested that the CPR "would be inclined to oppose the granting of any very large subsidy" to the GTPR.[22] In an interview published on 24 January 1903 he declared that federal subsidies to the GTPR would be "unfair" to existing railways in the prairie West. "In principle," he remarked, "I am opposed to the policy of government subsidies. It is demoralizing and unbusiness-like. If the projectors of the Grand Trunk Pacific desire to construct their lines, it should be essentially a private investment." Hays regarded the statement as clear evidence of CPR opposition to the GTPR scheme.[23] Shaughnessy's objections to federal subsidies for the GTPR seem rather self-righteous in view of his company's frequent requests for government aid for CPR lines on the prairies. However, he maintained that in 1903 the prairie West was rapidly filling up with agricultural settlers so that large subsidies, which had been justifiable in the 1880s when the region was sparsely populated, were no longer required. He was willing to support smaller subsidies to lines which opened up new territory on the prairies.

When the GTPR applied for a charter in April 1903, Shaughnessy was very critical of the proposed location of its main line on the prairies. He discussed his criticisms frankly with Sir Richard Cartwright, Laurier's minister of trade and commerce. The CPR president maintained that Cartwright and other cabinet ministers had assured him that the GTPR was designed "to open up new territory." However, the route map showed the GTPR paralleling the CPR main line west of Winnipeg for about 300 miles. Shaughnessy warned that such a proposal would be vigorously opposed by his company. "[The GTPR scheme]," he declared, "is such a complete and radical departure from their original proposition that it is sure to arouse the active opposition of the Companies whose interests will be injuriously affected by its construction." Shaughnessy also regarded the subsidizing of such a line – one that did not open up new territory – as "obnoxious by reason of its unfairness."[24] He enlarged upon these views in a long letter to Laurier written in May 1903 in which he asserted that from Kenora to a point 250 miles west of Winnipeg – a total of 400 miles – the proposed line would be within a 6 to 8 mile distance of CPR lines. The GTPR would therefore not open up new territory, and so its location "would seem to deprive the Grand Trunk Pacific of any grounds upon which to ask for Government aid in any form." Shaughnessy launched a strong attack on the GTPR. "Using the necessity for converging upon Winnipeg as an excuse," he charged, "they are going into the heart of our territory, and it is unnecessary for me to say that it would be monstrous if that were done with the financial co-operation of the Government." He proposed that the GTPR line bypass Winnipeg and be located north of the CPR line, through Prince Albert "or some other point to the north." Laurier replied in a conciliatory manner, observing that "any line marked on paper for the construction of a railway of such magnitude must be more or less approximative." He suggested that Shaughnessy's objections could be considered "if the time comes to consider any assistance which they [GTPR] may require from the Government."[25]

As discussed, the GTPR Incorporation Bill was amended to provide for government construction of the section from Winnipeg to Moncton. The bill then received third reading in the House on 10 August and in the Senate on 1 September.[26]

The CPR kept a low profile during the 2-month Commons debate on the government's National Transcontinental Railway Bill in August and September of 1903. Shaughnessy informed E.B. Osler of the rationale for this strategy. "Personally I have thought it best to avoid any open opposition because I would not wish to have investors in this country or elsewhere feel that we are apprehensive about the result of the project on our property because this might unduly affect our securities."[27] Conservative Opposition leader Robert Borden consulted Shaughnessy and four prominent supporters of the party in framing his railway policy, which he then presented to the House on 8 August.[28] The most important feature of his scheme was a proposal for the extension of the government-owned ICR from Montreal to a port on Georgian Bay, a policy supported by his five chief advisors on railway policy. The Conservative leader advocated this proposal for two main reasons. First, it would protect the interests of the Atlantic ports of Saint John and Halifax, for Borden was convinced that the NTR Bill would not prevent shippers from sending goods over the Grand Trunk line to Portland. Second, he wanted the ICR to obtain a share of traffic from the Canadian West that was shipped from the Lakehead via the Great Lakes water route. Another significant feature of his scheme was a proposal for government purchase of the CPR line from Fort William to North Bay, an idea that Shaughnessy had outlined to Borden. The Conservative leader advocated that the CPR, the Canadian Northern, the Grand Trunk, and the extended ICR all be given equal running rights over this line. Borden maintained that this was the most economical plan to provide the Grand Trunk and the ICR access to Western Canada, and the Canadian Northern access to Eastern Canada.[29] The Liberals charged that Borden's plan was inspired by the CPR, which wanted to get rid of an uneconomical section of its main line.

Postmaster General William Mulock made a bitter and sustained attack on Borden's scheme. He charged that the Conservative leader's proposal to purchase the CPR line from North Bay to Fort William would cost Canadian taxpayers $38 million for "the most unprofitable piece [of railway] in Canada." The result would be that the CPR would divert western traffic away from Fort William to the company's subsidiary, the South Shore line, (Duluth to Sault Ste Marie) at Duluth in the United States.[30] E.B. Osler, the Conservative MP for Toronto West, and a prominent CPR director, vigorously attacked the NTR Bill. His high profile in the railway debate reinforced the impression that the CPR was directing Conservative railway policy. One of the Western Liberal MPs, Walter Scott of Assiniboia, highlighted Osler's role in the railway debate by describing him as "one of these grafters ... [who] got away with this sum of $16,000,000" through the promotion of the Calgary and Edmonton Railway and the Qu'Appelle, Long Lake and Saskatchewan Railway. Osler protested against Scott's "very unfair attack" but the Western MP would only admit that Osler and his associates had made their money legally. Hays was pleased with the clash between Osler and Scott, feeling that it had drawn "the attention of the House and the country to the influence the Canadian Pacific is attempting to exort (sic) against our bill."[31]

Hays had information that the CPR hoped to defeat the NTR Bill in the Senate, where the Liberals had a majority of eleven. The Grand Trunk general manager was optimistic, however, and thought the bill would "be carried by a majority of five or six." Privately, Shaughnessy thought the CPR "might succeed in defeating the measure in the Senate, if we undertook it, but ... it would have to be done in a most roundabout way." But it appears that the CPR did not attempt this. The Conservatives were divided in the senate debates; for Mackenzie Bowell, a prominent Conservative and former prime minister, refused to endorse Borden's railway policy because he was opposed to government ownership of railways. Nonetheless, the bill received second reading on 19 October with a majority of seven and third reading the following day.[32]

Shaughnessy continued to keep a low profile during the 1904 parliamentary debate on the Liberal amendments to the GTPR-NTR project, but his sympathies remained with the Conservatives. He advised E.B. Osler of a weakness in the government's amending legislation. He praised Toronto Conservative MP E.F. Clarke's speech on railway policy. "Without any attempt at flattery," he informed Clarke, "I consider it one of the soundest and most comprehensive speeches that have [sic] been delivered in Parliament on the subject." The Toronto MP had maintained that all GTPR summer freight between Winnipeg and Port Arthur would be diverted to Grand Trunk lake carriers and thence over the GTPR system to Montreal and Portland. He called for the submission of the project to the people in the next general election.[33]

And in fact in the general election, held on 3 November 1904, the GTPR-NTR project was the centrepiece of the Liberal campaign. The Liberals suggested that the return of the Conservatives to power would involve the handing over of the entire project to the CPR, a point which Clifford Sifton made in a Calgary speech on 21 October. The Liberal Halifax *Chronicle* also stressed this theme.[34] Shaughnessy was determined to keep his company out of the campaign. When he learned that a CPR foreman at London, Ontario, was arranging to give Conservative employees a holiday on election day and to keep Liberal employees at work, he ordered his general supintendent at Toronto, H.P. Timmerman, to have the foreman stop such activities. Shaughnessy informed Timmerman that company policy was to give as many men as possible the chance to vote regardless of their politics.[35] (This action reflected his bitter experience in the 1891 election when the CPR had pulled out all the stops to defeat the Liberals.) It seems that the CPR was, however, involved in the *La Presse* affair of October 1904 in which Conservative English-Canadian business interests purchased the largest French-speaking daily in Quebec. Shaughnessy strongly and self-righteously informed Laurier that no CPR officer or director was in any way involved in the *La Presse* matter. However, it appears that the CPR pulled back from the scheme only when businessman David Russell gained control of the paper and was not willing to use it in the manner desired by the CPR.[36]

Laurier and the Liberals were returned with a large majority (138 to 75) in the 1904 election, while Conservative Leader Borden suffered a humiliating defeat in his own riding. Shaughnessy would undoubtedly have preferred a Conservative victory, for such a result would have dealt a serious blow to Laurier's GTPR-NTR project. However, he was pleased that voters had rejected Borden's policy of a government-owned transcontinental railway. He informed a Manitoba cabinet minister shortly after the election, "I think that the principle of Government ownership received such an emphatic black eye in the recent election that our Conservative friends will have no doubt as to the blunder of which they were guilty when they adopted it, and that they would surely avoid it in the future as a socialistic doctrine quite at variance with the precepts and principles of the Conservative party."[37] It is true that Shaughnessy had proposed a limited measure of government ownership in 1903 as an economical means of giving the Grand Trunk and the ICR access to Western Canada and the Canadian Northern access to Eastern Canada and of avoiding duplication of lines in the sparsely settled territory north of Lake Superior. However, the CPR president strongly objected to the federal government using public funds to build a transcontinental railway that would actively compete with the privately owned CPR. He felt the government's role should be to encourage private enterprise and, where necessary, regulate it in the public interest through agencies such as the federal Board of Railway Commissioners.

In 1905 a great deal was accomplished in launching the GTPR. Hays was elected president of the company. He appointed another Grand Trunk officer, Frank W. Morse, as general manager. An American who had started his railway career as a master mechanic, Morse proved to be an unwise choice.[38] Prime Minister Laurier officiated at the formal sod-turning ceremony held at Fort William on 11 September. Before a crowd of ten thousand, the prime minister stepped on a golden shovel and turned the first sod of what the *Manitoba Free Press* described as "Canada's second transcontinental railway." He flattered the citizens of Fort William by predicting that their city would soon become the "Chicago of the north." He also used the occasion to highlight the important role which his administration had played in reducing Western freight rates, by negotiating the Crow's Nest Pass Agreement and by assisting the Canadian Northern Railway. "By the construction of this Railway [GTPR-NTR]," he observed, "we shall further decrease the cost of transportation of wheat to the seaboard."[39] The location of the ceremony was significant, for it indicated that the GTPR planned to build its Lake Superior Branch (Fort William to NTR line) as soon as possible so that it could ship Western grain via the Lakehead rather than by the all-rail route.

At the start of 1905 the GTPR had announced that Edmonton would be the company's main divisional point between Winnipeg and the coast.[40] This decision indicated that the GTPR would be competing primarily with the Canadian Northern which, also in 1905, was completing its main line from Winnipeg to Edmonton, and that it would use the Yellowhead Pass rather than the more northerly passes which Hays had mentioned in 1902. The GTPR then did extensive surveys along almost the entire projected route. On 14 August the Cabinet approved its location plan from Portage la Prairie, west for a distance of 275 miles. Tenders were called, the contract was awarded to the Winnipeg firm of McDonald, McMillan and Company, and work started on 24 August.[41]

Charles Drinkwater, Shaughnessy's special assistant, appeared before a cabinet sub-committee early in August to protest the location of the line. He presented the company's case very forcefully, but could not convince the sub-committee to change the GTPR's location plan. There then followed a heated exchange of letters between Laurier and Shaughnessy. The president's basic objection to the GTPR plan was that it placed the company's line between the CPR and the Canadian Northern lines in a district where no farmer was more than 12 miles from a railway. Thus the GTPR would not open up new territory, as the Liberals had promised in 1903–4. Shaughnessy asserted that the Laurier government had "emphatically declared," in the House of Commons and during the 1904 election campaign, that the GTPR would open up new territory for settlers on "lands remote from existing lines." He reminded Laurier that in 1902 Railways Minister Blair had appeared before the House of Commons Railway Committee and declared that it was government policy "to keep a distance of thirty miles between railway lines" in the prairie West. The president concluded that it was now Laurier's policy to use the credit of Canada "for the purpose of making a vicious and unwarranted attack upon vested interests." Such a policy, he declared, would greatly weaken the confidence of foreign investors in Canadian railway bonds, "and would not help the credit of the country itself." Shaughnessy sent a copy of this letter to four senior Cabinet ministers.

Laurier rejected Shaughnessy's claims very emphatically. "Investors in railway securities, in a young country like Canada," he remarked, "are well aware that new conditions are all the time arising which may force parliament, at any moment, to aid in the construction of new lines." The prime minister asserted that it was now accepted in Canada "that the construction of another transcontinental railway is a commercial necessity." He admitted that in the vicinity of Winnipeg the GTPR would compete with CPR lines, but further west it would develop a section of the prairies not served by the CPR and would therefore receive "the universal approval of the whole section of the country" through which it would run. Finally, Laurier asserted that the interests of investors in Canadian railway securities "cannot be set up as a bar to deprive the people of more and much needed railway facilities." Shaughnessy replied, restating his arguments and stressing that the CPR objected to the GTPR location because the company was being assisted by the Canadian government.[42] He then advised Whyte that the CPR should "drop into the background" in the discussion of the GTPR, "and let the people of the towns whose interests will be injuriously affected" carry on the debate. The Conservative press vigorously protested the location of the GTPR line but the Cabinet and the Board of Railway Commissioners upheld the locations decided on by the GTPR.[43] The conflict over the location of the GTPR induced Shaughnessy to modify CPR land sales policy in the prairie West. In November 1905 he instructed F.T. Griffin, the company's land commissioner in Winnipeg, to increase the price of CPR agricultural lands in Canadian Northern and GTPR territory and to make sure that lands in company territory were sold at a much lower rate.[44] This policy was clearly designed to direct immigrants away from Canadian Northern and GTPR territory into areas served by the CPR.

In September 1905 the GTPR presented to the Laurier cabinet its route map for the main line from the Touchwood Hills in eastern Saskatchewan to 100 miles west of Edmonton. A lengthy delay ensued. Objections to the route map came from influential citizens in Saskatoon, Battleford, and Strathcona, as well as from the CPR. The GTPR had first proposed to build its main line 40 miles to the south of Saskatoon. A two-man Saskatoon delegation to Ottawa persuaded the company to route its line through that city.[45] However, the September 1905 route map projected a line 2 1/2 miles to the south of the town. This was a tactic frequently used by the GTPR to force concessions – cash grants, free land, or remission of taxation – from a city council in return for which the company would build a line into the town. The merchants of Strathcona were also upset because the GTPR route plan showed that the main line crossed the North Saskatchewan at Clover Bar, 3 miles east of Strathcona, and then ran into Edmonton's city centre. The town's hopes had been raised when Frank Morse, general manager of the GTPR, had visited Strathcona in March 1905 and assured residents that the town would be on the company's main line.[46] Finally, the residents of Battleford pressured the Laurier government to have the GTPR main line re-routed through their town. They had a strong case, since the wording of the 1903 GTPR charter called for the railway to be built through or near Battleford, although an escape clause provided for a "more feasible route as is hereafter located." Their demand, if granted, would result in a major change in the GTPR main line in Saskatch-ewan. Laurier made a special trip to Montreal to persuade Hays to make this change, but the GTPR president adamantly refused. Hays was convinced that the CPR was behind the pressure to route the line through Battleford, because the company had filed a route map for a line from the Touchwood Hills to a connection with the Calgary and Edmonton line at Wetaskiwin in the territory through which the GTPR would run.[47] In January 1906 Cabinet approved the GTPR route map, with the exception of the plans for Saskatoon and Strath-cona. Then in July Cabinet approved the Clover Bar crossing, and the GTPR bypassed Strathcona. As for Saskatoon, the GTPR reluctantly built a line into the city centre in 1907–8, but by such a roundabout route that it was known locally as the "spite route."[48]

In the 1906 parliamentary session, a private member's bill was introduced to incorporate the Grand Trunk Pacific Branch Lines Company and to authorize it to build numerous branch lines in British Columbia and the Prairie provinces. There was considerable debate on this bill in the House of Commons Railway Committee. As Hays informed Rivers Wilson, "The principal opposition has been from the Canadian Pacific who obstructed the passage of the bill on the same grounds as our original charter, i.e., that we were en-croaching on their territory and that we should be compelled to keep our lines at least thirty miles distant from theirs."[49] Minister of Justice A.B. Aylesworth informed the Railway Committee that a separate branch lines company would enable the GTPR to raise capital more effectively. Several Conservative MPs criticized the bill during the discussion in the House of Commons in the committee stage. Party leader Robert Borden expressed reservations about the bill, and wanted to ensure that it "will not take away from that company [GTPR] any business, any assets, any revenue in the future which it might reasonably be entitled to under the contract we made with it." R.A. Pringle maintained that the GTPR was "designed to open up and develop the northern zone of the Dominion." He asserted that the company was failing to do this, observing that its line from Winnipeg to Regina closely paralleled the CPR. He also noted that the Railway Committee had dropped a proposal in the bill for a line from Regina to Calgary that would have paralleled the CPR main line. Pringle had tried unsuccessfully to persuade the Railway Committee to adopt a policy that GTPR branches in Saskatchewan and Alberta should be not less than 20 miles from any other railway. H.R. Emmerson, the minister of railways, supported the intention of Pringle's principle, but argued that it could not be applied "as a hard and fast rule." David Henderson objected strongly to a clause giving the GTPR Branch Lines Company the right to build a line from Regina south to North Portal. The proposed line would run midway between the CPR's Arcola Branch and the CPR-controlled Soo line, which were only 24 miles apart. He observed that "it seems to be the policy of the promoters of this Bill to plunge into territory already supplied with railways." E.A. Lancaster moved 6 months' hoist of the bill on 29 June. This motion was defeated and the bill received third reading the following day. After a brief senate debate, the bill received third reading on 7 July.[50]

Increased competition from the Canadian Northern and the GTPR in the prairie West prompted the CPR to expand its branch line program in that region. Construction of the Wolseley branch was started in 1905; it ran from Wolseley, Saskatchewan, on the CPR main line east of Regina, in a southeasterly direction for 122 miles to Reston, Manitoba, on the Souris branch. Shaughnessy observed that the line was needed "to serve a large district that is being rapidly settled." The company sold 4 per cent debenture stock to provide the necessary funds to build this branch and others in the period 1905–14.[51] The most important work, started in 1906, was a line from Yorkton through Saskatoon to Wetaskiwin on the Calgary and Edmonton line. When completed this line would produce a "through connection" between Winnipeg and Edmonton via Yorkton and Saskatoon. In 1906 grading was done east from Wetaskiwin and west from Sheho, 40 miles northwest of Yorkton, where the CPR line ended. Another 142 miles of branch lines in Saskatchewan and Manitoba were begun in 1906. The two most important were the Moose Jaw branch, 50 miles from that city in a northwesterly direction, and a 36-mile line from Weyburn east to Staughton on the Souris branch. The Wolseley branch to Reston was completed in the autumn of 1906.[52] In 1907 a start was made on the building of a 165-mile branch from Regina to Saskatoon. The CPR also completed a bridge over the South Saskatchewan River in December that year to bring the railway into the centre of Saskatoon.[53]

In 1908 the company launched an extensive program of prairie branch-line construction. Vice-president Whyte announced the details at Winnipeg on 27 January. Construction centred in Saskatchewan, where two branches totalling 65 miles were begun. The most important new branch, however, was to go from Asquith (west of Saskatoon) west for 200 miles to connect with the line running east from Wetaskiwin, Alberta. As Whyte emphasized, this line would give a direct connection with Edmonton. Some of the necessary funds were raised by a 1908 issue of $24.3 million (par value) in common shares.[54] But this branch-line program was cut back by Shaughnessy in June 1908 because poor western crops in 1907 and unsettled economic conditions in 1908 had resulted in an "enormous shrinkage of earnings" on the Western Division.[55] He did respond, however, to a request from George P. Graham, Laurier's railways minister, that the CPR extend its Moose Jaw branch to Lacombe, Alberta. In June 1908 he sanctioned this extension, citing requests from the Saskatchewan government, provincial MPS and many area settlers.[56] In November Shaughnessy was advising Whyte that the CPR had to be more competitive west of Winnipeg, because the company would soon feel "most active competition throughout a considerable portion" of the prairie West. He admitted that the CPR handled the bulk of the prairie grain trade, but he was convinced that the Canadian Northern and the GTPR had larger shares than they should.[57]

From 1905 to 1909 the CPR carried out a double-tracking program on its main line from Fort William to Winnipeg, a distance of 427 miles. The single track had been improved in 1903–4, by reducing grades and laying 80-pound rails, so that it could carry a much larger tonnage. Then in May 1905 vice-president Whyte announced that a second track would be layed on the entire line. In part to finance this, the previous October shareholders had authorized an increase of $25.5 million (par value) in the company's common stock; $16,900,000 was offered to the shareholders at par, and all but 2,500 shares were subscribed. Some of the funds raised were used for the double-tracking program, for which some $5 million had already been earmarked under the earlier 1902 agreement with the Laurier government.[58] In 1910, double-tracking was started on the main line west of Winnipeg. By the end of 1911 double-tracking had been completed on the line from Winnipeg to Brandon, a distance of 129 miles. Shaughnessy gave the highest priority to this program, noting in 1913 that it was "absolutely essential to operation." By the close of that year another 314 miles of second track had been laid, mostly in Saskatchewan. Another 210 miles of double-tracking was completed in 1914. Thus, in nine years 1080 miles of second track had been laid on the 1255 miles between the Lakehead and Calgary. This major project greatly improved the railway's capacity and efficiency in the prairie region.[59]

In September 1911 Whyte retired as vice-president in charge of

Western lines and was succeeded by George J. Bury. Bury was a third generation Canadian of Irish descent, born at Montreal in 1866. He joined the CPR in 1883 as a junior clerk in the Montreal puchasing department at a salary of $1 a day. At that time the purchasing department was headed by Shaughnessy, who soon formed a high opinion of Bury's abilities. An "ambitious, dynamic, red-headed youth ... he established a reputation for driving energy and clear thinking that brought quick promotions." He then switched to the operating section and rose rapidly through the ranks to become general manager of Western lines in 1908. Then in 1911 he replaced Whyte as vice-president in charge of Western lines. Shaughnessy was confident that Bury would succeed in this important position. "Of course Bury was the natural successor at Winnipeg," he informed Augustus Nanton. "The position is a big one, and involves a good deal of work of a character apart from the mere operation of the railroad, but I am sure that he will prove equal to the occasion."[60] Bury's right-hand man in Winnipeg was Grant Hall, who was appointed assistant general manager of Western lines in 1911. Another career official, Hall had joined the company in Montreal at age twenty-seven in 1890. He soon became an expert on rolling stock and motive power. From 1908 to 1911 he was superintendent of motive power for the entire CPR system. In 1912 Hall was promoted to general manager of Western lines and thereafter acted as head in Bury's absence.[61]

The CPR's prairie branch-line construction program was fairly limited in 1909. Four branches were built in Alberta, the most important of them an extension of the Lacombe branch east of Stettler. But improvement in the Canadian economy in 1910 led Shaughnessy to revive an ambitious construction program. Branch-line construction was concentrated in Saskatchewan, where 346 miles were built in 1910.[62] The prairie construction program was even more substantial in 1911. Forty miles of siding would be built to accommodate the longer trains drawn by the new, more powerful Mogul locomotives. The main Winnipeg to Edmonton line consisted of the old Manitoba and Northwestern line to Yorkton, which had been extended to Saskatoon and then to the Alberta capital by way of Wetaskiwin and the Calgary and Edmonton line. Since many of its rails were light the company planned to lay 85-pound rails on 158 miles and do some heavy ballasting so that the road would be "capable of carrying the heaviest trains at the highest speed." A total of 339 miles of branch lines would be constructed in Saskatchewan and Alberta, 252 of them in the eastern province. The most important branch was the 80-mile Swift Current line. Whyte expressed both his faith in the west's potential and his amazement at the rapidity of its development by remarking that "Ten or twelve years ago ... if some one had told me that the time would come when large shipments of wheat would be made from Swift Current, I would have said that he was a fit subject for the asylum. Yet this year we carried from that point over half a million bushels."[63]

The autumn of 1911 saw a familiar Western problem, a grain blockage. Shaughnessy explained the CPR view to the new Conservative Prime Minister, Robert Borden. He pointed out that although his company had 100 more locomotives and 4,400 more cars in the West than in 1910, the 1911 harvest had been "very late." But the major cause of the congestion, in his opinion, was the 7-month coal miners' strike in British Columbia that had ended in November 1911. The railway had found it necessary to use much of its rolling stock to move "vast quantities" of coal into the prairies from Duluth and Fort William. Despite these difficulties, by the close of navigation on the Great Lakes, the CPR had handled 23 per cent more grain in 1911 than it had in 1910. The president promised George Foster, the trade and commerce minister, that he would discuss the whole issue at the end of December 1911 with George Bury, "to see what future plans should be adopted, based upon our experience in the past."[64] In 1912 the CPR ordered $48 million worth of new rolling stock. Thus, Bury was well prepared for the 1913 prairie crop, and before the close of navigation the CPR had moved 60 per cent of that year's production, a total of 112,084,000 bushels. As Shaughnessy proudly reported to Foster, "Mr. Bury has been marvellously successful in dealing with the grain situation this year."[65] Bury and Shaughnessy both realized, however, that the fundamental problem was the determination of prairie farmers and grain dealers to sell too much of the crop in a short period. Bury set out this problem very effectively in a 1913 Regina speech: "The CPR has been preaching for some years that it is not in the interests of the country in general to attempt to market too large a percentage of the Western crops in the three months intervening between the harvest and the close of navigation ... It is easy to offer counsels of perfection to the farmer who is anxious to get the money from his crop to pay his bills, but we really must prepare ourselves in some way to encourage and assist him to so market the crop that it will flow steadily and in moderation to the ultimate markets instead of descending in a flood."[66]

The CPR maintained an extensive prairie branch-line construction program in 1912–13. Shaughnessy had indications in 1911 that Premier Walter Scott of Saskatchewan, never a friend of the company, was "more inclined to cultivate our good will now than in the past."

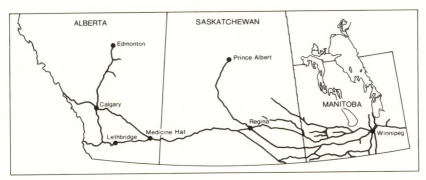

Figure 2 Canadian Pacific, 1905

On the president's advice, Bury showed the premier the company's 1912 branch-line program in advance to forestall government assistance to Canadian Northern and GTPR lines in territory the CPR served or proposed to serve.[67] That year the company planned 185 miles of branch lines in Saskatchewan and 55 in Alberta. The most important construction – 125 miles – would connect Weyburn, Saskatchewan, with Lethbridge, Alberta. When this section was complete, the CPR would have a through route from Winnipeg by way of the Crow's Nest Pass to Nelson, British Columbia, "entirely independent of the main transcontinental line." On the Winnipeg-Edmonton line about 500 miles of 85-pound steel rails would be laid to replace lighter ones.[68]

The 1913 program called for 439 miles of branch lines in the three Prairie provinces, the major portion of which was in Alberta. Work was continued west of Weyburn, where 145 miles were constructed. Shaughnessy was unhappy that year with the Western construction program, which seemed to "drag terribly." "We have made the mistake," he asserted, "of starting upon line after line before completing some of those already in hand. However, we shall not authorize one single additional mile until the work now in hand has been completed."[69] The trade slowdown that began in the fall of 1913 reinforced his attitude. When the Western appropriations were announced in January 1914 they were almost entirely confined to completing extensions and branch lines already under construction.[70]

The CPR also made additions and improvements to its railway system in the urban centres of the prairie West. Those relating primarily to passenger service – hotels and stations – are discussed in chapter 7, while the others are discussed in chapter 9.

The CPR had greatly expanded its prairie rail system from 956 miles of branch lines in 1896 to 4,318 miles in 1914. Manitoba branch

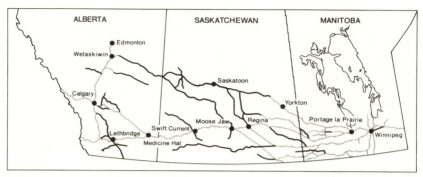

Figure 3 Canadian Pacific, 1914

lines in 1896 totalled about 687 miles and constituted a substantial network in southwestern Manitoba. By contrast, branches in the Territories in 1896, which amounted to only 344 miles, consisted of three lines: (1) Dunmore to Lethbridge – 109 miles – this was to link the CPR main line with the Crow's Nest Pass line; (2) North Portal to Pasqua – 160 miles – linked the CPR main line at Pasqua, just east of Moose Jaw, with the CPR-controlled Soo line in North Dakota; (3) Manitoba border to Estevan – 75 miles – connected the coal mines at Estevan with the Manitoba lines. By 1914 the company had increased its Manitoba branch lines to 1,777 miles, more than double the 1896 total. In addition, by that date the branch-line mileage in the Saskatchewan division totalled 1,902 miles, and constituted a substantial network in south and south-central Saskatchewan. By contrast the Alberta Division amounted to only 639 miles, including the section of the Crow's Nest Pass line from Lethbridge to the Crow's Nest Pass.[71] (See figures 2 and 3.) The most important line constructed by the company in the prairies between 1896 and 1914 was that from Portage la Prairie on the main line to Yorkton, Saskatoon, and Wetaskiwin, which constituted a through line from Winnipeg to Edmonton. Competition from the Canadian Northern and the GTPR was certainly an important factor in stimulating this tremendous expansion. But the CPR was also responding to the great influx of agricultural settlers into the prairies and building a system designed to obtain a large share of the expanding grain traffic of the prairies and the traffic from Eastern Canada into the prairie West. The double-tracking of most of the main line from the Lakehead to Calgary between 1905 and 1914 enabled the CPR to control this greatly increased traffic. Another important factor was the CPR's expansion of its terminal elevator capacity at Fort William. For example, in 1902 the company built two steel grain elevators with a combined capacity of 3.7 million bushels that increased the CPR's elevator capacity at Fort William to 9 million bushels. And Paul-André Linteau has demonstrated that from 1896 to 1914 most of the prairie grain crop was moved from the Lakehead to Montreal by water through the Great Lakes canal system or by water to ports such as Collingwood and Owen Sound on Georgian Bay and from there by rail.[72] Winnipeg was fast becoming the main distribution point for the entire Canadian West, as will be shown in chapter 9. Winnipeg's expanding wholesale houses were supplied with manufactured goods mainly from Toronto and Montreal by the CPR. Meanwhile, substantial expansion was taking place in the CPR system in BC as the company met competition from the Great Northern Railroad and the Canadian Northern Railway.

CHAPTER SIX

The CPR in British Columbia, 1898–1914

From 1898 to 1901 the CPR and the Great Northern Railroad (GN) maintained a truce in their struggle to secure control of the traffic of southern British Columbia. However, from 1901 to 1914 Shaughnessy and Hill fought vigorously and unceasingly for control of southern British Columbia. And competition was imminent from another source, the Canadian Northern, which constructed its main line from the Yellowhead Pass to Vancouver between 1910 and 1915.

The official who managed the CPR's Pacific Division for much of this tumultuous period was Richard Marpole. Marpole was appointed general superintendent of the division, with headquarters in Vancouver, on 1 June 1897 at the age of forty-seven. Emigrating to Canada from Britain in 1873, he served for eight years on the Northern Railway in Ontario and then joined the CPR as assistant to Harry Abbott, who was in charge of construction of several sections of the main line between the Lakehead and Lake Nipissing. When Abbott was appointed general superintendent of the Pacific Division, Marpole became his superintendent. A forceful and energetic person, Marpole was a good manager of the company's BC operations. After Marpole stepped down from his position in 1907, Shaughnessy praised him as a "valued officer of the Company" who had handled the post of general superintendent "with marked ability and great advantage to the Company."[1]

As was revealed earlier, the contest for control of the mining traffic of southern BC in the period 1893–8 had been between the CPR and D.C. Corbin's SF&N. But in July 1898 J.J. Hill acquired the SF&N and its subsidiaries, so that the GN now became the CPR's contender in this struggle. As Hill informed a business associate, "The Spokane Falls and Northern has cost more than it is worth, except for territorial reasons, and from that stand-point it is cheap enough."[2] Van

Horne and Shaughnessy were very concerned about Hill's action and were quick to respond. Under the charter of the Columbia and Western Railway, the CPR extended its Crow's Nest line west from Robson in West Kootenay for a distance of 100 miles to Midway in the rapidly developing Boundary mining district. Hill and Van Horne realized that unchecked competition between their companies could be very destructive, and so in July 1898 they began negotiations for a "territorial arrangement" in order to avoid "rate cutting and territorial contests in the future."[3] The first result of these discussions was a tripartite agreement between the CPR, the GN, and the Kaslo and Slocan Railway, reached in November 1898. Under the terms of settlement, the CPR and the Great Northern divided competing shipments of ore in the Slocan district equally, with "all parties to maintain rates in the meantime." In October 1899 Hill reported that this arrangement was working in favour of the Great Northern. "The result [of the tripartite agreement]," he observed, "has been that 80% of the competing ore has been shipped by the Kaslo and Slocan and Great Northern, and the Canadian Pacific has received the agreed difference in money. This shows quite clearly that the Canadian Pacific Railway on even rates would not carry ... 25% of the traffic."[4]

Upon taking over as president of the CPR in June 1899, Shaughnessy continued negotiations with Hill for a comprehensive settlement. Hill sent him a telegram congratulating him on his new appointment. The new president replied in a friendly manner. "I trust that we shall always be good friends," he informed Hill, "and that the Great Northern and Canadian Pacific may each continue to progress and prosper without any of the aggressive warfare that has proved so distructive [sic] to some lines in the past, and that does not belong to the present era of railroading."[5] The GN president responded very positively, expressing his intention of discussing with Shaughnessy in person matters "looking to the permanent protection of our respective properties and mutually strengthening our position ... You are North of the Boundary and we are South of it," he observed, "and surely there should not be any reason why we cannot work together for mutual protection, at least against all others." In September 1899 Shaughnessy sent Hill a conciliatory letter regarding the CPR's nearly completed line to Midway. The owners of the mining camp at Republic, Washington (in Great Northern territory), 25 miles south of Midway, proposed to haul their ores by wagon to the CPR line at Midway, and asked the company for a freight-rate quotation for shipping these ores to the smelter at Trail. Shaughnessy asked Hill if he had any objection to the CPR's concluding a smelting contract with the Republic mine owners, since the GN might be intending to build to the Republic mining camp. Hill informed Shaughnessy that the camp was "not sufficiently developed to warrant our Company in building a railway into it." although the Great Northern planned to build such a line later when the camp was more developed. Hill remarked that his company had "no reason to complain of your making the best arrangements you can covering the smelting" and thanked Shaughnessy for consulting with him on the matter.[6]

The improved relations between the CPR and the GN also resulted in further cooperation between the two systems. In November 1899 Shaughnessy made a request to purchase a 5-mile section of the Nelson and Fort Sheppard Railway (a SF&N subsidiary), between Five Mile Point and Nelson, which would become part of the CPR's Crow's Nest line to Nelson. He offered to give the GN perpetual running rights over the line. The proposal would give the Great Northern access to the centre of Nelson, since the Nelson and Fort Sheppard Railway stopped just outside the city. After extensive negotiations, an agreement was reached in June 1900. The CPR paid $75,000 for the 5-mile section, while the GN received perpetual running rights over it, and paid a fee of 50 cents per train mile for using it. The CPR undertook to handle GN business in its Nelson yards. However, when application was made the federal government refused to grant an $11,000-per-mile subsidy for the section since it had not been constructed by the CPR.[7]

Although the two companies did not settle all their differences, Shaughnessy reported in December 1900 that CPR-GN relations "continue to be of a most friendly character." "We have, consistently and persistently," he remarked, "refused to do anything that might be construed as a departure from our understanding [with the GN] about territorial encroachments, and, in turn, the Great Northern has not given us the slightest ground for complaint." Early in January 1901 Shaughnessy visited Hill in St Paul to discuss the negotiations between the Northern Pacific and the Roblin government regarding the sale of its Manitoba lines. He asked Hill to use his influence to persuade the Northern Pacific to retain these lines, rather than sell them to the Manitoba government. Hill gave Shaughnessy all the information he had on these negotiations, but was unable to pressure the Northern Pacific, which had by this time made a formal offer to sell its Manitoba lines to the Roblin government.[8]

Good relations were abruptly shattered in 1901 subsequent to three actions taken by Hill – the purchase of a controlling interest in the Vancouver, Victoria and Eastern Railway and Navigation Company (VV&E), the acquisition of a substantial interest in the Crow's

Nest Pass Coal Company, and the building of a railway to link this company's mines to the Great Northern system. From this date until 1914 the CPR and the GN were locked in a bitter struggle for control of southern British Columbia.

In April 1901 it was publicly revealed that the Great Northern had purchased a controlling interest in the VV&E.[9] The chief promoters of this project, which would link Vancouver and Victoria directly with the Boundary district and the West Kootenays, were the Vancouver contractors, the McLean brothers, (although it had Victoria backers as well). In 1897, the VV&E had received a charter from the BC legislature authorizing the company to build a railway from Vancouver to New Westminster, then across the Fraser River and easterly through the Hope Mountains by the most direct route to Rossland in the West Kootenays. The VV&E was also empowered to build a branch to some point on the Pacific coast between the international boundary and the Fraser River, where it could establish ferry connections with Victoria. The BC legislature passed a Loan Act in 1897 that offered a subsidy of $4,000 per mile for several railway projects, including the VV&E. The VV&E was strongly supported by Vancouver and Victoria businessmen as a means of ending CPR and central Canadian dominance of the trade of the mining districts of southeastern BC and opening that market to Victoria and Vancouver merchants. Both Vancouver and Victoria city councils strongly endorsed the project.[10]

Mackenzie and Mann had taken "a keen interest" in the VV&E from the start. A tentative agreement between the Turner government, the local promoters, and Mackenzie and Mann was signed on 15 June 1898. In return for building the railway, Mackenzie and Mann were to receive a majority of the company's capital stock. However, the provincial subsidy was conditional on the receipt of federal aid for the VV&E. In August 1898 Charles Semlin replaced Turner as premier. The new government decided that the June 1898 agreement was no longer in force because the VV&E had not secured federal aid. As a result, work on the railway stopped in August 1898.[11]

After the collapse of the Semlin government in February 1900, a new administration was formed on 15 June under the leadership of James Dunsmuir, the wealthy coal magnate. The new government passed a Loan Act authorizing the raising of a $5-million loan to assist the construction of railways and other public works. A cash subsidy was offered to any company that would build a line from Victoria (via ferry) and Vancouver, to Midway, in the Boundary district. Several conditions were placed on this aid: the BC cabinet was to have full control of the railway's freight and passenger rates, and 4 per cent of the company's gross earnings were to be paid to the government. A number of promoters were interested in obtaining the provincial subsidy, but as Roy remarks, "the contest for the subsidy lay between the VV&E and CPR."[12]

The VV&E had been placed under federal jurisdiction in 1898, so it was impossible for the company to meet the condition of provincial control of rates stipulated in the 1900 BC Loan Act. Hugh Sutherland, who looked after Mackenzie and Mann's interests in Victoria, visited Ottawa in March 1901 and attempted to persuade the Laurier administration to pressure premier Dunsmuir to subsidize the VV&E, using the threat that the federal government would not subsidize a northward extension of Dunsmuir's Esquimalt and Nanaimo Railway on Vancouver Island. He, however, failed in his mission, and so Mackenzie and Mann were not successful in getting federal aid for the VV&E. They sold their controlling interest in the company to the Great Northern in March 1901. At the end of 1901 construction crews were working on a VV&E line between Cascade and Carson City in the Boundary district, while surveyors plotted a route west to Penticton.

Shaughnessy had come out in opposition to any subsidy – provincial or federal – for the VV&E because the railway "would really be an extension of the Great Northern System from the Boundary Creek country to the Coast." The CPR had authority to build as far west as Penticton under the Columbia and Western charter. At Penticton, lake steamers would give the CPR connections to the whole of the Okanagan Valley.[13]

In July 1901 Shaughnessy protested strongly to Hill the GN's decision to start construction of the Washington and Great Northern Railway from Marcus, Washington, to the international boundary, where it would connect with the Cascade-Carson City section of the VV&E. "As the construction of this line on the Canadian side involves the invasion of territory tributary to our line between Cascade and Grand Forks," Shaughnessy warned, "it will be in direct contravention of the understanding that has existed for two or three years past between your Company and ours, and I presume may be accepted as a declaration by the Great Northern that that understanding is at an end."[14] Hill responded that the Great Northern "have no wish to invade the country served by your lines." He explained that he wanted to connect the SF&N with mines at Republic and elsewhere *south* of the international border. The mountainous terrain in the area dictated that "the only line with a low grade" was the one following the Kettle River, so that the railway would be built for 15

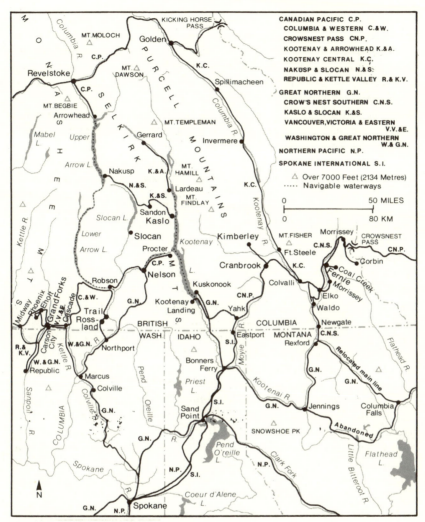

Figure 4 Railways in the Kootenays, 1912

miles in BC before re-entering the United States.[15] (See figure 4.) Shaughnessy did not accept Hill's explanation and so considered the territorial settlement with the GN to have come to an end. He then enlisted the support of Francis Carter-Cotton, a prominent Conservative MLA and publisher of the Vancouver *News-Advertiser*. Informing Carter-Cotton of Hill's plan to use the VV&E to drain traffic from southern BC between Vancouver and the West Kootenays to GN lines in the US, he warned that if Hill were successful in carrying out this scheme, it would do damage to "the best interests of the

Province."[16] Shaughnessy was prepared to appeal to public opinion through Carter-Cotton's newspaper, for he realized that there was a powerful anti-Hill sentiment in Vancouver and the lower mainland. This feeling was well expressed by the Vancouver *Province* which claimed in December 1901 that Hill's aim was "to render the Kootenay country, industrially and commercially, tributary to the cities and states immediately south of the boundary, in which his great interests are centred." Many in the province, Shaughnessy realized, wanted the coast-to-Kootenay railway built by an independent *Canadian* line to provide competition for the CPR.[17] He was concerned that this sentiment might lead the BC or Canadian governments to subsidize the VV&E. He met Premier Dunsmuir and his Attorney-General, D.M. Eberts, when they were in Ottawa in January 1901 and "impressed upon them the importance of only granting a subsidy to a [coast to Kootenay] line entirely within Canadian territory, every portion of it to be, at least, one mile North of the International Boundary." Such a condition would rule out the VV&E because it had connections with the GN. The CPR president also instructed W.F. Tye, the company's chief engineer of construction at Winnipeg, to have his engineers collect information on the practicality of building a railway from New Westminster to Midway, "keeping the railway entirely within Canada." At this point Shaughnessy was trying to forestall competitors from building a railway from Vancouver to the Boundary district.[18]

The railway situation in the Boundary district was made even more complicated by the entry of the Kettle River Valley Railway on the scene in the summer of 1901. This project was designed to bring ores from the Republic mining camp in Washington State to the Granby smelter at Grand Forks. The leading figure among its five promoters was Tracy Holland, British Columbia manager of the Dominion Permanent Loan Company. In the 1901 session of Parliament the promoters obtained a charter for the Kettle River Valley Railway (KRVR), the name used by Corbin for his railway, which had been defeated in the House of Commons in 1898. The new KRVR was empowered to build from the international boundary at Cascade City, westward via the Kettle River to Carson City, with branches from Grand Forks up the north fork of the Kettle River for 50 miles to the Franklin mining camp, and from Grand Forks westward via Greenwood to Midway. The promoters had a long and difficult struggle to get a charter in Washington State for their Republic and Kettle River Railway, which was authorized to build from the Republic mining camp to the international border at Carson City. Many Americans in Washington State were not pleased at the prospect of a Canadian railway hauling their ores to a Canadian smelter, but the charter was granted in 1901.[19]

The stage was now set for a fierce battle between Hill's Washington and Great Northern Railway and Holland's Republic and Kettle Valley Railway to be the first to reach the Republic mining camp. The conflict began in the autumn of 1901 and continued into 1902, as each railway sought court injunctions to halt the rival's construction.[20] Hill suspected that the CPR was secretly supporting the KRVR, for it appeared that the line would serve "as a healthy feeder to the CPR system." In March 1902 Shaughnessy attempted to persuade Hill to halt the construction of the VV&E line from Cascade to Carson City. He informed Hill's son James, who was president of the SF&N, that the GN's sponsorship of the VV&E "may have been inspired by the belief that we were back of the Kettle River Valley enterprise." The CPR president assured the younger Hill that his company had never promised or furnished financial aid to the promoters of the KRVR.[21] But Shaughnessy's attempt failed, for the GN proceeded with construction in June 1902. Though the KRVR line reached Republic in April 1902, several months ahead of Hill's line, the battle was not over. The KRVR had prevented the GN from building a spur line into Grand Forks, but Hill's lobbyist in Ottawa persuaded the House of Commons Railway Committee to give the VV&E the authority to construct this spur in late October 1902. Hill built his spur line into Grand Forks in early November, giving the GN-controlled VV&E a line to the Granby smelter. Hill then set low rates for hauling ore from the Republic mines to the Granby smelter, rates which the KRVR found very difficult to match.[22]

The other actions which destroyed good relations between the CPR and the GN were Hill's acquisition of a substantial interest in the Crow's Nest Pass Coal Company in 1901 and the building of a railway to link this company's mines to the Great Northern system. The coal company, which had its head office in Toronto, was controlled by a number of prominent businessmen including two powerful Liberals: Senator George A. Cox, president of the coal company and of the Canada Life Assurance Company, and Robert Jaffray, vice-president of the coal company and of the Imperial Bank. Cox was also an important member of the board of the Toronto *Globe* while Jaffray was President of the *Globe* Printing Company. The other major shareholders in the coal company were Elias Rogers, a wealthy Toronto coal merchant; J.W. Flavelle, head of a large Toronto pork-packing firm; and Toronto financiers E.R. Wood, A.E. Ames, and Henry M. Pellatt.[23]

On 30 July 1897 the CPR, the BC Southern Railway, and the Crow's

Nest Pass Coal Company had signed what came to be known as "the tripartite agreement." Under this important agreement, the CPR purchased the charter of the BC Southern Railway, with its 20,000 acres-per-mile land grant, for the sum of $85,000. However, the CPR would surrender to the Crow's Nest Coal Company about 250,000 acres of coal lands in the district from Elk River to the summit of the Crow's Nest Pass, and another 10,000 acres of coal- and oil-bearing lands in a district in the Crow's Nest region known as the Second Government Reserve, as soon as it earned them by constructing the BC Southern Railway, i.e., the Crow's Nest Pass Railway. The CPR also agreed to transfer 50,000 acres of coal-bearing lands in the Crow's Nest region to the federal government as a safeguard against a coal monopoly in that area. (This provision had been set out in the Crow's Nest Pass Agreement of 1897.) The CPR could only select six sections (3,840 acres) of coal lands in the Crow's Nest region, and could make its selection only after the federal government had designated its lands. As well, the CPR undertook not to operate coal mines on its lands for a period of 10 years after the construction of the Crow's Nest line unless the coal company failed to supply consumers on that line with sufficient fuel. The CPR agreed to the establishment of maximum freight rates for transporting coal along its Crow's Nest lines, and to build spurs to the coal company's mines. In return the coal company undertook to cooperate with the CPR in developing enterprises along the Crow's Nest line "by furnishing consumers a suitable and sufficient supply of coal and coke at reasonable prices."[24]

The Crow's Nest Coal Company proceeded to establish coal mines in the Elk River district at Coal Creek, Michel, and Morrissey and coke ovens at Fernie, Michel, and Morrissey. By February 1900 the company was producing an average of 622 tons of coal per day. Its coal and coke found a ready market in the smelters and businesses of the West Kootenay and Boundary districts and provided a very important traffic for the CPR's new Crow's Nest line. The CPR also purchased some of its coal requirements from the Crow's Nest Coal Company.[25]

However, early in 1900 a number of mines in the West Kootenays and the Boundary district closed down, thus reducing the demand for coke at the smelters. The coal company then obtained term contracts with a number of smelters in Montana, while the company's directors started negotiations with J.J. Hill of the Great Northern to supply his railway with coal. By March 1901 Hill and his associates had acquired 30 per cent of the stock of the Crow's Nest Coal Company. The coal company sought a federal charter for the Crow's Nest Southern Railway, which would run from the company's mines south to the international boundary, where it would connect with a Great Northern branch line from Rexford, Montana, north to the boundary.[26]

Shaughnessy vehemently opposed the development of close links between the Crow's Nest Coal Company and the GN. Early in January 1901 he protested to the coal company that its term contracts with Montana smelters were a violation of the 1897 tripartite agreement. He stated publicly that the coal company was unable to meet the fuel requirements of the CPR, the smelters, and other industries in southern BC. Robert Jaffray defended the coal company, assuring a reporter that it would supply "the legitimate demands of British Columbia" before it delivered coal to the Montana smelters. The Toronto *Globe* bitterly attacked the CPR for retarding the economic growth of southern BC, which it described as a "private preserve for exploitation by the Canadian Pacific Railway." Shaughnessy was furious at the *Globe*'s "vicious attacks" on his company and believed they were inspired by Jaffray. The coal company's arrangements with the GN were, he felt, a serious threat to the CPR's "vast investment" in southern BC which was "dependent on the mining and smelter interests for a return." He sought to block the coal company's attempt to secure a federal charter for the Crow's Nest Southern Railway by outlining his views on the issue in a lengthy memorandum sent to Prime Minister Laurier on 14 January.[27]

As well as seeking political support, Shaughnessy proposed a compromise solution to J.J. Hill, who did not respond to this conciliatory offer. He then met with Senator Cox and Elias Rogers, the coal company's managing director, who seemed to be "anxious to avoid friction, if possible." He informed them that the CPR's opposition to their proposed links with the GN "was due to the fact that we did not want to lose the Canadian traffic of their mines" since the GN had a number of lines in BC and might build more in the future.[28] On 1 April senior officials of the CPR and the coal company met in Ottawa and presented their views to Laurier, Tarte, Sifton, and Blair. Shaughnessy stated that he was convinced Hill would use his influence to make the price for coke at smelters on the GN cheaper than for coke supplied to Canadian smelters in BC. He had already informed Elias Rogers that he had "duly certified" invoices showing that in January 1901 "coke was shipped from your ovens to smelters at Great Falls, Montana, at the price of $3 per ton, while you were charging our Canadian smelters $4 and $4.75 per ton." Such price differentials, he stressed, would have a harmful effect on Canadian smelters. Rogers denied that his company was charging American smelters $3 per ton for coke, explaining that the figure was simply the valuation placed on the coke by US customs authorities, not the actual selling price. In fact, the price obtained by the Crow's Nest Coal Company for its coke at Great Falls, Montana, was "more than a dollar higher" than the price of coke delivered at any BC smelter. Rogers stressed that his company needed contracts with "a definite and assured tonnage which will in a sense be a backbone to our business." "The United States is the only place where we can get this trade at present," he asserted, "and there we will have to accept the best price obtainable, as we come in competition with coke from many different sources."[29] He assured the meeting that his company would supply Canadian smelters and businesses with all their coal and coke requirements. Shaughnessy and officials of the coal company met again on 10 April with Laurier, Tarte, Sifton, and Blair. Subsequently the application for the federal charter for the Crow's Nest Southern Railway was withdrawn while the bill was before the House of Commons Railway Committee. Instead, the Crow's Nest Company directors sought and obtained a provincial charter for the Crow's Nest Southern Railway. It passed the BC legislature on 24 April 1901.[30] It appears that the Laurier government agreed not to raise the constitutional issue of a provincially chartered railway crossing a provincial boundary.

The CPR protests had some effect, for the price of coke for its Trail smelter was reduced to that charged for American smelters at Great Falls, However, this reduction did not apply to the Granby and Greenwood smelters. In February 1902 the CPR president informed a correspondent that his company "consider[s] the price of coal and coke unduly high in British Columbia." He pointed out that the CPR had reduced its freight rates on the Crow's Nest line for coal and coke "to the lowest possible limit, without being able to induce the coal company to come down [on coal and coke prices] to a reasonable basis."[31]

In 1901 the Crow's Nest Coal Company exported 96,640 tons of coal and 85,047 tons of coke to the United States. These shipments were transported via the CPR's Crow's Nest line to Lethbridge, then south via the Alberta Railway and Irrigation Company's lines to Great Falls, Montana. The coke was sold to smelters at Great Falls.[32] The Crow's Nest Southern Railway was completed from the coal company's mine and coke ovens at Morrissey, BC, to Newgate at the international boundary in September 1902. There it connected with the GN's short line from Rexford, Montana, to the boundary. The coal and coke from the Crow's Nest Coal Company could now be shipped via this route to the GN which would then carry these products to smelters in Montana. The Crow's Nest Southern line was extended north from Morrissey 7 miles to Fernie in 1905. The coal company had large coke ovens at Fernie, which soon became the commercial centre of the coal-mining district in the East Kootenays.[33]

Negotiations between the CPR and the Crow's Nest Coal Company to implement all the terms of the tripartite agreement dragged on from 1901 to 1904. Shaughnessy had handed over most of the negotiations to Whyte but the CPR president insisted on seeing any agreement so that he could go over it with A.R. Creelman, the company's general counsel, to "be sure that nothing has been overlooked." He deeply mistrusted the coal company and especially its general manager, George Lindsey, and warned Whyte that Lindsey was "oily and adroit, and, unless you understand the situation thoroughly, he might get you to concede something that was not intended." Nevertheless, all outstanding questions between the CPR and the coal company were settled in December, 1904. The coal company received formal deed to 251,192 acres of coal-bearing lands (including the 10,000 acres of coal-and oil-bearing lands) as provided in the 1897 tripartite agreement. The CPR made arrangements for the GN to connect directly with the coal company's mines through leasing CPR branch lines to the mines.[34]

The federal government had selected its 50,000 acres of coal lands in 1902. Sifton's officials in the interior department had made a careful examination of the Crow's Nest coal fields the previous year, and Sifton followed their recommendations. They were ratified by an Order-in-Council passed on 19 May 1902. The CPR then selected its 3,840 acres of coal lands around Hosmer station on the Crow's Nest line between Coal Creek and Michel. W.H. Aldridge, manager of the Trail smelter, sent a party to prospect for coal in the Crow's Nest region and in June 1902 it discovered substantial seams near Hosmer station. Shaughnessy wanted the CPR to develop a coal mine there in order to "keep a check on the Crow's Nest Coal Company with reference to quantity, quality and price for Canadian consumers." However, under the terms of the tripartite agreement, the CPR could not build the coal mine until 1908.[35]

Hill was now putting pressure on the Crow's Nest Coal Company to increase substantially its production of coal and coke for the American market. To further his goal, in 1906 Hill and his associates purchased more of the company's stock and gained a controlling interest in the company. Hill was then able to issue directives to the company regarding production quotas for the US market. The company had exported a daily average of 468 tons per day of coal and coke combined to the US market in 1901; by March 1907 this figure had grown to about 4,000 tons per day.[36]

Hill was also active in the Boundary district of southern BC in the period 1902–6, as the GN challenged the CPR's control of the coke- and copper-ore traffic to the large smelter at Grand Forks. This smelter, owned by the Granby Consolidated Mining and Smelting Company, had begun operation in August 1900. The company was controlled by a syndicate headed by S.H.C. Miner, head of the Granby Rubber Company in Quebec, and J.P. Graves, an electric railway magnate from Spokane. The copper ore came from the Phoenix mines northwest of Grand Forks.[37] Rapid development of the Granby smelter and the Phoenix mines had been made possible by the arrival of the CPR subsidiary, the Columbia and Western Railway, which reached Midway via Grand Forks in early 1900. The Granby smelter received ore from the Boundary mines and coal and coke from the Crow's Nest Coal Company in the East Kootenays. In 1900 the CPR built a spur from Eholt, on the Columbia and Western between Grand Forks and Midway, to the Phoenix mines. (See figure 4.) The CPR carried an average of 700 tons of ore daily to the Granby smelter in 1900, 1,400 tons in 1901, and 2,000 tons in 1904.[38]

Hill had completed his line from Republic in Washington State to Grand Forks in late 1902, and began transporting copper ores from there to the Granby smelter. This was a victory for Hill, but he had a broader purpose – to wrest from the CPR the monopoly it held in hauling coke from the East Kootenays and ore from the Boundary district mines to the Granby smelter. By 1904 the Great Northern-controlled VV&E had completed its line from Laurier, Washington, west to Grand Forks, thus permitting the Great Northern to ship coke from the Crow's Nest Coal Company via its own lines to the Granby smelter. In that year Granby Consolidated was taken over by American interests. At its annual meeting on 3 October, Miner, the company's Canadian president, was replaced by an American and a new board composed exclusively of Americans was appointed. In 1905 Hill obtained a substantial interest in Granby Consolidated, whose directorate was interlocked with that of the Great Northern. The CPR up to this time had charged Granby Consolidated $1 a ton to haul ore from mines in the Boundary district to the Granby smelter. Negotiations between the CPR, the VV&E, and the Granby smelter were begun with the result that an agreement was reached under which both railways charged a freight rate of 25 cents per ton for shipping ore to the Granby smelter. This business was divided so that the VV&E received two-thirds and the CPR only one-third. The VV&E had completed a line from Grand Forks to the Phoenix mines in February 1905, so the freight-rate agreement also applied to ore shipments from Phoenix. Thus, by 1905 Hill had wrested control of the ore traffic in the Boundary district, and the coke traffic to that district, from the CPR.[39]

After the completion of the Columbia and Western Railway to Midway in early 1900, the CPR put a halt to railway construction in southern BC until 1905. A number of factors account for this. The company had made a very large investment in building the Crow's Nest and Columbia and Western lines from 1897 to 1900, but it did not appear that it was making much of a return on its investment. In July 1903 the president analysed the net earnings of CPR lines in southern BC for the 11-month period ending 31 May. The Crow's Nest Branch had made a "horrible showing": for that period 1902–3 it showed a deficit of $25,112, while for the same period in 1901–2 it had recorded net earnings of $484,690. The Columbia and Western Railway showed a decline in net earnings of $107,000 from 1901–2 to 1902–3. In both cases, the gross earnings of each line had declined substantially.[40] Another factor was the unsettled political and social conditions in the province. Shaughnessy informed a British investor in 1903 that "Provincial legislation, labour and other conditions in British Columbia have not, during the past three or four years, been calculated to encourage mine-owners in the work of development, and, as a consequence, we have not been receiving adequate returns on the investment in railway lines that we made for the purpose of opening up several mining districts."[41] Also, because of the province's rugged mountainous terrain, construction of railways in BC, as Shaughnessy remarked to one of his engineers, "is in almost every instance expensive, so that we cannot have too much intelligent information about the territory to be served by every line we contemplate building."[42] And finally, beginning in 1903, the CPR was spending large sums in the Prairie provinces on grade improvements, the installation of 80-pound rails, the building of branch lines, and the double-tracking of the main line from Winnipeg to Fort William (begun in 1905). This spending was essential to meet the competition from the Canadian Northern Railway and the GTPR. British Columbia thus had to take a back seat to the prairies in matters of spending.

Yet Shaughnessy was very interested in promoting the economic development of BC. He was pleased when Conservative Richard McBride formed the first party administration in BC history on 1 June 1903. It now appeared that BC was entering a period of political stability which would assist its economic growth.[43] The CPR had already contributed substantially to the development of mining in the province through its construction of the Crow's Nest line to Nelson and its extension to Midway, and by its purchase of the Trail smelter and the expansion of its smelting facilities. (The Trail smelter is discussed in chapter 10.) Shaughnessy also had a strong belief in the need to foster the agricultural development of BC. "It is a crying shame," he informed a CPR director in 1902, "that, with such beautiful and fertile valleys, and with such an excellent climate, British Columbia should, practically, be fed by the State of Washington." He was convinced that the provincial government had for some time seriously neglected the province's agricultural interests and that it needed to spend substantial sums on advertising promoting the settlement of BC lands. He was pleased when Vancouver *Province* editorials stressed that more attention should be given to agriculture in BC and "less to railway promoters and fakirs." The CPR had stimulated agricultural development in the Okanagan by building, under the charter of the Shuswap and Okanagan Railway, a branch line from Sicamous, south to the head of Okanagan Lake at Okanagan Landing near Vernon. This line was opened in 1892. The following year the company constructed a steamboat, thus giving communities as far south as Penticton access to the CPR main line.[44]

In July 1903 Shaughnessy signed an agreement with John Moore Robinson to form the Summerland Development Company. He personally provided the entire capital of $70,000 which would be used to purchase and irrigate agricultural lands at Summerland on the southwest side of Lake Okanagan, and to build houses for the settlers. Robinson would manage the company; he selected the land and prepared the irrigation plan. Robinson, who later became known as "the father of the Okanagan," had come to the district in 1897 and had established a successful irrigation project at Peachland, on the west side of Lake Okanagan; it demonstrated the excellent prospects of peach growing on irrigated land in the Okanagan. The plan for Shaughnessy's project was that the land would be sold off in small fruit farms, eventually allowing him to recoup his initial investment plus 5 per cent interest. He informed Marpole that he would be "quite satisfied" if his Summerland project would "give agriculture in that section of the country a little push." He was very pleased with the progress made by settlers at Summerland when he visited the project in September 1904 and ordered one of his officials to prepare a rate schedule for shipping the agricultural products to Nelson in the West Kootenays. His continuing interest in the development of fruit growing in southern BC led him to discuss some of the industry's problems, particularly the dumping of low-grade fruit from Washington State, with Premier McBride in 1909. And although Shaughnessy rarely served on volunteer organizations, in 1910 he accepted election as president of the First Canadian National

Apple Show because he was "interested in the continued development of the fruit growing industry of British Columbia."[45]

Shaughnessy was also interested in the development of BC's lumber industry. On a trip to the Pacific coast in May 1903 he was "very impressed" with the number of new lumber mills which had been and were being established on the CPR's main line and branches. "The influx of population to the North West has, of course, created a great demand for building material," he observed, "and all of the mills now in operation seem to be very busy."[46] And finally, the CPR president was deeply concerned with developing new sources of coal for the company's railway operations in BC. He advised Whyte in February 1903 that the CPR should give serious consideration to the establishment of three coal mines: one in the Crow's Nest coalfields, a second on the main line near Banff, and a third further west on the main line, to supply the western end of the Pacific Division. He was particularly concerned about the third location, since the coal supply question west of the Selkirks was "rapidly becoming one of paramount importance."[47] On 4 July 1903 Shaughnessy created a Mining and Metallurgical Department and appointed W.H. Aldridge its head. Aldridge would "have general charge of the smelting works and all of the Company's mining and prospecting operations, reporting direct to the President." Shaughnessy advised Aldridge to maintain "the closest relations" with Whyte and J.S. Dennis. (In December 1902 the latter had been appointed the company's superintendent of irrigation in the North-West Territories and land commissioner for BC, with an office in Calgary.[48])

Shaughnessy began to implement his Western coal policy with the assistance of Aldridge, Whyte, Dennis, and their officials. Work was started on the establishment of Bankhead, an anthracite coal mine in the Cascade Basin near Banff in 1903. Almost $2 million had been invested in it when the mine opened in 1905. It provided coal mostly for CPR main line operations in the Prairies and BC.[49] Coal discoveries in the Nicola Valley near the present city of Merritt, BC, represented an important supply for the CPR west of Kamloops. In December 1902 Shaughnessy had instructed Aldridge to have his coal experts investigate these deposits and draw up a report "without unnecessary delay." It must have been favourable, for in April 1903 Shaughnessy had his officials in Victoria lobbying in favour of the Nicola, Kamloops and Similkameen Coal and Railway (NK&S) charter. Promoted by a group of Ontario businessmen, engineers, and lawyers, the NK&S had been incorporated by the BC legislature in 1891 to build a railway from the western end of Nicola Lake to Princeton, on the Similkameen River and to Osoyoos Lake. In 1903 one of the few remaining members of the original NK&S sydicate, William Hamilton Merritt, petitioned the BC government to revive the 1891 charter and to add an extension from the western end of Nicola Lake to Spence's Bridge on the CPR main line. (See figure 5.)The provincial legislature passed the necessary legislation in 1903. The same year the Laurier government authorized a cash subsidy of $6,400 per mile for the 45 miles from Spence's Bridge to Nicola Lake. In 1903 the charter of the NK&S was controlled by Francis Carter-Cotton, publisher of the Vancouver *News-Advertiser* and several associates, including C.E. Loss, the president of the railway company, and Merritt, a Toronto mining engineer whom Shaughnessy had consulted about coal matters for many years.[50]

In September 1904 Shaughnessy met Premier McBride in Victoria for discussions on provincial aid for CPR lines in southern BC. It was agreed that J.S. Dennis would conduct the negotiations for the CPR, for the premier and his ministers in the past had been very dissatisfied with the absence of "some definite channel through which to deal with the President [of the CPR], and ... they never knew how far the large number of people who came before them with railway propositions were in touch with the Canadian Pacific Railway." Dennis had several meetings with McBride and R.F. Green, minister of lands and works, on 7 and 8 December 1904. Dennis requested a land grant of 20,000 acres per mile for the 85-mile Columbia and Western line from Midway to Penticton, with the lands to be exempt from taxation for 10 years. The government was agreeable to this proposition, provided that the CPR constructed the 12-mile section from Midway to Rock Creek in the first year. Dennis also proposed to use the charter of the NK&S to build a line from Okanagan Falls (about 10 miles south of Penticton) through the Similkameen and Nicola valleys to Spence's Bridge on the CPR main line, a distance of 188.5 miles. He requested a provincial government bond guarantee of $10,000 per mile and pledged that the CPR would build the 50 miles from Spence's Bridge to Nicola by the end of 1906. While he was conducting these negotiations, he received a telegram from Whyte informing him that Shaughnessy wanted a provincial cash subsidy of $5,000 per mile for the line from Okanagan Falls to Spence's Bridge, instead of a land grant. Dennis did not put forward this proposal during the negotiations because McBride, Green, Carter-Cotton, president of the executive council, and R.G. Tatlow, minister of finance, had stated emphatically that the province's financial condition "precluded any possibility of a Government [cash] bonus for lines in Southern British Columbia." Shaughnessy was particularly "annoyed and disappointed" at Carter-Cotton's opposition to a pro-

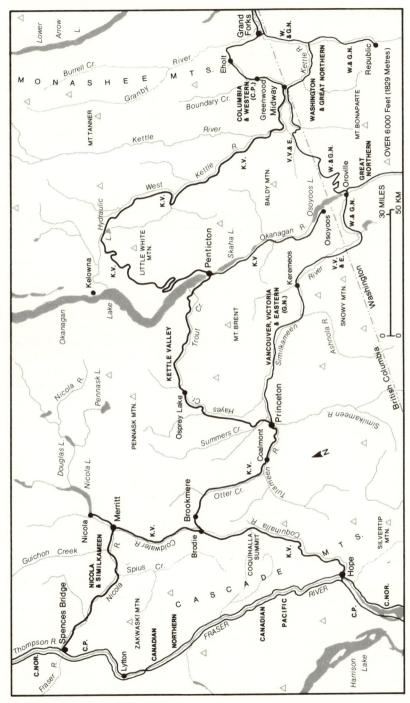

Figure 5 The Kettle Valley Railway

vincial cash subsidy. The premier made it "perfectly clear" to Dennis
that his government would not assist the NK&S unless the CPR owned
"a controlling interest" in its charter. Within the month the NK&S
board was reorganized to give the CPR control of the company, and
3 months later all the company's stock was held in the CPR interest.
McBride and his ministers then proposed to grant a provincial bond
guarantee of $10,000 per mile for the entire NK&S line. Shaughnessy
was disappointed. A provincial bond guarantee was of no special
value, he observed, because the CPR "can borrow money on a better
basis than the British Columbia government itself." However, McBride
clearly wanted the CPR to build the line, since he had previously
rejected a Great Northern proposal for aid to extend the VV&E to
connect the Great Northern with the Nicola Valley.[51] In March 1905
Dennis had further discussions with McBride requesting a $5,000
per mile cash subsidy for the Columbia and Western between Midway and Penticton as well as for the NK&S line, but McBride firmly
rejected these proposals.[52]

Shaughnessy decided that access to the rich coalfields in the Nicola
Valley was important and so he went ahead with construction of the
NK&S line from Spence's Bridge to Nicola Lake without a provincial
subsidy and using only the federal subsidy of $6,400 per mile. As
well, he and the BC government wanted the line built "in order to
head off any move from the south toward the Similkameen country
by our competitors." (At this time Hill was starting his drive to extend
the VV&E from Midway into the Similkameen district.) Shaughnessy
agreed to have C.E. Loss build the line, partly as a reward for his
efforts on the CPR's behalf, and also because he had offered to construct the line "at a figure somewhat less than our estimate of its
cost." At Shaughnessy's request, the NK&S appointed a CPR official,
H.J. Cambie, as chief engineer. Cambie had "general charge" of the
construction of the line, so the CPR could ensure that Loss built the
road according to company specifications.[53]

Construction took place in 1905 and 1906. In the spring of 1907
the NK&S line went into operation and was designated the CPR's Nicola
Branch. The CPR leased the line for 99 years at a rental equal to 4
per cent on the company's bonds. Shaughnessy's long-term goal was
to extend gradually the NK&S through the Similkameen Valley to
Princeton and Osoyoos Lake and eventually to Midway, thus connecting the Similkameen fruit-growing district with the Crow's Nest
line and heading off competition from Hill's Great Northern. He
informed Senator James Kerr in 1904 that "We would like to see
the country opened up, not only that we might have a new source
of fuel supply, but that an impetus should be given to farming, cattle

raising and mining." The Nicola Valley Coal and Coke Company developed a substantial mine at Merritt which, by the end of 1907, was turning out 225 tons of coal per day. Since this coal proved to be excellent for use in steam locomotives, the CPR secured most of the mine's output for its chutes on the main line as far east as Revelstoke. Soon a number of lumber mills were also developed along the Nicola Branch, to provide railway crossties and mine timbers. One example was the Nicola Valley Lumber Company, which opened a large mill in May 1908 at Canford, 10 miles northwest of Merritt.[54]

The conflict between the CPR and GN in southern British Columbia intensified. By 1905 J.J. Hill had wrested control from the CPR of most of the ore traffic in the Boundary district and the coal and coke traffic from the East Kootenays. In December 1904 Hill had publicly announced that he would start immediately building a railway from Curlew, Washington, to Midway, BC, and then west to Princeton and Vancouver on the Pacific coast. The VV&E would serve as the vehicle for this plan. Hill had already gained entrance into Vancouver that year by extending the tracks of his New Westminster Southern Railway across the Westminster Bridge over the Fraser River at New Westminster. This bridge, which had been constructed by the provincial government and completed in the summer of 1904, was a toll carrier for all railways, including those to the United States. It immediately provided a competitive route via GN subsidiaries from Vancouver to American railways and to Eastern Canada via these railways. Shaughnessy had gone public to denounce the McBride government's construction of the bridge as a "stupendous blunder" which would enable certain railways to enter BC and compete with the CPR.[55]

On 14 April 1905 Hill's son Louis, a GN vice-president, telegraphed the Victoria Board of Trade that the VV&E would be complete as far west as Princeton by the end of the summer and that soon after it would be pushed through to the coast. However, Hill had to obtain a Parliamentary amendment to the VV&E charter permitting the section from Midway to Princeton to cross the border into the United States at two points, in order to get the lowest grades and reduce construction costs. In June the bill amending the VV&E charter was placed before the House of Commons Railway Committee. A major battle then ensued, with most Liberal MPs, including all seven Liberals from BC, strongly supporting the bill. They maintained that the VV&E would break the CPR's monopoly in southern BC and open territory which the CPR had wanted to withhold from development until it was ready. The Conservatives, and some Quebec Liberal MPs, vigorously attacked the bill on the grounds that the VV&E would enable the GN to drain the wealth of the Similkameen Valley to Washington State and especially to Seattle. The Vancouver *Province* endorsed this view, commenting that Hill was building the line "purely and simply as a feeder that will drain Canadian mines and exhaust Canadian interests, steadily and surely, for the benefit of the Great Northern Railway Company." The Victoria Board of Trade supported the VV&E Bill on condition that "a binding guarantee be exacted that the Railway be built from Princeton to the British Columbia coast, and that a daily freight and passenger service be given to Victoria within four years." The Vancouver Board of Trade did not favour the VV&E; rather it sought aid for an independent Canadian company, the Vancouver and Coast Kootenay Railway, to build the line. As for the residents of the Similkameen Valley, according to Barrie Sanford, they were "solidly behind Hill. For them a railway was a railway and they were considerably less concerned about who built their railway than the armchair critics of the coastal cities, many of whom were already served by two or more rail lines." Shaughnessy put pressure on Laurier while the bill was before the railway committee. He informed Laurier on 19 June that construction of the VV&E line "is a distinct attack on our interests by the Great Northern Railway" and asked the prime minister to indicate to Liberal members of the committee that the bill should "stand over for another session for further consideration." Refusing to interfere in this matter, Laurier informed the CPR president he believed that "the people of British Columbia cannot be fairly refused this new line of communication between the coast and the mining regions." And on 27 June the VV&E Bill (Bill 139) passed the railway committee by a vote of 78 to 60.[56]

The next day the House began clause-by-clause study of Bill 139, a private member's bill sponsored by Liberal MP Duncan Ross (Yale-Cariboo). Although it was not a party measure, the prime minister strongly endorsed the bill. Laurier claimed he would have preferred the CPR to build the coast to Kootenay line, "But for some reason or other, the Canadian Pacific Railway ... have not given the people of British Columbia that communication which ... the people of British Columbia have been asking for years." The chief Conservative critics of the bill were Sir George Foster and David Henderson, who insisted that the VV&E be constructed entirely in Canadian territory. The bill obtained third reading on 11 July. There was little discussion of the measure in the Senate where it received third reading the next day. The Laurier cabinet then passed an Order-in-Council on 28 July permitting the VV&E to cross the international boundary.[57]

Hill was delighted at his victory. On 28 September 1905 he made a long speech in Vancouver outlining his company's policies for BC. He promised to have the VV&E across the Hope Mountains before any line which the CPR might build. The VV&E would soon provide the connection between the coast and the interior of southern BC, he maintained, and bring the region's trade to Vancouver. It would, he pledged, be "an all-Canadian line, with terminals at Vancouver. Mark my word: We will do more to upbuild Vancouver than any railway corporation has done yet."[58]

There was open conflict between the GN and the CPR as construction started on the VV&E just west of Midway in September 1905. Employees of the CPR and of the VV&E contractor, "staged a short private war when they both wanted to cross the same land." The first episode occurred when a CPR crew erected a fence of heavy timbers across the railway grade being built by the VV&E, 4 miles west of Midway. The CPR claimed that at this point the railway grade was being constructed across land that had been granted to the CPR as part of the Columbia-and-Western land subsidy and that the VV&E had failed to secure this land from the CPR before going ahead with construction. This dispute escalated quickly and soon more than 500 rival workmen had set up camp on opposite sides of the disputed territory. Inevitably some violence flared up as the men took axes and shovels against one another and the press referred to the incident as the "Battle of Midway." The provincial police were called in to restore order and the issue was referred to the courts. At the initial hearing it was discovered that the VV&E expropriation order did not apply to the piece of land over which blood had been shed! The correct expropriation order was finally granted in December 1905 so that construction could proceed.[59]

Construction of the VV&E commenced in the spring of 1906, but strikes and shortages of men and materials slowed building to a crawl. By July 1907 the section through Washington State had been completed and the line had reached the town of Keremeos on the Similkameen River about 15 miles north of the international boundary. (See figure 5.) During the business depression of 1907–8 Hill "gave the VV&E high priority in the allocation of the GN's limited funds." Tracklaying between Keremeos and Princeton was completed in November 1909 and on 23 December the first passenger train travelled over the line. A gala party in Princeton was organized to celebrate the event, during which the Similkameen River was unofficially renamed the Jimhillameen River. Hill had succeeded in reinforcing his already strong position in southern British Columbia.[60]

The CPR did not carry out much railway construction on its line from Midway west to Penticton, Princeton, and Hope in the period

1905–9, despite Hill's construction activities. The company did build a short line from Spence's Bridge to Nicola in 1905–6, but the line was not extended south into the Similkameen Valley.

Instead the CPR was developing a close relationship with the KRVR, the activities of which were overseen by James John Warren. Warren was a Toronto lawyer who specialized in commercial and corporate law. His friend James Stratton persuaded him to join the Trusts and Guarantee Company, and he was soon appointed its managing director (1905). Since it had been largely financed by capital from the Trusts and Guarantee Company, Warren made the KRVR one of his chief concerns. In February 1906 he made a trip to BC to familiarize himself with the railway and its financial problems. He did not think that extending the KRVR from Republic to Spokane would solve its problems, since D.C. Corbin was building a line from Spokane to the CPR in southern BC in order to divert traffic away from the GN and the NP. He realized that the Trusts and Guarantee Company did not have the financial resources to build what would be a very expensive railway from Midway through the Hope Mountains to the coast. A meeting with Premier McBride convinced him that there was "little chance" of the KRVR's getting assistance from the BC government to build from Midway west to Hope and Vancouver. Therefore he concluded that an alliance with the CPR or its takeover of the KRVR offered the best prospects for the trust company.[61]

In July 1905 the KRVR started grading the roadbed for a line from Grand Forks up the north fork of the Kettle River to Franklin mining camp. The long range plan was to extend this branch north to Vernon and then west to Quilchena, where it would connect with the NK&S, so that coal from the Nicola Valley could be carried to smelters in the Boundary district. The Laurier government had granted a $6,400-per-mile cash subsidy for the first 50 miles of this north fork branch. In July 1906 Shaughnessy informed Warren that the CPR would provide the KRVR with $10,000 to purchase land for the right of way on the north fork branch and would purchase the company's bonds to finance construction. By the end of the summer of 1907, when work on the branch stopped completely, only 18 miles of track had been laid to Lynch Creek, which was less than half the distance to Franklin Camp. The significant fact, however, was that the CPR was willing to give financial support for the construction of the KRVR. During the 1907 session of the BC legislature Dennis "pushed vigorously" for a provincial subsidy for the KRVR, with support from Carter-Cotton. Although he was unsuccessful, he was able to prevent the GN from obtaining a subsidy for the VV&E from Princeton to Hope.[62]

In April 1908 Warren had discussions with Shaughnessy during a voyage to London on the *Empress of Britain*. Warren proposed an alliance between the two companies, similar to that between Corbin and the CPR, for building a line into Spokane. The CPR president was very favourable to this proposal, and assured Warren "that for many years he had personally wanted to push CPR rails west from Midway and had only been awaiting the proper economic climate to justify the high construction costs." (Shaughnessy's determination to build a railway through southern BC to Vancouver had been evident as far back as 1898. In the spring of 1898 Shaughnessy met W.F. Tye to discuss construction plans for the Columbia and Western Railway and asserted, "Tye, I want you to build this line just as fast as you can, because I am going to make the Southern British Columbia line the through freight line to Vancouver.") Shaughnessy and Warren decided to cooperate in surveying the route of the KRVR between Midway and Hope, where it would join with the CPR main line to Vancouver. In September 1907 Shaughnessy had already assigned CPR engineer Henry Carry the job of revising the surveys which he had carried out between Penticton and Merritt during 1905–6. Carry's surveys of 1907–8 established a more satisfactory route, with lower grades, between Penticton and Merritt. In 1908–9 Warren had engineers complete the surveys on the line between Midway and Penticton. In the spring of 1909 Shaughnessy assigned CPR engineer W.I. Bassett the difficult task of establishing a railway location through the Coquihalla Pass in the Hope Mountains.[63]

Between 1905 and 1909 extensive survey work had been done for the KRVR line between Midway, Penticton, and Merritt, but no construction had taken place. What accounts for such lack of progress? Certainly the business depression of 1907–8 had restricted CPR construction plans not only in BC but also in the prairie West. Also, the CPR had many other projects in hand at this time, such as the double-tracking of its main line on the Prairies and the building of substantial hotels in Winnipeg and Victoria. In 1905 Shaughnessy advised Whyte that he did not want the company to make any promise on a time limit to extend the Nicola branch to Midway. "With so many other important works in hand," Shaughnessy asserted, "an undertaking to construct an additional mileage might prove burdensome, particularly in a locality where railway construction costs so much money."[64] Also, Shaughnessy was optimistic about receiving financial assistance for the KRVR from the McBride government which would permit construction of the line west from Midway to start in 1910. The CPR president and McBride were on very good terms. The premier informed a friend in 1909 that Shaughnessy "has always been very fair and reasonable in all that I have had to do with him and [he] has the best interests of our Province at heart."

While on his annual inspection tour of Western lines in September 1909, Shaughnessy visited Victoria and had a closed conference with Premier McBride. Shortly after, J.J. Warren met with the premier and signed an agreement for cash aid for the KRVR. Two major factors account for this important development: provincial finances were in excellent shape, for after 1907 there were several years of substantial surpluses in the provincial treasury, and the McBride government had a comfortable majority in the legislature as a result of the 1907 provincial election. McBride, who had sought to assist railways in developing BC ever since coming to power, could now safely provide substantial aid to railways. Roy remarks that the BC premier "had succumbed to the same railway mania that affected his predecessors in the province and his contemporaries elsewhere in the country."[65]

McBride dissolved the legislature on 18 October 1909 and 2 days later announced his railway policy, which was to be "the centrepiece" of the provincial election. The chief feature of this policy was an agreement with the Canadian Northern Railway for provincial bond guarantees of $35,000 per mile to finance construction of 600 miles of railway from the Yellowhead Pass to Vancouver and 100 miles of railway from Victoria along the west coast of Vancouver Island to Barkley Sound. McBride also had something to offer southern BC. On 20 October he and J.J. Warren signed an agreement under which the government would provide a $5,000-per-mile subsidy in cash or in 3 per cent provincial bonds for the construction of a maximum of 150 miles of the KRVR from Penticton to a connection with the NK&S at Nicola. The KRVR undertook to build the section from Midway to Penticton without provincial subsidy, but this section would be exempt from provincial taxation for a period of 10 years. The KRVR promised to employ no Chinese or Japanese as construction workers on the two lines, a restriction which also applied to the Canadian Northern Railway. No mention was made of the fact that the CPR was in the process of acquiring the KRVR. The agreement also required the KRVR to pay the debts which the defunct Midway and Vernon Railway had incurred with workmen and suppliers before it collected any of the subsidy.[66]

The criticisms of McBride's railway program were directed mainly at the lavish aid for the Canadian Northern while the restrictions on Asian labour were strongly supported. R.G. Tatlow, the minister of finance, felt strongly that this assistance was too extravagant, while minister of lands and works, F.J. Fulton, was convinced that railways would be built in BC without provincial aid. Both ministers resigned from the Cabinet though they did not publicly criticize McBride's policy during the election campaign. There is some evidence that the two ministers had CPR connections and had resigned because the CPR was strongly opposed to the aid for Mackenzie and Mann. However, these resignations did not hurt the McBride government, which won 38 of the 42 seats in the election of 25 November. The KRVR and Canadian Northern agreements were then embodied in legislation which passed the legislature in March 1910.[67]

Shaughnessy did succeed in obtaining substantial assistance from the Laurier government for the KRVR. In the 1910 session of Parliament, legislation was passed which granted it a cash subsidy of $6,400 per mile for a maximum of 250 miles from Midway to Merritt, and for a maximum of 50 miles from Brodie through the Coquihalla Pass to connect with the CPR main line at Hope. (See figure 5.) At a CPR board meeting in February 1910 Shaughnessy secured the directors' approval for financing the KRVR from Midway to Hope, and thus providing the coast-to-Kootenay railway which the coastal cities so strongly desired.[68] In May 1910 Shaughnessy chose Andrew McCulloch as the KRVR's chief engineer, the official who would be directly in charge of all aspects of the construction of the Kettle Valley line. Trained as an accountant in Kingston, Ontario, the forty-six-year-old McCulloch had abandoned his accounting career in 1889 to seek opportunities in the Canadian West. He first settled in Vancouver, but as jobs were scarce there he had signed on as an axeman clearing survey lines along the GN mainline in Montana. In 1897 he was hired as a surveyor on the CPR's Crow's Nest line. His competent performance had earned him a promotion to assistant engineer with the Columbia and Western Railway. He was then offered an excellent position by the GTPR locating that company's prairie lines, a job he did until 1905 when the CPR outbid the GTPR to employ him locating the CPR's Spiral Tunnels under chief engineer J.E. Schwitzer. In 1907 he was appointed divisional engineer of construction for the CPR's Eastern lines, with headquarters at Montreal. In view of his extensive experience locating railway lines in the American Northwest and the Canadian West, particularly British Columbia, McCulloch was a good choice as the KRVR's chief engineer. J.J. Warren, who had been elected president of the KRVR in 1909, was placed in general authority over the building of the line as manager of construction.[69]

McCulloch had a long interview with Shaughnessy in Montreal on 25 May 1910 during which the latter set down firm guidelines for the construction of the KRVR. The line was to pass through Penticton and the Summerland area, to connect with the CPR's Nicola Branch at Merritt and to go through Coquihalla Pass to Hope. All grades were to be 1.0 per cent or less except on the ascent out of the Okanagan Valley east and west of Penticton where 2.2 per cent grades could be used. The actual cost of construction would be underwritten by the CPR in return for KRVR bonds and debentures. Shaughnessy emphasized, in Sanford's words, that the KRVR "must be first class in every way, an enduring monument for all time to the CPR's faith and dedication to the service of the people of southern British Columbia."[70]

Construction began at Merritt on 9 July 1910, one day ahead of the 4-month deadline set by the BC subsidy legislation of 1910. This 30-mile section ran generally south, and at mile 25 it crossed the Coldwater River and took a 4-mile curve (known as "The Loop") to Brookmere. (See figure 5.) Rails reached Brookmere on 29 September 1911. On 29 November an inebriated federal government inspector arrived in Merritt and immediately declared the line to be satisfactory! Construction started at the other end of the railway at Midway in mid-June 1910. On 11 August a contract was let for grading and tracklaying from Midway west for 35 miles; this contract was not completed until the end of 1911. A major factor in slowing construction was the acute shortage of railway labour in Western Canada. The KRVR was competing for manpower with the Canadian Northern and the GTPR, both of which were heavily engaged in construction work in British Columbia from 1910 to 1914. Thus, in the autumn of 1910 the total number of men at work on the KRVR never exceeded 600. As Sanford observes, this was "a modest work force indeed for such a major construction project." Construction also took place in 1910–11 at Penticton where the KRVR's railway yard and terminal were to be located. Materials were shipped from the CPR main line at Sicamous via the Shuswap and Okanagan to Okanagan Landing and then by CPR boats to Penticton at the south end of Lake Okanagan. McCulloch decided to place the railway yard and terminal 1 mile south of Penticton because the high glacial terraces on Lake Okanagan were very unstable. A spur line into Penticton provided the necessary connection.

Federal legislation of 1911 changed the name of the railway to the Kettle Valley Railway (KVR). At the CPR annual meeting on 2 October 1912, shareholders approved the lease of the KVR, a transaction authorized by federal legislation passed in April 1913. On 2 June 1913 its directors approved an agreement which leased the KVR to the CPR for 999 years, effective 1 July 1913.[71]

The KVR faced a very difficult problem in finding a feasible route between the Kettle and Okanagan valleys, that is from the 4,100-foot summit at Hydraulic Lake to lake level at Penticton. This rapid descent was "along the edge of a rugged mountain which was cut by numerous transverse streams." In September 1910 a corps of KVR engineers started at Hydraulic Summit and searched 2 years before finding a practicable route to Penticton. As Warren informed a correspondent, "in the early summer of 1912 I almost dispaired [sic] of getting a line which we could build ... As a last resort our Engineers tried a line following the old Kelowna trail." They were finally able to get a location without the "prohibitive curvatures" of the line which they had tentatively decided to use. Warren was "very much relieved" and in September 1912 the contract for the Hydraulic Summit to Penticton section was let.[72] (See figure 5.)

In February 1912 the McBride government provided additional aid for the KVR: a subsidy of $10,000 per mile was authorized for the expensive and difficult section from Brookmere through the Coquihalla Pass to Hope and a subsidy of $200,000 was provided for the construction of a combined railway-and-traffic bridge over the Fraser River near Hope. This assistance program had been part of the 1912 election campaign which McBride had built around the Pacific Great Eastern Railway. When his government won a resounding victory in the 28 March provincial elections, the subsidy was assured. That same year the Borden government granted the KVR an additional $250,000 subsidy for the bridge. In 1913 the federal cash subsidy of $6,400 per mile for the KVR from Midway to Hope was reduced from the 1910 figure of 300 miles to a figure of 200 miles. The federal government subsidized the Merritt to Penticton section (145 miles), as well as the very expensive section from Brookmere to Hope, which already had a provincial subsidy of $10,000 per mile.

The poor outlook for the railway labour situation at the beginning of 1912 had changed radically by the end of the year. Immigration officials had resumed their attempts to limit the number of southern Europeans entering Canada as railway navvies. But under pressure from Mann, of the Canadian Northern, and Timothy Foley, a leading contractor for the GTPR, Robert Rogers, the minister of the interior in the Borden government, overruled his officials. The result was the free entry of alien navvies. This action greatly assisted the KVR, for by late 1912 the company had almost 5,000 workers on the line and construction was proceeding well, particularly on the section from Midway to Penticton.[73]

The only section of the KVR which was not completed or under contract by 1912 was that from Osprey Lake (about midway between

Penticton and Princeton) to the summit of the grade at Brookmere, at an elevation of 3,157 feet. The proposed route for this section ran north of the town of Princeton and bypassed the Tulameen Valley. (See figure 5.) However, Hill's vv&e had reached Princeton from the south in November 1909. Between 1909 and 1912 a growing trade was developing in the Similkameen and Tulameen valleys which the vv&e was capturing. Also, the Columbia Coal and Coke Company was developing a major coal mine at Coalmont, 12 miles west of Princeton along the proposed route of the vv&e. The coal from this mine was excellent steam coal, and in 1912 the GN signed a contract with the company for the delivery of 500 tons of coal per day. But most important, Warren was under strong pressure from Premier McBride and Conservative MLA L.W. Shatford to shift the KVR route through Princeton and the Tulameen Valley. Shatford, who took a keen interest in KVR matters, was managing director of the Southern Okanagan Land Company, which may have owned land in the Princeton district. Warren met the two politicians in Victoria in December 1911 and promised that his engineers would go over the country west of Penticton to see if there were a feasible route for the KVR through Princeton and the Tulameen Valley. On 27 February 1912 Warren informed McBride that his engineers had found a route that was "quite feasible though it involves considerably more expensive construction." He informed the premier that the KVR would now build its main line via Princeton and the Tulameen Valley to Brookmere. (See figure 5.) On 10 April Warren publicly announced the KVR's change of route. The new route created more conflict with the GN, since it represented an invasion of Hill's territory.[74]

In 1909 the vv&e had adopted as its route from Princeton to Hope a line to Coalmont, Tulameen, the Tulameen River, and an 8-mile tunnel to the Coquihalla River. This route would avoid the narrow and difficult Coquihalla Pass through which the KVR intended to build. Hill soon realized that the tunnel was too expensive and would take too long to construct, thus enabling the KVR to build to Hope several years ahead of the vv&e. Therefore, on 22 November 1910 the GN announced that survey work on the tunnel had been cancelled and that the vv&e was preparing for construction via Brookmere and the Coquihalla Pass. This route change, Sanford emphasizes, "placed the vv&e survey right alongside the KVR survey through the much more rugged upper canyon of the Coquihalla River where, due to the physical nature of the canyon, the construction of two railway lines would have been virtually impossible." Also the vv&e had been building eastward from Abbotsford in the Fraser Valley in 1910–11, and had reached Sumas Landing. On 22 May 1911 the vv&e allied itself with Mackenzie and Mann. An announcement stated that the Canadian Northern Pacific would build a line from Sumas Landing to Hope, with the vv&e receiving equal use of the line for its own trains. Hill was now in a strong position to make good his 1905 claim that the vv&e would be the first to build a railway from the Boundary district to Vancouver.[75]

The Board of Railway Commissioners now had to adjudicate the conflicting claims of the vv&e and the kvr to a route through the Coquihalla Pass. In 1906 the board had approved the vv&e location survey through the Coquihalla Pass to Hope, but the vv&e had abandoned this route in 1909. On 13 February 1912 the board issued an order approving the kvr location through the pass to a point 10.5 miles west of Coquihalla Summit, but did not rule on the route from that point to Hope. The kvr was now in a strong position, particularly in view of the fact that the McBride government had sanctioned a large subsidy for the kvr line through the Coquihalla Pass to Hope in February 1912. Hill ultimately decided to avoid a confrontation. In October 1912 L.C. Gilman, assistant to the president of the gn, publicly offered to allow the kvr to build the entire Coquihalla line if the kvr would lease trackage rights over it to the vv&e at a reasonable price. Gilman and J.J. Warren had a number of meetings in Victoria and Vancouver between November 1912 and April 1913. McBride played a key role in facilitating these talks. As Warren remarked to the premier, "You know the history of these negotiations because they have been practically carried on in your office." On 9 April 1913 Gilman and Warren emerged from their conference suite in the Vancouver Hotel and, in Sanford's words, "announced that the battle for Coquihalla Pass was over." An agreement had been reached for the construction and operation of a single line of railway, to be shared by both companies, through Coquihalla Pass. The kvr was to construct, own, and maintain a 54-mile line from Brookmere to Hope. The vv&e was to be granted trackage rights over the line for 999 years, for a basic annual rental of 2.5 per cent of the cost of construction. Sanford correctly asserts that this agreement was "a major concession to the cpr by the Great Northern." Later that year the gn began to cut back its operations in bc. In December 1913 train service to Princeton was cut from daily, except Sunday, to three trains a week. But the gn still competed with the cpr-kvr for the traffic of the Kootenay and Boundary districts to Vancouver.[76]

Construction of the unfinished sections of the kvr was carried out mainly in 1913 and 1914. In the April 1913 agreement, the gn had granted the kvr an option to use the vv&e trackage between Princeton and Brookmere, but because this track was unballasted the KVR built its own line for this section. Shaughnessy wanted the KVR completed as soon as possible, for he visualized the CPR-KVR-Crow's Nest line through southern BC as an alternate route to Vancouver to the company's main line. In July 1914, while appropriations for new prairie branch lines were being cancelled, the CPR president advised Warren, "It is very important that this Kettle Valley route should be available for use without undue delay, in order that we may have another string to our bow in the event of any serious difficulty on the main line." On 21 April 1915 the rails reached Princeton and tracklaying of the KVR main line was completed. Tracklaying superintendent Charles Taylor hammered down the last spike and remarked, "Well, the big stunt is done!" Shaughnessy was very satisfied with the quality of the work. W.F. Tye received a bonus of $5,000, J.G. Sullivan an extra $1,000, while the four division engineers each received a bonus of $500. On 31 May the KVR between Merritt and Midway was formally opened for service.[77] The coast-to-Kootenay railway, which had been strongly advocated by the businessmen of Vancouver and Victoria for almost two decades, was finally a reality. The CPR now dominated the traffic of southern British Columbia and the Crow's Nest Pass to Vancouver.

Another aspect of the intense rivalry between the CPR and the GN was Shaughnessy's support for the building of a railway by D.C. Corbin from Spokane to the CPR Crow's Nest line in the East Kootenays. Shaughnessy's alliance with his old arch-rival, Daniel Corbin, had begun in 1902. The CPR president was determined to obtain a portion of the GN's coal and coke traffic to Montana and Washington State, and to divert some of the GN-NP traffic in Washington State to the CPR in southern BC. In 1902 Corbin and George Turner, a senator from Washington State, joined forces to promote a rail connection between Spokane and the CPR's Crow's Nest line in the East Kootenays. In December 1902 the Spokane and Kootenai Railway was incorporated in the state of Washington to build this railway. Turner was at this time a director of the Sullivan Group Mining Company which sought to develop a large deposit of low-grade lead, silver, and zinc ore in the Fort Steele area in the East Kootenays. This company needed rail transportation to link its holdings with smelters in the West Kootenays and Washington State. The Spokane and Kootenai was supported by some prominent businessmen from the state. The company was to be financed by "interests friendly to the Canadian Pacific" and the CPR openly supported the new venture. Shaughnessy informed Senator Turner in April 1903 that the CPR was "more impressed than ever with the desirability of a connection just as soon as it can be provided." Spokane businessmen hoped to get low freight rates from the CPR, for they were convinced that the NP and the GN "treated Spokane shabbily when these transcontinental carriers had adjusted their rates to meet water competition at coastal terminals."[78]

However, the Spokane and Kootenai was unable to finance the road because of opposition from major US railways serving Spokane. In 1904 Corbin decided to reorganize the company. He brought in some of his old associates from the SF&N and dropped most of his original supporters, including Turner. The reorganized company – the Spokane International Railway – was incorporated in Washington State in January 1905. It absorbed the assets of the Spokane and Kootenai, which consisted chiefly of preliminary survey maps. Corbin negotiated a construction and traffic agreement with the CPR in January-February 1905. Under it, the CPR undertook to supply one-eighth of the Spokane International's construction costs in return for an option to purchase 52 per cent of its capital stock at a price to be determined not later than January 1917. The CPR purchased $300,000 worth of Spokane International bonds, the Soo line $200,000 worth, and Corbin was responsible for selling the remaining $3.5 million. The other part of the deal was a traffic-sharing agreement between the CPR and the Spokane International which, Shaughnessy remarked, "should make the line between Spokane and the International Boundary a fairly profitable one, unless Mr. Corbin be very much deceived as to the traffic that it will control."[79]

On 19 January Corbin formally announced that he would build a railway from Spokane to the international boundary where it would connect with the CPR's Crow's Nest line at the hamlet of Yahk in the East Kootenays. The Spokane International line was surveyed in the summer of 1905 and construction was started immediately. The railway, which ran through north-central Idaho via Bonner's Ferry to Eastport at the international boundary, was completed by September 1906. The CPR built a 12-mile branch from Yahk to Kingsgate at the boundary in 1905. (See figure 4.) The Spokane International opened for business on 1 November 1906.[80]

Shaughnessy was very pleased with his alliance with Corbin. The distance between Spokane and the Twin Cities of Minneapolis-St Paul via the Spokane International, the CPR, and the CPR-controlled Soo line was only slightly greater than via the GN, and about 20 miles shorter than via the NP. The GN and NP now faced serious competition for freight business between Spokane and the Twin Cities. West of Spokane to Portland, the CPR-Spokane International trains were handled by the Southern Pacific's Oregon Railway and Navigation line.

Corbin estimated that the CPR and his line would be able to obtain one-third of "the in and out freight business of Spokane," which amounted to about $7 million annually. In 1908 the American government dropped Hill's contract for handling the US mail between Minneapolis-St Paul and the Northwest and awarded it to the CPR and the Spokane International. Sanford observes that this was a coup "which Hill would never forget." The CPR did take away from the GN some of its exports of coal and coke from the Crow's Nest Coal Company to Montana and Washington State, though no figures are available. And finally, the CPR and the Spokane International started a through passenger service between Spokane and the Twin Cities on 1 July 1907, although it was not operated during the winter months.[81]

Not all CPR activities in British Columbia were related to the contest with Hill's Great Northern. In 1905 Shaughnessy took steps to acquire the Esquimalt and Nanaimo Railway (E&N) on Vancouver Island. The Esquimalt and Nanaimo Railway was incorporated by BC statute in 1884 to build a railway from Esquimalt through Victoria and along the island's east coast to Nanaimo, a distance of 73 miles. It was given an enormous land subsidy of 1,900,000 acres, in a 20-mile strip running north from Goldstream (a few miles west of Victoria) to Seymour Narrows, about 10 miles north of the town of Campbell River. The railway was financed by island coal baron Robert Dunsmuir and three wealthy American railway magnates. Dunsmuir possessed the right to nominate a majority of the E&N's directors and so controlled its financial policy. Construction began in September 1884 and the line was in operation in September 1886. The following year the E&N was extended from Nanaimo 4.8 miles north to Wellington, the site of Dunsmuir's huge coal operations. When Robert Dunsmuir died in April 1889, one son, Alexander, was elected president of the E&N, while his other son, James, took over full management of the Dunsmuir collieries. Traffic volume on the E&N increased steadily throughout the 1890's, but the deficit also rose regularly, reaching a peak of $200,000 in 1898. A turning point occurred in 1900 when the railway made a small profit of $5,440. In 1900 Alexander Dunsmuir died, leaving his entire estate to his brother James, who became the president of the E&N. The new president established a ferry service between Vancouver and Ladysmith (where some of the Dunsmuir coal mines were located) south of Nanaimo, and as a result E&N profits began to increase. By the autumn of 1902 he had bought out the three American shareholders and made himself sole owner of the railway.[82]

In late December 1903 and into the new year, Premier McBride negotiated with James Dunsmuir to have the provincial government purchase the E&N. Dunsmuir offered to sell the railway, its steamboats, and the remaining 1,500,000 acres of E&N lands for $3.5 million. He accepted McBride's proposal that Dunsmuir accept payment in 3 per cent inscribed provincial stock because the BC government could not raise a $3.5 million loan on the money market "on business terms." However, there were two points of contention. Dunsmuir was determined to "reserve absolutely" for himself all coal and coal rights on the unsold E&N lands. Also, the coal magnate adamantly refused to recognize the right of the BC government to tax E&N lands, "and shall resist to the utmost in my power any attempt to do so." McBride submitted Dunsmuir's terms to Cabinet, which rejected them. It appears that the sticking point was the land-taxation question, for the premier was willing to accept Dunsmuir's reservation of coal deposits on E&N lands.[83]

Dunsmuir was now however quite willing to sell the E&N. In January 1905 Shaughnessy instructed Marpole to open negotiations with Dunsmuir for CPR acquisition of the line. The president informed Whyte that "with the growth of population on the Island the property might become a valuable one." At the 1905 session of Parliament, the Laurier government passed legislation that authorized the CPR to lease the E&N. And on 7 June 1905 the CPR signed an agreement with Dunsmuir to purchase all the E&N's assets (including two steamships and a tugboat) and its land grant. Dunsmuir retained the coal rights to the land-grant property, which would continue to remain exempt from provincial taxation. The final price was $2,330,000, of which $1,080,000 was for the transportation system, while the balance covered the remaining 1,440,495 unsold acres of land grant. The old E&N board resigned on 7 June and was succeeded by W. Whyte, president, A.R. Creelman, vice-president, and directors R. Marpole, J.S. Dennis, and J.W. Troup. The CPR subsequently operated the E&N as a separate branch line.[84]

The acquisition of the E&N was planned in part to complement the CPR's Empress Hotel at Victoria, which was officially opened on 20 January 1908. Tourists would be encouraged to stay in the hotel and see some of Vancouver Island on the E&N. The CPR was probably also attempting to prevent the Canadian Northern from taking over the railway, although Shaughnessy privately expressed little concern over this possibility. He was interested in developing the "vast supply of timber" on the E&N land grant. He even considered having the CPR establish "a very big milling enterprise" on the Island but decided that existing mills were developing its timber industry at a satisfactory pace.[85]

In 1908 the CPR extended the E&N north along the Island's east coast in an attempt to win favour with the McBride government, which might then be persuaded to subsidize a CPR line from Midway to Hope. Marpole had stepped down as general superintendent on 1 March 1907 to become general executive assistant for BC. His new responsibilities were the E&N and the Vancouver townsite. He was eager to start construction of a line from Wellington to Alberni but Shaughnessy refused; at the time he was avoiding "any commitments for the present involving capital expenditures." However, in December 1908 he did approve an appropriation of $125,000 for clearing right of way between Wellington and Alberni. In 1907 the Laurier government passed legislation granting a cash subsidy of $6,400 per mile for a 55-mile line from Wellington to Alberni. In June 1908 Shaughnessy approved an appropriation of $574,294 to cover the cost of grading and bringing the E&N extension from Wellington to Alberni. This extension was undertaken in part to secure coal for E&N operations on Vancouver Island. In February 1908 the CPR signed a 5-year agreement with James Dunsmuir's Wellington Colliery Company at Alberni to purchase 5,000 long tons of steam coal per month at a price of $4.20 per ton. Some of this coal would be used by the *Empress* steamships and the coastal steamers. In May 1908 Marpole succeeded in getting a price of $3.50 per ton for lump coal for the CPR's steamships. At a banquet in his honour in Victoria on 22 October 1908, Shaughnessy stated that when the line to Alberni was completed the CPR would build a branch from Duncan to Cowichan Lake. He also envisaged the extension of the E&N to the north end of the Island. The Alberni extension was going to be expensive, for Whyte estimated its cost at $1,953,400, an average of $33,680 per mile. The line was completed late in 1911, and on 20 December the first through train ran from Victoria to Alberni.[86]

The CPR's monopoly position on Vancouver Island was challenged in 1910 by Mackenzie and Mann, who were planning to build several lines on the Island. In November Shaughnessy wrote Premier McBride expressing displeasure that the BC government was planning to approve the location of Canadian Northern lines on the Island parallel to the E&N railway as far as Duncan and the proposed E&N branch to Cowichan Lake. He remarked that he "would feel personally hurt by an action on your part indicating a feeling of animosity toward the Company." Finally, McBride did not approve these lines, but in his railway legislation of February 1912 he provided a $35,000-per-mile bond guarantee (principal and interest) for 150 miles of Canadian Northern Pacific line from Comox to Barkley Sound, part of which would parallel the E&N. By this time Shaughnessy was much less concerned about Canadian Northern competition on the Island. He was convinced that Mackenzie and Mann would have great difficulty completing their main line from the Yellowhead Pass to Vancouver, so that they would be unable to build on the Island for many years.[87]

The arrangements for a long-term lease of the E&N by the CPR were finalized with the passage of legislation by the McBride government in February 1912 affirming that E&N lands would continue to remain exempt from provincial taxation until sold. Under the legislation, the E&N undertook to extend its main line north from McBride Junction to the village of Courtenay before 31 December 1915. The CPR lease of the E&N, for a period of 99 years, was effective 1 July 1912 and was confirmed by federal Order-in-Council on 12 September. The E&N completed an 18-mile branch from Hayward Junction to Cowichan Lake in 1913, but the 45-mile extension to Courtenay was still under construction in June 1914.[88]

The last important line undertaken by the CPR in BC before World War One was the Kootenay Central Railway. This railway was incorporated in 1901 to build a line from Elko on the Crow's Nest line via Fort Steele and Invermere, to Golden on the CPR main line. It was also authorized to build a line from Elko south to the international boundary. (See figure 4.) In 1903 a federal subsidy of $6,400 per mile was granted to the company by the Laurier government, a subsidy which was revoted in 1906, 1910, and 1912. Some survey work had been done on the line when the CPR took control of the company in November 1904. Shaughnessy's concern at this time was to prevent a major railway (such as the GN) from acquiring the charter and thus controlling a major connecting link between the main line and the Crow's Nest line in BC. The line would also provide railway service to settlers in the valley of the Columbia and Kootenay rivers and encourage more settlement there. The CPR did survey work and some construction at the Golden end from 1905 to 1910 in order to keep the subsidy on the statute books and finally completed the survey of the entire line in May 1910. That year the short section from Elko to Fort Steele was built. At the CPR annual meeting on 5 October 1910 the shareholders authorized a lease of the Kootenay Central Railway. The lease, which ran for 999 years, was ratified by federal Order-in-Council on 31 December 1910 and came into effect 1 January 1911. Some construction work was done from 1911 to 1914, so that by June 1914, 41 miles had been completed from Golden, south to Spillimacheen. Shaughnessy now regarded the line as useful for the CPR's double-tracking work in BC. It could be part of an alternate route to Vancouver via the Crow's Nest-Kettle Valley lines when difficult sections of the main line were being double-tracked. It was completed to the Crow's Nest line by January 1915.[89]

And finally, the CPR took some important steps to improve its main line: the Spiral and Connaught tunnel projects and some double-tracking work. The Spiral Tunnels were designed to reduce the grade on the main line west of Kicking Horse Pass. The problem had been created in 1884 when construction crews, under Van Horne's instructions, laid tracks from the summit of this pass down what was supposed to be a temporary, short and steep (4.5 per cent) grade to the valley floor east of Field. This Field Hill section, which was the steepest on the whole CPR line, soon became known as the "Big Hill". As John Marsh points out, it was "notorious through twenty-four years of temporary use for its high operating costs and fearful accidents." In April 1907 a report on grade reduction at Field Hill was submitted to Shaughnessy, who had the company's chief engineer, F.P. Gutelius, analyse it. Then, after Whyte's engineering staff in Winnipeg studied both reports the Spiral Tunnels project went ahead.[90]

It was John E. Schwitzer, assistant chief engineer of the CPR's Western lines, who had devised the solution of looping the track through two long spiral tunnels so that it descended from the summit at a steady and acceptable 2.2 per cent grade. The idea had been used in Europe, but this was the first and only time that it was applied in North America. Schwitzer, born in Ottawa in 1870, had an engineering degree from McGill University and had started with the CPR in 1899. On 1 March 1907 he was appointed assistant chief engineer of the CPR's Western lines, only months before construction of the tunnels began. It was a major project requiring a 1,000-man work force and a budget of $1.5 million. The new line, which reduced the grade from 4.5 per cent to 2.2 per cent, was completed about the end of August, 1909. The great improvement in operating capacity it afforded was demonstrated by the fact that two engines could now draw a load of 980 tons up Field Hill, whereas before it had taken four locomotives to haul a load of 710 tons.[91]

The Connaught (Rogers Pass) Tunnel involved the building of a 5-mile-long tunnel beneath the summit of the Selkirk Mountains. As in the case of the Kicking Horse Pass, the problem was west of Rogers Pass, where the elevation was 4,300 feet (1,323 metres). The original line, built in 1885, had steep grades, for it had been laid down the exposed slopes of Avalanche Mountain, around a loop in the upper Illecillewaet Valley, and then around another loop lower down. It then continued more directly down the Illecillewaet River to reach the Columbia River at Revelstoke (elevation 1,400 feet [430 metres]). Due to the extreme danger of avalanches in this area, the CPR built 4 miles of snowsheds over the line in 1886–7: sixteen sheds east of Rogers Pass, one at the summit, and fourteen west of the summit.[92]

Most scholars have emphasized that the Connaught Tunnel was needed, in Marsh's words, "to give the line protection from avalanches that had been damaging the track and snowsheds, disrupting traffic and causing loss of life." Avalanches had claimed over 200 lives in the Rogers Pass area from 1885–1911. The winter of 1909–10 was particularly bad for avalanches. On 4 March 1910 an avalanche had come down Cheops Mountain and blocked the tracks west of the pass. A large CPR crew with a rotary snowplough was sent to clear the line, but just before midnight another slide descended on the men, killing 62 of them. In a recent study, Gary Backler effectively discounts the avalanche problem as a factor in the CPR's decision to build the Connaught Tunnel. Instead, he points out that the CPR in 1913 was faced with "unprecedented competitive pressures," notably "the imminent opening of two rival transcontinental railways and the Panama Canal." It was determined to secure westbound gradients comparable with those of its rivals, so that it could compete effectively for westbound grain. The Connaught Tunnel was the needed long-term solution to the operating problems of the Rogers Pass and a means of giving the CPR "a long-term competitive advantage."[93]

George Bury supervised the project, assisted by J.G. Sullivan, his chief engineer, and the engineering staff at Winnipeg. Bury was responsible for the decision to build a second line through the tunnel. The contract for building the Connaught Tunnel was awarded to the Foley Bros., Welch and Stewart, on 5 May 1913. The details were settled by 1 July 1913, and in August work began with the drilling of an exploratory bore. The bores from the east and west met on 19 December 1915, and just under a year later regular trains started using the tunnel. An official opening ceremony, held in the summer of 1917, was attended by many prominent people, notably the Duke of Connaught, who had served as Canada's governor general from 1911 to 1916. The tunnel was formally christened "The Selkirk," but it was soon renamed for the duke. The estimated total cost of reconstructing the route in Rogers Pass had been $8.5 million, of which $5.5 million was spent on the Connaught Tunnel. The tunnel reduced the length of the mainline by 4.3 miles, removed over 7 miles of the 2.2 per cent gradient on the east slope, and almost 6 miles on the west slope. At the summit of the Selkirks, the Connaught Tunnel reduced the gradient to less than 1 per cent for 8.8

miles. At the time the 5-mile-long tunnel was the longest railroad tunnel in North America.[94]

The CPR also improved the operating capacity of the main line in BC by carrying out a modest program of double-tracking from 1912 to 1914. Double-tracking of the main line outside the province had begun in 1905, and by 1909 had been completed between Fort William and Winnipeg. Between 1910–14 the company built 1,080 miles of second track for the 1,255 miles between Winnipeg and Calgary. In 1912 Shaughnessy announced that the CPR would start double-tracking the main line between Calgary and Vancouver, work which began that summer when Shaughnessy authorized the grading for a second track from Hammond Pit to Ruby Creek, in the Fraser Valley between Vancouver and Hope. At the CPR annual meeting on 2 October 1912 the shareholders approved an increase of $60 million (par value) in the company's capital stock. It would be offered to shareholders at $175 for each $100 share, and would thus raise $105 million. Shaughnessy informed Prime Minister Borden that some of the proceeds from this new stock issue would be used for the "extension of the double track to the Pacific Coast."[95]

Shaughnessy regarded the double-tracking program as "absolutely essential to operations." In March 1913 he advised Grant Hall, the general manager for Western lines, to be prepared to cut back severely on branch line construction on the Prairies, but not on the double-tracking program. In July 1913 the CPR president approved appropriations totalling $2,798,613 for double-tracking of the main line in BC from Revelstoke west (24 miles), Kamloops east (25 miles) and Kamloops west (9 miles). This work was completed by November 1914, along with 80 miles of double-track between Vancouver and Hope.[96]

By 1914 Shaughnessy had won the long battle with Hill for a dominant position for the CPR in southern BC, but he had not achieved a total victory, since from 1913 on the GN still competed with the CPR for the traffic of the Kootenay and Boundary districts to Vancouver. In 1915 the CPR finally completed a line from Lethbridge through the Crow's Nest Pass and southern BC to Vancouver which would serve as an alternate route to the company's main line. The Spiral Tunnels and the Connaught Tunnel reduced the steep grades on two parts of the main line and enabled it to compete in the 1920s for westbound grain traffic. And finally, the CPR acquired a railway on Vancouver Island and an enormous land grant rich in timber.

Most of the discussion of the CPR to this point has focused on plans and policies which were designed to increase the company's freight traffic. But in this period, when the automobile was in its infancy, passenger traffic also provided a lucrative source of revenue, particularly for transcontinental railways.

CHAPTER SEVEN

Serving the Traveller

The CPR's transcontinental passenger service developed to serve the needs of a number of different groups. First, it provided transportation for immigrants to Canada, particularly those who migrated to the prairie West in large numbers in the period 1900–14. Second, it served Canadians from Eastern Canada who were settling in the West. And finally, it enabled wealthy tourists from Eastern Canada, the US, Britain, and continental Europe to travel in comfort to the Canadian Rockies and then to the Orient on the company's *Empress* steamships which connected with the CPR at Vancouver. The transcontinental trains travelled from Montreal to Vancouver, with connections eastward to Quebec City and Saint John.

The CPR launched its transcontinental passenger service in June 1886. Senior CPR officials now put train crews "under strict discipline to adhere to schedules, something that had been less highly stressed in the past."[1] The day-to-day operation of the passenger service was looked after by the passenger traffic manager. This position, created in 1885, was held by Lucius Tuttle (1885–7) and then by David McNicoll (1887–99).[2] But it was Van Horne who shaped the main features of the company's passenger service and hotel system until his retirement as president in 1899.

Van Horne was particularly concerned about the comfort of CPR passengers, especially those who travelled first-class. There were three classes of passage – colonist, second-class, and first-class. The colonist cars were designed to serve the expected flood of immigrants from Britain and continental Europe. The colonist sleeping car was quite spartan; its berths were not upholstered, to facilitate easy cleaning and disinfecting, and passengers had to supply their own bedding or buy it from a CPR agent. The second-class car was, in Ted Hart's description, "a glorified version of colonist," but it had a different designation to meet the social concerns of middle-class passengers who did not wish to be classed as immigrants.[3]

But it was first-class passengers who brought in the largest revenue, and so Van Horne endeavoured to provide them with the best and most comfortable accommodation available. To do this, and to avoid paying the high lease rates of the Pullman Palace Car Company of Chicago, he decided not only that the CPR would acquire its own sleeping, parlour, and dining cars, but also that it would improve upon the Pullman cars. So he had the Barney and Smith Company of Dayton, Ohio, construct a number of cars to his specifications.[4] Sleeping cars in American railways were fitted with short berths that were uncomfortable to many passengers. Van Horne had commissioned cars "constructed of larger dimensions in height and width and equipped with longer and wider berths." In 1882 he began ordering wheels for the passenger cars from Krupp, the famous German steel company and armaments manufacturer, because the Krupp wheel seemed "to be the most economical and reliable wheel made for passenger service."[5] Accommodation in parlour and sleeping cars was sold separately from passage and was only available to those who held first-class tickets. By 1887 Van Horne was convinced that the CPR parlour and sleeping car service was "infinitely more popular with the travelling public" than the Pullman service. "It is to the vast superiority of our sleeping car service," he continued, "that our large transcontinental passenger business during the past year has been mainly due."[6] Van Horne also paid much attention to comfort and service in CPR dining cars.

The CPR hotel system began as an offshoot of the dining-car service. Many travellers on the CPR transcontinental trains could not afford the cost of dining-car meals, so with the company's blessing, privately owned restaurants were soon set up at divisional points where a quick, cheap meal could be obtained while the locomotive was being changed, watered, or fuelled. And in the mountainous sections in BC where it was impractical to haul heavy dining cars over the steep grades, the CPR established its own restaurants. At first, temporary quarters in the form of dining cars pulled to a siding were used. In the spring of 1886 work on restaurant stops began at three key locations: the Mount Stephen House at Field in the Kicking Horse Pass, the Glacier House at the foot of the Illecillewaet Glacier near Rogers Pass, and the Fraser Canyon House at North Bend. Mount Stephen House opened in the fall of 1886 and the other two in the following summer. All three buildings had been designed by Thomas Sorby, an English-born architect who at the time was one of the most prominent architects in Victoria,[7] though Van Horne had also participated in designing these dining stations. As Walter Vaughan observes, "Van Horne now began to realize a long-held dream by starting a chain of picturesque hotels commanding the choicest views in the Rockies and the Selkirks. He found recreation and delight in sketching, suggesting, or modifying the elevations and plans of these structures."[8] The three dining hotels had similar plans – three storeys in the centre, two storeys in one wing, and one storey in the other. The Mount Stephen House contained two dining rooms instead of one. Each building had six or seven bedrooms. With their clapboard siding and ornamental carving under the eaves and windows, they bore some resemblance to Swiss buildings. As Hart stresses, "the Swiss appearance was deliberate, planned to fit in with what would become a "Swiss" or "Canadian Alps" advertising theme for the CPR's mountain promotional material."[9]

The establishment of Mount Stephen House and Glacier House was also part of Van Horne's plan to "capitalize the scenery" of the mountains in British Columbia.[10] Well-to-do tourists would be induced to travel on the CPR to see the spectacular mountain scenery on the main line in British Columbia. This policy was best exemplified by the building of the Banff Springs Hotel in 1886–8. In 1885 CPR surveyors had discovered hot springs on the eastern slope of the Rockies near Banff Station. The federal government set aside 10 square miles around the hot springs as a national park, to protect the environment and to ensure that the hot springs would be available to the general public. Recognizing the tourist potential of the hot springs, Van Horne decided to build a luxury hotel on a magnificent site – a promontory overlooking the Bow Valley with a view toward the Fairholme Range. He chose Bruce Price, a prominent New York architect who had been hired by the company early in 1886 to design the CPR's new combined station and office building in Montreal (the Windsor Hotel) to design the Banff hotel.[11] Harold Kalman contends that Price wanted the hotel to be viewed as "a romantic structure," and the steep-hipped roofs, pointed finialed dormers, corner turrets and oriels "seem to have been freely derived from a medieval castle." He also maintains that the building was intended not as a French château but rather as a Scottish castle, for Van Horne, who influenced the design, seems to have regarded the environment as a reincarnation of the Scottish Highlands.[12] In any case it was to be a fine building in a magnificent setting. The plan specified two frame wings each five storeys high, with the top storey forming part of the dormer roof. A large central hall dominated the main floor, and tiered verandahs at the end of the wings provided visual access to the mountains. The hotel would accommodate 280 visitors, and the nearby bath house provided ten rooms and a swimming pool. The foundations were laid in the winter of 1886–7, while construction proper was started that spring and completed by the autumn. The finishing work on the interior was done in the winter of 1887–8 and the hotel opened in June 1888.[13] And finally, the company erected a small chalet at Lake Louise in 1890; it burned in 1892 and was rebuilt the following year.[14]

The Vancouver Hotel was the CPR's first city hotel. The boom town was just starting to develop in 1886–7. Van Horne realized that the CPR would need a first-class hotel there, when the western terminus was extended from Port Moody to Vancouver in 1887, to serve the present and future needs of CPR rail and steamship passengers disembarking at Vancouver. He chose a site at the corner of Granville and Georgia streets, which then was on "the fringes" of the city. The CPR sought to develop Granville as a commercial street, and make substantial real estate profits by selling its lands in this area. Construction was started in July 1886, and the luxurious Hotel Vancouver opened for business on 16 May 1887. It also was designed by Thomas Sorby. His plan called for a "simplified Château-style" building, but the architect later claimed that the CPR had not followed his design and had built the hotel "without the architecture." Although the six-storey brick building did retain some features of the château style, notably the steep-pitched tile roofs, it was a rather plain structure. The launching of the CPR's three Pacific *Empress* steamships in 1891 soon brought a substantial increase in the number of first-class passengers needing hotel accommodation in Vancouver, since each of the new ships could accommodate up to 160 first-class passengers. As a result, a block on the south side of the hotel was added in 1893.[15]

Shaughnessy, who became president in June 1899, continued the tradition of concern for the CPR's passenger services and hotel system. "We try to make our employees understand," he remarked shortly after assuming the presidency, "that every passenger on our train is entitled to, and must receive, just the same courtesy and consideration that he would if he were a guest of the Company."[16] Another of his ambitions was to improve and extend the CPR's hotel system in Western Canada, in order to meet the demands for first-class accommodation of the increasing number of well-to-do tourists.

Shaughnessy was concerned about the hotel situation in Vancouver because by 1900 there were not enough rooms in the company's hotel to accommodate the increase in travellers resulting from the popularity of the Pacific *Empresses* and the expansion of Vancouver. (The 1901 census revealed that the population of Vancouver exceeded that of Victoria.[17]) Shaughnessy, who visited Vancouver in October 1900 on his annual inspection tour of Western Canada, acknowledged the inadequacy of the Hotel Vancouver. He decided to tear down everything except the 1893 addition and build a new hotel with at least 250 rooms.[18]

After an architectural competition, in January 1901 the company awarded the commission to design the new hotel to Francis Mawson Rattenbury, a young Victoria architect. Born in Leeds, England, in 1867, Rattenbury had trained as an architect. An ambitious young man, he was inspired by reports in the British press of the rapidly expanding economy of British Columbia and emigrated to Victoria in 1892. He may have chosen Victoria over Vancouver because he hoped to obtain commissions for provincial government buildings. His hope was soon realized, for in March 1893 he was awarded the commission to design the new legislative buildings for the province. This was an astonishing coup for a young man of twenty-five who had only resided in the province for a year. However, his design for the legislative buildings (opened in 1898) was instrumental in establishing his reputation and he soon had numerous commissions for commercial buildings in Victoria and Vancouver. In November 1900 he submitted his plans in the competition for a new Hotel Vancouver,[19] the most important commission in BC since the construction of the legislative buildings. Rattenbury was called to Montreal in February 1901 to discuss his design, which was in the château style, strongly influenced by Bruce Price's Château Frontenac and Edward Maxwell's brick-and-stone CPR station in Vancouver. He got along well with the CPR officials, particularly David McNicoll, the company's general manager, who told Rattenbury that he would do a great deal of work for the CPR in the future. As Anthony Barrett and Rhodri Liscombe observe, "Rattenbury assumed the lucrative, if unofficial, position of architect to the CPR's Pacific Division."[20] He sent working drawings for the Hotel Vancouver to Montreal in April 1901. In June he was instructed to revise these drawings because the size of the project had been reduced to an addition to the old hotel. The revised design, accepted by the CPR in January 1902, retained some elements of the château style but it was mostly of the Italian Renaissance *palazzo* style. The design represented a shift in CPR policy to "preference for the Renaissance and Classical styles for metropolitan hotels," a policy which was continued by the Maxwells in the Royal Alexandra hotel in Winnipeg and the Palliser hotel in Calgary.[21]

Construction of the addition to the Hotel Vancouver began in December 1901, when the foundations were dug next to the original hotel. By November 1902 the roof was finished and internal plastering started. Most of the machinery was installed between the fall of 1903 and the summer of 1904, while the fitting up of the interior was completed in 1905. Rattenbury's addition was connected to the original hotel and linked on the exterior by a broad colonnaded verandah. The reconstructed hotel accommodated 300 guests, whereas the old hotel had served only about 200.[22] Barrett and Liscombe conclude that the Hotel Vancouver project was substantially curtailed "either because the CPR decided to reserve funds for a new hotel at Victoria, where land and labour prices were lower, or because the Hotel Vancouver became too busy to permit demolition."[23] The need for more first-class hotel accommodation in Vancouver continued to increase from 1905 to 1912. In 1912 the CPR began construction of a new Hotel Vancouver to replace the existing building. It was designed by Walter S. Painter, the CPR's former chief architect. After obtaining professional training as an apprentice in architects' offices in Pennsylvania and Michigan, Painter moved to Toronto in 1904 and established the firm of Brown and Painter, design engineers and contractors. This firm did a good deal of railway business, such as reinforcing concrete roundhouses and building machine shops and freight terminals. In 1905 he was hired by the CPR as chief architect and given responsibility for the design and administration of CPR buildings. Painter left the CPR in 1911 to form an architectural firm in Vancouver with Francis S. Swales. This firm supervised the design of the building, which had no château features and was finally completed in 1916 at a cost of $2 million.[24]

Shaughnessy's concern for the CPR's hotel development was evident on 13 June 1899, the day after he had become president, when he informed Whyte that he had decided on a site for a CPR hotel in Winnipeg. "We propose," he remarked, "to put up a large, handsome and expensive building, and to operate it on the lines of the Château Frontenac." The hotel was not to be located in "the heart of the City" on Main Street near Portage Avenue, since there were a number of good hotels in that district. Instead, it would be located next to the company's station on north Main Street, a poor neighborhood. Shaughnessy hoped that construction of a hotel in that location would improve "the class of buildings on that portion of Main Street, near the station."[25] After further discussions among CPR officials, he decided that the old station was inadequate and should be replaced by a new structure.

However, the combined hotel-station project necessitated negotiations with the city of Winnipeg for sharing construction costs for a subway on Main Street over which the CPR main line would pass. It would remove the dangers posed by the existing level-crossing on

Main Street and would be located just west of the proposed hotel and station. These negotiations were protracted; in December 1902 an exasperated Shaughnessy exclaimed to Whyte, "It is a disgrace that passengers arriving at and departing from Winnipeg should be furnished with no better accommodation than can be had at our present station, but this fact is due entirely to the obstructions that have been placed in our way by the City." The president asked Whyte to "take hold of this matter vigorously." Finally, on 12 September 1903, Whyte and CPR Solicitor J.A.M. Aikins attended a private meeting with the mayor and aldermen and reached a general agreement, which the CPR board tentatively approved on 15 September.[26] The formal agreement was signed by the two parties on 5 December, and then city council passed the required by-law on 15 January 1904. The CPR undertook to build a 100-foot-wide subway under its tracks at the crossing of Main Street, entirely at its own expense and to "indemnify ... the City from all damages and compensation" to businesses affected by the construction. The company also promised to construct a "more commodious" station, an office building, and a hotel just east of the subway. One unusual feature of the agreement was the CPR's promise that whenever snow melted or was blown away on Main Street under the subway, it would bring in snow "free of charge" so that sleighs could pass through without difficulty![27] The Manitoba government passed legislation in February 1904 which gave city council the authority to carry out the agreement.[28]

Shaughnessy stopped briefly in Winnipeg on 18 September 1903 on his annual inspection trip to Western Canada. He expressed to a reporter his pleasure at the subway agreement and promised that the hotel and station would be "proceeded with and completed as rapidly as possible." Whyte informed the press that excavations for the new station and hotel would be started right away and would continue until winter forced a halt. He indicated that construction would resume as early as possible in the spring of 1904, when the subway construction would commence. The estimated cost of the combined hotel and station was $3,000,000.[29]

The architects for the hotel, station, and office building were the Montreal firm of Edward and W.S. Maxwell, then one of the most prestigious firms in Canada. Its founder, Edward Maxwell, a native of Montreal, had opened his architectural firm in 1891. He designed a new CPR terminal building at Vancouver (1891) that was a bold composition of brick and stone in the château style popularized by the Château Frontenac in Quebec City. His younger brother, William Sutherland Maxwell, became his partner in 1902.[30] When the Maxwells presented preliminary plans for the Winnipeg project in February 1904, Shaughnessy had Whyte come to Montreal to discuss them. The new station was to house offices related directly to railway operations, as well as offices connected with other aspects of the company's activities in Winnipeg. The Maxwells submitted two plans for the station and offices. In one, the administrative offices would be located on several stories above the station offices, while in the second plan the former would be located in a separate building next to the station. Shaughnessy remarked to Whyte that "Architecturally, the low building for the waiting-rooms would be a decided improvement on a building several stories high with accommodation for offices above." Whyte evidently agreed with the president's view, and it was decided to have a separate office building.[31]

In May 1904, the contract for the hotel, station, and office building in Winnipeg was let to the lowest bidder, Peter Lyall and Sons of Montreal. This firm, one of the largest in Canada, had been founded in Montreal by a Scottish immigrant, Peter Lyall, and his five sons, in 1876. Lyall and Sons began work on the hotel in June 1904. Frederick J. O'Leary, an engineering graduate of McGill University who had some architectural skills, was appointed superintendent of the project, reporting directly to Whyte. He was assisted by a clerk of works who had drafting and surveying skills. The two men were to supervise construction and ensure that the contractor followed the architect's plans. Shaughnessy informed Whyte that "We have found O'Leary thoroughly competent and very reliable in connection with other works that he has supervised for us."[32] The station and office building were completed in April 1905. Whyte was pleased with his "new quarters" which, he informed Van Horne, "are much brighter and [more] pleasant than the ones just vacated." The hotel was completed in March 1906 and opened in July.[33] The station had six storeys, the office building five, and the hotel eight.

Shaughnessy believed that the name of the new hotel would be important for attracting business, since the hotel would be in competition with a number of other large establishments in Winnipeg. At one point he thought that the most suitable name would be "The Canadian Pacific Hotel."[34] However, the name "Royal Alexandra" was selected, although it is not known who proposed it. The association of the hotel with King Edward VII's consort was no doubt designed to enhance its reputation as a first-class hotel. The Royal Alexandra Hotel was a simple block in a Renaissance style with classical detail and a flat roof. The lower two storeys were all stone while the remaining six were pressed red brick with stone trimmings. The beaux-arts style was reflected in the design, no doubt due to the influence of W.S. Maxwell who had studied at the École des beaux-arts in Paris. The hotel had over 300 bedrooms, most with an adjoining private bathroom. The kitchen enabled the hotel to serve 500 people at one sitting; the main dining room was very spacious – 50 feet by 125 feet.[35] Most of the design work for the furnishings, linens, and the interior of the hotel was done by Kate Reed, the wife of Hayter Reed, who had been appointed manager of the company's new hotel department in January 1905.[36] On occasion Shaughnessy passed judgment on her proposals. Mrs. Reed had chosen a sheaf of wheat as the dominant design for the hotel's carpets, linen, and chandeliers. "I am afraid," he remarked, "that it [sheaf of wheat] would be a bit monotonous if used to such an extent as would be necessary in a large hotel situated at the most important point on our system west of Montreal where people from all directions will be guests. I think that the Winnipeg hotel should be made characteristically Canadian Pacific, and ... that our crest, the shield with the beaver, as used on our folders, could be made very attractive, besides being a most valuable advertisement."[37]

The Royal Alexandra soon became a popular hotel for businessmen and tourists who wanted first-class accommodation in Winnipeg. In 1910 Shaughnessy decided that it needed to be enlarged, and the Maxwells were hired to design an addition. The existing building would not support the addition of three storeys, so the expansion involved an extension at ground level. The work, completed in 1913, added 184 rooms, a large ballroom and a substantial banquet hall to the hotel.[38]

Shaughnessy's desire to expand the CPR's passenger business was also reflected in his establishment of a steamship service on the Pacific coast. Although the CPR had been interested in developing such a service as early as 1885, funds were scarce and the necessary ships could not be obtained. The company therefore relied on the Canadian Pacific Navigation Company (CPN) to provide a steamship service connecting Vancouver, Victoria, and Puget Sound. This company, partly owned by the Hudson's Bay Company (HBC), had long dominated the BC coastal trade. Then, in 1894, the CPR invested $221,000 in the construction of a fast, steel-paddle steamer, the *Prince Rupert*, for service between Vancouver and Victoria. The CPN, realizing that the world depression of the time left it in a poor position to compete with the CPR's trim new ship, fomented an agitation against the CPR in Victoria. And CPR officials, realizing the unpopularity of their company in Victoria, decided not to press the issue. The *Prince Rupert* was placed on the run between Digby and Saint John in 1895.[39]

Dissatisfaction with the CPN's ships and services grew steadily after

1894. Many of its ships were out-dated and not in good repair. In Victoria there was much unrest because the CPN's best steamer had been diverted to the Alaska run and the important Vancouver-Victoria service was being maintained by a slower and smaller steamer, the *Charmer*. In the summer of 1898 the Victoria Board of Trade approached the CPR to see if it might be interested in providing steamship service between Victoria and Vancouver. Shaughnessy replied that the CPR had been trying for some time to improve the Victoria-Vancouver service. "The navigation company [CPN]," he remarked, "has promised to build a suitable passenger boat for the service. If this be not done within a reasonable time we shall resort to other means." It soon became clear that the CPN, with an aging fleet and inadequate financial reserves, was not interested in improving its service. The HBC consequently sought to dispose of its large block of CPN shares, which might soon be a liability rather than an asset. Shaughnessy saw the opportunity for the CPR to obtain a coastal steamship service. The company's interest in the coastal trade had been stimulated by the Klondike gold rush, when the CPR transferred two of its ocean-going vessels to the Vancouver-Skagway run.[40] Negotiations for CPR acquisition of the CPN, which were carried on late in 1900, were kept secret so that the CPR could, as Shaughnessy remarked, "secure the [CPN] stock at the price we were willing to pay." Clarence Chipman, chief commissioner of the HBC in Winnipeg, acted for the CPR and quietly bought up most of the CPN stock which the HBC did not already own. This procedure undoubtedly prevented a substantial increase in the price of CPN stock which would have resulted if the CPR's intention to take over the Navigation Company had become known. The CPR president was very grateful to Chipman and praised "the prompt and efficient manner" in which he had carried out the stock transaction. The negotiations were completed in Victoria on 10 January 1901 and the next day Shaughnessy was informed by telegram that the CPR was in control of the CPN. The CPR had acquired nearly all of the Navigation Company's stock, for $531,000. Shaughnessy regarded the takeover as a means of obtaining "a larger percentage of the passenger business" to and from northern BC, the Yukon, and Alaska for the ports of Victoria and Vancouver, although the Klondike boom was over by 1901.[41]

The formal transfer of the CPN to a new board of directors took place on 5 March 1901. The CPR's Captain, James W. Troup, was appointed manager, but the fleet and services continued to be owned and operated by the CPN. At the time of the takeover, the CPN fleet was heavily mortgaged. In March-April 1903 these mortgages were paid off so that the CPN steamers could be registered in the name of the CPR. Then in May 1903 the company announced that all its coastal steamers would be operated as the CPR's British Columbia Coast Service, with Captain Troup as general superintendent (a title which was later changed to manager).[42]

Captain Troup was an excellent choice for manager of the CPR's coastal steamers. Born in Portland, Oregon, in 1855, Troup took to the river early in life, following the example of his father and grandfather, both of whom were well-known steamboat captains on the Columbia River. By the age of 20 he was already master of a small river steamer. Later he went to the upper Columbia, where he gained fame as "a daring and skillful swiftwater pilot." In 1883 Captain John Irving persuaded him to come to BC. At about this time Irving was organizing the CPN. Troup served with the company until 1886 when he returned to Oregon and worked for 6 years as superintendent of the steamer services of the Oregon Railway and Navigation Company. He then returned to BC to manage the lake and river steamers of the Columbia and Kootenay Navigation Company, in which Irving was a major shareholder. Early in 1897 the CPR purchased the company and retained Troup as manager.[43]

The fourteen-ship fleet of the CPN consisted of a motley assortment of vessels, "varying in size from 175 to 1525 tons and in age from a few weeks to nearly 40 years." Troup sold most of them as opportunities arose and replaced them with the famous *Princess* steamers which he put into service on the Vancouver-Victoria and Alaska runs. The *Charmer* also sailed between Victoria and Vancouver but its slow speed was a source of constant irritation to passengers. Troup decided that it had to be replaced by a new, fast, specially designed vessel. Although he was not a qualified naval architect, he had "a vast practical knowledge of ships and shipbuilding," and he became involved in designing the new steamer, the *Princess Victoria*. He felt that it was desirable that the new ship should be capable of running to Skagway if necessary, and for the Alaska service a propeller-driven vessel was preferable. Troup finally requested a steamer 300 feet long and of nearly 2000 tons gross. He appeared before the CPR board of directors to support his proposal. Most of the directors were opposed to his plan, Shaughnessy included. He declared that such a ship would be "a white elephant, and nothing but a liability to the Company." However, R.B. Angus strongly supported Troup's proposal, declaring that Troup "was a pretty shrewd young man, and that they should give him his ship and let him have a try with it." After much discussion the directors approved Troup's plan.[44]

The *Princess Victoria* was launched at Newcastle-on-the-Tyne on 18 November 1902, and on 26 January 1903 she started for Victoria, reaching her destination on 28 March. It had been decided to build the *Victoria*'s elaborate wooden superstructure in Vancouver in order to avoid a threatened strike of carpenters and joiners at Newcastle. On the evening of 17 August the completed steamer entered regular service. The next day she made the trip from Vancouver to Victoria in 3 hours and 48 minutes, the fastest trip yet made by a merchant ship between the two cities. In some respects the *Victoria* was a luxury ship, for there were four large *en suite* rooms with private bath. The dining saloon seated 90. There were 152 berths in the 78 state-rooms, and on day runs the *Victoria* was licensed to carry 1000 passengers. Victoria and Vancouver now possessed a fast, first-class steamer service. The *Princess Beatrice*, a much smaller ship than the *Princess Victoria*, was built at Esquimalt in 1903 and made her first sailing from Vancouver to Seattle on 20 January 1904. The CPR's Pacific coastal fleet expanded rapidly in the period 1907–14, when the company commissioned nine new Princess steamships.[45]

The CPR's Pacific coastal fleet carried passengers to Victoria and Vancouver from northern BC, the Yukon, Alaska, and Washington State. The fast Vancouver-Victoria service enabled first-class passengers on the Pacific *Empresses* from the Orient to stop in Victoria and then travel in comfort to Vancouver. Similarly, passengers travelling on the *Empresses* to the Orient could spend a few days in Victoria before leaving for their destination. These factors increased the demand for first-class hotel accommodation in both Vancouver and Victoria. The CPR had increased the size of its Hotel Vancouver with an addition which was opened in 1905. Next in Shaughnessy's field of vision was the hotel situation in Victoria.

By the late 1890's Vancouver had emerged as the province's largest city and its metropolitan centre. As Robert McDonald observes, "With the shift in B.C. from an outward to inward economic orientation, lower transportation costs, made possible by its fine harbour, mainland location, and CPR connection, gave Vancouver a crucial trade advantage over Victoria." Vancouver took the lead over Victoria as the principal port of entry on the coast in 1899, a lead which widened in the period 1900–14.[46] A number of Victoria lawyers, politicians, and businessmen who were concerned about their city's economic decline proposed to use Victoria's advantages of a mild climate and "English" ambience to develop tourism as a means of arresting this trend. The most important among them was Harry Barnard, a successful Victoria lawyer. By 1902 he was convinced that in order for Victoria to develop as a tourist resort, the city needed a large, first-class hotel, and that the CPR was the only company with sufficient financial resources to build it. In 1902 he was elected to the Victoria City Council and began lobbying his fellow aldermen to have the city offer concessions to the CPR to induce it to build a Victoria hotel.[47] Supporting him was his brother-in-law, John A. Mara, a wealthy Victoria businessman who had moved from his native Toronto to Kamloops at the age of twenty-two in 1862. He became a prosperous Kamloops merchant and also made a good deal of money from his promotion of the Columbia and Kootenay Steam Navigation Company which was sold to the CPR in 1897. Another important figure in the group was David R. Ker, chairman of the Brackman-Ker Milling Company. In 1882 he became a partner in this firm which he expanded in the 1890's by building a new mill and processing imported as well as local cereals. By the turn of the century he was one of the city's most prominent businessmen.[48]

The Victoria Board of Trade took the first steps to interest the CPR in building a hotel in Victoria on 3 December 1901 when it appointed a hotel committee, chaired by John A. Mara. The committee wrote to Shaughnessy enclosing a clipping from "an Eastern paper" which stated that the CPR was considering the construction of a tourist hotel in Victoria "at an early date." The CPR president replied, denying that his company was contemplating such a project. Shaughnessy visited Victoria in mid-June 1902 on his annual inspection trip of Western Canada. Mayor Charles Hayward and the hotel committee met the CPR president and presented "the advantages which Victoria offered for a first class tourist hotel under the management of the c.p.r." Shaughnessy seemed "impressed by the arguments advanced" and promised to discuss the matter with his board of directors. Soon after the meeting, David McNicoll, the CPR's general manager, and Richard Marpole, general superintendent of the company's Pacific division, visited Victoria. The hotel committee arranged a meeting with the two officials, and invited members of city council and the executive of the Victoria Tourist Association. After a long and "satisfactory" meeting, the hotel committee took McNicoll and Marpole to the Douglas Gardens to show its advantages as a site for the hotel. These were the gardens of James Douglas' former residence, and were located close to the legislature buildings, although a building occupied the site. McNicoll agreed to discuss the matter with Shaughnessy on his return to Montreal. The hotel committee secured an option on the Douglas Gardens site and submitted it to McNicoll "who replied that the company had decided not to build."[49]

Late in September 1902 Rattenbury had a meeting in Vancouver with Sir William Van Horne and broached the subject of a CPR hotel in Victoria. Van Horne who was still a member of the CPR's executive committee, was interested in the proposition, and at his request Rattenbury sent him the plan of a hotel on the Douglas Gardens site. On 17 October the president and secretary of the Board of Trade invited Shaughnessy to build a hotel in Victoria. The CPR president was non-committal, observing that the Driard House had an excellent reputation as a tourist hotel and could easily be expanded. If the Board of Trade found that the Driard's owner was unwilling to enlarge his hotel Shaughnessy indicated that the CPR might give further consideration to the hotel question.[50]

The Board of Trade responded by requesting that the city council offer concessions to the CPR for the building of an hotel. In December 1902 the hotel committee persuaded the mayor, city council, and the Victoria Tourist Association to form a committee (which would include a representative from the Board of Trade) to draft "definite proposals which would be likely to meet with the approval of the ratepayers and which would be submitted to the railway company." This "joint committee" drew up three proposals:

1 If the CPR built a tourist hotel on the Douglas Gardens site, the company would be given free water and exemption from taxation for 25 years, subject to ratepayers' approval.
2 If the CPR wished to build the hotel on the James Bay flats, the city would give the land to the company free, subject to ratepayers' approval, but would withhold the exemptions in the first proposal.
3 If the CPR wanted to purchase the Driard Hotel and expand it, the company would receive the same exemptions as in the first proposition.[51]

When the "joint committee" learned that Shaughnessy would be in Victoria on 19 May 1903 to testify before a legislative committee inquiring into the CPR's Columbia and Western land grant, it appointed a four-member sub-committee to present the proposals to Shaughnessy. The members of this sub-committee were Mayor Alexander C. McCandless, J.A. Mara (representing the board of trade), David R. Ker (representing the tourist association), and Herbert Cuthbert (secretary of the tourist association). The sub-committee met with the CPR president on 19 May at 6:15 PM at the Driard Hotel. After the three propositions were presented, there followed a discussion of the relative merits of the Douglas Gardens and the James Bay flats as hotel sites. Shaughnessy then declared: "If the city will supply the site and exempt us from taxation and give us free water for 20 years, we will build a hotel to cost not less than $300,000."

Shaughnessy was clearly determined to obtain the land for the hotel free, which meant building on the James Bay flats which the city owned. Shaughnessy requested that the water and tax concessions be reduced to 20 years, since the company would not have to purchase the land. The sub-committee was delighted with what was the first offer made by the CPR to build a hotel in Victoria. Mayor McCandless thought the only difficult point would be the duration of the tax exemption. The meeting then ended.[52]

The "joint committee" then asked Rattenbury to map out "a ground plan of an hotel he thought likely to meet Sir Thomas' views," hoping that the support of the CPR's "unofficial architect" for BC would help their cause. The sub-committee (minus Ker, who was out of town) and Rattenbury met with Shaughnessy on 20 May. Rattenbury explained that his ground plan envisaged a five-storey building of 150 rooms. The CPR president stated that this was not large enough and that he preferred a hotel plan "of not less than 250 or 300 rooms" even if it cost more than $300,000. There was a full discussion of the term of the tax exemption; the CPR president and the sub-committee agreed "that 15 years should be the term for exemption from taxation and for free water." Shaughnessy then requested that he receive all the requisite documents before 8 June so that he could present the proposition to his board of directors, which was scheduled to meet that afternoon. He expressed confidence that the board would ratify the proposition, observing that "my board has never refused to grant any recommendation of the kind that I have made."[53]

On 9 June the headline on the front page of the *Victoria Colonist* triumphantly proclaimed: "The CPR Decide To Build Tourist Hotel." The CPR board had met on 8 June and endorsed the proposal which Shaughnessy and the "joint committee" had drawn up. It appears that the directors felt they had been presented with a *fait accompli*.[54] Shaughnessy immediately telegraphed the good news to Mayor McCandless: "Our Board has adopted the Hotel project on the general lines indicated in the letter of June First signed by yourself and the other members of the Committee [the "joint committee"]." He emphasized that the city was responsible for filling in the James Bay flats "to the level contemplated by the plans." Shaughnessy wrote the "joint committee" the same day requesting a draft copy of the municipal by-law that would be submitted to the ratepayers, to ensure that it met with the company's approval. "I hope sincerely," he concluded, "that the hotel may assist in bringing to Victoria every season a great many additional tourists and that the Company's action in this matter will be accepted by the citizens of Victoria as an earnest of the Company's good-will and ... its appreciation of the kind treatment that it has always received at the hands of Victoria merchants and shippers."[55] The *Victoria Colonist* urged the city to prepare the James Bay flats for the hotel site as soon as possible and extolled the benefits of the hotel for Victoria. "A hotel accommodating 300 guests," it editorialized, "is worth more to a city, a good deal more, than a factory employing 300 workers, especially when we remember that the c.p.r. to fill that hotel and keep it filled will have to develop and stimulate the steamboat traffic of the port."[56]

The next important step was the ratification of the by-law, passed by council on 24 August 1903, authorizing the city to give the James Bay site to the CPR, to exempt the land from taxation for 15 years from the opening of the hotel, and to grant the CPR a free water supply for 15 years. In return, the CPR undertook to build on the James Bay site "a first class modern hotel of stone or brick" at a minimum cost of $300,000. Throughout the spring and summer of 1903 Harry Barnard campaigned vigorously for ratification of the by-law. He was assisted by several other councillors and by Mayor McCandless. The vote was held on 15 September and the ratepayers approved the by-law by a vote of 1810 to 85.[57] An overjoyed Mayor McCandless immediately telegraphed the results to Shaughnessy who replied, "The good will indicated by the vote is a source of gratification to all of us here. We shall commence work on the plans immediately."[58]

Late in November 1903 Rattenbury was in Montreal to discuss his sketch plans for the hotel with Shaughnessy and Hayter Reed, the company's most influential adviser on hotel operations and plans. Reed had been a career civil servant in the Department of Indian Affairs, starting in 1881 as Indian agent at Battleford and reaching the top position in the department – deputy superintendent-general – in 1893 at the age of forty-four. The rise of the Liberals to power in Ottawa in 1896 spelled the end of Reed's career, for he had been a staunch Conservative. In 1897 he retired from the department on a pension. In January 1900 Shaughnessy was looking for a new manager for the company's most important hotel, the Château Frontenac, and Reed applied for the job. The CPR president was impressed with Reed who, as well as being a good administrator, was a cultivated, well-educated man who had some knowledge of French. Shaughnessy hired Reed. He began his duties as manager of the Château Frontenac on 1 April and remained in this position until he was promoted to the position of manager of the CPR's Hotel Department, effective 1 January 1905.[59]

Reed's wife Kate was soon actively involved in designing furnishings, linens, and chandeliers for the interiors of the new CPR hotels.

Reed had married in 1888, but his wife had died the following year. Kate Armour, eldest daughter of the chief justice of Ontario, married a successful New York lawyer in 1880 and moved to New York City where she made many friends in high social circles. Her husband died in 1893 and she returned to her girlhood home of Cobourg. As a young woman, Kate Armour had been engaged to Hayter Reed, then a young businessman in Cobourg, but the two had quarrelled violently and the wedding had been abandoned. In the winter of 1893–4 she visited Ottawa and met her former lover. A second courtship followed, and the two were married in Ottawa on 16 June 1894.[60]

During the meeting with Shaughnessy, Hayter Reed instructed Rattenbury to divide his commission into three stages to be built in the following order: the main block, the north wing, and the south wing. Rattenbury's exterior plan was a classical reinterpretation of the château style as embodied in the Château Frontenac. Barrett and Liscombe characterize his plan as "a reformed CPR style, an orderly structure, as much Scottish Baronial as French Château"; this was reflected in the entrance which was covered by English Tudor cloisters and flanked by baronial style turrets. Rattenbury was much more eclectic in his design for the interior: an "Old English" style panelled hall, a Chinese glass-roofed palace-garden, a grand dining room with carvings and frescoes, a "Marie Antoinette" style oval ladies' saloon, and a "Queen Anne" style reading room. On 7 May 1904 Rattenbury sent Shaughnessy the working plans, carefully emphasizing that he had used Reed's "valuable suggestions." He expressed regret that the constraints imposed by a $350,000 budget had compelled him to limit the fireproof construction to that part of the building above the kitchen.[61] Shaughnessy forwarded the working plans to Reed in Quebec on 16 May for he wanted to get his "further criticism" before approving them. The CPR president had some of his own comments on the interior design. "It strikes me," Shaughnessy remarked to Reed, "that the space devoted to bathrooms is unnecessarily large, and that our bedroom accommodation is cut down accordingly; and he does not seem to have taken into account the necessity for linen rooms, housemaids' closets, etc. on the different floors."[62] On 26 May Rattenbury received "a shattering telegram" from Shaughnessy: "Plans very incomplete and proposed arrangements will require [a] good many alterations. Returning them to you with [Reed's] memorandum today." Shaughnessy asked Rattenbury either to adopt Reed's proposed changes, "or lay out his suggestions on some separate sheets of tissue paper, so that we may be able to compare the present scheme with his." He then wanted to go over the final revisions with Reed and Rattenbury in Montreal. Reed made a number of major criticisms. He recommended that the bar and billiard room be separated by "arches, or some like structure." He was emphatic that the main drawing room be moved from the ground floor to the first floor, with the ladies drawing room running off it, as in the Château Frontenac and Place Viger hotels. There would then be space for private dining rooms connected to the main dining room. It would also permit the ladies' drawing room to overlook the harbour, "a great feature." He also wanted to avoid the necessity for guests, particularly ladies, to cross the main-floor hallway, which would be used by people from the city, to get to the dining room. Reed also agreed with some of Shaughnessy's criticisms, particularly the absence of linen rooms, and the need to reduce the size of bathrooms and use the space to enlarge the bedrooms.[63]

Rattenbury replied on 3 June. He thought there could be "little difficulty" in meeting most of Reed's suggestions. However, he would not agree with Reed's proposal to put the main dining room and the ladies' drawing room on the first floor. He claimed that Reed had not made this proposal at their conference in November 1903 and maintained that this arrangement had worked very well in popular American hotels in cities such as Boston and Portland, Oregon. He observed that the townspeople would frequent the bar, billiard room, and grill room in the basement rather than the main hall on the ground floor. Then, pleading poor health, he sent his assistant, John Pearce, to confer with Reed in Montreal. He eventually won this point, for the main dining room and the ladies' drawing room were on the ground floor in the final set of working drawings.[64]

The city proceeded to fill in the James Bay flats, a foul-smelling slough and garbage dump, with silt dredged from the harbour and thousands of yards of gravel. It also built a stone-and-concrete causeway across James Bay. But with the "reclaimed" land site ready and waiting, the CPR delayed construction of the hotel by deciding that the hotel could not be properly centred on the causeway using only the land that the city had donated. The company then quietly purchased land west of the reclaimed hotel site. By June 1904 it had bought out all property owners except one, who refused to sell. The city council co-operated by promptly expropriating this lot and extending the tax-free status to the newly acquired land, an action ratified by a large majority of ratepayers.[65]

Tenders for the hotel contract were received in December 1904. Shaughnessy was very concerned at the high figures in the tenders; one from Peter Lyall and Sons was 50 per cent above the CPR's estimate.[66] The contract was finally awarded to J.L. Skene of Gribble and Skene of Victoria, for the sum of $465,000, and was signed on 25 March 1905. The foundations were tendered separately. The total cost of the hotel was about $765,000.[67] Marpole supervised construction for the CPR. A cost-conscious Shaughnessy advised him that his approval was necessary for "changes of any nature or description." "I take it for granted," the CPR president warned, "that you will not permit ... a single change."[68]

Construction of the hotel finally got underway in August 1905. In November Shaughnessy hired Frederick J. O'Leary "to supervise work connected with additions and alterations to any of our hotel buildings." He had been impressed with O'Leary's performance as supervisor during the construction of the Royal Alexandra in 1904–6. "I believe," he informed Whyte, "that he [O'Leary] can save us a great deal of money and at the same time secure better arrangement of hotel buildings for practical operation." Shaughnessy told Rattenbury that the CPR "would like to give Victoria merchants as much of the trade connected with the construction of the building as possible."[69] The CPR president was determined to use the hotel project to build up good relations with Victoria's business community.

Relations between Rattenbury and the CPR grew strained as construction proceeded. In June 1906 Shaughnessy commented that "Mr. Rattenbury, like most architects, is adhering to his own ideas without special reference to the working of the hotel."[70] The situation was further complicated when W.S. Painter was appointed the CPR's chief architect in 1905. In October 1906 the CPR president had a conference with McNicoll, Reed, and Painter regarding the construction of the Victoria hotel. Shaughnessy was upset at learning that Rattenbury "has in many cases proceeded utterly regardless of Mr. Reed's recommendations, with the result that we have not only been put to unnecessary original expense, but we must now spend further money to make corrections." He asked Painter to prepare "sketches and memoranda" regarding Rattenbury's unauthorized changes, which would be sent to Marpole as soon as possible. Marpole was instructed to inform Rattenbury that the company had decided not to erect false columns in the main room on the ground floor, as Rattenbury had proposed.[71]

The situation came to a head on 4 December 1906 when Rattenbury announced that he was severing his connection with the CPR because he refused to change the arrangement of the office and drawing room on the ground floor, as ordered by Painter. Rattenbury's biographer, Terry Reksten, contends that the main reason for the architect's resignation was that Kate Reed had taken charge of the interior design of the hotel. Rattenbury's departure partly resulted from Shaughnessy's "growing displeasure" with the architect's involvement with the GTPR, for in November 1906 Rattenbury announced that he had completed plans for a GTPR hotel in Prince Rupert. Shaughnessy was particularly concerned about Rattenbury's disregard for Hayter Reed's views on the design of the hotel. It is possible that there was a cabal against Rattenbury, for Kate Reed had her sister, Mrs Stewart Gordon, assist her in designing the hotel's interior. With Rattenbury's departure, Kate Reed now had full control over interior decorations; she was also entrusted with the design of the gardens around the hotel. The Vancouver architect G.D. Curties was appointed in Rattenbury's place.[72]

The pace of construction had slowed in 1906 because of city council's delay in preparing the grounds for landscaping. However, construction of the six-storey steel frame central block, which had 163 bedrooms, was completed in the autumn of 1907.[73] Shaughnessy had decided that the new hotel would be named the Empress Hotel, a title which appropriately linked it with the CPR's Pacific steamships.

The official opening of the Empress Hotel was held on Monday, 20 January 1908. Over 50 newspaper men from all "the principal papers" of BC, Washington State, and Oregon were invited as guests of the CPR to attend an afternoon banquet, presided over by Hayter Reed and George Ham, the CPR's manager of public relations. This opening was intended to provide widespread publicity for the hotel, particularly in the American Northwest, and to illustrate the company's desire to develop the American tourist trade. The first speaker at the banquet was Seattle newspaper man Percy Parkinson, who announced his conviction that the beautiful new hotel "will surely attract an army of American visitors." J.S.H. Matson of the *Victoria Colonist* offered a toast to the artistic taste of Hayter Reed and his wife, and to Mr and Mrs Stewart Gordon. Mr Gordon was the manager of the Empress, and his wife had assisted Kate Reed in designing the interior of the hotel and its furnishings. In the evening a dinner was held in the main dining room, to formally open the hotel to the general public. It was attended by many people from Victoria and other areas of Vancouver Island, as well as from the mainland. After the dinner, "the spacious palm room was thronged by the visitors in evening dress. Coffee and liquors were partaken of and to the strains of the orchestra a general promenade was formed." The *Victoria Colonist* reporter exhausted his stock of superlatives in describing the hotel, which would he felt attract many wealthy tourists to the city. "It [the Empress] is a permanent token to the wealthy travelling public," he remarked, "that Victoria can offer them entertainment that is not to be surpassed in any city on the continent." On 22 October 1908 the Victoria Board of Trade held a lavish banquet in the Empress Hotel with Shaughnessy as the guest of honour. In his speech the CPR president expressed his pleasure with the new hotel, declaring, to great applause, that "of all the company's works which have been completed in my time none has given me more satisfaction."[74]

The north and south wings of the Empress, planned in outline by Rattenbury, were built between 1909 and 1914 under the supervision of Walter Painter, who also added a ballroom at the rear. The château design, as represented by the Empress Hotel, influenced other Canadian architects. The Château Laurier in Ottawa (1912), the Fort Garry Hotel in Winnipeg (1913), and the Macdonald Hotel in Edmonton (1915) were all designed in the château style by the Montreal firm of Ross and MacFarlane.[75]

The last major CPR hotel built in Western Canada before the First World War was the Palliser Hotel in Calgary. Calgary's economic growth was closely connected with the development of the livestock industry and the city's key position as the main transportation centre in Alberta. The opening of southern Alberta to farming in the early 1900s produced rapid growth in Calgary, where population increased from 4,398 in 1901 to 43,704 in 1911. Shaughnessy was impressed by this expansion, and decided to construct a large new CPR station in the city in May 1907. "There can be little doubt," he observed, "that Calgary itself will continue to grow and that a building which at this time would appear almost extravagant will in the not remote future be quite warranted by the traffic." Walter Painter drew up a plan of a four-storey main building and two wings, each two storeys in height. Since the board of trade building occupied the chosen site, it had to be demolished before construction could begin. The station opened in 1912.[76]

Throughout 1910 Whyte pushed very strongly for a CPR hotel in Calgary. Shaughnessy opposed the project at first, not wishing to antagonize existing hoteliers in a city "which has become such a large commercial centre and is growing so rapidly." By November, however, he had changed his mind. He was now convinced that a CPR hotel in Calgary was "almost an essential link in our mountain hotel system"; it could provide additional accommodation for the large number of tourists who wanted to visit the mountains in the summer and fall, and so relieve the pressure on the company's mountain hotel system. After lengthy negotiations the CPR extracted valuable tax concessions in return for building a large 350 room hotel – named the Palliser – next to the new CPR station. The city agreed on a fixed annual assessment of $4,000 and a provision that it would never ask for further concessions or increases because of local improvements. Since property in the vicinity of the Palliser was valued at around $1,000 a frontage foot in 1911, with land assessed at fair value and buildings at 50 per cent of actual value, Calgary was paying considerably for the new luxury hotel.[77]

The chief architect for the hotel was William Maxwell, who with his elder brother had designed the new CPR hotel, station, and office building in Winnipeg. Shaughnessy was delighted with his plans. "I think that the layout of the proposed hotel in Calgary," he informed Whyte in May 1911, "in the amended drawings that Maxwell showed me to-day, is everything that could be desired." The contract was awarded to Peter Lyall and Sons, the builders of the Royal Alexandra, who by then had a branch office in Regina. Construction, which began in March 1912, was supervised by F.L. Ellingwood, an American architect who had recently been appointed as the company's superintendent of building construction and whose abilities Shaughnessy greatly respected. The hotel was completed in the summer of 1914 at a total cost of almost $2 million. The nine-storey hotel was, at 120 feet, the tallest building in the city. It was modelled on the big-city hotels of the East coast of the United States, with an E-block plan of three towers and each of its major rooms in a different style. The lobby and exterior facade were Renaissance revival, and the immense dining room (142 x 38 feet) was done in Tudor style. It had 350 rooms, each with private bath. The Palliser boasted the longest bar in the Canadian West; it connected directly with the station platform at the side of the hotel. An architectural historian has suggested that the configuration of three towers made the hotel resemble the grain elevators which in 1914 were located just down the street. Calgarians fondly nicknamed it "the castle by the tracks" and it "soon became the pride and joy of the town and a centre of social activities [for the well-to-do] ... Even then [1914], the hotel established a reputation of supplying the utmost in comfort and convenience for its guests."[78] The building was to dominate Calgary's skyline for over 50 years.

Shaughnessy directed a substantial expansion of the CPR's mountain hotels in Western Canada in the period 1899–1914. The first to receive his attention was Château Lake Louise: a small hotel was on the site but even in the depression of the 1890s its limited number of guest rooms could not meet the demands of mountaineers and mountain lovers. Construction of a new hotel began in 1899 and small portions were built each year until it was completed in 1908. Francis Rattenbury designed at least one of these extensions in 1902, in a picturesque arts and crafts style. In 1912 construction began on a large concrete wing, containing 350 rooms, which Walter Painter had designed.

Rattenbury also designed a major addition to Mount Stephen House in 1901 in the chalet style. It contained 50 rooms and was completed in 1902. The hotel at Glacier House consisted of a small central building connected to an annex of 30 rooms. In 1904 the CPR started work on a second wing (designed by Rattenbury), which was completed in 1906. It contained 54 rooms and had conveniences such as baths, steam heating and an elevator. The addition was designed in keeping with the chalet style.[79]

The most important of the CPR mountain hotels was the Banff Springs Hotel. The 1894 *Baedeker Guide to Canada* listed it as one of the five top hotels in the country. It was especially noted for its excellent cuisine and good service. By 1900 it had become "one of the top two or three mountain resorts on the North American continent," and was turning into a very profitable venture for the CPR. The hotel was open from 15 May to 15 October. In the 1902 season hotel guests numbered 3,890; in 1904 this figure had risen to 9,684, and many potential guests had been turned away for lack of accommodation. The hotel was now serving an international clientèle, for the 1905 hotel register showed names from South Africa, Holland, France, Austria, England, Japan, Hong Kong, and the United States.[80]

To meet the demands of an expanding international clientèle, in 1900 the CPR started a program of extending and improving the hotel. From 1900–10 all modifications related directly to the original building. The most extensive addition was made in 1902–3. The west wing of the original structure was duplicated on a site a few feet south of the copied wing. The two wings were joined by a low, split-level wooden passageway. This added 200 rooms to the hotel. When the refurbished hotel opened in May for the 1907 season, it was filled to capacity with 450 registered guests. The years 1907 to 1910 were overflow seasons; in the summer of 1910 almost 400 persons were sent back to the CPR station in Banff to find shelter in sleeping cars! The 1911 season was even busier, for over 22,000 people stayed at the hotel.[81]

In 1910 the CPR decided that further modifications of the Banff Springs should be directed toward the ultimate end of a new hotel. Although this plan was not accomplished until 1928, considerable planning was done from 1911 to 1914 by Walter Painter. He was strongly influenced by Price's works and by the entire CPR château tradition. Although the company had moved away from the château design for its city hotels, "the château was still held to be an appropriate mode for all mountain resorts." While the hotel was closed in the winter of 1911–12, the existing centre portion of the hotel was torn out and a new reinforced concrete wing was built. It was designed to become part of an eleven-storey centre tower. Two swimming pools were also constructed at this time. During the off-seasons of 1912–13 and 1913–14, Painter undertook the contract to complete the centre wing, which was called the Painter Tower. It had a dining room, a large rotunda which became the hotel's central lobby, and bedrooms for over 300 guests. The Painter Tower was ready for business when the hotel opened in May 1914. The total cost of the new tower was about $2 million.[82]

Kate Reed was responsible for designing the new interiors of the Banff Springs Hotel. She also was involved in designing much of the interior decoration for Glacier House and Château Lake Louise. At the latter hotel she even became involved in landscaping; it was she who introduced the famous Iceland poppies to the grounds at Lake Louise.[83]

The CPR also added several new small hotels in the BC interior. In 1896 the company constructed a hotel at Revelstoke. This hotel, which had a distinctive gambrel roof and may have been designed by Rattenbury, was built immediately behind the station with a view over Mount Begbie. The Hotel Sicamous was built in 1898 on the shore of beautiful Shuswap Lake, at the junction of the main line and the Shuswap and Okanagan (which served the northern Okanagan Valley). Both these hotels were minor extensions of the CPR's mountain hotel system; they served those who wished to hunt or fish or who wished to transfer to branch-line trains to the south.[84]

Under Shaughnessy's firm guidance, the CPR had greatly expanded its hotel system in Western Canada from 1899 to 1914 to serve the needs of the first-class traveller. Three large luxury hotels were built in Winnipeg, Calgary, and Victoria, while the Hotel Vancouver was first expanded, then replaced by a new structure. The company's system of mountain hotels, the brainchild of Van Horne, was greatly enlarged. The most extensive work was done on the Banff Springs Hotel, which developed a world-wide reputation as a first-class luxury hotel. The Château Lake Louise, Mount Stephen House, and Glacier House were all expanded to meet the demands of both mountaineers and mountain lovers. Apart from being profitable ventures in themselves, all these hotels and the *Empress* steamships generated considerable first-class passenger traffic for the CPR. The policy of expanding passenger services begun by Van Horne and continued under Shaughnessy proved quite profitable. The CPR obtained substantial revenues from transporting immigrants and Canadians to the prairie West, for the company had envisioned the major shift of population westward in Canada and was well prepared by the time the heaviest migrations began.

CHAPTER EIGHT

Land and Settlement
Policies in the Prairie West

From its inception, the CPR had been a large landholder in the prairie West, for under its 1881 charter the federal government granted the company a land subsidy of 25 million acres in that region. The conferring of large land subsidies to railways was a practice imported from the United States, where it flourished from 1850 until 1871. The 39 million acres awarded to the Northern Pacific Railroad in 1864 was the largest grant made to an American railway.[1]

The CPR land subsidy differed from American practice in several important respects. First, it was not awarded on a mileage basis, for it provided, as Kaye Lamb observes, "a fixed acreage, regardless of the length of the line."[2] Second, in the United States the land was granted on either side of the railway line as constructed, so that although the railway lands would represent the average quality of land in a particular territory, the differences in land quality between sections could be quite substantial. Under the CPR charter, the company was not required to accept lands which "consist in a material degree of land not fairly fit for settlement."[3] James B. Hedges, an authority on CPR land policies, concludes that this "fairly fit for settlement" clause was the result of the experience of the CPR promoters who, through their control of the St Paul and Pacific Railroad in the late 1870s, "knew at first hand the workings of land subsidies in the United States, who knew what pitfalls to avoid and what concessions to obtain." The CPR used this clause to ensure that it obtained the best land available in the Canadian prairie West.[4] Third, in the United States there were many railways in the West in competition with each other for land sales as well as for traffic. So most railways set up land-selling organizations to move the land fast, with the result that much land speculation occurred before permanent settlement. In Canada, the CPR was the only connection inside the national boundaries between the Prairies and the outside world in the period 1883–1902. Any settlement therefore generated traffic to its main line.[5]

The lands the CPR selected were in Manitoba and the North-West Territories, where the federal government controlled all public land (it did not have such control in Ontario or British Columbia). The BC government did agree to reserve a railway belt of 10 million acres along the CPR main line, but the company declined to select any of its lands from this largely mountainous region.[6] In 1871–2 the Canadian government adopted the American system of a square township of 36 sections and a free homestead of 160 acres (a quarter-section). Much of the CPR's land grant was expected to be along the main line, and was to consist of "alternate sections of 640 acres each, extending back 24 miles deep, on each side of the railway" from Winnipeg to Jasper House. The practice of making grants in alternate sections was borrowed from the United States.[7] In Canada, most of the odd-numbered sections in a township were reserved for railway lands. But even if all the land in the enormous reserve (a belt of land 48-miles wide) had been available and acceptable, it would have supplied only about 10 million acres. Some of the land in this reserve had already been alienated, some could be claimed by the Hudson's Bay Company, while sections 11 and 29 in each township were set aside as "school lands." Thus, a large part of CPR lands had to be found away from the main line reserve.[8]

Although the stated policy of making such a large land grant was to enable the CPR to raise revenue for the construction of the main line, it is doubtful if either the Macdonald government or the CPR promoters expected to raise much revenue from land sales or land-grant bonds in the construction period, if American experience were a reliable guide. For example, the construction costs of the Union Pacific Railroad were covered mainly by federal government bonds ($27 million) and the company's first mortgage bonds ($23,700,000); land-grant bonds raised less than $6,064,000.[9] The Canadian Pacific promoters had raised substantial sums from the sale of St Paul and Pacific lands in Minnesota, but this railway ran through a heavily settled area, while the CPR would be constructed through the prairie West which had few white settlers in 1881. The CPR's objective in the 1880's was to attract the individual settler and farmer and encourage him to stay on his holding and develop it, in order to create traffic for the railway. As CPR president George Stephen wrote in May 1881, "It is *settling*, not *selling* that we must aim at ... if our lands won't sell we will give them away to settlers."[10]

In March 1881 the CPR appointed a land agent in London, England, and by autumn an advertising campaign for CPR lands had been started in Britain. In May 1881 the company established a Land Department in Winnipeg and appointed J.H. McTavish, the Hudson's Bay Company factor at Fort Garry, as land commissioner. The *Manitoba Free Press* was pleased with this appointment, praising McTavish's "well-known business capacity and administrative ability" and his devotion to Western interests. He was succeeded in 1887 by Lauchlan A. Hamilton. A native of Ontario, the thirty-five-year-old Hamilton had extensive experience as a provincial land surveyor in BC and as a dominion land surveyor. He surveyed much of the city of Vancouver at its inception in 1886–7, and served as an alderman on Vancouver's first city council in 1886. In 1900 Hamilton resigned as land commissioner and was succeeded by Frederick T. Griffin, who had served as his assistant since 1890. Ontario-born Griffin completed high school in Hamilton and then worked for the Ontario Department of Education from 1875 to 1882. After a brief stint with the Canada North-West Land Company, he joined the CPR Land Department in 1883.[11]

In April 1881 the CPR board authorized the advertising of its lands in major Canadian newspapers at a selling price of $2.50 per acre. The CPR directors met in Winnipeg in August and adopted a plan to sell land only to the actual settler. The settler was required to pay one-sixth of the purchase price in cash, with the remainder to be paid in five equal annual instalments. The purchaser was obligated to "bring under cultivation and sow and reap a crop on three-fourths of the land" within 4 years, a provision designed to discourage speculative buying. An added incentive to the actual settler was a rebate of $1.25 per acre for every acre cultivated and cropped within 4 years. However, these land regulations made no provision for forfeiture of the land if the cultivation and cropping conditions were not met. The CPR's Land Department removed this loophole early in 1882 by inserting a forfeiture provision in the land regulations which would be applied if the purchaser failed to carry out the conditions of his contract within the specified time.[12]

CPR land sales started in 1881. The CPR's momentous decision that year to change its route to run through Kicking Horse Pass meant that the main-line belt would be located on the southern part of the Prairies. In December 1882 the CPR land department ended the flat price system and offered land in the 48-mile belt at prices ranging from $2.50 to $7 per acre, with no settlement conditions. At the same time it placed 2.5 million acres in southern Manitoba and eastern Assiniboia on the market. But the company was still following a policy of trying to attract the *bona fide* settler. In the 48-mile belt it instituted a price differential between lands that were cultivated and those that were not: (1) land prices ranged from $2.50 per acre up with cropping conditions and from $4 per acre up without such conditions; (2) for cultivation, a rebate of one-half the purchase price was allowed on the area cropped, to be applied on the next payment falling due; (3) land within 1 mile of the main line and in the vicinity of towns and stations (previously withheld from sale) was put on the market in April 1883 with large rebates for cultivation. Since land sales were very slow, in 1888 the Land Department reduced the minimum price of land in the main-line belt to $2 per acre without cropping or cultivation provisions. For actual settlers, the department extended the time of payment from 6 to 10 years.[13] As a result, the department experienced some success in selling lands in the main-line belt to people who had been successful farmers on adjacent lands and who wanted to expand their acreage. This trend was confirmed in the company's 1894 annual report; 3 years later Van Horne informed a correspondent, "we sell practically no lands at all to people newly arrived in the country, our sales being almost entirely to people who have already made a start on Government lands and who wish to add to their holdings."[14] In fact, the CPR had started extensively advertising free government homestead lands after the collapse of the Manitoba Land Boom in 1882.

In January 1892, the Land Department reduced the price scale on lands in the main-line belt and in the land grant of the Manitoba South Western Colonization Railway, which the CPR had leased in 1884. Land offered at $4 per acre was now priced at $3 per acre, while land at $6 per acre was reduced to $4 per acre. At the same time the CPR made its first serious effort to sell lands on the main line west of the third meridian and in the large reserves to the north, remote from the railway. Land sales for 1892 were higher than for any year since the early 1880's. However, the economic depression worsened in 1893 and brought "a sharp decline in sales which continued unabated until 1896."[15]

Early in 1882 the CPR instituted provisions permitting individuals and companies to buy large amounts of land in the 48-mile reserve. This decision was a response to the federal government's policy, adopted in December 1881, allowing companies to purchase lands remote from the CPR for colonization purposes. During the 1880s the government signed contracts covering 2,842,742 acres, with twenty-six colonization companies. If these companies were able to sell substantial amounts of land, settlement might be diverted from areas near the CPR main line. The CPR therefore adopted regulations for the sale of land in bulk, as a means of attracting colonization companies to the 48-mile belt along its main line. Lands were to be taken in as compact a form as possible on both sides of the main line, in such a manner that the mean distance from the CPR was not less than 12 miles. Land was priced at $5 per acre, payable one-quarter in cash and the balance within 5 years. One-half the land was to be cultivated, and a crop sowed and reaped, within 5 years. If the cultivation conditions were carried out, the purchasers were released from the balance of the purchase price over and above the initial payment of $1.25. "In short," Hedges observes, "if the lands were brought under settlement and cultivation, they could be acquired at the price of $1.25 per acre."[16]

The CPR sold 808,200 acres to colonization companies formed to take advantage of the regulations of December 1881 (leaving aside the special case of the Canada North-West Land Company). Several of these companies failed to comply with the conditions respecting cultivation and settlement, so the CPR cancelled their contracts. By 31 December 1886 it had cancelled contracts for 696,330 acres. A few of the remaining companies had some success in selling their lands, but on the whole they failed to bring in as many settlers as the CPR had hoped. "It is not surprising, therefore," Hedges remarks, "that Canadian Pacific confidence in large land companies revived but slowly at the turn of the century."[17]

The Canada North-West Land Company, a corporation organized under the laws of Great Britain, was a special case. The CPR was in financial trouble in the spring of 1882, and so it attempted to convert some of its land grant into cash with which to continue construction. On 6 June 1882 George Stephen, the CPR president, and Charles Drinkwater, its secretary, signed an agreement with E.B. Osler and William B. Scarth, both of Toronto, and two New York financiers. Under the terms of this agreement, the CPR would sell to Osler and his associates 5 million acres of land in designated sections in every township in the main-line belt between Brandon and the eastern boundary of BC. The land, priced at $3 per acre, a substantial discount from the contract price of $5 per acre, would be paid for in CPR land-grant bonds, at a 10 per cent premium, plus accrued interest. The land company would also receive half the area of all townsites established on the main line between Brandon and the BC border. On 26 July 1882 Osler and his associates transferred all their rights under the 6 June agreement to the Canada North-West Land Company, which had its head office in London, England. On 14 April 1883 the CPR transferred a first instalment of 1.5 million acres to Canada North-West Land, for which it paid $275,000 in cash and $4,200,000 in CPR land-grant bonds. Despite the fact that the land company had contracted to purchase six sections of CPR land per township in the main-line belt, the bulk of its lands were taken in southern Manitoba. This was made possible because, under the 1882 agreement, Canada North-West Land agreed to select only those lands judged fit for settlement. Canada North-West Land did not have sufficient capital to carry out the original agreement, so a new agreement was signed on 20 December 1883. The land company reduced its land area from 5 million to 2.2 million acres and its bond purchases to $6 million. This left a balance of about 700,000 acres to be selected. This land was to be taken between range 33 west of the first meridian and Moose Jaw.[18]

Canada North-West Land sold farmland on the basis of a one-sixth cash down payment, with the balance to be paid in five equal annual instalments at 6 per cent interest. The company had a successful year in 1883, with land sales (including townsites) of 65,621 acres and a profit which enabled it to pay a dividend of 5 1/2 per cent. But thereafter land sales dropped substantially, as did profits, and the English investors began to lose confidence in the company. During the 10 years from 1882 to 1892 the company managed to sell only 274,553 acres of its 2.2 million-acre purchase. In 1893 the original company went into liquidation and a new one with the same name was incorporated in Canada to take over its business and property. Control of the new company, which had its head office in Toronto, passed to the CPR. In September 1893 the stockholders met and elected Van Horne president, E.B. Osler, vice-president, and Donald Smith, Shaughnessy, and R.B. Angus among the directors. Sir Thomas Skinner, a CPR director and a prominent financier resident in London, England, was elected chairman. With the land company then a CPR subsidiary, the CPR Land Department took over the administration and sales of Canada North-West Company farm lands. Since these lands represented an initial investment of $3 per acre, they were sold at substantially higher prices than CPR lands of the same quality and location.[19]

By the end of 1896, the CPR had disposed of 3,623,066 acres from its main-line grant. However, 2.2 million acres should be deducted from main-line sales, since the CPR sold this amount to the Canada North-West Land Company. Also the figure of 274,553 acres, which represents Canada North-West Land sales, should be added to main-line sales. This gives a figure of 1,697,619 acres for main-line sales from 1881 to 1896. In the period 1881–8 the CPR sold land-grant bonds that realized a total of $23,676,359.[20]

Apart from its sizeable original land grant the CPR increased its landholdings in the prairie West after 1881 even more through the purchase on long-term lease of other railways, which had been awarded substantial land grants by the federal government, and through the land awards that accompanied its branch-line construction program. (The federal government policy of land grants to railways in the prairie West continued until 1894.)[21] The CPR for instance received a federal land subsidy to build its Souris branch. In 1890 and 1891 the Macdonald government authorized a land grant of 6,400 acres per mile for construction of a railway from Kenmay, just west of Brandon on the CPR main line, south to Souris, and then in a southwesterly direction to Estevan (157 miles), which was the site of some valuable lignite coal fields. Also subsidized were two connecting lines, one from Napinka east to Deloraine (18 miles) and another from Souris east to Glenboro (45 miles). These lines, which constituted the Souris branch, totalled 220 miles, and earned 1,408,000 acres for the CPR. The company was required to pay 10 cents per acre to the government to cover the cost of surveys, and any *bona fide* settler had the right to purchase 320 acres at not more than $2.50 per acre. The "fairly fit for settlement" clause was inserted in this land grant. Since there was not enough land along the Souris Branch to provide the land required, the CPR was permitted to select some of its lands from odd-numbered sections in the Battleford Block – two strips of 12 miles each on either side of a line from Saskatoon through Battleford to the fourth meridian–and in a triangular tract to the southwest of the Battleford Block. In 1894 a further grant to the CPR of 6,400 acres per mile was made for the Pipestone extension of the Souris Branch, a 31-mile line from Lauder west to Reston in the Pipestone valley, for a total value of 200,320 acres. Construction of the Souris Branch lines began in 1886 and was completed in 1893. The Pipestone extension was opened in 1893.[22]

The first land-grant railway acquired by the CPR was the Manitoba South Western Colonization Railway, which was chartered by the federal government in 1884 to build a line from Winnipeg southwest to Rock Lake, near the town of Crystal City. In 1885 the company was authorized to build several branch lines and to extend its main line to the Souris coal fields. All lines were to receive a land subsidy of 6,400 acres per mile. The CPR leased the company in 1884. Its line, completed in 1886–7, consisted of a railway from Winnipeg to Glenboro (103 miles) where it connected with the Souris Branch, a line from Manitou to Deloraine (100 miles) connecting with the Souris Branch, and a short 12-mile line from Elm Creek on the Winnipeg-Glenboro line south to the town of Carman. It received a total of 1,396,800 acres for these lines.[23] The Manitoba South Western and the Souris Branch together created "something approaching a system" for the CPR in southwestern Manitoba.[24]

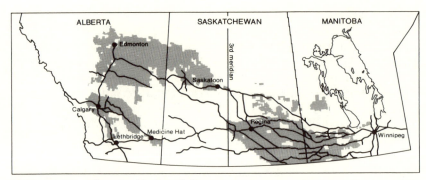

Figure 6 Canadian Pacific Land Grants

The CPR took over two land-grant railways in 1900: the Great North West Central Railway and the Manitoba and North Western Railway Company of Canada. In 1891 the Great North West Central built a line from Chater, just east of Brandon on the CPR main line, north and west toward Miniota, for a distance of 50 miles, for which it received a grant of 320,000 acres. This grant passed to the CPR when it leased the Great North West Central in perpetuity in March 1900. The Manitoba and North Western, first chartered in 1880, built a line from Portage la Prairie to Minnedosa in 1883, and later extended it northwest to Yorkton. Only 3,153 acres of its land grant remained unsold when the CPR leased it on 1 May 1900. However, in 1887 the Manitoba and North Western had leased the Saskatchewan and Western Railway for 99 years. This company was authorized to build a line from Minnedosa to Rapid City, a distance of 18 miles. The federal government granted it a land subsidy of 6,400 acres per mile in 1894. The CPR built from Minnedosa south to Gautier (near Rapid City) a distance of 15.5 miles, for which it received 98,880 acres. (Gautier was located on a CPR branch line to Hamiota.)[25]

The CPR took over the Calgary and Edmonton Railway in 1903. (See chapter four.) This was a colonization railway that had earned a large land grant of 1,888,000 acres. However, well before the CPR takeover the company had transferred its land subsidy to the Calgary and Edmonton Land Company, which hired the Winnipeg firm of Osler, Hammond and Nanton to act as selling agent for the lands. The Calgary and Edmonton Railway had been required to deposit 407,402 acres of its land subsidy as "security lands" with the federal government. These lands became the property of the CPR when it purchased control of the Calgary and Edmonton Railway. The CPR Land Department in Winnipeg was very active in selling these lands

Table 1
Land Grants to the CPR in the Prairie West, 1881–1914

Grants	Acres
Grants for Construction	
Main-line grant	25,000,000
Souris Branch	1,408,704
Pipestone Extension, Souris Branch	200,320
Grants made to other companies[1]	1,396,800
Grants earned by other companies[2]	
Alberta Railway and Irrigation Company	181,249
Calgary and Edmonton Railway	407,402
Great North West Central Railway	320,000
Manitoba and North Western Railway	3,153
Saskatchewan and Western Railway	98,880
Sub-total	29,016,508
Land relinquished to the federal government in 1885	6,792,014
Total	22,224,494

Sources: McDougall, *Canadian Pacific,* 126–7; Hedges, *The Federal Railway Land Subsidy Policy,* 139–40.
[1] Earned by CPR after the purchase of charter, Manitoba South Western Colonization Railway
[2] Later passed in part to CPR by purchase of those companies' stock

from 1903 to 1906. Most of these lands were located in the foothills region of Alberta, from Red Deer south to the boundary.[26]

The last colonization railway taken over by the CPR was the Alberta Railway and Irrigation Company (AR&I CO) which was leased on 1 January 1912 for 999 years. The AR&I CO had received land subsidies totalling 1,114,368 acres for building a line from Dunmore to Lethbridge and from Lethbridge to the international boundary. Under the 1912 agreement the CPR acquired the company's unsold lands in the Lethbridge area, comprising 181,249 acres, together with the irrigation system that the company had developed in the early 1900s. These lands and the irrigation system, which became the third unit of the CPR's irrigation project, are discussed later in this chapter.[27] (Table 1 outlines CPR land grants in the prairie West in the period 1881–1914. The company obtained a total of 22,224,494 acres. Figure 6 gives the geographical distribution of these grants.)

The CPR and colonization railways were permitted to delay the selection and patenting of their lands. As Hall remarks, "The longer the railways could put off the selection and patenting process, the longer they could put off paying taxes on those lands earned, while the lands increased in value."[28] When Clifford Sifton became minister of the interior in November 1896 he was determined to have the railways select and patent their lands as quickly as possible. During the negotiations for the Crow's Nest Pass Agreement, Sifton came up with a different policy for dealing with this problem in so far as it involved the CPR. He proposed to Van Horne that the CPR sell to the federal government all its unsold lands east of the third meridian at $2 per acre. These amounted to 2,617,000 acres: 1,850,000 acres from the main-line reserve and 767,000 acres of the Manitoba South Western land grant. Van Horne was quite cool to this proposal, since these lands formed "the cream of our grant," but he did suggest that the company's directors might accept a price of $2.50 per acre. Sifton them made a counter-proposal of $2.80 per acre. But the two parties failed to reach an agreement on this matter. Van Horne informed Sifton that the CPR directors were reluctant to sell these lands because they expected an increase in immigration to the prairies, which would cause increased demand for CPR lands and a resulting rise in land prices. The directors may have expected that the low Crow's Nest freight rates would attract more settlers into the prairie West. (See chapter two.) The directors also regarded the company's lands as a major factor in the company's credit rating; a substantial reduction in the size of the land grant might weaken its credit.[29]

Locating the main-line land grant was a long and complex process, extending over a 22-year period from 1881 to 1903. The CPR had relinquished 6.7 million acres of its main-line grant to the federal government in 1886 as part payment for a federal loan (see table 1), so the grant was reduced from 25 million acres to 18,206,986 acres. Under the terms of the CPR charter, the company was to receive the odd-numbered sections in a belt 24 miles deep on each side of the main line, except for sections 11 and 29 which were reserved for "school lands." The CPR, using the "fairly fit for settlement" clause, selected only 5,255,870 acres from the main-line belt. The shortage was to be made up from other prairie lands between the 49th and 57th parallels. Here the company might select the odd-numbered sections in a belt 24 miles deep on each side of any CPR branch line constructed or projected. However, as Hedges remarks, "in actual practice the company, in searching for lands fairly fit for settlement, went far afield and eventually found itself with millions of acres far removed from either main or branch lines."[30]

The major portion of this land fell into four large land reserves, which the CPR acquired in the period 1882–1901. (See table 2.) The First Northern Reserve was created in 1882. The CPR had requested and obtained the lands already earned along the main line and along

Table 2
Location of CPR Main-Line Land Grant in 1901

	Acres
The Main-Line Belt	5,255,870
The First Northern Reserve	6,620,000
Southern Reserve	2,244,130
The Lake Dauphin Lands	400,000
The Second Northern Reserve	386,000
Total	14,906,000

Source: Hedges, Building the Canadian West, 56.

a branch, from Winnipeg southwest to the Pembina Mountains, which had been located. At the same time, it requested the reservation of an additional tract of land extending south from the proposed Pembina Mountain Branch to the international boundary, but the government refused the request. The company, through its secretary, Charles Drinkwater, protested this decision, pointing out that the maximum available land in the main-line belt was 6 million acres, so that the CPR would need large tracts of land from other parts of the prairie West. Accepting the company's arguments, the government passed an Order-in-Council on 24 October 1882 creating the First Northern Reserve, located between the 52nd and 54th degrees of latitude and the 104th and 116th degrees of longitude. It covered the fertile North Saskatchewan Valley, from about 35 miles east of Saskatoon west to the foothills of the Rocky Mountains and to 40 miles north of Edmonton.[31] The minister of the interior also agreed to create a large reserve south of the main-line belt. This Southern Reserve was established by Orders-in-Council passed on 3 November 1882 and 25 January 1883. It comprised all odd-numbered sections between the main-line belt and the international boundary, and between the Red River and the original western boundary of Manitoba.[32] Although these two reserves were too remote to make a substantial contribution to the CPR's traffic, they were important assets. As Hedges observes, "they guaranteed the larger portion of the grant, assured the Canadian Pacific of a significant influence in the future development of the country, and afforded a measure of control over rival transportation enterprises."[33]

In the 1890s two additional reserves were created in partial satisfaction of the main-line grant. The first of these, the Lake Dauphin Reserve, was established by a federal Order-in-Council passed on 18 February 1895. It called for the setting aside of the odd-numbered sections still at the government's disposal in a block immediately west of Lake Dauphin.[34] An Order-in-Council of 18 December 1895 created the Second Northern Reserve, situated to the east and northeast of Edmonton.[35]

In 1901 the CPR had selected 14,906,000 acres of its main-line grant, leaving 3,300,986 acres yet to be designated. After making no headway in negotiations with Van Horne to select these lands, Clifford Sifton took up the problem with Shaughnessy. They finally agreed on the main features of a settlement in July 1903; Whyte then went to Ottawa to work out the details with officials of the Department of the Interior. On 22 August Cabinet passed an Order-in-Council ratifying the agreement. Under its terms, the CPR accepted a block of 2,900,000 acres between Medicine Hat and Calgary that would be developed under its proposed irrigation project. The balance of the CPR main-line grant – 400,986 acres – would be selected from the odd-numbered sections in the reserve of the Manitoba and North Western Railway.[36]

CPR land sales increased substantially from 1899 until 1914, with the exception of the 1908 fiscal year. (See table 3.) A massive influx of settlers into Canada from Britain, the United States, and continental Europe took place in the period 1902–14, reaching a peak of 400,870 in 1913.[37] Many of these immigrants took up farming in the prairie West, with the result that the price of agricultural land there rose steadily. In 1899 the average price of CPR lands sold was $3.18 per acre; this had increased to an average price of $5.92 in the 1907 fiscal year. There were then large increases from fiscal 1908 to fiscal 1912, a slight decline in fiscal 1913 followed by a substantial increase to $16.57 per acre in the 1914 fiscal year. Figures are available on land sales for two of the land-grant railways acquired by the CPR. For the Manitoba Southwestern Railway in the period 1 January 1897 to 30 June 1913, 1,229,148 acres were sold and total proceeds were $4,805,786 for an average price per acre of $3.91. For the Great North West Central Railway in the period 1 May 1900 to 30 June 1913, 237,742 acres were sold and total proceeds were $1,083,783 for an average price per acre of $4.56. As Hedges points out, the rush of land speculators and settlers to the prairie West from 1902 to 1914 prompted the CPR to "revise upward periodically the price of land in small units." As a result, in July 1903, land east of the third meridian was priced up to $10 per acre, according to location.[38]

The CPR had lost faith in colonization companies as instruments for selling its lands to settlers as a result of its experiences in the 1880s. However, the company decided to try this approach again after the turn of the century. The reasons for this decision are not

Table 3
CPR Land Sales in Prairie West, 1896–1914 (Excluding Townsites)

Year	Amount (in acres)	Proceeds	Average price per acre
1896	87,878	$ 308,928	$ 3.51
1897	199,482	665,740	3.38
1898	348,608	1,121,744	3.22
1899	416,806	1,327,667	3.18
1900–01[1]	668,477	2,122,230	3.17
1902[2]	1,362,852	4,442,136	3.26
1903	2,639,617	9,695,673	3.67
1904	928,854	3,807,248	4.10
1905	509,386	2,446,300	4.80
1906	1,115,743	6,513,452	5.84
1907	994,840	5,887,377	5.92
1908	164,450	1,586,853	9.54
1909	306,083	3,354,669	10.96
1910	829,609	10,602,403	12.78
1911	631,777	8,914,373	14.11
1912	666,369	10,561,948	15.85
1913	466,854	7,096,180	15.20
1914	253,053	4,193,088	16.57
Totals	12,590,738	83,835,446	6.66

Source: CPR, *Annual Reports,* 1896–1914. For the years 1897 to 1912 these figures include only sales from the main-line grant (including irrigated lands) and the Souris Branch. After that they include sales from all of the company's lands.
[1] The years 1896–9 are calendar years. The 1900–1 report covers the 18-month period 1 January 1900 to 30 June 1901.
[2] 1902–1914 are fiscal years, starting 1 July of the previous year to 30 June of the year listed.

clear; the company may have needed a cash influx to carry out extensive branch-line construction on the prairies, and it seems that it was confident that colonization companies would sell the land rapidly, bringing in settlers who would provide more traffic for the CPR. From December 1901 to July 1906 it sold 2.3 million acres to thirteen different colonization companies. This accounts for the large land sales in the years 1902, 1903, 1904, and 1906. The first such sale was to an American company headed by Beiseker, Davidson and Martin – three North Dakota businessmen and land speculators. Land Commissioner F.T. Griffin had urged senior CPR officials to sign a contract with the trio since they had been very successful in selling land to settlers in North Dakota. A contract was signed on 13 December 1901 under which Beiseker and his associates purchased 170,297 acres on the CPR's Pasqua section in eastern Assiniboia, at a price of $2.75 per acre. They then created the Canadian-American Land Company, with headquarters in Minneapolis. Within 5 months this company had retailed the entire area to settlers from the US. Another important purchaser was a Canadian, J. Heber Haslam, who in December 1901 contracted to purchase at $2.50 per acre 82,584 acres of land south of Weyburn on the CPR-controlled Soo line. Haslam had for some time been promoting the movement of settlers into southeastern Assiniboia. He now proceeded to build up an extensive land-sales organization in the middle Western states, expecially in Iowa and Illinois.[39]

The most important of the colonization companies dealing with CPR lands in Assiniboia was the Northwest Colonization Company, owned by a group of Minneapolis bankers and businessmen, and capably managed by O.A. Robertson and F.B. Lynch, two of the most well-known land promoters in the American Northwest. Robertson and the CPR signed a contract on 8 April 1902 for the purchase of 337,090 acres of CPR and Manitoba South Western lands at $2.50 per acre. A clause in the contract requiring Robertson to sell the land to settlers at not less than $4 per acre protected the interests of the Canada North-West Land Company whose lands sold at prices considerably higher than $2.50 per acre. The Northwest Colonization Company purchased 412,859 acres in Assiniboia in December 1902, bringing its total holdings to 749,949 acres. Robertson and Lynch advertised these lands very extensively in the American Northwest, combining that with high-pressure sales methods, with the result that by the spring of 1905 the entire area had been retailed to American settlers.[40]

Other large sales to colonization companies between 1902 and 1906 were as follows:[41]

1	Union Trust Company of Toronto	76,765 acres
2	Ontario and Saskatchewan Land Corporation	150,055 acres
3	Great West Land Company	200,004 acres
4	Alberta Central Land Corporation	116,483 acres
5	Alberta and Saskatchewan Colonization Company	127,200 acres
6	Western Canada Land Company	500,000 acres
7	Luse Land Company of St Paul	102,510 acres
	Total	1,273,017 acres

The lands obtained by the last four companies were located in northern Alberta and, as Hedges observes, "represent the first serious effort of the Canadian Pacific to sell and settle that portion of the

West." All these organizations appear to have recruited settlers mainly in the United States. However, it should be stressed that from 1897 to 1914 when it carried on extensive advertising and publicity campaigns, the CPR Land Department was very active in selling company lands primarily in the regions tributary to the main line in Manitoba and Saskatchewan and the southern reserves in those two provinces.[42] In the period 1897–1906, sales to settlers had numbered 26,241, covering an area of over 6 million acres.

In 1908 the CPR set up a "development department" in Calgary to manage the company's irrigable lands, which were located in southern Alberta. In 1910 this department was also given the responsibility for selling ordinary lands along the Lacombe and Wetaskiwin branches of the CPR, where most of the government sections had been sold. The decision to transfer some responsibilities for the sale of lands from the Land Department to the Development Department was probably influenced by the fact that the Calgary office had built up an extensive advertising and selling organization in the United States, while the Land Department had no comparable organization.[43]

Irrigation had become an important aspect of CPR land development in 1903 when the company accepted a block of 2.9 million acres between Medicine Hat and Calgary. The company used this land, Hedges observes, "to develop perhaps the largest irrigation scheme in North America, as well as a program of assisted settlement and colonization far more extensive than anything which other land grant railway companies had attempted."[44]

The man who was chiefly responsible for interesting the CPR in the irrigation of prairie lands was William Pearce. Pearce was born on the family farm in Elgin County, Ontario, in 1848. After graduating from the St Thomas grammar school, he enrolled in the School of Engineering at the University of Toronto. Though he greatly enjoyed the practical survey work in the wilderness of northern Ontario, he was bored by his university studies. So he withdrew from the university in the fall of 1869 and began a 3-year apprenticeship with a Toronto engineering firm. During the apprenticeship he did much exploration surveying in northern Ontario and gained a wide reputation for excellent work. In October 1872 he became a certified land surveyor for the province of Ontario. The following year he accepted an offer from the partners of his apprenticeship firm of a position at a monthly salary of $100 plus all his travelling expenses.[45]

In the spring of 1874 Colonel J.S. Dennis, the deputy minister of the interior, recruited Pearce for a post in the department's surveys branch in the North-West. (Pearce had been highly recommended by surveyors who had observed his work as an apprentice.) He did excellent work in his position, but was dissatisfied with the fact that he was hired on the basis of a one-year contract. After his marriage in the fall of 1881 he decided to seek a permanent position outside the government service in order to obtain financial stability for himself and his wife. When he informed the Surveyor-General, Lindsay Russell, of his decision, Russell and the deputy minister of the interior, not wanting to lose such a capable official, recommended him for the post of inspector of dominion lands agencies in the newly formed Dominion Lands Board, at a salary of $3,200 a year plus travelling expenses. Pearce accepted the offer without hesitation and was officially appointed to his new position in February 1882.[46]

Pearce's new position was an important one. From his office in Winnipeg he administered the interior department's employees working in Manitoba and the North-West Territories, established regulations to help control the land rush of 1881–3, and devised means to eliminate land speculation on the frontier. In the summer of 1884 he was appointed superintendent of mines, with an office situated in Calgary. Pearce still retained his seat on the Dominion Lands Board but had to relinquish his post as inspector of lands agencies. The federal government had created the position of superintendent of mines in anticipation of a mining boom in the eastern foothills of the Rocky Mountains. The mining rush did not take place, so Pearce – now located in Calgary – spent much of his time as a government troubleshooter, investigating numerous matters relating to federal policy in the prairie West. From the time of his appointment as inspector of lands agencies, he had been encouraged to write Prime Minister Macdonald on any matter which he felt worthy of consideration relating to Western development. He thus became Macdonald's "personal representative on the frontier," and a number of his reports were to form the basis of the government's Western policies. In the period 1885–90 he played a major role in the development of stock water reserves, the adjudication of the CPR land grant, the establishment of a national parks system, and the conservation and development of territorial water resources.[47]

In the period 1890–1904 Pearce was mainly concerned with the promotion of irrigation as a solution to drought conditions on the southern prairies. His interest in irrigation dated back to his first trip across the southern plains by train in September 1883, when he had been struck by the similarity in landform and vegetation between the southern Canadian plains and the states of Utah and Colorado. He had visited reclamation projects in the semi-arid districts of Utah and Colorado in 1881. Remarking on the similarity to a traveller from Colorado, the fellow replied that the Canadian plains would be a very good agricultural country, if the waters of the Bow River, which ran deep in its channel, could be placed on the dry soil. "Before the train arrived in Calgary," Pearce's biographer, Alyn Mitchner, asserts, "he [Pearce] had decided that the diversion of river water onto the short grass plains was not only advisable but essential for the future economic prosperity of the Territories." He soon became known as the "irrigation crank" in the department of the interior![48]

In order to promote his ideas he had, at about this time, arranged a "chance" meeting at the CPR station in Winnipeg with W.C. Van Horne, then the company's general manager. Van Horne invited him to come to supper and the two soon became close friends. On return trips to Winnipeg Pearce often stayed at the Van Horne home.[49] The growing support for irrigation in the prairie West in the early 1890s gave Pearce the opportunity to impress upon CPR officials – notably Van Horne, who had become president in 1888 – the financial benefits to be gained from irrigation on the western plains. He proposed that the remaining lands owed to the CPR be transferred in a single block. He was certain that he could arrange for the company to obtain title to all the even-numbered sections as well as the lands reserved for school purposes and the Hudson's Bay Company. He pointed out that the CPR already had its own engineering and survey staffs to plan the development of the block and possessed the heavy equipment needed for the construction of canals and headgates. Since the block was to be located near the CPR main line, the company would benefit through increased freight and passenger traffic as well as from sales of lands whose value would be greatly enhanced by irrigation. Pearce also felt that this might be the only way the railway could close out its land grant. This latter argument may have carried some weight with the CPR directors who, Pearce knew, were then desperate to close out the company's land grant. The directors may have been concerned that if the Liberals came to power in Ottawa, the remainder of the CPR land grant might be put in jeopardy.[50]

In January 1894 Pearce had several lengthy discussions with Van Horne in Montreal in which he made a proposal which came to be known as the Bow River Scheme. Pearce's plan called for transfer to the CPR of all unclaimed land in a block, with an average width of 41 miles, running 170 miles east of Calgary along the Bow River. This area encompassed 4.5 million acres, of which 2 million were considered irrigable. Van Horne presented the Pearce proposal to his board of directors as his own in order to give it more weight. In any case the directors were interested in the project and in January 1894 authorized funds for carrying out a preliminary survey. Then Pearce, A.M. Burgess, deputy minister of the interior, and CPR officials Van Horne, George M. Clark, and Drinkwater examined the many aspects of the Bow River Scheme.[51]

The preliminary survey of the Bow project was carried out in the summer of 1894 by government surveyors in the company of Jacob L. Doupe, of the CPR's Land Department. It indicated that the best place to divert the Bow River would be close to Calgary, where the Calgary and Edmonton Railway crossed the river. A diversion at that point, close to ground level, would provide sufficient elevation to command over 2 million acres of arid land running as far east as Medicine Hat. Pearce urged the CPR to take immediate action to acquire the lands before rumours of the scheme caused a rush of new settlers into the district; in 1894 there were 38,000 acres within the tract already settled. Van Horne was delighted with the result of the preliminary survey and remarked that he would make the country "fairly stink with blossoms through irrigation." He had his officials file applications for river diversions at Banff, Kananaskis, Logan, Calgary, and Crowfoot Crossing. He then ordered more detailed topographic surveys of the block to be done in the summer of 1895, to see what lands were at a lower elevation than the main canal. At the same time Pearce started reserving from settlement all unclaimed lands in the block. The CPR then submitted proposals to the minister of the interior indicating that it was ready to close out its land grant through the receipt of lands east of Calgary *en bloc*.[52]

Negotiations for the transfer of these lands were broken off early in 1895 because of the CPR's insistence on obtaining clear title to water rights from the Bow River before construction started. Interior department officials felt that the company could guarantee their water rights under the North-West Irrigation Act of 1894, which also contained the proviso that lands not developed within 10 years would revert to the government. The directors were not prepared to risk losing their claims if they did not complete the project within the period stipulated. The government then proposed to guarantee water rights even if it meant diverting some of the flow from the Red Deer River into the block. However, the company did not agree to this plan because it faced a financial crisis brought on by a general world-wide business depression. "We cannot let a penny go this year that we are not pretty sure of getting back immediately," Van Horne informed Pearce in July 1895, when directors decided to shelve the irrigation project until the company's financial position improved.[53]

The CPR directors decided they needed more detailed information about the Bow River Scheme. They were especially concerned as to whether it would divert enough water from the Bow River to irrigate the entire block. J.S. Dennis Jr, the chief inspector of surveys, had his officials carry out a survey of the proposed block in the autumn of 1895 which indicated that a 40-mile canal moving east from Calgary would supply an area of 2,304,000 acres.[54] At Van Horne's request, the CPR's Chief Engineer, P.A. Peterson, estimated how much material would be excavated for a 34-mile canal, and arrived at a figure of 5,373,145 cubic yards. Van Horne remarked to Pearce that these quantities "run a long way beyond my expectations. Is it quite certain that so large a canal will be needed?" Using Peterson's figures, Pearce estimated the cost of this canal, including supervision and engineering expenses, at $537,315.[55] These figures did nothing to allay the director's concerns about the cost of the project. In any case by the end of 1895, the building of the Crow's Nest Pass Railway had top priority, and CPR officials were seeking substantial financial aid from the federal government to build it. The Bow River Scheme would have to be shelved until the costly Crow's Nest Pass Railway was completed.

The advent of the Liberals to power in Ottawa in July 1896 brought a substantial turnover of the civil service staff. The new Minister of the Interior, Clifford Sifton, was under pressure to remove Pearce but decided to retain his services because, as Mitchner asserts, "he had found Pearce to be a clever and valuable servant with an exhaustive knowledge of the West whom the government could not easily replace." Pearce undertook to win Sifton's support for the Bow River Scheme. In November 1896 he sent the minister a synopsis of the plan. Sifton was impressed with the magnitude of the scheme and gave it his unqualified support. He also promised to reopen negotiations with the CPR and to pursue the project in Cabinet.[56]

Pearce endeavoured to renew the CPR's interest in the project by writing to Van Horne in December 1897 to inform him of the plans of the Mormon Church to irrigate 200,000 acres of land between Stirling and Lethbridge. The Alberta Irrigation Company, a subsidiary of the Galt enterprises, had undertaken to build the main canal for the Mormons. Van Horne informed Pearce that he had looked over Galt's plans for the Mormon irrigation scheme. "If his [Galt's] scheme ... is successful," he observed, "we will no doubt then be able to arrange with the Govt. about the lands east of Calgary and in reference to water, etc. So we have decided to await his results before making a further effort." This view was shared by the company's Land Commissioner, L.A. Hamilton. "Further effort" came the following year when the CPR, having decided that if the project were successful it would generate more traffic for the railway, began paying the Alberta Railway and Irrigation Company a grant of $5,000 every six months, until a total of $100,000 had been paid out. The Alberta Irrigation Company completed the main canal to Stirling in the fall of 1899 and to Lethbridge in 1900, thus opening large areas of southern Alberta for agricultural settlement.[57]

In the autumn of 1899 CPR and government officials reopened negotiations on the Bow River Scheme. Pearce was called to Ottawa to help present the government's case to Shaughnessy, who had succeeded Van Horne as president in June 1899. According to Mitchner, the new CPR president "was cool to the idea of the railway's involvement in irrigation." However, by this time the Mormons' large irrigation scheme was almost complete and operating successfully. The talks helped convince Shaughnessy that the scheme was economically feasible and that it would generate year round passenger and freight traffic for the CPR.[58]

At this point the directors insisted that an independent engineering report on the scheme should be prepared, apart from the surveys of the Irrigation Branch and the company's Land Department, both of whose employees were regarded as having a vested interest in the project. Shaughnessy accepted Pearce's recommendation that the best man to carry out this investigation was George G. Anderson of Denver, Colorado, who was one of the best irrigation engineers in the United States. At this time Anderson was resident engineer for the Alberta Irrigation Company; he had proved his abilities by his successful direction of the Mormon irrigation system (the St Mary project). Though delayed in beginning his investigation of the Bow River Scheme until the spring of 1901 because of his responsibilities on the St Mary project, Anderson was able to complete his investigation and report to Shaughnessy in the latter part of June. He recommended that the CPR should immediately embark on the implementation of Pearce's plan, which he found to be structurally and economically sound. Shaughnessy was pleased with Anderson's "lengthy favuorable report" but was still cautious in committing his company to the Bow River Scheme. "Indeed," he remarked to a CPR official in October 1901, "we are not inclined to give the subject the slightest attention until we know that Parliament and the Government will give us such legislation as may be necessary to ensure land in solid blocks, water supply without interference, and reasonable taxation."[59]

The Laurier government prepared a draft bill to carry out the transfer of lands to the CPR during the 1902 session. However, Frank Oliver, the outspoken Liberal MP for Edmonton and a stern critic of the CPR, was opposed to the company getting lands on both sides of the Bow River for any distance. Sifton obliged Oliver by delaying the bill for the session, for he was not strong enough to force it through the House in the face of his opposition. Shaughnessy was sympathetic to Sifton's situation. "I am sure," he informed William Whyte, "that the Minister of the Interior is very anxious that there should be no unnecessary delay, but he did not want to have Oliver bucking a Government bill." Pearce, who had an interview with Sifton on 5 May, thought that the minister was "greatly annoyed with Mr. Oliver."[60]

At this time J.S. Dennis raised the question as to whether special legislation was necessary to establish the Bow River Scheme. He consulted with a lawyer regarding clause 11 of the CPR charter under which the CPR, with the consent of the federal government, could select any unoccupied lands in the North-West Territories as a means of fulfilling its main-line land grant. Dennis informed Pearce that he had concluded "that under that section the Minister can give the Company any unoccupied land he likes." Pearce shared this view which he discussed with Shaughnessy and CPR Chief Solicitor A.R. Creelman in Montreal on 17 May. Creelman was concerned about the last sentence in clause 11 which stated that "such [land] grants shall be made only from lands remaining vested in the Government." This provision meant that the government could not transfer title of the Hudson's Bay Company's lands to the CPR.[61] Dennis talked to Griffin about the land commissioner's visit to Montreal to discuss the Bow River Scheme with Shaughnessy and reached the conclusion "that the President is not very keen about the Bow Scheme." "I am afraid," he lamented to Pearce, "that there are too many 'bosses' in [the] CPR and too much delay and red tape for an aggressive move to make a scheme like the Bow Canal a success under them. If Mr. Whyte and Griffin had a free hand things would be different." Pearce responded that Shaughnessy's problem was that "he attempts to do too much, that is to look after details." But he was optimistic that the CPR would soon undertake the scheme and that Whyte would supervise it.[62]

On 31 May Shaughnessy left Montreal for his annual inspection tour of Western Canada, accompanied by directors E.B. Osler and W.D. Matthews. Dennis joined the three men at Winnipeg and while travelling to Calgary, discussed the Bow project at great length with them. Then Shaughnessy, Osler, and Matthews visited Pearce in Calgary and were shown his own irrigation works on the Bow River near Calgary. Pearce was upset that the CPR officials had arrived in a driving downpour and remarked to Whyte that "it is unfortunate ...

that such a wet season prevailed at his [Shaughnessy's] visit here. It looked almost absurd to suggest an irrigation proposition under the present conditions." The CPR president indicated to Pearce that he was pleased with the advantages of closing out the railway's land grant. He was impressed by the Calgarian's remark that the Bow project would provide enough capital from land sales in the irrigated block to build profitable spur lines into the project area. Pearce felt that Shaughnessy was "very favourably disposed towards the scheme" as was Osler, and that Matthews would probably support it.[63]

Shaughnessy was still cautious regarding the cost of the project. Whyte had discussed this matter with him in Winnipeg. The CPR president had used Anderson's report to arrive at a low estimate of $750,000 as the total cost. "When I pointed out to him," Whyte observed, "that it would take between four and five million dollars it seemed to stagger him." However, Whyte and Dennis showed the CPR president that a "handsome return can be had from these lands if water can be put upon them beside the large traffic the lands will bring to the Road."[64] In 1902 the CPR was in an excellent financial position. Earnings from January 1899 to June 1902 had been very good, enabling the company to pay a 5 per cent dividend on common stock for 3 consecutive years.[65] Also, the Crow's Nest Pass Railway had been completed and extended to Midway by early 1900, with no further extensions planned at that time. The CPR had the financial resources to undertake the Bow project.

Shaughnessy had decided in the summer of 1902 to go ahead with the project. He made "little progress" with the government in settling the land question. Pearce visited Whyte in Winnipeg at the end of September 1902 and strongly urged that the CPR should apply "at once" to the department of the interior for all even-numbered sections in its proposed irrigation block. In the latter part of October Whyte initiated this action, applying for the even-numbered sections between the fifth meridian and Range 19 and later for the same sections between Range 19 and Medicine Hat.[66] When James Smart, deputy minister of the interior, left for England early in January 1903, Clifford Sifton dealt directly with the matter. On 9 February the CPR president sent Sifton a letter outlining the company's proposal for a settlement of its land grant. The company wanted the lands between Medicine Hat and Calgary for its irrigation project to be made available in a solid block, including the even-numbered (homestead) sections as well as the odd-numbered and school sections. It estimated the total amount of land available as a block at 2.5 million acres. This would leave a deficiency of 800,000 acres in its main-line subsidy, which the company wished to select out of the Manitoba and North Western Railway reserve. Sifton then left for England to discuss the Alaska Boundary Question, further slowing down the negotiations. But in July 1903 Sifton and Shaughnessy finally reached a settlement. The irrigation block would comprise 2.9 million acres, and the remaining 400,000 acres would be selected out of the Manitoba and North Western Railway reserve. Whyte was then sent to Ottawa in early August to settle the details and the arrangement was ratified by a cabinet Order-in-Council passed on 22 August 1903.[67]

Shaughnessy now looked for a capable person with experience in the irrigation field to direct the Bow River Scheme. George Anderson hoped that the CPR would ask him to superintend the work. But Pearce, Charles Magrath, an irrigation expert with the Alberta Railway and Irrigation Company, and Elliot Galt all warned the CPR that Anderson was an extremely vain man who disparaged the work of others, so he was not offered the position. The CPR also considered Pearce and Dennis for the post. Pearce did not accept the offer because, as his biographer observes, "he was not interested in the detailed planning of the scheme but rather in the overall engineering aspects." At this time Dennis was deputy commissioner of the department of public works of the North-West Territories government and in charge of its irrigation branch. Because the conflict between the department of the interior and the territorial assembly over his administration of the irrigation branch had never been resolved Dennis felt that his position was precarious and that he would soon be forced to leave the government service.[68] He applied for the position in October 1901, and had G.M. Clark, the CPR's recently retired chief solicitor, and Charles Drinkwater, now assistant to the president, support his application.

Dennis was successful in his application and on 1 January 1903 he became the CPR's superintendent of irrigation and British Columbia land commissioner, with an office at Calgary. He soon became one of the most important CPR officials dealing with Western matters, particularly land and resource policies. John Stoughton Dennis Jr had been born at Weston near Toronto in 1856. His father, Colonel John Stoughton Dennis, was an excellent and experienced land surveyor who had been Canada's first surveyor general (1871–8) and deputy minister of the interior (1878–81). His son received an excellent education at the elite institutions of Trinity College School and Upper Canada College. He received much practical experience as a surveyor on special federal surveys of Manitoba and the North-West Territories between 1872 and 1878. During this period he took a year of private study, passed his examination, and received a commission as dominion land surveyor and dominion topographical surveyor. He then worked as a surveyor and engineer for the Land Department of the Hudson's Bay Company and in 1885 joined the Topographical Surveys Department of the Department of the Interior, rapidly rising to the position of chief inspector of surveys. Between 1895 and 1897 he was in charge of the general irrigation surveys in the North-West Territories, which involved him in location surveys for the St Mary's, the Bow River, and the Red Deer irrigation canals. In June 1897 he had resigned as chief inspector of surveys to take up his position with the North-West Territories government. He was admitted into the Canadian Society of Civil Engineers in November 1901.[69]

The surveys of 1894 and 1895 had indicated that a diversion of the Bow River near Calgary could supply enough water to irrigate 2.3 million acres of land, and Anderson's investigation of 1901 had concurred with this plan. However, detailed surveys by CPR engineers showed that the area naturally divided into three sections, each comprising about 1 million acres. These were designated as Western, Central, and Eastern. Only the Western section, it was determined, could be adequately served from the intake near Calgary.[70]

The CPR decided to complete the Western section before working on the other two. Shaughnessy, who was still being cautious in his approach, decided that initially water would be supplied to only 300,000 of the 1 million acres in the Western section. In 1904 the main canal leading from the Bow River east of Calgary was located and construction was started. The following year secondary canal "A" was located and construction begun. By the spring of 1906 the main canal, the secondary canal, and the irrigation ditches for the 300,000 acres were finished. Shaughnessy noted that the cost estimates had been exceeded "by a considerable amount" because the CPR had built lateral ditches (not part of the original plan) on the recommendation of Elwood Mead, an irrigation expert with the US Department of Agriculture. The CPR president wanted to see how this scheme worked in practice before completing the Western section. He was satisfied with the results, so that work on the irrigation canals and ditches in the rest of the Western section was begun. By 1910 the system was in full operation; it consisted of an 18-mile main canal, 150 miles of secondary canals, and irrigation ditches totalling 800 miles, which produced about 353,000 acres of irrigable land in a total area of 995,000 acres.[71]

There was one obstacle to the CPR's obtaining control of *all* lands in the irrigation block: the federal government could not transfer the Hudson's Bay Company (HBC) lands to the CPR. Before the railway started construction of the Western section, CPR officials in the

West had discussions with Clarence Chipman, the HBC's chief commissioner, who had his office in Winnipeg. A proposal for the HBC to become a partner in the project "by contributing its pro rata proportion of the cost," was fully discussed. The CPR officials did not think it fair that the HBC should have to pay a portion of the costs of the main canal, which would serve the entire Western section, when the CPR would only be developing one-third of this section for the first few years. It was suggested that the HBC be charged its share of the costs of the secondary canal and lateral ditches, but this arrangement was rejected because it "would have been a complicated and unsatisfactory transaction." Finally, the CPR officials were cool to the plan for a partnership with the HBC because, as Shaughnessy remarked, "we preferred to have a free hand in determining the rapidity with which the balance of the work [on the Western section] should be carried out." After considerable discussion, Chipman and the CPR officials decided that "the simplest and most satisfactory solution" was an exchange of lands between the two companies: the HBC would transfer its lands in the irrigation district to the CPR and would receive good CPR agricultural land in return. An agreement along these lines was signed by Chipman, William Whyte, and F.T. Griffin in the autumn of 1904. This agreement was passed by the CPR board of directors, but Chipman evidently believed that he had the necessary authority to ratify the agreement and did not submit it to the HBC board of governors.[72]

However, the HBC board did not approve this agreement, so Shaughnessy took the matter up with Lord Strathcona, the governor (chief executive officer) of the HBC. Reviewing the negotiations between the two companies, he stressed that he was determined to be "absolutely fair" to the HBC. He then expressed his willingness to consider "any other feasible solution more acceptable to the Hudson's Bay Company" although he considered the proposition for an exchange of lands as the best and simplest arrangement. Strathcona proposed a partnership in the irrigation project. Shaughnessy and his officials gave this proposal "very careful attention" but decided that it was not feasible. "We wish to have a free hand in dealing with these lands," he informed Strathcona, "because we may find it desirable to secure an advantage for our carrying business at the expense of the lands, and this would not be fair to any other partner whose interest was centred in the lands themselves." The CPR president concluded by stating that the only alternative to the exchange of lands proposal was for the CPR to purchase "right of way through the H.B.C. lands for our irrigation ditches." He sent a copy of his letter to Whyte and asked him to discuss "a reasonable price" for right of way with Chipman. In December 1907 the original exchange of lands proposition was agreed upon, although it applied only to the Western section of the irrigation project. By January 1908 the exchange of lands between the two companies was well underway.[73]

Shaughnessy kept a close watch over the selling price of the CPR's irrigable lands. He insisted that a price schedule for these lands be approved by the board's executive committee. "Considering the enormous cost of our irrigation work, and the comparatively small area estimated to be irrigable," he informed Whyte in 1905, "we must try to sell as many acres as possible at the higher prices fixed for the irrigation lands."[74] The CPR president was very critical of Dennis's actions regarding the sale of irrigable lands. In June 1905 Dennis received an offer from T.L. Beiseker and C.H. Davidson, two North Dakota land promoters who had purchased a large amount of CPR land in southeastern Assiniboia in 1902. They proposed to join with A.J. Sayre to form a colonization company which would sell 110,000 acres of CPR irrigable land and 30,000 acres of non-irrigable land in the Western section. They undertook to guarantee the CPR $11 an acre for irrigable land and $6 per acre for non-irrigable. Dennis was very favourable to this proposition, since these men had a good record of colonizing CPR lands in eastern Assiniboia, but Shaughnessy was "appalled" that Dennis had practically closed the transaction with Beiseker and Davidson. Dennis was informed that no agreement for selling irrigable lands in a block would be approved. The CPR president was also unhappy with the guaranteed price of $11 an acre. Galt's Alberta Railway and Irrigation Company was getting $18 per acre for many of its irrigated lands, and Galt expected an average price of "well above $14 per acre." On Shaughnessy's instructions, Whyte proposed that the contract should cover only 30,000 acres of irrigable land, and if the group were successful in the sale of this area, a new agreement for a larger tract of land could be arranged. Dennis informed Whyte that these men, who were forming the Canadian Pacific Irrigation Company (CPIC), would not accept a grant of 30,000 acres since their initial expenses – establishing agencies, printing promotional material, bringing in delegates, setting up a demonstration farm – were such that they would make no profit on the first 30,000 acres. Dennis persuaded Whyte that the CPIC needed the larger tract of 110,000 acres, and the latter won Shaughnessy over to the idea. The CPR executive committee approved the larger area on 1 September 1905.[75]

The CPR and the CPIC signed a contract on 1 November 1905 which covered 110,000 acres of irrigable land and "such non-irrigable lands as may be grouped with and attached to the irrigable lands by the railway company." Under the terms of this contract, the CPIC acted as the CPR's exclusive agent for the sale of these lands for a 3-year period beginning 31 December 1905. The CPIC guaranteed the CPR $11 an acre and $6 an acre for irrigable and non-irrigable lands respectively, and retained as profit all proceeds in excess of these prices. The purchaser was required to pay one-tenth of the selling price at the time a contract was signed, and the balance in nine equal annual instalments, with interest at 6 per cent. Dennis was to maintain close supervision of the work of the CPIC and was given the authority to terminate the agreement with 15 days' notice if he were dissatisfied with its results or methods. Dennis grew increasingly critical of many of the CPIC's practices. The colonization company set a flat price of $25 per acre for irrigable land, and $15 per acre for non-irrigable land. Dennis maintained that the land should be priced according to quality, location, and proximity to the CPR, and that maximum prices should be $20 and $10 respectively for irrigated and non-irrigated lands. Shaughnessy and Whyte were unhappy with the slowness of sales, despite the CPIC's extensive efforts in promoting the lands in the United States. In its first 15 months of operation, the CPIC sold slightly less than 23,000 acres of irrigated land and 14,000 acres of non-irrigable land. The two CPR officials also wanted to eliminate the middleman's (CPIC) profit and use it to pay substantial commissions to agents and sub-agents in the field, particularly in the US. All these factors led the CPR to take over the CPIC, effective 1 January 1908. The CPIC now became the CPR's Land and Colonization Department for lands in the irrigation block. Beiseker and Davidson were paid $50,000 for the surrender of their equity in the existing contract. Although Hedges rightly emphasizes the CPR's primary concern to settle its lands, its takeover of the CPIC demonstrates that the company was also determined to obtain the maximum profit from these lands. The CPIC had sold irrigated land at $25 an acre which netted the CPR only $11 an acre. With a program of sales by the CPR, allowing $5 an acre as the cost of selling, the company would net the substantial sum of $20 an acre.[76]

When the CPR took over the CPIC, it retained its manager, Charles Peterson, and the Calgary staff. The CPIC had hired Peterson in September 1906 in response to Dennis's criticisms of the company, and he had cooperated with Dennis in making some changes. Born in Denmark in 1868 and educated in England, Peterson had organized the department of agriculture for the government of the North-West Territories and served as its first deputy minister from 1898 to 1902. He then organized the Territorial Live Stock Association and served as its secretary, before joining the CPIC.[77] Under Beiseker and Davidson, there had been little coordination between the Calgary office and the CPIC's extensive agency organization. Within a year Dennis and Peterson brought about reforms which made the CPIC, in Hedges' view, "a model of efficiency." They worked out a standardized procedure to be used for every inquiry about CPR-irrigated lands: the prospective settler was sent four letters, with accompanying literature, at intervals over a 40-day period. The most useful pamphlet for the settler was *Starting a Farm*, which was sent with the fourth letter. It contained testimony from practical farmers who had started homes in the irrigation block. Other reforms related to the arrangements for commissions to agents. The CPIC had paid its agents a commission of $1.50 per acre on irrigable lands and $1 on non-irrigable land. Under the CPR regime, commissions were increased substantially. Irrigable land selling between $18 and $24 per acre now paid a commission of $2.25 per acre, while the commission on non-irrigable land was to be $1, $1.25, or $1.50 an acre according to the price at which it was sold. A drastic change was made in the method of paying the commission. Under Beiseker and Davidson, a fraction of the commission was paid at the time of sale, while the balance was paid as subsequent payments were made on the land. This practice limited the agent's working capital and made it difficult for him to pay commissions to his sub-agents. Under the new regulations, the proportion of the total commission paid the agent in cash was graded according to the amount of the cash payment that the purchaser made at the time of purchase. For example, for irrigable land which carried a commission of $2.50 per acre, the agent received the entire amount when the buyer paid at least one-fifth cash. These and other reforms provided a strong incentive for agents to promote the CPR's lands as vigorously as possible.[78] Subsequently, there was a substantial improvement in land sales in the irrigation block, amounting to 185,000 acres in 1908 and 215,000 acres in 1909. In addition, the cost of selling the land had decreased from $3 per acre under Beiseker and Davidson to $2.42 per acre in 1908 under CPR administration. The contract with Beiseker and Davidson had netted the CPR $11 per acre for irrigable and $6 for non-irrigable land, while the net for 1908 was $19 and $8 respectively.[79]

The sale of lands in the Western section of the irrigation block was almost completed by December 1909. Further surveys of the Central section of the block undertaken in 1909–10 indicated that only a small amount of the land was irrigable. The CPR directors therefore decided in 1910 that the company should undertake to irrigate the Eastern section. They estimated that this work would take 3 years to complete at a cost of approximately $8.5 million. The

Eastern section would be more costly to irrigate than the Western section for several reasons. It would require 3,500 miles of ditches compared to 1,600 for the Western section, while the structures in the Eastern section would need to be more substantial than those in the Western section. The money required for the project would come from the CPR's accumulated land funds.[80]

The start of work in the Eastern section was, however, delayed by a serious dispute with the HBC over its lands in this area. The HBC no longer wished to employ the exchange-of-lands procedure used to settle the matter in the Western section. Instead, the company's Chief Commissioner, Clarence Chipman, proposed to F.T. Griffin that the CPR pay the HBC the market value for its lands in the Eastern section as irrigated lands. Griffin visited Shaughnessy in Montreal in May 1909 and explained Chipman's proposal. Shaughnessy was adamantly opposed and informed Whyte that the CPR might seek authority at the next session of Parliament to expropriate the HBC lands. He was certain that Lord Strathcona "will see the unfairness and impropriety of demanding for these lands the value that has been given them by our irrigation project, without which they would have been almost valueless." Lord Strathcona, who was in Canada in the autumn of 1909, discussed this sensitive issue with both Chipman and Shaughnessy. In October 1909 Shaughnessy agreed on $8 an acre as the minimum price for HBC lands in the Eastern and Central sections. When the CPR president was in London in January 1910, he discussed the matter with Strathcona and some members of the HBC board. They informed him that the Southern Alberta Irrigation Company had offered $15 an acre for HBC lands in its area, so that they considered the CPR price of $8 per acre "too low." Shaughnessy then consented to increase the minimum price for HBC lands to $10 an acre. In an interview with Shaughnessy in Montreal in March 1910, Chipman stated "that he had instructions to carry out the transaction" on the basis of a minimum price of $10 per acre. Subsequent to this, construction of the irrigation works of the Eastern section went ahead that spring. The agreement between the CPR and the HBC to purchase 102,174 acres of HBC lands in the Central and Eastern sections at an average price of $13.50 per acre was signed only in November 1910.[81]

The focal point of the system was a large dam constructed at Horse Shoe Bend on the Bow River, about 3 miles south of Bassano. It was necessary because the Bow runs in a very deep valley in this area; the dam would raise the water level sufficiently to facilitate its flow into the main canal. The Bassano Dam was designed by Hugh B. Muckleston, a CPR engineer who was assistant to A.S. Dawson, chief engineer for the Eastern section. Dam construction proceeded through the summer and into winter, when the concrete work was suspended only if the temperature dropped to -26° Celsius. Nonetheless, the structure was not ready for operation until April 1914. Shaughnessy and a large party of CPR officials, including George Bury, J.S. Dennis, P.L. Naismith, and Hugh Muckleston, inspected the Bassano Dam on 26 April 1914. Shaughnessy formally opened the main canal by "thrusting over the handle himself and allowing the waters to rush through into the main canal." The concrete spillway section of the dam was 720 feet long with an earthen embankment 7,200 feet in length, which raised the level of the river 50 feet. A flow of 100,000 cubic feet (3000 m²) could pass through its five open sluice gates without danger of damage to the structure. The dam provided a substantial amount of hydroelectric power, some of which was used for the CPR's new Ogden Shops in Calgary. Muckleston had also drawn up the plans for all other major structures of the irrigation system in the Eastern section. By the summer of 1914 these were completed and water was flowing in the ditches. The system brought water to 245,000 acres of land.[82]

The CPR's activities in the irrigation field had been a major factor in the company's two-stage takeover of Galt's AR&I CO. In 1908 the CPR spent $2 million to acquire a controlling interest in Galt's company, to prevent the Canadian Northern Railway or the GTPR from gaining control of it. The AR&I CO. had close links with the CPR, for its Lethbridge colliery supplied substantial amounts of coal to the railway and settlers along it, while the Canadian Pacific received considerable revenue from the traffic interchanged with it. Then in 1910 the two rival transcontinental railways had filed plans for lines through the CPR irrigation block. These actions prompted the CPR to acquire full control of the AR&I CO. At the CPR annual meeting in October 1911 the shareholders ratified a 999-year lease of the AR&I CO. This lease was authorized by federal Order-in-Council on 28 December 1911 and came into effect on 1 January 1912. The CPR guaranteed interest on the AR&I CO's debenture stock and agreed to purchase all the company's outstanding capital stock at a price of $150.[83]

In December 1909 the Calgary office was given jurisdiction over all CPR lands in Alberta. Dennis had proposed this policy in discussions with Shaughnessy, who strongly supported it. The CPR president realized that since the sales of lands in the Western section were almost completed at this time, there was little work to keep the Calgary office and its agencies going. It would take some time before lands in the Eastern section could be sold; "in the meantime," Shaughnessy informed Griffin, "it is important that the organization that has been created at the cost of a good deal of trouble and money should not be broken up." Griffin was strongly opposed to what would represent a reduction in the jurisdiction of the Land Department in Winnipeg, but he was unable to change the new policy. As Hedges points out, most of the activities of the Land Department had been confined to selling lands tributary to the CPR main line in Manitoba and Saskatchewan, as well as the lands in the southern reserves in these two provinces, although it had also sold much land in areas tributary to the CPR line to Saskatoon.[84] However, the reorganization went ahead in January 1912 when the CPR created the Department of Natural Resources (DNR) with headquarters at Calgary. The existing Calgary organization formed the basis for the new department. J.S. Dennis, appointed its head with the title of assistant to the president, was mainly responsible for policy formation. P.L. Naismith, the AR&I CO's general manager, was to administer the department with the title of manager.

The CPR acquired substantial coal and timber resources by taking over the AR&I CO. (Its policies for the development of these resources are discussed in chapter ten.) In addition, the CPR acquired the Galt company's holdings of a 500,000 acre tract of land, located directly south of Lethbridge, which had been purchased from the federal government in 1902 for $500,000, to be paid in ten equal instalments, commencing 1 December 1907. However, the federal government had set a maximum price of $5 per acre on these lands, while all lands in the parcel not sold by the end of the agreement (1917) had to revert to the Crown. These obligations were circumvented by having the AR&I CO. sell all the land to one buyer, its parent company, the CPR. Thus the CPR could legally sell the 500,000 acres for prices as high as the market would bear.[85]

The CPR placed the administration of *all* the company's land under the control of the DNR, which was divided into five branches – Land, Engineering, Coal Mining, Treasury, and Accounting – each with its own organization. The result was that the company's Land Department in Winnipeg was no longer required. However, the office of Manitoba Land and Immigration Agent was set up there. The agent, who reported directly to Dennis, was in charge of lands and townsites in Manitoba only and was also responsible for the forwarding of immigrants to all points west of Winnipeg. Similar offices for Saskatchewan and Alberta were established at Saksatoon and Calgary and the agent at Lethbridge was put in charge of the lands

Table 4
Sales of CPR Irrigated Lands, 1908–14

Year	Amount (in acres)	Proceeds	Average price per acre
1909	69,963	$1,728,785	$24.71
1910	145,421	3,866,744	26.59
1911	19,097	642,232	33.63
1912	3,270	144,697	44.25
1913	7,944	388,303	48.88
1914	6,318	422,864	66.93
Totals	252,013	7,193,625	28.54

Source: CPR, *Annual Reports,* 1909–14.

and town lots of the AR&I CO. The DNR also controlled substantial agricultural and timber lands and mining properties in BC and valuable town properties in Vancouver.[86]

On 1 January 1913 the CPIC as a land-selling organization went out of existence and its staff was transferred to the DNR. The DNR's Land Branch was responsible for administering and selling the CPR's irrigated lands, primarily those in the Eastern section, although some irrigable lands in the Western section were still unsold in 1912.[87] In July 1912 Naismith approved a reclassification of unsold CPR lands in the Western section. There were now six classes of land, ranging from irrigable loam land at $35 an acre, non-irrigable loam land at $20 per acre, to slough land at $10 an acre. After Dennis gave his approval to this price schedule, the Land Branch's sales division took over the selling of the lands.[88] In March 1914 the DNR's Land Branch started a vigorous campaign to colonize the irrigable lands in the Eastern section. Special terms of payment were adopted to facilitate their sale. While they were sold on the 20-year plan (as were irrigable lands in the Western section), the settler was excused from the second payment of the principal until the end of 3 years' residence, and was exempted from payment of water rental for 2 years.[89]

The figures for sales of CPR irrigated lands are shown in table 4. Some irrigated lands were sold in the period 1906–8, but the company's *Annual Reports* for these years do not list these separately. The table demonstrates that the largest sales of irrigated lands in the Western section were made in the 2-year period from July 1908 to June 1910. The steady increase in the price of irrigated lands is similar to that for non-irrigated lands in this period.

The "primary concern" of the CPR in its land policies, asserts Hedges, was "with the occupation of the land as rapidly as it was sold." Settlers would soon produce valuable traffic for the railway. This over-whelming concern for colonization was particularly the case from 1908 to 1914. In 1908 the company set up a Development Branch at Calgary to assist land purchasers in starting farming operations, mainly on irrigable lands. This branch offered the preliminary work – fencing the land, preparing it for crop, and seeding – to be done under contract. Since it could contract annually for the work on thousands of acres, the branch was able to obtain from contractors "the highest grade of work at the lowest possible prices." The com-pany made no charge to land purchasers for the personal services of the development staff.[90]

In 1908 the CPR introduced another innovation which illustrated its commitment to colonization rather than just land selling. This was the "crop payment plan." A similar scheme had been used by the Northern Pacific Railroad in the 1890s and subsequently by other American railways. J.S. Dennis introduced the policy to the CPR. He engaged R.B. Bennett, the Calgary solicitor for the CPR, to draw up a draft contract allowing for the sale of land by crop pay-ment. Dennis then presented the proposal to Shaughnessy in August 1908. He stressed that the crop payment plan was a good method for encouraging agricultural production, because under it the CPR would take only a small part of the farmer's capital in a cash payment, while the farmer was required to use the rest of his capital to develop his farm and to pay the company with part of his crop. Under the plan, Dennis remarked to Shaughnessy, "our security for the de-ferred payments is absolute, while at the same time we are creating traffic and improving the value of the land."[91] It should be noted that this plan was used only for lands in the CPR irrigation block.

The crop payment plan was approved by the Canadian Pacific board of directors in the autumn of 1908 and thereafter a publicity campaign was mounted to sell it to American farmers. The main features of the plan were as follows: a farmer could purchase up to 160 acres of irrigable and 480 acres of non-irrigable land. The farmer paid one-tenth of the purchase price in cash. The balance was paid in a portion of the annual crop; each year the farmer would deliver to the CPR one-half of the grain grown on his land and the company would give the farmer the market price prevailing on the day of delivery. The farmer agreed to put in crop at least 50 acres in the first year, and a similar area annually thereafter. The plan seems to have been designed to promote mixed farming, for the farmer was to keep an accurate record of all crops raised on his land – grain, sugar beets, alfalfa, and timothy. The crop payment plan was not very popular in the pre-War period, though its popularity increased after World War One.[92] It was overshadowed by the ready-made farm policy started in 1909.

The ready-made farm policy (often referred to as "assisted group settlement") was launched because the crop payment plan did not, in its first year of operation, solve the problem of land settlement in the irrigation block. In October 1909 an official of the CPIC estimated that only 10 per cent of those who had purchased land were actually in residence. It appears that many of the "settlers" were purchasing land for speculative purposes and were staying in the US.[93] Charles Peterson, the manager of the CPIC, was convinced by this time that his organization had expended too much effort on land selling and needed to "immediately institute a vigorous campaign to persuade those who had purchased to go into occupation." The policy adopted to achieve this goal was the "ready-made farm." Peterson believed that the need in the irrigation block was for compact settlement, so he proposed farms of 80 acres rather than 160 acres. However, in 1909 the CPR decided to build 24 farms on quarter-sections, in the Western section of the irrigation block. The company erected on each quarter-section a small house and barn, fenced the land, dug a well, and prepared part of each farm for seeding in the spring of 1910.[94]

Hedges, who termed this a "revolutionary" policy for land and railway corporations in North America, suggested that its original inspiration came from the Salvation Army in England, which in 1909 wanted to sponsor a program of assisted land settlement in Canada. However, Shaughnessy had seriously considered such a policy in 1904 as a means of attracting British settlers to farm in Western Canada. During a trip to the UK in March and April 1904 he discussed his idea with people who were well informed on agricultural and immigration matters. These experts all agreed "that the better class of farmers in the British Isles can only be induced to emigrate if they know that they will have a home immediately on arrival. They know nothing of the methods of our hardy westerners," he informed F.T. Griffin, "who will live in a sod shack, for a year if necessary, before investing in farm buildings. The Englishman wants to have his house and his stable all ready for him." The CPR president did not pursue his idea at that time because of the difficulty of creating a group settlement when the company controlled only the alternate sections in a township. However, in the irrigation block where the CPR controlled all the land such a policy could be implemented.[95]

The ready-made farm policy adopted in 1909 was designed to attract British settlers to Western Canada. The following year in March a group of settlers embarked from the UK to take up the 24 ready-made farms. In the spring of 1911, 100 British families were to arrive and take up additional farms. But having discovered that there was insufficient contiguous land in the Western section for group settlement, company officials turned temporarily to lands outside the irrigation block. The region selected was in the vicinity of Sedgwick, on the CPR's Westaskiwin-Saskatoon line in central Alberta. Each farm was built on a quarter-section. Alternate sections in four townships were available for the development of ready-made farms, and "the Sedgwick colony became," Hedges asserted, "one of the largest and most prominent of such group settlements."[96]

In 1912 the policy of ready-made farms for British settlers was extended to the Eastern section of the irrigation block. At this time Dennis decided that Peterson's idea of an 80-acre farm was a mistake for several reasons. First, poorly broken land, alkali sloughs, or undesirable pockets would reduce the cultivable area on the farm and render it uneconomic. Also, under Dominion land surveys the road allowances were designed for farms of 160 acres or more, and the provision of road allowances for smaller farms would involve additional expense. Dennis therefore ordered the proposed ready-made farms in the Eastern section reclassified on the 160-acre basis. The DNR's Land Branch sought for these farms British immigrants who were farmers with at least £200 of capital or urban workers with capital and some farming experience. By the spring of 1914 there were two ready-made farm colonies, one at Bassano, the other at Rosemary, ready for settlers. The company no longer restricted these farms to British settlers, for in 1914 23 Colorado families were successfully established at Bassano. In the period 1909–14 the CPR had developed 1,622 ready-made farms.[97]

Another important program of assisting settlers was the "loan farm." The initiator of this policy was J.S. Dennis, who outlined it in a long letter to Shaughnessy in March 1912. The plan was designed to attract tenant farmers from the American Midwest who had little cash but "a large capital in the form of farming experience, large families, implements, and stock." The main features of the program were that the CPR reserved the right to select the settler. It accepted only married men with agricultural experience; four horses valued at about $1,000; machinery to the extent of $750; cows, pigs, or other stock worth $300 to $400; and household furniture of the value of about $200. The company would determine the amount of land to be purchased by the settler and would loan the farmer up to $2,000, to be spent under the DNR's direction, in erecting a house and barn, fencing the farm, drilling a well, and placing part of the land under cultivation. Although the drilling and fencing would be done under contract, the DNR could hire the settler and his equipment in cultivating the land, paying him the going rates. Shaughnessy was very favourable to this plan, and in May 1912 he recommended it to the board of directors, which approved it. In the period 1912–14, 297 of these farms were developed.[98]

Hedges concluded that the Calgary office – the CPIC and then the DNR's Land Branch – was very successful in promoting the settlement of CPR lands. Between 1 January 1908 and 15 December 1913, net sales through Calgary amounted to 2,485,669 acres for total proceeds of $38,749,226, at an average price of $15.59 per acre. The cost of selling these was an average of $1.84 per acre, while under Beiseker and Davidson (1905–7) it was about $3 per acre, a disparity which, Hedges remarked, "bears out the contention of the Canadian Pacific as to the efficiency of its land-selling organization.[99]

One of the most difficult problems in CPR land policy was that of dealing with the purchaser who was seriously in arrears in his payments. When the farmers' financial problems were the result of short crops or depressed prices for farm products, the CPR carried over the purchasers' accounts, rearranged contracts, cancelled interest, and reduced prices which the farmers had contracted to pay for the lands. However, the number of speculative purchases gradually increased after 1900, so that by 1912 the problem of arrears on the lands had become acute. Paul Voisey has shown that land speculation was widespread in the Vulcan farming district between Calgary and Lethbridge in the period 1904–14 and suggests that this phenomenon was predominant in all those parts of the Canadian Prairies settled after 1900. In March 1912 the CPR laid down a firm policy. "Our general policy," Dennis stated, "will be not to cancel contracts except where they have got so much in arrears that there is no hope of collecting the amount, or, in case there is no indication on the part of the purchaser to go into occupation of land and it is clear to us that it is being held for speculative purposes only." In October 1913 a cancellation policy was adopted, with the proviso that the purchaser be allowed to salvage his equity in the land. Between October 1913 and 30 April 1914, contracts covering 61,181 acres of irrigable land and 201,059 acres of non-irrigable land in the irrigation block were cancelled.[100] Table 5 shows the number of land grants cancelled in the period 1897–1913.

From 1896 to 1914 the CPR carried out a number of programs to promote better agriculture in the prairie West. Hedges has stressed that while the company borrowed some ideas from American railways, it also "adopted novel methods and policies."[101] Though Hedges has fully examined these policies, a summary is appropriate to this

Table 5
Cancelled CPR Land Grants, 1897–1913

Year	Cancellations (in acres)	Year	Cancellations (in acres)
1897	46,898	1907	50,960
1898	33,093	1908	33,957
1899	19,841	1909	34,621
1900–1901	19,232	1910	55,952
1902	17,224	1911	54,006
1903	23,802	1912	59,046
1904	64,347	1913	100,829
1905	33,092	Total, 1897–1913	744,201
1906	97,301		

Source: Hedges, *Building the Canadian West*, 388. These figures include only sales from the mainline grant and the Souris branch, for the years to 1912. After that date they include sales from all CPR grants.

discussion. In 1882 the CPR had transported Red Fife wheat from Ontario to the Prairies free of charge in an attempt to induce farmers to use a hardy strain of wheat which matured rapidly. In 1905, when the company was promoting the agricultural development of southern Alberta, it encouraged farmers to use winter wheat by importing Turkey Red wheat from Kansas City and transporting it free of charge over its lines from Portal to Calgary.[102] But its most innovative policies for promoting better agriculture were those connected with its irrigation project and those devised by the DNR. Initially, the CPR had cooperated closely with the AR&I CO in pioneering the development of irrigation in the prairie West. Galt's company had encouraged the cultivation of sugar beets on its irrigated lands, but for production to be profitable a sugar refinery was needed close at hand. In 1901 the AR&I CO signed an agreement with Mormon businessman Jesse Knight to establish a sugar beet factory, which came to be known as the Knight Sugar Factory, at Raymond. The CPR actively supported this project. It held 52,000 acres of land for sale at prices to be determined by agreement with Knight. If Knight completed his factory by September 1903, the railway would give him two-thirds of the proceeds of land sales in excess of $5 an acre. The CPR also leased to Knight 226,000 acres of land until the completion of his factory, when it would sell him the entire area at the low price of $2 an acre. These terms were carried out and the Knight Sugar Factory became a successful operation.[103]

The CPR was an active promoter of dry farming methods in southern Saskatchewan and Alberta from 1905 to 1914. In 1905 J.S. Dennis made inquiries of the US Department of Agriculture regarding Hardy W. Campbell of Nebraska, who was at this time "the most conspicuous propogator" of the dry farming faith in the United States. Dennis was so impressed with the results achieved by dry farming that he sought to interest important CPR officials, notably William Whyte, in it. In 1906 the CPR cooperated with the Saskatchewan government in distributing a pamphlet, *Hints to the Grain Growers*, issued by the Saskatchewan Department of Agriculture. This pamphlet was, in Hedges' words, "an adaptation of Campbell's *Manual* to Canadian conditions." The dry-land farming techniques were applicable to the irrigation block because many of the farms there consisted of both irrigated and non-irrigated or "dry" lands. The CPR sponsored Campbell's speaking tour of the irrigation block in the summer of 1909, and the following summer the company established two "dry land" demonstration farms there. The dry-land farming idea led the CPR to sell large areas in the Central and Eastern sections of the irrigation block as "dry land farms" in advance of the completion of the irrigation system in these areas. For reasons which are not clear, the company was unable to establish a successful dry farming community in the Eastern section. In a recent study, David Jones makes a convincing case that dry-land farming in the prairie dry belt of southeastern Alberta (which includes the Central and Eastern sections of the irrigation block) and southwestern Saskatchewan proved to be a disaster in the 1920s.[104]

However, the CPR's main interest was the development of irrigation farming. The first demonstration farm in the irrigation block was opened at Strathmore in 1905. It was supervised by the trained agriculturalist, Professor W.J. Elliott. Not only did it have excellent equipment, it also had an irrigation instructor who was in charge of the farm's irrigation operations and was available for service to independent farmers. Additional demonstration farms were set up in the Eastern section; by 1914 such farms existed at Tilley, Brooks, Cassils, and Latham. The CPR realized that as settlement developed in the irrigation block and the land was fenced, there would no longer be free grass on what had once been cattle ranges. The company therefore stressed in its literature and on its demonstration farms the importance of fodder crops, especially alfalfa. The railway "preached alfalfa," imported alfalfa seed – selling it at cost to the farmer – and provided an expert to give advice to farmers on growing alfalfa. The CPR also introduced livestock in the irrigation block as a means of promoting mixed farming.[105]

When the Department of Natural Resources was established in

1912, the CPR's agricultural work, Hedges asserted, "was greatly enlarged, not only in the irrigation block but throughout the prairie provinces." Professor Elliott was put in charge of the DNR's Agricultural Branch in Calgary. With Shaughnessy's support, Dennis set up demonstration "mixed farms" on CPR lands in the prairie provinces in order to prove that prairie farmers should adopt mixed farming. By 1914 thirteen farms were in operation: three in Manitoba, four in Saskatchewan, and six in Alberta. Also, the DNR's Agricultural Branch issued monthly bulletins which were widely distributed and which stressed the advantages of mixed farming. And finally, Dennis created the Animal Husbandry Branch of the DNR in 1912 to promote the raising of livestock on mixed farms. It was headed by Dr. John G. Rutherford, who had been veterinary director general of the federal Department of Agriculture since 1904.[106]

Some general conclusions can be made about CPR agricultural land policies in the prairie West in the period 1896–1914. Hedges has claimed that "the most distinctive feature of Canadian Pacific land policy [in the prairie West], the one which differentiated it most sharply from that of other land grant railways on the American continent, was its program of assisted settlement which officials of the company commonly referred to as 'colonization.'" The key features of this program were the ready-made farms and the loan farms.[107] Hedges' emphasis on the CPR's overriding concern for settlement of its lands in order to generate more traffic for the railway needs to be modified. The directors of the company were determined to maximize profits from the sales of the railway's lands, as their refusal to sell a large part of the main-line grant to the federal government in 1897 demonstrates. We have seen that the setting of maximum freight rates for some commodities in the prairie West in the Crow's Nest Pass Agreement of 1897 may have been a factor in convincing the CPR directors that the price of its prairie lands would increase substantially in the near future. The proceeds from land sales were very substantial in the period 1897–1914. Shaughnessy was extremely pleased in July 1906 when he issued a cheque for just over $1.5 million which paid off the remaining prairie land-grant bonds. "Few things in our history," he informed his close friend E.B. Osler, "have given me greater pleasure than the liquidation of the indebtedness, thus leaving the balance of our lands as a free, unencumbered asset."[108] These proceeds were largely invested in additions and improvements to the railway. In January 1914 the CPR president calculated that his company had spent $95 million of the proceeds of its land sales in additions and improvements to the CPR, or about 90 per cent of the total. This policy does not seem to have favoured the interests of the shareholders. However, the fact that the company did not have to take large sums from general revenue for additions and improvements was undoubtedly a factor in determining its dividend policy and enabling it to pay shareholders a handsome 10 per cent dividend on common stock from 1912 to 1914.[109] These findings – a high rate of reinvestment and a generous dividend policy – support Mercer's recent study which concludes that the CPR needed land grant aid, but that the amount of aid given was excessive.[110]

From 1881 to 1907 the CPR Land Department in Winnipeg was the centre of land-selling activities in the prairie West, but from 1908 to 1914 the Calgary Land Department emerged as the leader in this field. The Calgary office developed in the United States an extensive agency organization which was very effective in recruiting settlers, with the result that during this period the majority of those purchasing CPR land in the prairie West came from the US.[111]

CHAPTER NINE

Urban Policies

The CPR strongly influenced the pattern of urban growth in Western Canada by determining the sites of hundreds of communities along its lines and by contributing substantially to the economic and spatial growth of these centres. Although this chapter focuses on urban policies in the period 1896–1914, a discussion of the company's urban policies before 1896 is essential for understanding later developments.[1]

One of the CPR's most important decisions was its choice of a site for the railway's Western terminus. The Macdonald government in 1879 had finally decided that the transcontinental railway would terminate at Burrard Inlet rather than cross to Esquimalt on Vancouver Island. The CPR charter of 1881 located the Western terminus at Port Moody at the head of Burrard Inlet. However, as Patricia Roy remarks, "Van Horne ... decided that the limited amount of land for industry and railyards, the tidal mud flats, and the need for ships to go through the treacherous Second Narrows to reach it made Port Moody an unsuitable terminus." After visiting Burrard Inlet in August 1884, Van Horne announced that the CPR would be extended 12 miles west from Port Moody to Coal Harbour and English Bay, which would then become its Pacific terminus. The company needed a first-class harbour to obtain, with the assistance of its Pacific steamers, traffic from Asia to the east coast of North America, and to provide, with Atlantic steamers, an Imperial "All-Red Route" linking Britain with her colonies in Asia and Australia.[2]

Construction of the line west of Port Moody was completed in time for the first scheduled train from Eastern Canada to reach the terminal at Vancouver at 12:45 P.M. on 23 May 1887. It was a festive occasion to which almost all the citizens of Vancouver turned out. "Businesses were closed, city council adjourned its meetings, ships in the harbour were decorated, and the fire brigade and city band led a parade of hundreds to the station." In his welcoming address, Mayor MacLean praised the CPR, predicted a bright future for Vancouver, and called for three cheers for the company. Then Harry Abbott, the company's general superintendent of the Pacific Division, spoke. He discussed the many obstacles the CPR had overcome to reach Vancouver, but promised "Here we are and here we will remain." On 13 June the CPR liner *Abyssinia* reached Vancouver from the Orient. The company had established a regularly scheduled steamship service to China and Japan and, as Norbert MacDonald observes, Vancouver "was firmly established as a major depot in the all-British route to those distant lands."[3]

The CPR acquired substantial landholdings in the new city. The BC government had agreed in 1884 that in return for the extension of the main line from Port Moody to Coal Harbour and English Bay, it would grant the company about 6,000 acres of land in the vicinity of the new terminus – 480 acres in the Granville townsite, between Coal Harbour and False Creek, and some 5,795 acres south of False Creek, an immense tract which in 1885 was largely untouched forest. Private owners in Granville gave land to the CPR, realizing that real estate values would soar if Vancouver became the Western terminus. As a result, the CPR acquired 6,458 acres in the heart of the future city of Vancouver, which represented, in Norbert MacDonald's words, "the most significant land transaction in Vancouver's entire history." In time, CPR plans would shape "the street layout and the general location of the city's commercial, industrial and residential areas."[4]

The town of Granville was incorporated as the city of Vancouver by special charter on 6 April 1886. The incorporation bill, introduced into the legislature by the Smithe administration, provoked a lengthy and heated debate which focused mainly on the new city's name. Van Horne had proposed the name "Vancouver" because he thought Britons would remember Vancouver Island and Captain Vancouver and would therefore have some idea of the city's geographical location. Many legislators argued that the city's name would cause endless confusion with Vancouver Island. Victoria MLAs were outraged that this upstart city should steal the name of their Island. Underlying these attacks was the opposition of residents of Port Moody and the realization by Victoria merchants that the provincial capital would soon be overtaken as the province's commercial centre.[5]

The preparation of a plan for the city was undertaken by L.A. Hamilton, the CPR's surveyor and a member of the first city council elected in May 1886. Under the direction of Hamilton, who was assisted by the CPR officials, Henry Cambie and Harry Abbott, the entire area was surveyed in 1885 and 1886. As MacDonald observes, "the CPR's detailed plans ultimately shaped the layout of much of the city." The location of the CPR station, office, and Hotel Vancouver on the Granville-Street axis "pulled the centre of the city well to the west of the existing townsite." This placement avoided the extensive settlement in Gastown, gave the CPR room to develop its own facilities and allowed it to monopolize real estate profits. Development continued on the original townsite, which became the working-class, industrial section of the city, while the area west of Granville Street "attracted a more prosperous clientele, commanded the highest prices and held the greatest prestige."[6]

Vancouver City Council exempted the CPR yards from taxation for 20 years in order to have the company build its yards north of False Creek. The CPR took steps to develop a retail area along Granville Street. The CPR's luxurious Hotel Vancouver opened in May 1887 at the corner of Georgia and Granville streets, and soon after the CPR constructed a 1,200 seat opera house nearby. Shaughnessy later justified the CPR's decision to build an opera house in Vancouver – an unusual venture for a railway – on the grounds that "we were endeavouring to establish a city on a site selected by ourselves for the terminus of our railway line."[7]

Robert McDonald has demonstrated that Vancouver's economic growth from its founding in 1886 to the end of its first expansion phase in 1893 was mainly the result of CPR activities. "More than any other factors," he asserts, "it was the CPR that created Vancouver's first phase of development as a city." As a railway terminus, Vancouver became an important centre for servicing CPR equipment, and extensive machine shops developed there. The city's role as a breakpoint between land and water transportation systems also generated much economic activity in the city. The links with the Orient were expanded in 1891 by the arrival in port of the CPR's three new *Empress* steamships. Shipping required the construction of CPR wharves along the Coal Harbour waterfront. As more passengers were drawn into the city from both land and sea, the company constructed its luxurious Hotel Vancouver (1887). A survey of the city's economy in 1890 showed that the CPR employed 600 workers and paid out $400,000 annually in wages in Vancouver alone. This made the railway the largest single employer in the city, with a wage bill exceeded only by Vancouver's lumber and construction industries. By 1898 the CPR's annual expenditure in Vancouver had reached $2,040,000, including a monthly payroll of $88,000. The company also stimulated local economic growth by selling its large landholdings. J.B. Browning, who in 1888 succeeded L.A. Hamilton as CPR land commissioner in Vancouver, presided over the extensive selling and improvement of company land in the upper-class west end, and induced CPR magnates William Van Horne, Sir Donald Smith, and Lord Mount Stephen to invest substantially in Vancouver real estate. And finally, the CPR provided the crucial factor of expectations for Vancouver. The company's extensive facilities in the city convinced capitalists, entrepreneurs, and workers alike that Vancouver had a magnificent future as a metropolitan centre, a vision that helped draw capital and labour into the city.[8]

Another major decision taken by the CPR was the location of its major centre on the eastern edge of the Canadian plains at Winnipeg. Winnipeggers assumed from the beginning that their city would be on the main line. As Allan Artibise remarks, "The city was ... the largest community in the Northwest [in the 1870s] and it ... seemed reasonable to assume that it would receive special consideration." When the Liberals under Alexander Mackenzie came to power in November 1873, they had Sandford Fleming, engineer-in-chief of the transcontinental project, survey the route across the prairies. Fleming had proposed that Selkirk, not Winnipeg, would be on the main line, a decision the government announced in December 1874. Fleming proposed that the railway be built from Fort William to Selkirk, 20 miles north of Winnipeg, there cross the Red River, and run in a northwesterly direction to Edmonton. This route was shorter than the one through Winnipeg, and had engineering and economic advantages. The banks of the Red River at Selkirk were more stable than those at Winnipeg, and more importantly, were considerably higher, so that the bridge, railway, and townsite would be safe against flooding. The site at Winnipeg had been flooded seven times since 1812, while Selkirk had never been flooded. Delegations of important Winnipeggers lobbied with the prime minister for a crossing at Winnipeg, but without success. Winnipeg then reduced its demands to a branch line from Selkirk 20 miles to Winnipeg.[9]

The hopes of Winnipeggers for a location on the main line were again raised by the return of the Conservatives to power in the federal election of September 1878. During the campaign the Tories had broadly hinted that if elected they would have the transcontinental line pass through Winnipeg. At a mass meeting in the city on 8 November a memorial was drawn up, sponsored by the Board of Trade and endorsed by city council, containing an offer of a $300,000 bonus to assist the construction of a bridge across the Red River at Winnipeg. This memorial was sent to Ottawa and a by-law was drafted which provided for the raising of $300,000 by the city. In April 1879 the Macdonald government announced that the Prairie section of the Pacific Railway would be built on a more southerly route than proposed by the Mackenzie administration, and that as far as possible it would be built through existing centres of population. However, federal Minister of Public Works Charles Tupper made it clear that the main line would *not* pass through Winnipeg.

Clearly more pressure was necessary to protect Winnipeg's interests. At another meeting in Winnipeg yet another petition was drawn up and a new delegation sent to Ottawa. The Winnipeg delegates proposed that the government build a colonization line, which would be part of the Pembina Branch (Winnipeg to Emerson at US boundary), across the Red River at Winnipeg and running in a northwesterly direction to link up with the proposed main line north and west of the city. Tupper promised the delegates that the government would build this colonization line if the city built a bridge over the Red River. Although the colonization railway was not nearly as acceptable to Winnipeggers as having the main line pass through the city, it at least gave them an indirect connection with the main line. In September 1879 city council passed the by-law to raise $300,000 to finance construction of the railway bridge. At that time also the federal government called for tenders for construction of 100 miles of track west of Winnipeg, stipulating that the line was to be completed within 12 months. By January 1880 the Winnipeg City Council was ready to let tenders for the construction of the Louise Bridge across the Red River at Point Douglas.[10]

The Macdonald government signed a contract with a syndicate of capitalists headed by George Stephen to build the Pacific Railway in October 1880. Then in February 1881 Parliament passed legislation which provided extensive aid to the privately owned Canadian Pacific Railway for the construction of the transcontinental railway. One of the chief members of the CPR syndicate was Donald Smith, a major stockholder of the Hudson's Bay Company, which stood to make large financial gains if Winnipeg were chosen as the western headquarters of the CPR, since the HBC owned 1,750 acres of land in and around the city. "In the boom that would surely follow the passing of the CPR through Winnipeg," Artibise observes, "this property could be sold at high prices."

A delegation made up of members of the Board of Trade and the city council quickly made its way to St Paul, Minnesota, to interview members of the CPR syndicate. If the CPR would locate its main shops in Winnipeg, the city would provide the company with 30 acres of land within city limits, free of cost. The city delegates also offered to exempt CPR property from all city and school taxes for 20 years. When the syndicate had not reached a decision by May

1881, the city council and Board of Trade met and sweetened the offer by extending the tax exemption to perpetuity. On 16 June 1881 the CPR syndicate formally offered to locate its workshops in Winnipeg, which effectively involved the location of the city on the CPR main line. When the city by-law was drawn up, CPR property "now owned or *hereafter to be owned*" was exempted from taxes forever. The city provided the company with lands suitable for a passenger station and gave the CPR free use of the Louise Bridge which had been constructed by the city. This by-law was ratified by the ratepayers in September 1881. The CPR at once started construction of workshops, a freight shed, and a passenger station. With the consent of the federal government, the CPR in the latter part of 1881 built a new line directly from Winnipeg to Portage la Prairie, shortening the rail distance by 17 miles. Winnipeg had become the western headquarters for the CPR.[11]

The history of Winnipeg as the metropolis of Western Canada, as Ruben Bellan observes, "properly commences in 1886." In that year the recently completed CPR opened the western plains to large scale agricultural settlement, giving Winnipeg a hinterland of more than 100 million acres. Although the city had suffered economically as a result of the collapse of the real-estate boom of 1881–2, its economic base had grown substantially since 1880, due to the CPR's establishment in Winnipeg of its shops, yards, and offices, the continuing construction of the CPR in the West, and the steady growth of agricultural settlement. The city had a population of 21,164 in 1885, more than double what it had been in 1880.[12]

In the 1870s, despite the influx of Ontario businessmen into Winnipeg, members of the old trading houses remained dominant. By the mid-seventies five establishments – headed by such powerful figures as James Ashdown and A.G.B. Bannatyne – "all of whom could trace their origins to pre-confederation Winnipeg, controlled most of the trade." Through their particiaption in city council and the Board of Trade, Winnipeg traders "exerted considerable influence on the growth of the city."[13] Their first important victory was the defeat of Selkirk as the western headquarters of the CPR. Their next achievement was the modification of the CPR's rate structure in favour of Winnipeg. After the completion of the CPR, the Winnipeg Board of Trade made repeated complaints that the existing freight-rate structure favoured Toronto and Montreal in the distribution of items such as sugar, provisions, and heavy hardware. In 1886 the CPR recognized the city's status as a distributing centre by granting a 15 per cent reduction on freight rates west from Winnipeg. After further pressure from the Board of Trade, these lower freight rates were applied to goods manufactured in Winnipeg as well as merchandise imported from Eastern Canada. In 1890, again after pressure from the Board of Trade, the CPR introduced lower rates on merchandise shipments from Eastern Canada to Winnipeg. As Bellan observes, "These reductions applied only to shipments to Winnipeg, and were particularly significant in clothing, dry goods, and machinery." The CPR's freight-rate reductions contributed substantially to the development of Winnipeg as the major distribution centre for the prairie West. By 1890 there were eighty wholesale firms in Winnipeg – many of them branches of Eastern Canadian houses – which did an aggregate turnover of $15 million annually.[14]

The CPR's policy of levying higher freight charges from Eastern Canada to Winnipeg on manufactured goods rather than on raw materials assisted the development in Winnipeg of industries that manufactured heavy raw materials into products sold wholly or mainly in Western Canada. "Thus," Bellan points out, "the lower freight charges on pig iron and steel billets, compared to iron wares and structural steel forms, contributed substantially to the establishment in Winnipeg of foundries and metal works, which obtained their basic materials from Eastern Canada or the United States. Local scrap iron afforded additional support to local foundries."[15]

By 1897 the policies of the federal government had established Winnipeg as "the undisputed headquarters of the Western grain trade." This in turn made Winnipeg the main railway centre of Western Canada. The CPR built large yards there to handle the huge number of boxcars which carried the western grain harvest to Winnipeg, to be graded, sorted, and sent on to the Lakehead. The CPR's Winnipeg workshops serviced and repaired all rolling stock used on the company's lines in the prairie West. By 1884 the CPR roundhouse and workshop employed 2,000 people. The city's population rose steadily from 21,164 in 1885 to 38,500 in 1895.[16] Thus, the CPR, though it had required some pressure at first from the city's business elite, had played a major role in the development of Winnipeg as the metropolis of Western Canada by 1896.

In the early 1880s the CPR decided to place a divisional point, steamer terminals, and large grain elevators at the Lakehead in order to move the prairie grain crop to markets in Eastern Canada and Europe. This decision, Max Foran asserts, "precipitated a bitter struggle between the neighbouring communities of Fort William and Port Arthur." In 1889 the CPR chose Fort William (which did not gain town status until 1892) as this important service centre, despite the fact that Port Arthur was a larger town with a more substantial commercial section. Elizabeth Arthur rejects the argument that the tax dispute between the CPR and Port Arthur was the direct cause of this action and suggests that the decision was strongly influenced by Donald Smith, since the Hudson's Bay Company had substantial landholdings in Fort William. The CPR's decision did stimulate the growth of Fort William in the 1890s; by 1901 its population exceeded that of Port Arthur for the first time.[17]

In 1881 the CPR directors had decided on a southerly route across the prairies, a decision which had a major impact on the development of the prairie West. On the advice of Sandford Fleming the Mackenzie government had chosen a northerly route across the prairies, from Selkirk across Lake Manitoba at The Narrows to Battleford, then south of the North Saskatchewan River to a point not far south of Edmonton, and west through the Yellowhead Pass. In 1880 the Macdonald government made a slight change so that the Pacific Railway would run south of Lake Manitoba. This route was written into the CPR charter of incorporation approved by Parliament in February 1881. Later that year the directors moved the company's western headquarters from Selkirk to Winnipeg and decided to build directly westward from Brandon and through the Kicking Horse Pass. The change of pass was authorized by legislation passed by Parliament in 1882. This important decision shifted settlement – both urban and rural – away from the valley of the Saskatchewan to the southern plains. It led the Macdonald government to move the territorial capital from Battleford to Regina on the CPR main line, in 1883. The CPR's adoption of a southerly route also left towns in the valley of the Saskatchewan such as Battleford, Prince Albert, and Edmonton without rail facilities for another decade, since the CPR was not active in constructing branch lines north of its main line in the 1880s. And, as Foran points out, "the southern route ... gave the CPR more arbitrary power over townsite selection than did the original survey, which traversed existing settlements. The choice of a southern route enabled the CPR almost literally to build urban western Canada from bald prairie, and primarily on its own terms."[18]

Foran stresses that the profit motive was very important in the CPR's townsite selection. This may have been accentuated by the role of the Canada North-West Land Company, which under its charter of 1882 was entitled to half the area of all townsites established on the main line between Brandon and the British Columbia border. CPR policy called for a townsite to be located in each township crossed by the railway, while the locations of larger centres were determined by company requirements for divisional points. A number of examples will illustrate the importance of the profit motive in the selection of the larger townsites. When land speculators bought much of the land in Grand Valley because it was known that a divisional point would be required near this location, the CPR simply moved 2 miles west and built its station at Brandon, where it owned the land. Brandon soon became an important town in western Manitoba, while Grand Valley did not develop at all. The location of the CPR townsite in Regina, the territorial capital, was another example of the profit motive at work. The Regina townsite was on a dry, treeless plain but it appears that this location would promote substantial land sales in the vicinity. The federal government – in the person of Edgar Dewdney, lieutenant-governor of the North-West Territories – chose land in Regina for the legislative buildings, a government house, and the new headquarters of the North-West Mounted Police. The CPR, however, built its station on its own land half a mile east of Dewdney's location, and began selling town lots there. The result was that the fledgling town of Regina was spread out over 2 miles and deprived of the advantages of a core of institutional facilities. The acrimony that developed between Dewdney and the CPR convinced the company to establish Moose Jaw (some 40 miles to the west) as the divisional point rather than Regina. As a result, Moose Jaw became "the emergent industrial capital of Saskatchewan when that role could have fallen just as easily to Regina." A final example of the importance of the profit motive was the CPR's involvement in the development of Calgary. By 1882 a good-sized community had developed on the east bank of the Elbow River and around Fort Calgary at the confluence of the Bow and the Elbow. The railway reached Calgary in 1883. But instead of bringing the railway to the existing town the company decided to place its townsite a mile to the west on land that it owned. As Foran remarks, this decision "ignored topography as well as the strongly expressed feelings of the resident community."[19]

After 1896 and prior to World War One, there was a slight shift in CPR urban policy. It resulted from the phenomenal growth of the population and the economy of Western Canada in that period. Clifford Sifton's vigorous immigration policies contributed substantially to the tripling of the population of the prairie West, from 419,512 in 1901 to 1,328,121 in 1911. This was the period of the wheat boom in the West, when wheat production rose from 31,455,633 bushels in 1898 to 208.4 million bushels in 1911. In British Columbia, the population more than doubled, from 178,657 in 1901 to 392,480 in 1911. Mineral production in this province increased from $10,906,861 in 1898 to $30,296,000 in 1913. The amount of lumber that had been cut in the decade 1891–1900 amounted to 1,227,000 board feet while the figure for the 1901-1910 decade was 5,921,000 board feet, an increase of 374 per cent.[20]

The Western city that benefitted most from CPR policies after 1896 was Winnipeg, which reached "the apogee of its power and influence in the West" in the year 1912. As Shaughnessy correctly prophesied in 1899, "Winnipeg is destined to be a large city, and its growth within the next ... ten years will ... be phenomenal." Because of congestion in its yards and the overloading of its repair shops, the CPR in 1903 started a major program of expanding these services. When completed, the CPR's Weston Shops employed 4,000 people.[21] Shaughnessy believed that it was important for CPR passengers arriving at and departing from Winnipeg to have first-class hotel accommodation. Therefore, the company built a luxurious hotel at the corner of Portage and Main streets – the Royal Alexandra – which was opened in 1906 and had over 300 bedrooms. The hotel was expanded in 1913 by the addition of 184 rooms. A new station and office building next to the hotel were opened in 1905.

In 1898 the CPR introduced Tariff 490, generally known as the "Traders' Tariff" which, as Bellan explains, was "designed to ensure that Winnipeg wholesalers, in shipping to Western points [i.e., in the prairie West], paid freight charges no greater than those paid by Eastern firms shipping to the same points. Under this tariff, firms which purchased goods in the East paid the low through rate for transportation to Winnipeg, and after breaking bulk, sorting and storing at Winnipeg, paid only the balance of the through rate on consignments shipped out to Western points plus a small charge of eight cents per hundred for cartage and handling." That same year the other railways operating in and out of Winnipeg adopted the same rates as those set under the Traders Tariff. Under this system of tariffs, Winnipeg wholesalers effectively obtained a 15 per cent reduction in freight rates. The 1901 Canadian Northern Agreement with Manitoba brought an additional 15 per cent reduction in freight rates from the Lakehead to Winnipeg. These two reductions gave Winnipeg "a commanding advantage over other cities, both in the East and West, in distribution across the Prairie." As late as 1896 Eastern Canadian firms had handled the bulk of the Western wholesale trade, but by 1901 Winnipeg handled the greater part of this trade.[22]

Winnipeg's position as the centre of the Prairie grain trade and the Western wholesale trade, and as the Western headquarters of the CPR (and later the Canadian Northern Railway and the GTPR) resulted in a substantial expansion of its population, from 44,972 in

1901 to 144,040 in 1911. However, other prairie cities, supported by the Pacific coast cities, attacked Winnipeg's freight-rate privileges, and in 1903 the railways cancelled the Traders' Tariff to points east of the city, raised terminal charges in the city by two cents per 100 pounds, and increased the through rate from Winnipeg to the Kootenay district of southern BC. In 1907 Portage la Prairie, with support from the Pacific coast cities, demanded the complete elimination of the Traders' Tariff out of Winnipeg on the grounds that it discriminated against other Western cities. At first the Board of Railway Commissioners ordered the railways to post new tariffs which would eliminate the discrimination in favour of Winnipeg. Following strong protests from the Winnipeg Board of Trade, the railway commissioners instructed the railways to delay the introduction of new rate schedules in order to allow it to consider the issue further. The new schedules, when finally introduced, retained some discrimination in favour of Winnipeg, but the city started to lose some of the Prairie distributing trade to Eastern distributors and wholesalers in other prairie cities.[23]

It was the Regina Board of Trade Case which undermined the remaining discriminatory features of the freight-rate structure favouring Winnipeg. In 1909 the Regina Board of Trade (supported by the Moose Jaw Board of Trade) formally complained that the existing freight-rate structure favoured Manitoba wholesalers in territory that belonged to Regina and Moose Jaw. The railways – including the CPR – opposed the Regina application, claiming that the differential in favour of Manitoba derived from the Manitoba Agreement of 1901 with the Canadian Northern Railway, which had been confirmed by federal legislation. The Board of Railway Commissioners handed down a major decision in favour of Regina: it ruled that the Manitoba Agreement did not override the provisions of the federal Railway Act which specifically prohibited discrimination in freight rates between communities with comparable traffic and operating conditions. The Board also declared that other Western cities were by then established wholesale centres enjoying a considerable density of traffic, and were thus entitled to the same rates as Winnipeg. The Board therefore ordered the railways to file new rates before 1 April 1911 to end the existing discrimination in favour of Winnipeg. When the railway companies appealed this decision to the Supreme Court of Canada in 1914, it confirmed the Board's judgment. In the meantime, to comply with the Board's order, the railways introduced a new tariff in 1910 in which, for rate-making purposes, the distance from the Lakehead to Winnipeg was assumed to be 250 miles instead of the actual 400 miles. This procedure conferred a differential advantage on Winnipeg. In 1911 the railways, on their own initiative, granted distributors' rates to several smaller prairie centres, including Weyburn, Yorkton, and Medicine Hat, enabling wholesalers in these towns to ship to surrounding districts on the same basis as wholesalers in larger cities. The CPR, assisted later by the Canadian Northern Railway and the GTPR, had consistently endeavoured to maintain Winnipeg as the main distribution centre for the prairie West. As Bellan concludes, "Rising Western centres had begun [by 1912] to challenge Winnipeg's sweeping authority, but its supremacy was virtually intact."[24]

Calgary was profoundly influenced by CPR policies after 1896. The company decided the nature of Calgary's business and wholesale districts. By selective sale of lots around its townsite, the CPR established a retail core around its station and north of its tracks. In 1898 the city gave the company $25,000 for the erection of freight sheds. "The CPR's decision to build these facilities right in the downtown area east of its terminal," Max Foran asserts, "virtually ensured the development of the area near the tracks for wholesale purposes. The resulting brand of wholesale activities with its need for spur-line trackage was a buffer to future retail and business expansion."[25] The building of the Crow's Nest Pass Railway and its extension to Vancouver enabled Calgary to become a major supplier of flour and meat to the towns and cities of southern BC, while the development of the irrigation block created a large new hinterland for Calgary. Calgary, Shaughnessy remarked in 1911, is "one of the most important business centres on our Western lines."[26]

The most important CPR decision affecting Calgary after the choice of townsite was the company's location of its new locomotive and car shops at Calgary. Until this time the company's Weston Shops in Winnipeg had monopolized locomotive and car repair work in the prairie West. But when an additional site was chosen, Calgary won out in preference to Medicine Hat and Lethbridge. The CPR had favoured Medicine Hat for a time because of its cheap power, in the form of natural gas. However, in 1910 the Calgary Power Company had completed the Horse Shoe Falls power project, providing the city with a source of cheap electric power. With the power question resolved, the CPR went looking for a site. It found one on 360 acres outside the city boundary and east of the Bow River. The company and the city council reached an agreement in 1911 under which the site was annexed to the city, and the city undertook the construction of access roads and bridges, a streetcar service, and the provision of water and light at cost. Ground for the shops was broken on 1 April 1912 and construction was completed in early 1913. The locomotive shops were designed to handle between 20 and 25 engine repairs per month, while the freight car facilities had a capacity of 500 cars per month. The shops were named in honour of CPR vice-president I.G. Ogden. The Calgary *Albertan* estimated in 1913 that with 2,000 people employed at the Ogden shops, at least 10,000 people would be added to the community. Max and Heather Foran conclude that the building of the Ogden shops "was easily the most important single factor in the economic development of Calgary before the post-1945 oil boom." The city's population rose from 4,392 in 1901 to 43,704 in 1911 and to 56,514 in 1916.[27]

The CPR also constructed a large new station in Calgary, which consisted of a four-storey main building and two wings, each two storeys in height. "There can be little doubt," Shaughnessy observed in 1907 when the project was started, "that Calgary itself will continue to grow and that a building which at this time would appear almost extravagant will in the not remote future be quite warranted by the traffic." After its completion in 1912 the company began construction of a large nine-storey luxury hotel with 350 rooms – the Palliser Hotel – which opened two years later. Between 1909 and 1912 the CPR developed the exclusive suburbs of Mount Royal and Sunalta in the southwest quarter of the city and opened up the working-class suburb of Bridgeland on the more remote high bluffs on the north side of the Bow River.[28]

Edmonton, which had become the capital of the new province of Alberta in 1905, was also growing. The population of the city increased from 5,547 in 1901 to 31,064 in 1911, a total which was augmented by 5,579 in 1912 when Edmonton amalgamated with the city of Strathcona.[29] In recognition of its economic emergence the CPR started work in 1906 on a line from Yorkton through Saskatoon to Wetaskiwin, on the Calgary and Edmonton line. It would produce a through line from Winnipeg to Edmonton, but, while construction was underway, complex negotiations with the Edmonton and Strathcona city councils proceeded regarding the construction of a bridge from Strathcona across the North Saskatchewan River to the centre of Edmonton. On completion of the Low Level Bridge (1902), Mackenzie and Mann had built the Edmonton, Yukon and Pacific from the CPR Strathcona terminus across this bridge into Edmonton. This was not a very satisfactory arrangement for the CPR, since passengers and freight destined for Edmonton had to transfer at Strathcona.[30] The company's purchase in 1903 of the Calgary and Edmonton Railway touched off a flurry of speculation that the CPR would build a bridge from Strathcona to Edmonton. It was not until 1905, however, that definite plans began taking shape. In May the Edmonton

Bulletin published the CPR scheme for a line northwest from the company's Strathcona station to 109th street in Edmonton. The railway would cross the river on a "high-level" bridge about 150 feet above water level. On the north (Edmonton) side it would run between 109th and 110th streets and cross over Jasper Avenue, the city's main thoroughfare. In June 1905 vice-president Whyte visited Strathcona to discuss the plans, which were becoming more imperative.[31] The move was timely. The Canadian Northern main line from Winnipeg reached Edmonton in November 1905, crossing the North Saskatchewan River at Fort Saskatchewan, east of the city. The GTPR also came into Edmonton from the east, crossing the river at Clover Bar in 1909.[32] A line into Edmonton would give the CPR a share of that city's growing commerce and tap some of the developing traffic from northern Alberta.

Bridge negotiations between the city of Edmonton and the CPR began in earnest early in 1906 and dragged on until October 1909. The project involved a combined rail-and-road bridge (it was Strathcona residents who sought a road deck below the rail level).[33] Shaughnessy was concerned that the CPR's Edmonton terminus would be a considerable way from the city's business section, whereas the competition was in the heart of that district.[34] There were two major obstacles to an agreement. First, there was opposition from the Edmonton Board of Trade which acted as the spokesman for residents on 109th and 110th streets whose property would be depreciated by the CPR line. Second, the CPR's proposal to close some Edmonton avenues was a matter of serious concern to city council. However, in November 1906 council accepted the CPR's proposition – except for the closing of Peace and Athabasca (102nd and 103rd avenues). In 1907 Shaughnessy considered an entrance into the city from the east, possibly as joint user of the GTPR bridge, because it seemed to him that the High Level Bridge was going to be "enormously expensive, and we may yet have to consider whether the game is worth the candle."[35] Then, when the company refused to compensate owners of property backing on the route, in February 1909 the railway commissioners held hearings on this issue and ruled that the property owners must be compensated to the value of their lots.[36] By the end of March the company had purchased the Edmonton lots it needed. In September 1909 Strathcona City Council granted $50,000 towards the project; Edmonton City Council had been promised a $100,000 provincial grant for the bridge by Premier Rutherford. An agreement among all the parties was reached on 21 October 1909: the CPR would contribute $842,727, the city of Edmonton $585,000 for the road decks, sidewalks, and street-railway lines, and the municipalities of Edmonton and Strathcona and the provincial and federal governments would pay the rest of a total estimated cost of $1.5 million. Edmonton ratepayers ratified the agreement by a three-to-one majority on 18 November 1909.[37]

The parties signed this agreement on 30 November. The city of Edmonton had given way and agreed to close Peace and Athabasca avenues. Construction was to begin within 3 months of approval by the Alberta legislature, which came early in 1910, with the province agreeing to put up $175,000 as its share of construction costs. The Alberta and Great Waterways Railways scandal of March 1910 ended in Premier Rutherford's resignation, but his successor, A.L. Sifton, advised civic officials to start work immediately, saying he would issue a cheque for $50,000 as the first instalment of the province's share. Construction began in earnest in August 1910 on a steel-span structure 2,500 feet in length with four main piers rising 125 feet above water level. On 2 June 1913 the first passenger train steamed into Edmonton over the new bridge: at last the city had a direct link south to the CPR main line.[38]

The CPR had a major impact on the urban development of BC in the period 1896–1914. The major towns in the interior of the province were located on CPR lines. One of the most important was Kamloops, a divisional point on the CPR main line and the location of major repair shops. Its population increased from 500 in 1893 to 3,772 in 1911, although in the latter year the city council conducted its own census which recorded a figure of 4,266. The construction of a CPR line from the Crow's Nest Pass through southern BC to Vancouver stimulated urban development in this more southerly region of the province. A number of urban centres were established and expanded – notably Cranbrook (a CPR divisional point), Nelson, Midway, Trail, and Penticton. Trail, where the large CPR smelter was located, was incorporated as a city in 1901; the tiny community of 1895 had developed rapidly as the smelter expanded. By 1914 it had a population of 1,500, about 600 of whom worked in the smelter. Their monthly payroll of $60,000 enabled city council to make improvements to the town.[39]

On Vancouver Island, the CPR's takeover of the Esquimalt and Nanaimo Railway in 1905 was instrumental in consolidating Nanaimo's urban status. The CPR also operated rail and passenger ferries between Vancouver and Nanaimo. Finally, Nanaimo's proximity to the Dunsmuir coal deposits coupled with Vancouver's energy demands enabled Nanaimo to expand significantly prior to 1914.[40] In Victoria, the CPR carried out activities which assisted the development of the province's capital. In 1901 it took over the Canadian Pacific

Navigation Company which had long dominated the BC coastal shipping trade. In 1903 a luxurious new vessel, the *Princess Victoria*, began
a fast daily steamship service between Victoria and Vancouver. The
CPR continued expanding its coastal fleet in the period 1907–1914,
when it commissioned nine new *Princess* steamships. The fleet developed a substantial passenger and freight business between northern BC, the Yukon, and Alaska, and the cities of Victoria and
Vancouver. This corresponded to Shaughnessy's determination to
obtain for the two port cities "a larger percentage of the passenger
business to and from the Northern country." The CPR opened a six-
storey luxury hotel – the Empress Hotel – in Victoria in 1908 which
attracted more tourists to the city, particularly from Washington
State and Oregon.[41]

The CPR continued to assist the development of Vancouver in the
period 1896–1914, although "the utter dependence of the early years
was over." In 1901 the city's population of 27,010 exceeded that of
Victoria (20,919) for the first time. This disparity was to widen considerably in the next decade, as Vancouver, like Winnipeg, experienced phenomenal growth. By 1911 Vancouver had a population
of 100,401 while for Victoria the figure was 31,660.[42]

By 1900 Vancouver and Victoria were obtaining a substantial share
of the traffic of BC, as revealed in statistical data which Shaughnessy
had his officials prepare. These figures dealt with the freight traffic
forwarded from Winnipeg and Vancouver for the fiscal year ending
30 April 1900. The Vancouver statistics included freight from Victoria, "because everything is rebilled from Vancouver." Winnipeg
derived 80 per cent of its revenue from the Western Division (the
prairie West and the line to Fort William) and only 4 per cent from
BC. Vancouver obtained 50 per cent of its revenue from BC and 35
per cent from the Western Division. Shaughnessy observed, "These
figures show most conclusively that Winnipeg is serving the territory
East of the Mountains, and that Vancouver and Victoria have the
trade of the territory between the Mountains and the Coast." He
also explained that Vancouver received a large part of its earnings
from the Western Division because "the through traffic from our
Pacific Steamships via Portal [Soo line] and Winnipeg is very considerable."[43] Winnipeg dominated the trade of the prairie West but
not that of BC. The figures also demonstrate that Vancouver and
Victoria were able to obtain a substantial share of the trade of the
Kootenays using the CPR main line to Revelstoke, the Arrowhead
branch, the Nakusp and Slocan line, and Kootenay lake steamers to
Procter and Kootenay Landing. (See figure 1.) Robert McDonald's
contention that BC's coastal cities "still had little commercial presence

in the Boundary and Kootenay regions of the province" as late as 1916 clearly requires substantial revision.[44]

After 1900, many Vancouver businessmen were still convinced that Winnipeg's special freight rates gave that city most of the Kootenay business, although the 1900 statistics do not support this contention. In 1905 Shaughnessy was privately critical of "the agitation aroused by some Vancouver merchants because of our unwillingness to concede their unreasonable demand that their rates to points east of the Rocky Mountains be placed on the same footing as the Winnipeg rates."[45] In 1907 the Vancouver Board of Trade Council informed the Board of Railway Commissioners that the CPR should not be allowed to set rates giving Winnipeg most of the Kootenay business, and it was supported in this by the McBride government. The Board, which was sitting in Vancouver, upheld the CPR's contention that it should be able to charge higher rates on its BC lines because they cost more for construction, maintenance, and operation than did its prairie lines and they furnished less traffic. The Board also ruled that the CPR should be allowed to charge a higher rate to interior points so as to recoup losses on the coast, where it had to compete with American and water transportation. It did however order a reduction of rates on goods covered by the Crow's Nest Pass Agreement. Vancouver and the CPR reargued their cases in 1908 in the *Coast Cities Case*, but the Board reconfirmed its previous decision.[46]

Vancouver attempted to become an export centre for Alberta grain starting in 1907, when the first flour shipments to Japan started. The following year the first bulk grain shipments were exported to Japan via Vancouver. Although the amount was small – 215,000 bushels – it represented 25 per cent of that year's grain crop in southern Alberta. In 1908 the CPR installed at Vancouver improved machinery for filling grain sacks and set special rates on the export of grain from Alberta. Then in 1914 the federal grain commissioners completed Vancouver's first grain elevator. However, it saw little use until the 1920s. Vancouver needed lower freight rates on grain and better rail links with northern prairie points to become a centre of the grain trade.[47] In the 1920s the Crow's Nest Pass freight rates were applied to grain and flour moving west to Vancouver, while the Canadian National Railways provided good access to northern Alberta. With the Panama Canal providing a water route to ship grain to Britain and continental Europe, Vancouver expanded rapidly as a grain trading port.

Vancouver's maritime trade increased substantially in the period 1900–14, partly due to the activities of the CPR. In 1908 the company erected two new piers to accommodate its tri-weekly *Empress* service to China and Japan as well as the monthly visit of the Canadian-Australasian Royal Mail Service. Throughout the period an increasing number of tramp steamers called at Vancouver to pick up cargoes of lumber, sacked grain, and flour. In 1912 the federal department of customs designated Vancouver as "a first class port" in order to give it an adequate customs service. Finally the expansion of the CPR's coastal fleet was important in increasing Vancouver's port business.[48]

"The rapid growth of freight and passenger traffic over the CPR and the expansion of Vancouver," Robert Turner observes, "required the development of new terminal facilities by 1912." The Montreal firm of Barrott, Blackader and Webster designed a new station and office building while the New York firm of Westinghouse, Church, Kerr and Co. served as project engineers. Construction of these new facilities, located on Cordova Street just east of the old station, began in 1912 and was completed by the summer of 1914. The station was designed to service four passenger tracks and to provide for quick and easy transfer between the company's rail and steamship operations. The estimated cost of the new terminals was almost $1,250,000.[49] The CPR expanded its hotel in Vancouver in 1905 and later constructed a new hotel, located near the CPR station, which opened in 1916.[50]

The CPR also constructed new major freight yards about 18 miles east of Vancouver at Coquitlam in 1912–14. Vancouver had limited space for freight yards and the downtown property was too valuable to be used for additional yards. The Coquitlam yards, capable of handling 5,000 cars, were designed to manage freight arriving from the East and to assemble traffic originating in the West. The facilities included a 12-stall roundhouse for servicing both main line locomotives and switch engines.[51]

The CPR decided to subdivide certain portions of its extensive landholdings in Vancouver as an exclusive residential neighbourhood. In 1907 Richard Marpole, the company's general executive assistant in Vancouver, made the proposal to the CPR board, which consented with some misgivings. The new subdivision was christened "Shaughnessy Heights," in honour of the company's president, and four streets – Osler, Nanton, Angus, and Hosmer – were named after CPR directors. The company employed the town planners Frederick Todd, a Montreal landscape artist, and M. Davick, a Danish engineer, to plan the subdivision. Lots were large, and the streets contoured across the steep hills, allowing for a good view and gentle road grades. Before house construction commenced, the CPR installed sewers, water mains, paved roads, curbs, and sidewalks – it even planted the boulevard.

Shaughnessy himself took a great interest in developing the area. No home built in Shaughnessy Heights could cost less than $6,000 – "the price of an ordinary, everyday mansion." The selling of lots began in 1909 and by 1914 there were 243 householders. One of the most magnificent mansions in pre-war Shaughnessy Heights was "Hycroft," built for Vancouver lumber tycoon General A.D. McRae. This estate contained a 2,000 bottle wine cellar, greenhouses, squash and tennis courts, a swimming pool, and an Italian garden with a tea house. The CPR wanted to put the subdivision which was in the municipality of Point Grey, into its own municipality. Although the provincial government refused this request, it did pass the Shaughnessy Settlement Act in 1914 permitting only single family dwellings in Shaughnessy Heights. This legislation effectively sanctioned the CPR's plans and preserved the elite character of the subdivision.[52] In a sense, Shaughnessy Heights was not only a profitable real estate development but also a tribute to Thomas Shaughnessy's strong interest in the economic development of BC and its metropolis, the CPR-located city of Vancouver.

CHAPTER TEN

Natural Resource Policies

The most important of the CPR's natural resource policies was its acquisition of the Trail smelter in 1898 and the expansion of this enterprise in the period 1898–1914. The CPR also developed several coal mines, promoted the exploration for oil on its lands, sold some of its lands in southern BC, and began to develop its large timber holdings on Vancouver Island.

The establishment of smelters in the West Kootenays took place in 1895–6. Three major ore discoveries had occurred in this region in the previous decade: the silver-copper deposits on Toad Mountain near Nelson (1886) and on Red Mountain near Rossland (1890), and the silver-lead deposits in the Slocan north of Rossland (1891). Most of the ores were shipped on steamers by lakes and rivers south to the Northern Pacific and the GN, to be smelted in Washington State and Montana in the United States.

This situation changed in 1895 with the building of a smelter at Nelson by the British-owned Hall Mines Limited, which owned the Silver King and other valuable mines on Toad Mountain. The Hall smelter, with a capacity of 100 tons, blew in its first furnace on 14 January 1896 and its second, 275-ton capacity furnace the following 5 September. Harold Innis observes that the construction of this smelter, close to the mines in the area, "permitted rapid expansion [of West Kootenay mines] through the possibility of handling lower-grade ores." By 1898 the Nelson smelter had become an important purchaser of ores; in particular it treated large quantities from the War Eagle mine at Rossland. It also smelted limestone ore from Kaslo in the Slocan area. Labour troubles that year, however, brought a steep decline in the smelter's production of copper matte.[1]

In 1895 a successful mining entrepreneur from Butte, Montana, Augustus Heinze, decided to build a smelter on the Trail townsite, located at the mouth of Trail Creek where it flows into the Columbia River. His investigators assured him that a narrow-gauge railway could be built from Trail to the mines at Rossland. The two owners of the townsite gave Heinze a 40-acre site for the smelter on a bench above the Columbia River. The American mining promoter then obtained a valuable contract from the Spokane-controlled Le Roi Mining Company to smelt 37,500 tons of copper ore from its rich Le Roi mine at Rossland. Construction of the Trail copper smelter began in the summer of 1895. On 1 February 1896 the smelter furnace blew in and began treating ores from the Le Roi mine. As the historian of the city, Elsie Turnbull, remarks, "Trail was at last a smelter town."[2]

Heinze approached D.C. Corbin, the promoter of the SF&N railway, requesting a reduction of the rates to carry copper matte between Trail and Spokane. Corbin, however, rejected the proposed alliance. But Heinze was in a strong position, for he had the contract with the Le Roi and his smelter could earn 50 cents a ton from the federal government, up to a limit of $30,000, as a bonus for silver-lead ore smelted in the Dominion.[3] Ore for the smelter was initially hauled from the Le Roi mine in large horse-drawn freight wagons. Under the Columbia and Western charter, a 13-mile narrow-gauge railway was built from the Rossland mines to the Trail smelter, which when completed in June 1896, enabled the smelter to treat larger quantities of ore each day. Heinze also intended to direct to his smelter the ores from the mines opening in the Boundary district west of Trail. In 1896 his Columbia and Western Railway was authorized to build a line from Rossland, west to Midway in the Boundary district, and then to Penticton, for a large land subsidy of 20,000 acres per mile.[4]

At this point Corbin took a number of steps to outmanoeuvre Heinze. Early in 1897, the SF&N and the War Eagle mining company in Rossland enticed E.H. Wedekind, the man who had helped design the Trail Creek smelter and had supervised its construction, to leave Heinze and join a new company that would establish a smelter at Northport, Washington, on the SF&N. This company would smelt the ores from mines within a 60-mile radius of Northport, which would take in mines representing "virtually all the American capital invested in major Rossland mines other than the Le Roi."[5] In the spring of 1897 this company – the Le Roi Mining Company – announced that it would build a smelter at Northport. Corbin undertook to give the company free land, water rights, and special railroad rates. The Le Roi Mining and Smelting Company was registered in BC in August 1897. Apart from Wedekind, James Breen and another important Trail smelter official also resigned from Heinze's staff to join the new company. Heinze countered by trying to persuade Laurier to impose a duty on ore shipped to the us, but he was unsuccessful in his bid. Construction of the Northport smelter was begun in August 1897 and the smelter blew in on New Year's Day, 1898. Heinze's smelter was by then in serious trouble, for not only had many of his best men been lured away to the Northport smelter, but "most of the American-controlled mines of Rossland shipped to Northport."[6]

Corbin had incorporated two railway companies – one in British Columbia (1893) and one in Washington State (1894) – to build the Columbia and Red Mountain railway from Northport to Rossland. This railway reached Rossland in the first week of December, 1896, although a bridge over the Columbia River was not completed until October 1897.[7] Heinze proceeded to build a 19-mile section of the Columbia and Western Railway from Trail north to Robson; this line was ready for provincial inspection in October 1897. However, he could not afford to extend this line west into the Boundary district as originally planned because he had too much capital tied up in his Montana mining properties. He did request a federal subsidy of $8,000 per mile for construction of 100 miles of railway west from Robson, but the Laurier cabinet does not appear to have given this request serious consideration. By late 1897, as Corbin's biographer, John Fahey, observes, "F. Augustus Heinze had run his course in British Columbia."[8]

Van Horne and Shaughnessy kept a close watch on the activities of Corbin and Heinze in 1896–7. They were particularly concerned about Heinze's plan to build a railway into the Boundary district, since such a line would occupy a large part of the route the CPR hoped to follow to the Pacific coast and would enable Heinze to control the traffic from the Boundary mines.

The stage was now set for serious negotiations between the CPR and Heinze. Heinze could no longer meet the competition from Corbin, while the CPR wanted to prevent Heinze from expanding into the Boundary district. Shaughnessy was in charge of the negotiations with Heinze. He and Van Horne met with him in Montreal and offered him $750,000 for his smelter and railway. Van Horne informed Railways Minister Blair that this meeting had achieved nothing: "We offered him an extreme price for his railway – a price certainly very much in excess of its cost, leaving him his lands as additional clear profit, but he refused our offer. We are at a loss to see what more can be done."[9] On the advice of a personal friend, Arthur Dwight, the manager of a large Kansas smelting and refining company, Van Horne hired an American mining engineer, Walter

H. Aldridge, in November 1897 to look after CPR interests in Trail. Born in Brooklyn in 1867, Aldridge had trained at Brooklyn Polytechnic and the Columbia University School of Mines, where he was a classmate of Augustus Heinze's, and from which he graduated in 1887. He worked 5 years as assayer, chemist, and metallurgist in Colorado and was then hired by the United States Smelting and Refining Company as manager of its plants in Great Falls and Helena, in Montana. Van Horne sent him to Trail to value Heinze's smelter.[10] From Aldridge's inspection, the CPR estimated Heinze's total expenditure for the smelter and railways at $550,000. This confirmed Shaughnessy's and Van Horne's view that their initial offer to Heinze had been a generous one.[11]

At this point Heinze asked T.G. Blackstock, the vice-president of War Eagle Consolidated Mining and Development Company, to act as an intermediary in the negotiations. (The War Eagle mine was one of the most valuable at Rossland. The company, which was originally controlled by Spokane businessmen, was taken over by Toronto interests, chiefly the Gooderham family. George Gooderham was company president.) The CPR made a second offer: $750,000 for the smelter and railways, and 640,000 acres of land − part of the subsidy which the CPR-controlled Columbia and Western Railway would earn for building the railway from Robson to Midway. Blackstock advised Heinze "that I thought the offer was a liberal one and did not see that I could say anything to get it changed."[12]

Blackstock was strongly interested in seeing the CPR and Heinze reach a settlement because the railway was willing to charge the War Eagle mine lower smelter rates than Heinze had. Shaughnessy had presented Blackstock with an offer of $8.00 per ton for freight and smelter costs for ore from the War Eagle mine. In turn the Toronto businessman offered to give the Trail smelter a 5-year contract on the mine's output if the CPR would fix a rate of $7 per ton. Heinze had charged a rate of $14.50 per ton in his contract with the Le Roi mine.[13]

Blackstock then visited Ottawa to obtain more information on the government's position in the CPR-Heinze negotiations. He judged that the Cabinet wanted the CPR to acquire Heinze's interests and to extend its Crow's Nest Pass Railway from Nelson to the Boundary district, although Blair wanted the line to Boundary Creek to be operated as an independent enterprise. Clifford Sifton informed Blackstock that "the real struggle between Heinze and the C.P.R. was ... as to which of them should obtain the bonus [land grant] for the Road from Robson to Penticton."[14] At Trail, Aldridge and Heinze could not agree on a figure for the Trail smelter, so the two men asked J.S.C. Fraser, manager of the local Bank of Montreal, to adjudicate the dispute. Late one night in January 1898 the two men visited Fraser and put their cases before him. Aldridge was pleased with the outcome, which he felt was in the CPR's favour.[15] In the final settlement, reached in late January 1898, the CPR paid Heinze $800,000 and 640,000 acres of land for his copper smelter, the narrow-gauge railway from Trail to Rossland, and the Columbia and Western line from Trail to Robson. The War Eagle board insisted on a rate of $7 per ton for freight and smelter costs, and eventually a figure of $7.50 per ton was agreed upon.[16] Van Horne triumphantly wrote Lord Mount Stephen: "We have got rid of Heinze by taking over his railway from Robson to Rossland, Smelter [sic] and all ... He and his railway were full of danger to us. There is nobody now save Corbin to dispute the territory with us."[17] In 1898 Parliament passed a private member's bill which brought the Columbia and Western Railway under the provisions of the federal Railway Act, and authorized the lease of the company to the CPR. On 3 August 1898 Cabinet sanctioned the lease of the Columbia and Western Railway to the CPR. Thus, the CPR obtained charter rights to build a railway from Robson west to the Boundary district (and as far west as Penticton), for which it would receive a handsome provincial land subsidy of 20,000 acres per mile.[18]

The CPR was now in the smelting business. Several authorities on the CPR agree with Lamb's assertion that "the Canadian Pacific had no great wish to enter the smelter business, but it did attach considerable importance to getting rid of Heinze."[19] However, evidence from the CPR Archives clearly demonstrates that the CPR board was convinced by Shaughnessy that the company should enter the smelter business. In June 1897 Shaughnessy had informed the publisher of the Victoria *Colonist* that the CPR did *not* intend to erect any smelter in BC, since such undertakings were "more properly a matter of private enterprise." However, he hoped that "the increase in mineral development" and the building of the Crow's Nest Pass Railway "will warrant experienced people in establishing smelters at several points in British Columbia."[20] But a trip to the mines in the West Kootenays in August 1897 led Shaughnessy to change his views on this subject drastically. The vice-president met with a group of mine owners at Rossland, who informed him that "the low grade character of a large percentage of the Red Mountain ores made it impossible to mine them at a profit at the present cost of freight and smelting." They strongly urged the CPR to extend the Columbia and Kootenay Railway from Robson to Rossland, so that Rossland would be directly linked with the Crow's Nest Pass Railway. The mine owners also recommended that the CPR lower its freight charges on Rossland ore, which would "increase the output [of the Rossland mines] substantially." "With this c.p.r. connection," Shaughnessy observed, "they [Rossland mine owners] feel confident that smelters would be established on the Columbia River, where they could have the ores treated on a lower basis than at present seems possible." He also talked with mine owners in the Slocan district who were very concerned about the recent decrease in the price of silver. They were convinced that "their ores would have to be treated nearer home so as to save transport charges." The Slocan mine owners also asked for support from the CPR "in obtaining from the smelters the guarantee that the smelting would be done for a very moderate profit." Shaughnessy believed that it would be very difficult to make such a guarantee effective. He was however convinced that the CPR should establish a smelter on the Columbia, and he strongly supported this policy at a CPR board meeting in September 1897. Shaughnessy informed Sir Richard Cartwright, Laurier's minister of trade and commerce:

Our Board decided that not only should we build to Rossland immediately but that we should secure the immediate establishment at some point on the Columbia River, of a large and modern plant that would be controlled by the Company in such a way as to cause it to be operated not with a view to any special profit from the smelting but with the object of reducing the cost of treatment to the lowest figure possible, so that all mine owners shall have opportunity to ... ship their ore of any grade, down to the lowest practicable limit. If by this means we can increase the tonnage of ore that will be mined to the figures given to me at Rossland the advantage to the country will be enormous and we shall receive our own compensation from the business of the important community that will be built up in that vicinity by such large operations.[21]

Van Horne and several CPR directors visited the West Kootenays in October 1897. They were, Van Horne reported, "all very much impressed with what we saw and learned in the mining district, especially in the Slocan district."[22]

W.H. Aldridge was appointed manager of the Trail smelter, and as Lamb observes, "from this small beginning were to develop the vast operations of Cominco." Shaughnessy consulted with the CPR's chief solicitor, G.M. Clark, and decided in July 1898 to name the Trail smelter "The Canadian Smelting Works." The term "Canadian" emphasized that the smelter was now under Canadian control. That summer the CPR began widening the narrow-gauge line between Trail and Rossland. Winter snows forced a halt to rail laying, but it was resumed the following spring and completed in mid-June 1899.[23]

Shaughnessy and Van Horne had decided "that in order to reduce the cost of treating the ores of the West Kootenay to a minimum it would be necessary to practically rebuild the smelter." Thus Aldridge's first step as manager was to close the smelter for re-designing and re-equipping from February to August 1898. After taking an inventory, Aldridge announced that $100,000 would be spent on improvements. New copper blast furnaces were installed. Aldridge also wanted the smelter to treat large quantities of the silver-lead ores from the Slocan. He therefore strongly recommended the building of two lead furnaces and the installation of Bruckner mechanical roasters for preparing the Slocan ores. Shaughnessy approved these proposals, although he was concerned about the $35,000 price-tag for the roasters. "This expenditure," he informed the smelter manager, "is rather in excess of our anticipation, but inasmuch as we are in the smelting business we must try to do it well." The open roasting stalls would be replaced with forty-eight roast ovens and a tall chimney to carry away the disagreeable sulphur fumes. Shaughnessy visited Trail on 8 June to inspect the smelter and to discuss the renovation program with Aldridge. By mid-July the CPR vice-president informed Aldridge that the company was "exceedingly anxious to get the smelter started because it will have a good effect in British Columbia, and besides this, of course, each week's delay will involve the investment of additional capital in ores." The smelter was continuing to purchase ores from the War Eagle, Centre Star, and other Rossland mines and was borrowing money from the Bank of Montreal at 6 per cent to pay for these purchases. On 13 July the smelter had ores to the value of $140,000 on hand.[24]

The Trail plant was to be operated by electricity. "Heinze had used steam, burning cordwood for fuel," Turnbull observes, "and had supplemented this with a small amount of electricity from the power station he built at the foot of Smelter Hill on Pine Avenue." In the summer of 1898 the owners of the Centre Star mine had formed the West Kootenay Power and Light Company. It constructed a powerhouse at Bonnington on the Kootenay River and laid a transmission line into Rossland to supply power for the mines. A branch line was run to a substation in the Trail smelter yards. On 21 July 1898 Aldridge signed an agreement with the power company to supply electricity to the smelter for a 5-year period. Soon after the Bonnington station was enlarged to supply all the electricity for the mines, smelter, and the town of Trail.[25]

On Sunday 7 August 1898 the Canadian Smelting Works blew in its copper furnaces and the modernized plant began operations. The new stack for the lead roast stalls, 175 feet high, was completed in December and in honour of the event four flags were raised from the top – three Union Jacks and one Stars and Stripes. Coke and coal replaced cordwood as fuel for the roasting stalls. At first the smelter had to obtain its supply from Vancouver, and this was expensive. But by the middle of November 1898 the Crow's Nest Pass Railway was completed to Kootenay Lake and ready for operation; the smelter now used much cheaper coal and coke from the Crow's Nest Coal Company's mines in the East Kootenays, which had just started production. Shaughnessy advised Aldridge to insist on the same price for "screened coal" as the CPR paid – "there is no reason why you should pay anything more."[26]

Aldridge made his first report on production to Shaughnessy on 3 October 1898. In the period from the reopening of the smelter to the end of September, the plant had shipped out twenty carloads of copper matte which brought in net revenue of $168,567. One of the two blast furnaces was producing high-grade concentrates (45 to 50 per cent) of copper matte while the other was turning out low-grade concentrates. The smelter could handle about 280 tons of copper ore per day. By the start of May 1899 Aldridge reported that "the works are in excellent condition and we are in a position to handle over four hundred tons of copper ore per day, which is more than we are able to get." A third copper blast furnace would be blown in by the end of the month, and would enable the plant to handle "easily" 600 tons of copper ore daily. Thus the smelter would be able to smelt the ores from all the Rossland mines (except the Le Roi) and from all the Boundary mines. The plant was also producing 75 tons of lead ore per day.[27] In December 1898 Shaughnessy had authorized plans for another CPR smelter in the Boundary district, the construction of which was to start in the spring of 1899, but this no longer appeared to be necessary since the modernized and expanded Trail plant was handling ore production from that district. Nevertheless, the CPR vice-president was still seriously considering the establishing of a CPR smelter at Cascade in the Boundary district in May 1899.[28] In the period 1898–1901 Aldridge attempted to contract for large tonnages from the recently discovered copper deposits at Phoenix and Greenwood in the Boundary district. However, the low grade of the ores and the long haul to Trail made them uncompetitive. Two smelters had already been built in the Boundary district to process its ores: a large one at Grand Forks, owned by Granby Consolidated Mining and Smelting Company, which opened in August 1900, and a smaller one at Greenwood, owned by the New York-based British Columbia Copper Company, which began operations in February 1901. Therefore, Shaughnessy abandoned the project for a company smelter in the Boundary district.[29]

In January 1901 the CPR offered to sell the Trail smelter to the Gooderham-Blackstock syndicate. T.G. Blackstock had initiated these negotiations when he discussed the matter with Aldridge in Toronto in July 1900. The Toronto syndicate had expanded its mine holdings in the West Kootenay by acquiring the Centre Star Mining Company in September 1898 and the Red Mountain Gold Mining Company in December 1899. Shaughnessy was reluctant to sell but, he had been persuaded to make the offer "because the opinion seemed to prevail that the mines [in West Kootenay] could be more profitably operated if the Mining Companies had their own reduction plant."[30] There is no evidence to indicate why the offer was rejected.

In June 1901 Shaughnessy made an important decision regarding the Trail smelter – he approved Aldridge's proposal for building a refinery to process the lead produced by the smelter. The decision to establish a lead refinery had been precipitated by the withdrawal of the American-owned American Smelting and Refining Company from BC early in 1901. As the *Canadian Annual Review* reported, "the only way of meeting the situation was to establish a Lead Refinery in Canada." This would be an expensive undertaking. On 15 April a large delegation from the Kootenay district, representing mine owners and local boards of trade, arrived in Ottawa and presented a petition to the government requesting a bounty of $5 per ton for 5 years on pig lead produced from ores smelted and refined in Canada. The Laurier government acceded to this pressure. On 21 May the Minister of Finance, W.S. Fielding, moved a resolution in the House of Commons authorizing Cabinet to pay bounties on lead refined in Canada. The bounty for 1902 was set at $5 per ton, and in each succeeding year it was reduced by $1 so that it would be $1 per ton in 1906. "The conditions in Canada are favourable," Fielding declared, "and we ought to be able to establish the [lead] industry on a permanent basis." Fielding's proposal was accepted by the House.[31]

Shaughnessy was rather concerned about the estimated costs of $250,000 for setting up a lead refinery. However, he had a great deal of confidence in Aldridge, and expected that he would keep costs down. "I have found him [Aldridge] a most competent, trustworthy and satisfactory man in every way," he informed T.G. Blackstock, "and, if I were going into the smelting business myself, I know of no man whom I would sooner get." The federal subsidy would now make it possible for the silver-lead ores of the Slocan to be refined in Canada. However, the refining process could not yet be done entirely at Trail; the lead bullion had to be sent to a refinery in Tacoma, Washington, for final processing. The Trail smelter's contract with the Tacoma refinery specified that the bullion had to be carried as far as practical over CPR lines. Two lead furnaces were installed in the Trail smelter in the latter part of 1901.[32]

Aldridge soon found a solution to completing the lead refining process at Trail. He began by purchasing the Canadian rights to the Betts patent, a new method of lead extraction by an electrolytic process developed by Dr. A.G. Betts of Troy, NY. As Lorne McDougall remarks, the Betts Process "was a tremendous technical breakthrough, for it produced a purer product at a lower cost than the processes using heat, which it displaced." Aldridge commissioned Betts in 1901 to design and supervise the construction of the first commercial application of the process at the Trail smelter. Dr Betts submitted a cost estimate of $156,500 for a 50-ton lead refinery. The refinery was constructed in the early months of 1901 for only $121,900. The equipment consisted of 240 asphalt-lined wooden cells housed in a frame building with a rated capacity of 10 tons per day. McDougall emphasizes the significance of the establishment of the lead refinery at Trail. It was, he remarks, "the very beginning of the modern Cominco" for it represented "the transition from a gold-copper base to a wider range of metals, and ... a receptiveness to new inventions." Since the lead refinery was the first of its kind in the world, it attracted much attention. Japanese engineers even arrived to see it in operation. By February 1904 Aldridge wrote jubilantly to Shaughnessy, "We now control the supply and price of pig lead throughout Canada as well as in China and Japan." Constant improvement and changes in the equipment steadily increased the refinery's daily output.[33]

In February 1904 Aldridge made a controversial proposal to put in pipe-making and rolling machines at Trail to manufacture lead pipe and sheets of lead. "There is no reason," he informed Shaughnessy, "why we should ship pig lead to Montreal, have it manufactured there and returned to Winnipeg and Western points in the form of pipe and sheet." This smelter manager was threatening powerful industrial interests in Central Canada, which manufactured their products from Western Canadian resources. Some months later Aldridge installed machinery in the smelter to make lead pipe in sixty different styles and sizes. The CPR president was upset at Aldridge's initiative and informed him that the railway could not afford to compete with lead pipe manufacturers in Ontario and

Quebec. These companies were "amongst the largest shippers over our line," he informed Aldridge, "and any advantage that you would receive from the utilization of your lead product in the manufacture of pipe would be a mere bagatelle as compared with the loss of revenue to the Company if these important interests were antagonized." Shaughnessy advised Aldridge to direct his efforts to persuading Canadian lead manufactureres to use only Canadian lead in their factories "in consideration of your pipe plant being shut down. This strikes me as a good proposition, and one that should meet your case fully." The CPR president also opposed Aldridge's proposal on grounds of cost. He informed him that he would like to see "corroding works [for manufacture of lead pipe] established on a good sound basis, but this Company will not invest any more money in that direction. We have gone rather farther than we should in providing refining works, and that must be considered the limit of our investment." In December 1904 a representative of the oldest and largest metal manufacturing firm in Canada, Thomas Robertson and Company of Montreal, called on Shaughnessy to discuss the whole matter. "In the meantime," Shaughnessy informed Aldridge, "I am convinced that to avoid friction, the manufacture of lead pipe should be discontinued at Trail." Aldridge's bold initiative had been defeated.[34]

Aldridge now concerned himself with the problem of ore supply. The Trail smelter received most of its ore from the War Eagle and Centre Star mines in Rossland and the St Eugene mine at Moyie in the East Kootenay. None of these mines was controlled by the CPR; Aldridge and Shaughnessy were concerned that the Le Roi Mining Company might gain control of these mines, with the result that their ores would be shipped to the Northport smelter which was controlled by the Le Roi. Aldridge strongly favoured the purchase of these mines. Not only would this assure the Trail smelter of a steady supply of ore, but also, Aldridge believed, there would be a saving in "general expenses" and a "great economy in the reduction of the ores." He was confident that the proposed consolidation "will convert the several properties, now individually unprofitable, into a money-making concern." Shaughnessy continued to have "great faith" in Aldridge's judgment and approved the plan.[35]

The death of George Gooderham on 1 May 1905 and the poor health of T.G. Blackstock evidently were factors which led to the takeover of the Gooderham-Blackstock's controlling interest in the three mines by a syndicate headed by CPR directors E.B. Osler and W.D. Matthews in late June 1905. The syndicate paid $825,000 to purchase a controlling interest in the three mines. The CPR provided most of the purchase money and obtained a 54.3 per cent interest in the new Consolidated Mining and Smelting Company of Canada (CM&S) which was incorporated under a Dominion charter in January 1906. CM&S owned the three mines and the Trail smelter. Matthews became president of the new company, which had its head office in Toronto; E.B. Osler and Charles R. Hosmer (Montreal), both CPR directors, were members of the seven-member board. W.H. Aldridge was appointed managing director of the company, which had its office in Trail. He was elected to the board and received a salary from CM&S. He continued to look after mining interests for the CPR, for which he was paid a yearly salary, which was set in 1907 at the substantial figure of $12,500.[36] However, the key figure in CM&S was its president, Wilmot D. Matthews. Born in 1850, Matthews was the son of a prominent Toronto grain dealer. After receiving an education at the Toronto Model School, he started in the grain trade in 1873, with Toronto as his base. His business success is attested to by his election as president of the Toronto Board of Trade in 1888 –9 and as a director of the CPR in May 1888. He was to become engaged in the promotion of many companies such as the Canadian Mining Trust Company (1897) and the Pacific Coal Company (1901). In 1907 *Saturday Night* magazine rated him a millionaire. He remained president of CM&S until his death in May 1919.[37]

In 1905 the CPR attempted to bring the London-based Le Roi Mining Company into CM&S. Shaughnessy sent Aldridge to London in November 1905 to buy up Le Roi Mining Company stock, with the assistance of George S. Waterlow, an Englishman who had substantial holdings of Le Roi stock. At "a stormy meeting" of 500 Le Roi shareholders on 8 December 1905, the proposal to amalgamate with CM&S was defeated by a large majority. Despite this setback, Shaughnessy was delighted when the Trail smelter's operations in October 1905 produced an increase of $700,000 in net revenue over the previous month. "It is gratifying to know," he informed Matthews, "that the consolidation of the Centre Star and the War Eagle properties was successfully carried out. I am sure that it will prove to the advantage of everybody concerned in the two mining companies."[38]

While the negotiations for the Gooderham-Blackstock properties were in progress, the CPR purchased a controlling interest in the West Kootenay Power and Light Company in February 1905 and decided to spend $1 million in increasing its output of electric power, since much of the company's output would be consumed by the Trail smelter. But Shaughnessy also felt that CPR control of the power company would be useful "in keeping the mining and smelter interests of the Kootenay in close touch with us." He also had plans to

use some of the power to run CPR trains between Nelson and Rossland, and possibly as far west as Greenwood in the Boundary district.
Richard Marpole and W.R. Baker were elected as directors of the
power company in October 1906 and acted as the CPR representatives
on its board. In 1916 West Kootenay Power was merged into CM&S,
but the plans for electrifying the Nelson to Rossland line were never
carried out.[39]

The financial policy of CM&S was quite sound. From November
1907 to October 1912 no dividends were paid as profits were used
to build up reserves and finance improvements. By 1909 it owned
two mines in Phoenix in the Boundary district – Snowshoe Mines
and Phoenix Amalgamated Mines – and one in Sandon in the Slocan
– Richmond-Eureka Mines. Aldridge reported in June 1910 that for
the last few months CM&S had averaged a monthly gross profit (not
allowing for depreciation) of $45,000. "Considering the continued
low price for metals and the low grade of the ore we are treating,"
he remarked, "this showing is certainly very good." In 1911 CM&S
purchased the Le Roi Mining Company, even though Shaughnessy
regarded its mine as "practically an abandoned mine." In the fiscal
year ending 30 September 1914, CM&S paid out a substantial dividend
of 8 per cent in four instalments.[40]

The most important decision made by CM&S in the years 1906 to
1914 was its takeover of the Sullivan mine at Kimberley in the East
Kootenays in 1910. The Sullivan property had been discovered in
1892 and was known to have huge deposits of lead-zinc ore. However, under four successive owners no practical method had been
devised to separate out the zinc which, at the time, was considered
an impurity in the lead. In 1909 Federal Mining and Smelting, which
owned the mine, decided to sell the property. Aldridge sent two of
his men, Robert H. Stewart, manager of mines, and S.G. Blaylock,
superintendent of the St Eugene mine, to examine the property.
They reported that the lead ore deposit was extensive and that it
was worth taking the chance on finding a solution to the metallurgical
problems which, they admitted, were considerable. Aldridge accepted their advice and in 1910 CM&S leased the mine with an option
to purchase.

In February 1911 Aldridge resigned as managing director of CM&S
to take a position in the United States. He was succeeded by Robert
Stewart, who was appointed general manager. A thirty-seven-year-
old curly haired native of Saint John, New Brunswick, Stewart took
his engineering training at McGill University. He then made his way
to BC in 1896 and worked as a mining engineer with a number of
companies, including the Le Roi. In 1906 he was hired as manager

of mines for CM&S. Stewart recalled Selwyn G. Blaylock from the St Eugene mine to become his chief assistant. Blaylock, then thirty-two years of age, had come to the Kootenays after graduating as an engineer from McGill in 1898. At the Sullivan mine, Stewart and Blaylock followed a policy of searching for those parts of the ore body which were high in lead, and of hand sorting the ore after it had been raised. By 1913 the mine was making a modest profit, so CM&S exercised its option and purchased the mine. By 1914 it was the largest lead mine in Canada. During the war, under pressure of strong wartime demand for zinc, CM&S developed processes for extracting large quantities of zinc from the ores.[41]

The CPR's contribution to developing the mining and smelting industries of southern BC was significant. It also played a very important role in developing the extensive coal reserves of Western Canada. Since Western coal was located so far from Ontario, which obtained cheap and readily available coal from Pennsylvania, the market for Western Canadian coal was limited to the Prairies and the BC interior. Coal mines here became dependent on the railway because it was the only efficient means of moving coal. The railway was also the chief consumer of coal, until the massive immigration to the Prairies after 1900 created an important domestic consumer market. "In western Canada," den Otter concludes, "rail founded the coal mine: coal did not create the railway."[42]

The CPR's decision in 1881 to use a more southerly route on the Prairies prompted the Montreal entrepreneur Sir Alexander Galt to go ahead with plans for establishing a coal mine in southern Alberta. That year government surveyors from the Geological Survey reported that there were enormous coal seams beneath most of southern Alberta. Galt negotiated a fuel contract with the CPR, and persuaded some London financiers to form the North Western Coal and Navigation Company in April 1882. This company decided to locate Alberta's first large coal mine near present-day Lethbridge, and to build a narrow-gauge railway from Lethbridge to Dunmore on the CPR's main line. Both projects were completed in 1885. Since there was little immigration into the prairie West in the period 1885–1900, the Galt company's coal was consumed mainly by the CPR. For example, in April 1886 Galt secured a one-year contract with the CPR in which the railway agreed to use Galt's coal exclusively between Winnipeg and the Rockies.[43] In 1892 H.W. McNeill and Company opened a mine at Canmore, just east of Banff on the CPR main line. Since the Canmore colliery promised to produce a fairly cheap but good-quality bituminous coal, the CPR guaranteed a loan for its establishment, built a siding to its tipple, and paid a bonus for its coal.

Thus by the early 1890s the CPR had "a cheap and reliable coal supply on its western division." It burned McNeill coal from Kamloops to Medicine Hat and Galt coal from Medicine Hat to Winnipeg.[44]

The CPR built the Crow's Nest Pass Railway in 1897–8 primarily to counter the competition from the SF&N and the Great Northern, which then dominated the mining traffic of the Kootenay region. One by-product of this decision was the creation of the Crow's Nest Pass Coal Company which began establishing coal mines in the East Kootenays in 1898. The CPR had effectively created this company by turning over most of the coal lands from its British Columbia Southern land grant to the Toronto-based company. And the coal company created a substantial traffic for the Crow's Nest line since it supplied coal and coke to the Nelson and Trail smelters, and also to the Granby and Greenwood smelters which were later established in the Boundary district. However, J.J. Hill and his associates gained control of the Crow's Nest Coal Company in 1901 and proceeded to divert some of its coal and coke production to the Great Northern Railroad and to smelters in the United States. After a major controversy, the coal company agreed to meet the coal and coke requirements of the smelters in BC, but Shaughnessy was convinced that it was charging lower prices for coke delivered to American smelters than for coke delivered to BC smelters. Only CPR pressure on the federal government brought a reduction in coke prices for the Trail smelter. (See chapter 6.)

In 1903 Shaughnessy became deeply concerned with developing new sources of coal for the company's operations in BC. He advised Whyte in February that the CPR should in the near future give serious consideration to the establishment of three coal mines: one in the Crow's Nest coalfields, a second on the main line near Banff, and a third on the main line in BC, to supply the western end of the Pacific Division. He was especially concerned about opening production at the third location, since the coal supply west of the Selkirks was becoming restricted. In February 1905 he informed Whyte that west of Winnipeg all coal for CPR locomotives should come from "mines located on our own line," except for the western end of the Pacific Division where it was necessary to obtain coal from Nanaimo.[45]

On 4 July 1903 Shaughnessy had appointed W.H. Aldridge as chief of the Mining and Metallurgical Department, a post he held until his resignation in February 1911. Aldridge retained his position as manager of the Trail smelter and in addition was placed in charge of all the CPR's mining and prospecting operations in Western Canada. He reported directly to Shaughnessy. He was to keep in close touch with J.S. Dennis, BC land commissioner, since the development of mining in BC would have "an important effect upon the value of the Company's lands in the vicinity of the mines."[46] Aldridge then directed the activities of those CPR officials who did prospecting work, particularly in regard to coal deposits in BC and Alberta. In June 1903 Shaughnessy appointed A.H. Reeder, an American coal expert, as superintendent of coal mining operations in the West at an annual salary of $6,000. Aldridge, who was Reeder's superior, did not think he was suitable for the job because his coal mining experience was in West Virginia and Pennsylvania where conditions were very different from those in BC and Alberta. The two men came into open disagreement over the location for the CPR's proposed anthracite coal mine at Banff. As a result, Reeder resigned his position in October 1903.[47]

In 1903 Aldridge's department dug several prospecting tunnels at Bankhead, about 5 miles north of Banff. Development work continued over the next 2 years, with Shaughnessy expressing concern about the high costs involved. Nevertheless, the Bankhead mine went into production in 1905. Shaughnessy commented that the mine's operations for the first three months of 1906 "do not furnish an encouraging outlook for the property." By the latter part of 1906 the mine employed over 250 underground workers to extract an average of 600 tons of coal a day. This coal was used mainly for main-line operations in the prairies and BC. There were serious problems with this mine, however. The coal produced was poor in quality – soft and friable. A briquetting plant was built to process some of the soft coal, but the costs exceeded the revenue from the sale of the briquettes. In February 1909 Aldridge informed the CPR president that "excepting under most favourable conditions, the mine cannot be operated at a profit," and that even under ideal conditions the profits would be used up maintaining the plant in satisfactory operating condition. About $2 million had been invested in establishing the mine and the briquetting plant. Bankhead was continued in operation, but was finally closed down in 1923.[48]

In 1903 Shaughnessy had wanted the CPR to establish a coal mine on the railway's main line in BC to provide coal for the railway west of the Selkirks. This policy was modified to one of assisting the development of coal mines in BC near the main line. In 1904 the CPR took over the charter of the Nicola, Kamloops and Similkameen Coal and Railway Company (NK&S), which had authority to build a line from Spence's Bridge on the CPR main line southeast through the Nicola Valley to Nicola Lake, and a federal cash subsidy of $6,400 per mile to assist in its construction. The NK&S line went into operation in the spring of 1907 and was designated as the Nicola Branch. There were rich coalfields in the Nicola Valley. The Nicola Valley Coal and Coke Company established a large mine at Merritt on the Nicola Branch which by the end of 1907 was turning out 225 tons of coal per day. This coal proved to be excellent for use in steam locomotives, so the CPR secured most of the mine's output for its coal chutes on the main line from Spence's Bridge east to Revelstoke. This greatly assisted the CPR's requirements on the main line west of the Selkirks.

Shaughnessy's next move to implement his 1903 coal policy was the establishment of a coal mine at Hosmer in the East Kootenays. Under its 1897 agreement with the Crow's Nest Coal Company, the CPR could select six sections (3,840 acres) of coal lands in the Crow's Nest district, but only after it had transferred 50,000 acres of coal-bearing lands in this area to the federal government. In 1901 Clifford Sifton hired Colonel E.F. Taylor, a mining engineer from Pittsburgh, along with William Pearce and W.F. Leach, an official from the Geological Survey, to make a careful examination of the coalfields in the district. In a report of 4 October 1901 Taylor suggested how the 50,000 acres could be selected. Sifton accepted his recommendations, and the selection was confirmed by cabinet Order-In-Council on 19 May 1902.[49] The CPR then selected its 3,840 acres of coal lands at Hosmer, about 5 miles north of Fernie. However, under the 1897 agreement, the CPR undertook not to operate coal mines on these lands for a period of 10 years after the construction of the Crow's Nest line, so it could not sell coal from such mines until 1908.

Shaughnessy was appalled when Aldridge informed him that the total capital cost of the Hosmer mine would be about $2 million. "Never at any time," he reminded Aldridge, "has $2,000,000 been fixed as the estimate of cost at Hosmer. The highest ever mentioned was $1,500,000." By the summer of 1908 a large colliery and a row of coke ovens had been completed, and the mine was in production. Hosmer was never profitable; the seams were severely faulted and this made mining difficult and expensive. Shaughnessy was very upset with both the Hosmer and Bankhead operations, which had entailed a total capital expenditure of about $4.5 million. He was critical of Aldridge, whose favourable predictions for the two properties were "very wide of the mark." The Hosmer mine was closed in July 1914, after producing 984,000 tons of coal and coke.[50]

The CPR's only profitable coal-mining investment was at Lethbridge. The CPR purchased a majority interest in Galt's Alberta Railway and Irrigation Company (AR&I CO) and signed a 999-year lease of the company, effective 1 January 1912. The AR&I CO, which operated the Lethbridge colliery, was placed under the jurisdiction of the CPR's new Department of Natural Resources (DNR), which was managed by P.L. Naismith, who had been general manager of the AR&I CO. (See chapter eight.) The colliery was administered by the DNR's Coal Mining Branch. As den Otter points out, the Lethbridge coal mines were large and efficient. The CPR operated them until they were sold in 1935 to a new company, Lethbridge Collieries.[51]

It was in the period 1904–12 that the CPR, under Shaughnessy's guidance, developed a policy regarding mineral rights on its prairie lands, particularly in regard to petroleum and natural gas. The CPR's title to its prairie lands granted before the federal land regulations of September 1889 conferred not only surface rights but mineral rights as well. It was in southern Alberta that the discoveries of oil and natural gas occurred, and this was a region where the remaining company lands happened to be concentrated.[52]

The CPR's interest in oil and natural gas appears to have been sparked by the action of the city of Medicine Hat which, in 1904, formed a municipally owned utility to supply natural gas fuel for home and commercial use. The natural gas came from wells first discovered in 1890 near the city. As David Breen observes, "an added inducement" for the CPR was that oil could be expected to exist in combination with natural gas. After negotiations in 1905, in February 1906 the company hired Eugene Coste, an experienced Canadian geologist, to drill for oil under CPR lands in southern Alberta. Breen contends that a "deliberate decision to look for a mineral for which it had no immediate use was something of a departure from company practice." He acknowledges that the CPR operated the Trail smelter, but accepts the contention of Lamb and Mcdougall that the smelter had been acquired "almost by accident." As this author has shown, the Trail smelter had been taken over in order to encourage the mining of low-grade ores in the Kootenays and thus to increase traffic for the CPR's new Crow's Nest line. At about this time, Shaughnessy became interested in experimenting with oil as a fuel source for the company's Pacific coastal steamers. It is possible, as Breen suggests, that Lord Strathcona influenced the CPR's decision to explore for oil, since he was deeply involved in Middle Eastern oil exploration at the time and would become the founding chairman of the powerful Anglo-Persian Oil Company in 1909.[53]

Under Shaughnessy's 1906 agreement with Coste, the CPR would finance the drilling program and the geologist would collect $25,000 above his expenses and salary if he made an important discovery. The forty-seven-year-old, Ontario-born geologist had served with the Geological Survey of Canada from 1883 to 1889 and had acquired a first-hand knowledge of the geology of the southern prairies. He decided to explore in the Medicine Hat district because of the previous natural gas discoveries there. Coste's expertise was in the field of natural gas; as a private entrepreneur, since 1889 he had opened up and equipped the Welland natural gas field and had visited natural-gas sites all over the world. In 1906 Shaughnessy had the deed that transferred title to company settlement lands changed to reserve petroleum rights for the railway. As Breen rightly observes, this was "a turning point in the company's thinking about its western lands." The CPR no longer saw the lands strictly in terms of agricultural settlement, but also in terms of their potential mineral deposits. The CPR had at first included sub-surface rights with the title passed on to homestead buyers. After 1904 coal rights were withheld, and in 1912 the reservation was extended to include all mines and minerals.[54]

After Coste launched his exploration program, the CPR was approached in 1907 by A.W. Dingman, manager of the newly incorporated Calgary Natural Gas Company, for financial assistance for its exploration program to develop a gas supply for Calgary. Dennis supported Dingman's request, but Coste used his influence with Whyte to have it turned down. Whyte reminded Dennis that the CPR was looking for oil and that it was best to concentrate on Coste's exploration.

The Dingman consortium sank its second well on the Colonel Walker estate in east Calgary, and an encouraging gas flow was discovered in October 1908 at the 800-foot level. Dennis reminded Whyte that this well was near land on which the CPR was developing a new industrial subdivision. Then in February 1909 Coste made an important natural gas strike at Bow Island, northwest of Medicine Hat. However, this discovery was a substantial distance from Calgary, the most important market, so the CPR's officers agreed to help finance completion of the Dingman well. Its $5,000 investment was rewarded in May 1909 by a gas strike in east Calgary.[55]

Coste started drilling more wells in the Bow Island area to determine the size of the gas field, and began assessing promising sites closer to Calgary, near Brooks and Bassano. Whyte and Dennis were strongly in favour of the company entering directly into natural gas distribution, by laying the pipeline to Calgary along the CPR right-of-way. Shaughnessy was not swayed by their arguments, for his main aim was to discover a substantial supply of oil which could be used as fuel for the company's Pacific coastal steamers. In November 1909 the CPR president therefore rejected Coste's "elaborate scheme" on the grounds "that we were looking for oil and not gas," and proposed that Coste's new gas wells be capped. The CPR drilling program under Coste's direction was completed in the spring and summer of 1910. Six wells had been drilled – all natural gas producers. However, Coste had still found no oil and his most productive gas well was at Bow Island, 150 miles from Calgary.[56]

Despite no company oil finds, its experiment with oil as fuel for the Pacific coastal steamers began on 28 March 1911 when the *Princess Mary*, refitted to burn oil, made her first trial run. It was so successful that her engineers felt that the conversion might have added a knot and a half to her speed. The *Princess Alice* was converted to oil during her regular annual overhaul at Esquimalt later in 1911, and the refitting of the *Princess Victoria* was completed in April 1912. As Lamb remarks, "the new fuel was a tremendous boon. It was much cleaner than coal; a steady head of steam could be maintained much more easily; refueling became a quick and simple matter." The experiment which Shaughnessy had actively furthered had been a great success.[57]

In 1910 Coste and several associates put together a strongly capitalized company called the Prairie Fuel Gas Company, which made a far-reaching proposal to the CPR. Coste proposed to lay a gas pipeline to Lethbridge and Calgary, purchase gas from CPR wells for 10 per cent of the gross monthly receipts from the sale of that gas, and turn over any oil discovered to the CPR. He also wanted the exclusive right for 20 years to drill for and sell gas from selected CPR lands and the right to lay pipeline through and along the CPR right-of-way. Since the Calgary Natural Gas Company held an exclusive franchise to supply Calgary, Coste's group made its owners an attractive purchase offer which was accepted on 12 November 1910. The CPR and Coste's company then signed an agreement in February 1911. The CPR obtained a number of important concessions from Coste's 1910 proposition. At least 50 per cent of the gas required by the gas company had to come from CPR lands, and it would be charged at 6 per cent of the gross monthly receipts instead of 10 per cent. The railway could buy all the gas it required at 10 cents per thousand cubic feet at the wellhead or 15 cents if delivered by pipeline. Coste's company, capitalized at $8 million, was obliged to transfer $200,000 in fully paid capital stock to the CPR. As Breen concludes, the CPR had opted for a junior partner role in the development of Alberta natural gas, with others bearing the risk and cost of development, while at the same time being "reasonably rewarded for any success." Shaughnessy took a very cautious approach, partly because natural gas was not vital to the CPR's primary function of transportation.[58]

The only important CPR policy decision on oil and natural gas between 1912 and 1914 came as the result of the stampede for drilling rights on lands running south along the Alberta foothills. This occurred when the Calgary Petroleum Products Company struck naphtha-saturated gas near Calgary on 14 May 1914. The CPR responded by reserving from sale not only mineral rights but also surface rights to all its lands south of the city and west of the Calgary-Fort Macleod railway.[59]

In BC, the CPR concentrated on developing the timber resources on its extensive lands in that province, particularly those on Vancouver Island. The company became a substantial landholder in BC much later than it had in the prairie West. The provincial government transferred to the federal government in 1883 a 20-mile strip of land on either side of the CPR main line in BC containing 10,976,000 acres. The company was authorized to select some of its main-line grant from this "railway belt," but did not do so since very little of it was good agricultural land. The federal government disposed of 4.9 million acres of this land and transferred the remainder back to the province in 1930.[60]

The CPR obtained its first large BC land grant in 1892, when it leased the BC-chartered Columbia and Kootenay Railway and Navigation Company and built under this charter a 28-mile line from Robson to Nelson, for which it received a grant of 188,593 acres. Then in 1898 it leased the British Columbia Southern Railway and under its charter built the Western section of the Crow's Nest Pass Railway from the pass to Nelson. The CPR received a land subsidy of 20,000 acres per mile for this work, for a total of 3,755,733 acres. The BC Southern land grant was settled in 1901. In 1898 the CPR took over the Columbia and Western Railway and used its charter to build west from Robson to Midway in the Boundary district in the period 1898 to 1900. The Columbia and Western was eligible for a provincial land subsidy of 20,000 acres per mile, so this construction earned the CPR a land grant of 1,348,225 acres.[61] However, this grant was the subject of great controversy and was not settled until 1906. In June 1905 the CPR leased the Esquimalt and Nanaimo Railway (E&N) and obtained the remainder of its land grant on Vancouver Island, which amounted to 1,440,495 acres. All of these subsidy lands (outlined in table 6) had timber rights attached to them.[62]

A major controversy erupted in 1906 regarding the land grant to the CPR-owned Columbia and Western Railway. In 1896 the Turner

Table 6
Land Acquired by the CPR in BC, 1886–1914

	Acreage acquired
British Columbia Southern	3,755,733
Columbia and Kootenay	188,593
Columbia and Western	1,348,225
Esquimalt and Nanaimo	1,440,495
Vancouver townsite	6,275
Total	6,739,321

Sources: Cail, Land, Man and the Law, 167; MacDonald, "The Canadian Pacific Railway and Vancouver's Development to 1900," in Ward and McDonald, eds., British Columbia: Historical Readings, 400.

government had passed legislation granting the Columbia and Western a subsidy of 20,000 acres per mile to assist the construction of a railway from Trail to Penticton. The company undertook to complete the line and to survey all subsidy lands within 7 years. The company, controlled by F.A. Heinze, built a line from Trail to Robson in 1897. The CPR purchased the Columbia and Western from Heinze in 1898 and quickly constructed a line from Robson west to Midway in the Boundary district by 1900, but it did not build west of Midway. The BC legislature in 1897 chartered the VV&E to build a railway from Rossland (near Trail) west by the most direct route through the Hope Mountains to Vancouver. J.J. Hill acquired this charter in 1898 and began building west from Midway in 1905.[63]

In 1905 the CPR put pressure on the McBride government to settle the Columbia and Western land subsidy. In February and May 1905 the government passed two orders-in-council recommending legislation to confirm the Columbia and Western land subsidy upon completion of surveys of the selected lands. McBride promised the CPR's J.S. Dennis that the legislation would be passed in the 1906 session of the legislature. When Dennis arrived in Victoria on 7 January 1906 to look after the company's interests in this matter, he learned that the government had decided that it would not grant subsidies to any railways in the 1906 session, except for settlement of the Columbia and Western question. This decision created dissension in the Conservative caucus, for some members regarded the Columbia and Western Bill as a special favour to the CPR. Though the government had a slim majority in the legislature, it appeared that the two Labour MLAS who usually supported the government would vote against the legislation, as would three Conservative MLAS, so that the government might be defeated.[64]

On 26 February Minister of Finance R.F. Green introduced a bill authorizing the government to issue Crown grants for 808,872 acres of land – the balance owed to the Columbia and Western – when the surveys were completed. The Liberals charged that the CPR was not entitled to this grant since it had not built the entire line from Trail to Penticton in 7 years nor had it completed the surveys for the lands in question, as required by the 1896 legislation. The McBride administration was portrayed as a "creature of the CPR." The premier vigorously defended the legislation, maintaining that the Turner government had relieved the Columbia and Western from building the section from Midway to Penticton by chartering the VV&E in 1898 and observing that the Semlin government in 1900 had declared that the Columbia and Western grant (for the line to Midway) had been earned. McBride then declared that the Columbia and Western "had been of immense service to the Boundary country and deserved its subsidy on every ground of equity and justice." Carter-Cotton, a minister in the McBride government, stated that, although he had voted against the Columbia and Western land subsidy in 1896, he "now favoured settlement as a matter of equity." The bill passed on 9 March by a vote of 18-12. James Dunsmuir had personally lobbied among the members for the bill. Dennis informed Shaughnessy that without Dunsmuir's support, it would have been defeated. Attorney General Charles Wilson, who privately opposed the bill, resigned at the end of the session, but made no mention of the Columbia and Western matter. He stated simply that he was resigning to devote himself to his own business.[65]

The official chiefly responsible for BC land matters was J.S. Dennis, who had joined the CPR in January 1903 as superintendent of irrigation and BC land commissioner, with an office in Calgary. In 1908 Dennis was relieved of responsibility for E&N land matters, which were now handled by Richard Marpole, the company's general executive assistant in Vancouver. However, Dennis continued to supervise the BC Southern and Columbia and Western land grants. Shaughnessy felt that Dennis had enough work dealing with irrigation matters in Alberta, and wanted the BC Southern and Columbia and Western lands handled through a land commissioner in Marpole's office. However, this change was not carried out. The formation of the Department of Natural Resources in January 1912 brought all BC lands under the general jurisdiction of the new department's Lands Branch in Calgary. However, a British Columbia Land and Timber Agent in Vancouver supervised the CPR's lands and the tie-and-timber operations in that province, while the E&N

organization with its office in Victoria continued to handle the sale of E&N lands.[66]

In January 1904 the CPR drew up detailed regulations for the sale of its BC Southern lands. Lands suitable for agriculture were divided into three classes; the most valuable, first-class, was to be sold at $5 per acre. But as William Whyte observed, about 90 per cent of these lands were "only of value as timber land." Under BC land law, any land with more than 5,000 board feet of timber per acre was required to be sold as timber land. The CPR did not set fixed prices for this land, but did approve a schedule of fees which the purchaser was required to pay for the timber cut. The fees ranged from $1 per thousand board feet for commercial lumber to $1/_2$ cent per foot for cribbing timber and telegraph posts. The purchaser was also liable for provincial timber royalties. These regulations were approved by the BC Cabinet in April 1904. It appears that similar regulations were adopted for the Columbia and Western lands.[67]

The existence of substantial amounts of commercial timber on the BC Southern and Columbia and Western lands did add considerably to their value. Much of this timber found a ready market in the prairie West. In April 1909 the CPR sold 10,560 acres of BC Southern lands to the BC Lumber Company for $1.90 per acre. This price was based on the timber on the land – about 1900 feet per acre. However, no figures are available on the timber fees which were paid to the CPR. For the 12-year period 1900–12, total sales from the BC Southern and the Columbia and Western land grants were 434,696 acres. The net revenue from these sales amounted to only $769,412, or an average price of $1.77 per acre.

Dennis carried on negotiations with the McBride government to sell a large portion of these lands back to the province. In 1912 the CPR and the McBride administration signed an agreement by which the province purchased 4,065,076 acres of these lands at 40 cents an acre. The CPR retained 543,496 acres of the lands for its timber and tie requirements. The company was eager to divest itself of most of these lands which had originally been free from provincial taxation but by 1912 were subject to taxation.[68]

The most valuable CPR lands in BC were the E&N lands. The CPR had paid $1,330,000 to acquire the stock of the E&N, for which it received the railway and 1,440,495 acres of land on Vancouver Island. These lands were free from provincial taxation until they were sold. At first, Shaughnessy wanted to sell the entire land grant for $2.5 million, and there were negotiations on this proposition with "parties" in New York and Seattle. "I am ambitious," the CPR president informed J.S. Dennis in June 1905, "to get back out of the [E&N] lands the entire cost of the railway and lands, and a profit." When Dennis drew up regulations for the sale of E&N lands, the name of the CPR was used. Shaughnessy was quick to inform Dennis and his superior, William Whyte, that the name of the CPR should not be used in connection with the E&N land grant, "otherwise we are sure to have trouble about taxation."[69]

The CPR kept the E&N organization in place, and had its land examiners begin classifying and evaluating the lands. By November 1905 their reports indicated that the E&N land grant was, Shaughnessy observed, "worth a great deal more money than any price that we before had in mind." He therefore abandoned the idea of selling the entire land grant to a single purchaser. By October 1906 the land examiners had gone over 800,000 acres, about 60 per cent of which had been classified as agricultural lands. These lands had a maximum of 10,000 feet of timber per acre and were being sold at $5 an acre. Shaughnessy wanted them brought under cultivation "as soon as possible." J.S. Dennis had outlined this in a policy speech to the council of the Victoria Board of Trade on 7 July 1905. He stressed that an increase in the settled agricultural land near Victoria would help the city develop, just as the settlement of the irrigation lands had greatly increased the population and business of Calgary. The CPR closed an agreement with the British-based British Columbia Development Company late in 1906. Under it the development company agreed to clear 150,000 acres of E&N agricultural lands within an 11-year period. The CPR would receive $5 an acre when these lands were sold, the development company would recoup its expenses for clearing the land, and any remaining funds would be divided between the two companies "on an agreed basis." The revenue for clearing the land would come from the sales of timber on it.[70]

Shaughnessy's concern for agricultural development in BC had led him to neglect the value of E&N lands as timber lands. On 4 December 1906 he had an interview with a man who was very well informed about timber areas in Washington State and who had some knowledge of the timber resources of Vancouver Island. This man "rather opened my eyes on the subject of the value of timber land," the CPR president informed Dennis. The timber expert asserted that the E&N had "the finest body of Douglas fir remaining on the Continent." If this were so, the CPR president felt that the CPR's prices for E&N lands had been "too modest" and that the company could afford to "go slowly about the sale of our timber lands, even at twenty-five dollars per acre." He also realized that E&N land classified as agricultural would be used for timber, not agricultural purposes, because it contained much valuable timber. He therefore approved Dennis's amendment to the land regulations for agricultural lands requiring a payment of $1 per 1,000 feet of timber as well as the $5 an acre fee. In the period 1905–12, the CPR sold 250,000 acres of E&N lands for $3,364,000, which represented an average price of $13.46 an acre.[71] The sale of E&N lands had already paid more than double the purchase price of the railway and its lands! The McBride government passed legislation in 1912 confirming the exemption of E&N lands from taxation until sold, while the E&N undertook to pay an annual tax of 1.5 cents per acre on its unsold lands.[72]

CHAPTER ELEVEN

The CPR West

CPR policies in the prairie West and BC in the period 1896 to 1914 were designed to connect the West's economy as closely as possible with that of Central Canada and to enable the CPR to meet competition from the Great Northern, the Canadian Northern, and Grand Trunk Pacific enterprises. The most decisive move in extending these policies was the CPR's decision in 1896 to build the Crow's Nest Pass Railway, which came as a response to mining developments in the Kootenay region of southeastern BC and to the efforts of American railways to divert this mining traffic to the United States. The CPR wanted not only to secure the rapidly increasing mining traffic of this region but also to link the Kootenays with Central Canada via the CPR's main line, so that the industries of Ontario and Quebec could sell their goods in this developing region. The prairie West would also benefit by gaining a new market for its grain and cattle.

The Laurier government furnished substantial cash assistance to the CPR for this project and secured benefits for prairie farmers, by persuading the company to reduce some of its freight rates in the prairie West, under the historic Crow's Nest Pass Agreement of 1897. The Crow's Nest Pass Railway was completed from Lethbridge to Kootenay Landing, BC, in 1898. Between Kootenay Landing and Nelson freight cars were carried on barges along Kootenay Lake and the Kootenay River. But since it was difficult for CPR car ferries to use the Kootenay River in winter, the CPR then built the 18-mile section from Nelson, east to Procter, on Kootenay Lake, that was opened in 1902.

Although the Crow's Nest rates were to be fixed in perpetuity, the CPR was basically satisfied with them because under prevailing economic conditions it could still make a profit with this rate structure. The company realized that these rates would assist the expansion of prairie agriculture, which received additional aid in 1901 when the Canadian Northern Railway reduced its rates on grain moving from Winnipeg to the Lakehead and on a variety of commodities shipped from the Lakehead to points in Manitoba. In 1903 the CPR not only decreased its rates to these levels but also cut its rates to points in the districts of Assiniboia and Saskatchewan which were not then served by the Canadian Northern.

The Crow's Nest Pass Railway contributed to the rapid development of mining in southeastern BC, promoted permanent settlement there, and enabled Central Canadian business to develop a market in the region. Although the CPR was initially effective in meeting competition from the Great Northern in the West Kootenays, J.J. Hill was determined to control the mining traffic of southeastern BC. In 1901 he acquired 30 per cent of the stock of the Crow's Nest Coal Company, the largest coal mining corporation in the East Kootenays. The next year the coal company built a railway from its mines to the international boundary, where it connected with the GN. Coal and coke from the company's mines were shipped via this route to the GN, which then carried them to smelters in Montana. This development threatened the operations of Canadian smelters in the West Kootenays and the Boundary mining district further west. Shaughnessy was able to persuade the coal company to meet the fuel requirements of the Canadian smelters, but it also expanded operations to produce coal for the GN's operations in the states of Montana and Washington as well as coal and coke for smelters there. When Hill consolidated his position by gaining a controlling interest in the coal company in 1906, the GN clearly held a dominant position in southeastern BC.

Hill had also taken steps to control the traffic of the Boundary mining district by seeking a federal charter for the KRVR in 1898, but the CPR used its influence to have the legislation defeated by Parliament. The CPR countered by acquiring the charter of the Columbia and Western Railway and building a line from Robson to Midway in the Boundary district with a provincial cash subsidy of $4,000 per mile. It was completed early in 1900. Hill responded in 1901 by acquiring the charter of the VV&E, which was authorized to build a railway from Vancouver east to Rossland in the West Kootenays. This project was strongly supported by Vancouver and Victoria businessmen, who sought to end CPR and Central Canadian dominance of the trade of the mining districts of southeastern BC and to open that market to Victoria and Vancouver merchants. The CPR then took control of the charter of the Kettle Valley Railway (KVR) which was authorized to build a line from Midway to Vancouver. A major battle then ensued between the two railways. By 1909 the VV&E was complete from Midway to Princeton whereas the CPR had not carried out any construction west of Midway. However, in 1910 the BC government granted the KVR a $5,000-per-mile cash subsidy for 150 miles west of Princeton, while the federal government awarded it a cash subsidy of $6,400 per mile for the section from Midway to Hope. The BC government provided additional aid for the KVR in 1912 – a cash subsidy of $10,000 per mile for the expensive section from Brookmere to Hope. The CPR began building west of Midway in 1910. In 1913 the GN made a major concession to the CPR by agreeing that the KVR could build the line from Brookmere to Hope and that the VV&E could have trackage rights over the line for an annual rental. Although the GN began to cut back its operations in BC, it was still competing with the CPR-KVR for the traffic of the Kootenay and Boundary districts to Vancouver, since the VV&E had reached an agreement with the Canadian Northern in 1911 for use of its line from Vancouver to Hope. However, the CPR was to complete the KVR to Vancouver in 1915. The CPR succeeded in turning the tables on Hill by negotiating a traffic agreement with the Spokane International Railway, which was completed from Spokane to a connection with the Crow's Nest Pass Railway in 1906. This agreement enabled the CPR to take from the GN some of the freight business between Spokane and the Twin Cities, to the east, and Portland, Oregon, to the west.

In the period 1896–1914 the CPR greatly expanded its branch-line network on the prairies, in part as a response to competition from the Canadian Northern Railway and the GTPR. The official directing this policy, in consultation with Shaughnessy, was William Whyte, who had a strong faith in the agricultural potential of the prairie West, a view shared by his successor, George Bury. Total CPR branch lines in the prairie West increased from 856 miles in 1896 to 4,212 miles in 1914. The CPR also laid double-tracks on the entire main line from Winnipeg to the Lakehead and 828 miles of the main line between Calgary and Winnipeg and invested heavily in new rolling stock so that it could handle the prairie grain crop more efficiently. These measures enabled the company to move 60 per cent of the large 1913 prairie grain crop to the Lakehead before the close of navigation in December 1913. Finally, the CPR increased its terminal elevator capacity at Fort William. So the CPR was able to move a substantial portion of the prairie grain crop from the Lakehead to Montreal by water through the Great Lakes canal system or by water to ports on Georgian Bay and from there by rail. The building of the Spiral and Connaught tunnels reduced the steep grades on two sections of the main line in BC, putting the CPR in an excellent position to handle grain exported westward to Vancouver (and beyond, when the Panama Canal went into full operation after World War One).

By the time Shaughnessy became president in 1899, the CPR had a substantial mountain hotel system as well as a hotel in Vancouver. The new president improved and expanded the mountain hotels and established new luxury hotels in Victoria, Winnipeg, and Calgary in order to meet the demands of the increasing number of well-to-do tourists who wanted first-class hotel accommodation. The most impressive of the new city hotels was the château-style Empress Hotel in Victoria, opened in 1908, which attracted many tourists to the city, especially Americans. Another attractive hotel was the beaux-arts style Royal Alexandra Hotel in Winnipeg which opened its doors in 1906. The rising metropolis of Calgary obtained a CPR luxury hotel in 1914 – the Palliser – which was to dominate the city's skyline for over half a century. The Hotel Vancouver was considerably enlarged in 1905, and in 1912 the CPR began construction of a new and larger hotel to replace the existing building. It opened in 1916. The most important of the company's mountain hotels was the Banff Springs Hotel which was extended and improved, beginning in 1900, to meet the demands of an increasing international clientèle. In the 1902 season guests at the Banff Springs numbered 3,890 while during the 1911 season over 22,000 stayed there. Other mountain hotels that underwent considerable expansion were the Château Lake Louise, Mount Stephen House, and Glacier House. All these resort hotels were very profitable and attracted many first-class passengers to the CPR.

The CPR had its strongest impact on urban growth in Western Canada in the period before 1896. The company's momentous decision in 1881 to adopt a southerly route across the Prairies shifted settlement – both urban and rural – away from the valley of the Saskatchewan to the southern plains. Subsequently, the CPR determined the sites of hundreds of communities along this main line and on its branches. Before 1896 most prairie communities were south of the transcontinental line. As late as 1901 the majority of centres of urban population in the prairie West were concentrated along the CPR main line and those branches under the company's control. By 1912 the CPR's monopoly position was faltering, though nine of the largest urban centres in the prairie West and BC were located on CPR lines.[1]

Most CPR urban policies from 1896 to 1914 resulted from decisions taken in the earlier period. With policies such as the Traders' Tariff of 1898, the company continued to support Winnipeg's position as the centre of the prairie grain trade and the Western wholesale trade.

The expanding wholesale houses of Winnipeg were supplied with manufactured goods mainly from Toronto and Montreal via the CPR. Vancouver experienced substantial growth after 1896 because of its position as the Western terminus of the CPR. The city's maritime trade increased substantially, partly due to the company's expansion of its *Empress* service to the Orient and its coastal steamship service. This expansion also benefitted Victoria. The CPR improved its rail connection with Edmonton by the construction of the High Level Bridge, which opened in 1913. A departure from pre-1896 policies was the company's actions in promoting Calgary as a major urban centre in the prairie West. The CPR's establishment of the irrigation block created a large new agricultural hinterland for the city. In 1912 the company established the Department of Natural Resources (DNR) with headquarters in Calgary, a measure which involved the transfer of the CPR's Land Department from Winnipeg to Calgary. But most important was the company's decision to establish large locomotive and car shops in Calgary. When they opened in 1913, Winnipeg's monopoly on locomotive and car repair work in the prairie West was over.

The authority on CPR land policies in the prairie West, James Hedges, has emphasized the company's overriding concern for settlement of its lands in order to generate more traffic for the railway. The study shows that this generalization needs to be modified. It is true that the CPR did not follow the policy of the Hudson's Bay Company in the period 1900–13 of withholding from sale "specified sections in each [prairie] township to gain the benefits of increased value arising from the occupation of adjoining areas."[2] However, CPR directors were determined to maximize profits from the railway's agricultural lands, as their refusal to sell a large part of the mainline grant to the federal government in 1897 demonstrates. Proceeds from prairie land sales, excluding townsites, were very substantial, amounting to $83,835,446 for the entire period 1896–1914. This revenue was used mainly for additions and improvements to the railway, eventually allowing the CPR to increase dividends on common stock, which stood at a high of 10 per cent in the years 1912 to 1914. One of the CPR's most innovative land schemes was its vast irrigation project in southern Alberta, adopted from a proposal by J.S. Dennis and William Pearce. The Western section of this project was in full operation in 1910 and produced 353,000 acres of irrigable land; the Eastern section, completed in 1914, irrigated 242,000 acres.[3] The company also introduced new techniques, such as the ready-made farm and the loan farm, to encourage settlement in the irrigation block.

The most important of the CPR's natural resource ventures was the acquisition and expansion of the Trail smelter. It was Shaughnessy who convinced the cautious CPR directors to purchase the Trail smelter in 1898 and who then had the smelter lower its rates for treating ores, a policy which stimulated the mining of ores in the Kootenay and Boundary districts and provided valuable traffic for the CPR lines in southern BC. Van Horne appointed the New York mining engineer W.H. Aldridge manager of the smelter. He proved to be a very capable and resourceful official. Aldridge introduced the Betts process that enabled the smelter to complete the lead refining process at Trail, making it the first lead refinery of its kind in the world and marking the transition of the Trail smelter from a gold-copper base to a wider range of metals. Aldridge's proposal to produce lead pipe and sheets at the smelter was however firmly rejected by Shaughnessy, who did not wish to challenge the interests of manufacturers of these products in Ontario and Quebec. The CPR also developed several coal mines, but its only profitable investment in this field was the Lethbridge colliery, purchased in 1912. The company adopted a new policy for its settlement lands in Alberta by promoting the exploration of oil there from 1906 to 1914.

Western Canada in the years 1896 to 1914 can be aptly described as "the CPR West"[4] for in this period the CPR played a crucial role in the region's settlement – both urban and rural – and its economic development.

Notes

The following abbreviations or shortened references are used in the notes:

CAR   *Canadian Annual Review of Public Affairs*
CHCD   Canada, House of Commons, *Debates*
CHR   *Canadian Historical Review*
CRMW   *Canadian Railway and Marine World*
CSD   Canada, Senate, *Debates*
Dorman   Robert Dorman, Compiler, *A Statutory History of the Steam and Electric Railways of Canada 1836–1937* (Ottawa: Department of Transport, 1938)
GAI   Glenbow-Alberta Institute
GC   James J. Hill Reference Library, James J. Hill Papers, General Correspondence
LP   NAC, Sir Wilfrid Laurier Papers
MCHS   Milwaukee County Historical Society
Morgan 1912   Henry James Morgan, ed., *The Canadian Men and Women of the Time*, Second edition (Toronto: William Briggs, 1912)
NAC   National Archives of Canada
PABC   Public Archives of British Columbia
SLB   NAC, CPR papers, T.G. Shaughnessy Letterbooks
SLI   CPR Archives, CPR Papers, T.G. Shaughnessy Letters Inward
VHLB   NAC, CPR Papers, W.C. Van Horne Letterbooks
WSA/SHSW   Wisconsin State Archives, State Historical Society of Wisconsin

PREFACE

1 VHLB 54, Van Horne to Harry Moody, 9 November 1897. Emphasis in the original.
2 The CPR retained the originals and also has microfilm copies.
3 W. Kaye Lamb, *History of the Canadian Pacific Railway* (New York: Macmillan, 1977).
4 I.B. Scott to author, 22 September 1982.
5 J. Lorne McDougall, *Canadian Pacific: A Brief History* (Montreal: McGill University Press, 1968).
6 Pierre Berton, *The National Dream* and *The Last Spike* (Toronto: McClelland and Stewart, 1970, 1971).
7 Robert Chodos, *The CPR: A Century of Corporate Welfare* (Toronto: James Lewis and Samuel, 1972).
8 The discussion of these books is taken from my article, "Railways and Canadian Development," *Acadiensis* 73 no. 2 (Spring/Printemps 1978), 159–64.
9 Hugh A. Dempsey, ed., *The CPR West: The Iron Road and the Making of a Nation* (Vancouver: Douglas & McIntyre, 1984).

CHAPTER ONE

1 Cited in Pierre Berton, *The Last Spike* (Toronto: McClelland and Stewart, 1971), 416.
2 Montreal *Star*, 29 June 1886; W. Kaye Lamb, *History of the Canadian Pacific Railway* (New York: Macmillan, 1977), 143; Norbert MacDonald, "The Canadian Pacific Railway and Vancouver's Development to 1900," in W. Peter Ward and Robert A.J. McDonald, eds., *British Columbia: Historical Readings* (Vancouver: Douglas & McIntyre, 1981), 398–9.
3 CPR, *Annual Report*. The figure of 6,476 miles excludes three railways which were "worked for account of owners": Montreal & Atlantic Railway, Calgary & Edmonton Railway, Qu'Appelle, Long Lake & Saskatchewan Railway.
4 For the period 1896–1914 I have used the "implicit price index" in M.C. Urquhart, "New Estimates of Gross National Product, Canada, 1870 to 1926: Some Implications for Canadian Development," Discussion Paper no. 586, Institute for Economic Research, Queen's University, 1984, 93–4. For the period 1914–1973 I have used series K8–18, "Consumer Price Index for Canada 1913–1975," in F.H. Leacy, ed., *Historical Statistics of Canada*, 2nd edition (Ottawa: Ministry of Supply and Services Canada, 1983). For the period

1973–1988 I used Statistics Canada, *The Consumer Price Index*, April 1988, table 2, 11. The precise figure arrived at was $8.30.

5 CPR, *Annual Reports*, 1892–1896; Lamb, *Canadian Pacific*, 188–9; VHLB 52, Van Horne to Adolph Boissevain, 30 September 1896; NAC, T.G. Shaughnessy Papers, vol. 2, file 3, "Memoranda re Canadian Railway Problems." I am very grateful to the present Lord Shaughnessy for permission to consult this important collection and cite material from it.

6 SLB 72, Shaughnessy to A.A. Housman, 27 October 1900; Canadian Railroad Historical Association Archives, Private Correspondence of Sir William Van Horne, 1856–1938, microfilm copy in Glenbow-Alberta Institute (hereafter GAI), file 82.5.308, "Canadian Pacific Railway Company, Office of the Secretary, Distribution of Common Stock," 9 December 1901.

7 CPR, *Annual Reports*, 1894, 1899, 1900–1, 1914.

8 SLB 5, Shaughnessy to Richard White, 13 February 1891, "Personal"; A.W. Currie, *The Grand Trunk Railway of Canada* (Toronto: University of Toronto Press, 1957), 357–76.

9 Walter Vaughan, *The Life and Work of Sir William Van Horne* (New York: The Century Company, 1920), 3–11.

10 Cited in ibid., 17–18.

11 Cited in ibid., 20–1.

12 Ibid., 30–9; Stephen Mayles, *Willam Van Horne* (Don Mills, Ontario: Fitzhenry & Whiteside, 1976), 10.

13 Vaughan, *Van Horne*, 39–53.

14 Vaughan, *Van Horne*, 53–4; NAC, Katherine Hughes Papers, vol. 2, "Manuscript of life of Sir Wm. Van Horne with notes," 78–9.

15 Vaughan, *Van Horne*, 54–62; Heather Gilbert, *Awakening Continent: The Life of Lord Mount Stephen*, vol. 1, *1829–1891* (Aberdeen: Aberdeen University Press, 1965), 49. The Manitoba road's title was the St Paul and Pacific, but Hill had it renamed after he and his associates took over.

16 James Jerome Hill Reference Library, James Jerome Hill Papers, Letterpress Books, Railroad Series, vol. R 21, James J. Hill to George Stephen (in Montreal), 17 October 1881; Berton *Last Spike*, 45; Vaughan, *Van Horne*, 45.

17 Mayles, *Van Horne*, 16; Berton, *Last Spike*, 45–9; *Canadian Pacific Facts and Figures* (Montreal: Canadian Pacific Railway, 1946), 38. Easton's comment is cited in Berton.

18 Mayles, *Van Horne* 20; Berton, *Last Spike*, chap. 2 & 3.

19 Montreal *Gazette*, 15 May 1884; NAC, Shaughnessy Papers, vol. 2, file 3, "Memoranda re Canadian Railway Problems," which lists all CPR

directors 1881–1923, with dates of appointment and retirement. Angus was re-elected as a vice-president of the company.

20 Gilbert, *Awakening Continent*, 219, 286–7 (letter to CPR shareholders); GAI, Van Horne Private Correspondence, file 82.5.276, George Stephen, R.B. Angus and E.B. Osler to W.C. Van Horne, 15 August 1889, file 82.5.54, W.C. Van Horne to Sir George Stephen, R.B. Angus, E.B. Osler, 17 August 1889; NAC, J.S. Willison Papers, vol. 46, W.C. Van Horne to Willison, 1 December 1898, "Private."

21 NAC, Shaughnessy Papers, vol. 2, file 2, "Pedigree charts"; MCHS, naturalization papers of Thomas Shaughnessy, Sr; Old Settlers Scrapbook, Thomas Shaughnessy Sr obituary, 15 November 1903, Mary Shaughnessy obituary, 23 June 1906; Kathleen Neils Conzen, *Immigrant Milwaukee 1836–1860* (Cambridge: Harvard University Press, 1976), 142–3. For a fuller account of Shaughnessy's life in Milwaukee, see my article, "Baron Thomas Shaughnessy: The Peer That Made Milwaukee Famous," *Milwaukee History* 6, no. 1 (Spring, 1983): 28–40. One son, James, was drowned in 1878 at the age of twenty.

22 Milwaukee *Sentinel*, 6 June, 9 July 1866, 4 November 1867, 6 June 1878, 5 September 1868; J.R.H. Weaver, ed., *Dictionary of National Biography, Twentieth Century, 1922–1930* (London: Oxford University Press, 1937), 764; SLB 68, Shaughnessy to H. [sic] C. Spencer, 26 July 1899.

23 Herbert W. Rice, "Early History of the Chicago, Milwaukee and St Paul Railway Company" (PH D. thesis, State University of Iowa, 1938), 173–7; August Derleth, *The Milwaukee Road* (New York: Creative Age Press, 1948), 98–9.

24 Milwaukee *Sentinel*, 20, 26, 28 July 1875, 31 January, 5 April 1876; NAC, Shaughnessy Papers, vol. 1, file 3, Shaughnessy to E.M. Hopkins, 12 June 1917.

25 WSA/SHSW, Milwaukee Council Proceedings, 24 April, 22 October 1877, 12 August 1878, 2 April 1879; Milwaukee *Sentinel*, 5 and 19 April 1882.

26 Milwaukee *Evening Wisconsin*, 12 January 1880; NAC, Shaughnessy Papers, vol. 2, file 2, "Pedigree Charts." Elizabeth Nagle was born 24 August 1850 at Moher, Country Clare, Ireland.

27 WSA/SHSW, WPA field notes on Thomas Shaughnessy, circulars issued by Chicago, Milwaukee and St Paul Railroad, dated 4 and 31 December 1879 and signed by S.S. Merrill; Milwaukee *Sentinel*, 10 November 1879; MCHS, newspaper clipping dated 20 September 1953 by Alan E. Kent; Vaughan, *Van Horne*, 57–8; Katherine Hughes Papers, vol. 2, "Manuscript life ... of Sir William Van Horne," 83–4.

28 WSA/SHSW, Milwaukee *Sentinel*, 11 December 1923, obituary of Lord Shaughnessy; MCHS, newspaper clipping, 20 September 1953.

29 Milwaukee *Sentinel*, 10 February 1882; J.M. Gibbon, *Steel of Empire* (New York: Macmillan, 1935), 229–30; D.C. Masters, "Financing the C.P.R., 1880–1885," *Canadian Historical Review* 24 (1943): 355–6.

30 Milwaukee *Sentinel*, 31 October 1882. Mallory, admitted to the New York State bar in 1848, moved to Milwaukee in 1850. He was elected district attorney for two full terms. Appointed a municipal judge in 1860, he was re-elected to hold office for 29 years. I am indebted to Professor Frederick Olson of the University of Wisconsin-Milwaukee for this information.

31 SLB 1, Shaughnessy to W.B.H. Gaylord, 10 March 1884.

32 SLB 83, Shaughnessy to Editor, Milwaukee *Sentinel*, 29 October 1903.

33 NAC, Shaughnessy Papers, vol. 2, envelope containing original page from the register of St Lawrence Hall, 2 November 1882; *Lovell's Montreal Directory*, 1883–4, 518.

34 D.C. Coleman, "Rt. Hon. Lord Shaughnessy, G.C.V.O.," in *Canadian Pacific History: Four Addresses*, pamphlet in CPR Archives, 20.

35 Lamb, *Canadian Pacific*, 110; D.C. Masters, "Financing the CPR, 1880–1885," *Canadian Historical Review* 24 (1943): 350–61.

36 SLB 1, Shaughnessy to Archer Barker, 13 March 1884, to James Worthington, 25 March 1884; SLB 3, Shaughnessy to W. Whyte, 11 November, 3 December 1884.

37 SLB 3, Shaughnessy to Hon. Frank Smith, 14 January 1885, "Private"; SLB 4, Shaughnessy to H. Abbott, 12 February 1885, "Private and Confidential"; Berton, *Last Spike*, 320–1. Lord Shaughnessy also recounted this story to this author.

38 SLB 24, Shaughnessy to W.D. Marvel, 16 October 1890. The announcement of Shaughnessy's promotion is in SLB 19.

39 Montreal *Gazette*, 24 February 1891; Vaughan, *Van Horne*, 189–94, 346–7.

40 NAC, Shaughnessy Papers, vol 2, file 1, Shaughnessy to Walter Vaughan, 8 May 1920 (copy); SLB 99, Shaughnessy to J.L. Garvin, London, 11 April 1911; SLB 100, Shaughnessy to Jacques Bureau, 23 September 1911, "Private."

41 Cited in Peter B. Waite, *Canada 1874–1896: Arduous Destiny* (Toronto: McClelland and Stewart, 1971), 224–5.

42 Montreal *Gazette*, 19 June 1891; Waite, *Ardous Destiny*, 228–30; J.K. Johnson, ed., *The Canadian Directory of Parliament* (Ottawa: National Archives of Canada, 1968), 1–2; NAC, Shaughnessy Papers, vol. 2, file 3, "Memoranda re Canadian Railway Problems," vol. 2, file 2, "Pedigree Charts"; CPR, *Annual Report*, 1891. Sons William and

Alfred were born in 1883 and 1887 respectively. The Shaughnessy's last child, Edith, was born in 1892.

43 Shaughnessy Papers Private (in possession of Lord Shaughnessy), Shaughnessy diary of trip to Orient; SLB 29, Shaughnessy to Right Hon. Viscount Enoye, 3 February 1892, "Private"; SLB 30, Shaughnessy to The Naval Construction and Armaments Company, 8 March 1892; Vancouver *Daily World*, 26 January 1892; Gibbon, *Steel of Empire*, 336. I am greatly indebted to the present Lord Shaughnessy for permission to consult the papers in his possession.

44 SLB 100, Shaughnessy to W. Whyte, 12 December 1911; CPR, Report of Proceedings at the Eleventh Annual Meeting of Shareholders, 11 May 1892. The date for board meetings was fixed by company by-law.

45 D.M.L. Farr, "Donald Alexander Smith, 1st Baron Strathcona and Mount Royal," in James H. Marsh, general ed., *The Canadian Encyclopedia*, 3 vols. (Edmonton: Hurtig Publishers, 1985), 3: 1708; Gilbert, *Awakening Continent*, 38–49; Morgan 1912, 1068–71.

46 W.S. Wallace, ed., *The Macmillan Dictionary of Canadian Biography*, 3rd edition (Toronto: Macmillan, 1963), 16; Morgan 1912, 29; Merrill Denison, *Canada's First Bank: A History of the Bank of Montreal*, 2 vols. (Toronto: McClelland and Stewart, 1967), 2: 126, 164, 196, 298–9, 411–12; Gilbert, *Awakening Continent*, 49, 90; Albro Martin, *James J. Hill and the Opening of the Northwest* (New York: Oxford University Press, 1976), 210, 214; NAC, Shaughnessy Papers, vol. 2, file 3, "Memoranda re Canadian Railway Problems."

47 Johnson, ed., *Directory of Parliament*, 451; Morgan 1912, 874–5; Augustus Bridle, "E.B. Osler, Constructive Citizen," *Saturday Night*, 1 April 1911; Donald M. Wilson, *The Ontario and Quebec Railway* (Belleville, Ontario: Mika Publishing Company, 1984), 48, 51, 62–4, 73. The information on Osler's trip to Aberdeen was supplied by Mr Paul Nanton of Victoria in an interview on 25 February 1986.

48 Morgan 1912, 789; CAR, 1903, 422; interview with David McNicoll, Montreal *Standard*, 21 October 1905; NAC, Shaughnessy Papers, vol. 2, file 3, "Memoranda re Canadian Railway Problems."

49 Ibid., CPR, *Annual Report*, 1914. Holt was elected to the CPR board on 8 May 1911.

50 Henry James Morgan, ed., *The Canadian Men and Women of the Time* (Toronto: William Briggs, 1898), 284; CPR, *Annual Report*, 1908; CAR, 1908, 573, 637; Public Archives of Nova Scotia, W.S. Fielding Papers, vol. 466, Fielding to A.R. Creelman, 18 May 1908, "Personal"; SLB 74, Shaughnessy statement, dated 1 May 1901, re Charles Drinkwater.

51 Morgan 1912, 54; CPR, *Annual Report*, 1908; T.D. Regehr, *The*

Canadian Northern Railway (Toronto: Macmillan of Canada, 1976), 43–4; SLB 71, Shaughnessy to W.R. Baker, 9 May 1900.

52 CPR, *Annual Report*, 1896; SLB 49 and 50, passim; Alfred D. Chandler, *The Visible Hand: The Managerial Revolution in American Business* (Cambridge: Harvard University Press, 1977), 176–81; SLB 76, Shaughnessy to Lord Strathcona, 16 November 1901, "Personal."

CHAPTER TWO

1 F.W. Howay, W.N. Sage and H.F. Angus, *British Columbia and the United States*, ed., H.F. Angus (New York: Russell & Russell, 1970), 272–3; G.W. Taylor, *The History of Mining in British Columbia* (Saanichton, BC: Hancock House, 1978), 128; Harold A. Innis, *Settlement and the Mining Frontier* (Toronto: Macmillan of Canada, 1936), vol 9, part 2, *Canadian Frontiers of Settlement Series*, eds., W.A. Mackintosh and W.L.G. Joerg, 270–9.

2 Ronald H. Meyer, "The Evolution of Railways in the Kootenays," (Master's thesis, University of British Columbia, 1970), 11–13.

3 John Fahey, *Inland Empire: D.C. Corbin and Spokane* (Seattle: University of Washington Press, 1965), 60–1.

4 Ibid., 60, 62.

5 Ibid., 77, 90. Washington achieved statehood in 1889.

6 Ibid., 112–18; *BC Statutes*, 1890, c. 41, c. 62; *Statutes of Canada*, 1890, c. 2, c. 87; Dorman, 169, citing P.C. 1997, 20 August 1890; Howay et al., *British Columbia and the United States*, 251.

7 Howay et al., British Columbia and the United States, 251; SLB, 26, Shaughnessy to Collingwood Schreiber, 30 April 1891, "Private"; SLB 28, Shaughnessy to Mackenzie Bowell, 3 August 1891, "Private."

8 Fahey, *Inland Empire*, chap. 9. Fort Sheppard was the place where the Columbia River crossed the international boundary. The Hudson's Bay Company had once had a post there named Fort Sheppard.

9 NAC, J.S. Willison Papers, vol. 46, W.C. Van Horne to Willison, 11 April 1896, "Confidential."

10 A.A. den Otter, *Civilizing the West* (Edmonton: University of Alberta Press, 1982), chap. 1 to 7. The company's original name was the North Western Coal and Navigation Company.

11 Ibid., 156–8; SLB 36, Shaughnessy to W. Whyte, 4 July 1893.

12 VHLB 47, Van Horne to R.L. Gault, 14 November 1894; VHLB 50, Van Horne to J.H. Turner, 7 February 1896.

13 Meyer, "Railways in the Kootenays," 17.

14 W. Kaye Lamb, *History of the Canadian Pacific Railway* (New York: Macmillan, 1977), 82 and chap. 14.

15 Innis, *Settlement and the Mining Frontier*, 278–9.

16 NAC, CPR Papers, Van Horne to Stephen Letterbrook 1894–1898,
    Van Horne to Stephen, 11 October 1894. These are typed copies of
    Van Horne's letters to Lord Mount Stephen.
17 Ibid., Van Horne to Stephen, 6 November 1894; Meyer, "Railways
    in the Kootenays," 13–14.
18 Meyer, "Railways in the Kootenays," 17; SLB 44, Shaughnessy to F.S.
    Barnard, 14 December 1895.
19 Van Horne to Stephen Letterbook 1894–1898, Van Horne to Ste-
    phen, 8 August 1895.
20 Meyer, "Railways in the Kootenays," 18; Patricia E. Roy, "Railways,
    Politicians and the Development of the City of Vancouver as a
    Metropolitan Centre, 1886–1929," (Master's thesis, University of
    Toronto, 1963), 31; SLB 44, Shaughnessy to J.A. Mara, 21 September
    1895, "Personal."
21 Van Horne to Stephen Letterbook 1894–1898, Van Horne to Ste-
    phen, 8 August 1895; SLB 43, Shaughnessy to H. Abbott, 8 August
    1895.
22 SLB 44, Shaughnessy to F.D. Underwood, 29 November 1895,
    "Personal."
23 SLB 43, Shaughnessy to J.H. Susman, 6 August 1895, "Personal"; SLB
    44, Shaughnessy to H. Abbott, 10 September 1895, Shaughnessy
    to J.H. Susman, 27 September 1895.
24 SLB 43, Shaughnessy to N. Clarke Wallace, 21 August 1895.
25 Ibid.
26 H.G.J. Aitken, "Defensive Expansionism: The State and Economic
    Growth in Canada," in W.T. Easterbrook and M.H. Watkins, eds.,
    Approaches to Canadian Economic History (Toronto: McClelland and
    Stewart, 1967), 183–221.
27 Meyer, "Railways in the Kootenays," 54. Citing CPR *Annual Report*,
    1896, 10.
28 SLB 51, Shaughnessy to Sir Oliver Mowat, 15 April 1897 with attached
    "Memorandum."
29 Willison Papers, vol. 46, W.C. Van Horne to Willison, 11 April 1896,
    "Confidential," author's emphasis.
30 SLB 47, Shaughnessy to Reverend A.E. Burke, 3 July 1896.
31 SLB 46, Shaughnessy to John Haggart, 15 April 1896; LP, vol. 19,
    Shaughnessy to Wilfrid Laurier, 12 September 1896, "Personal."
    Shaughnessy asserted that he prepared the 15 April 1896 memoran-
    dum for Premier Sir Charles Tupper. Tupper did not become
    prime minister until 1 May. Undoubtedly Shaughnessy discussed the
    terms of his letter to Haggart with Tupper. See also VHLB 40, Van
    Horne to John Haggart, 18 March 1892, in which Van Horne

says the CPR will be applying for a charter to build the Crow's Nest Pass Railway.

32 Ottawa *Daily Citizen*, 23 April 1896, 5; SLB 46, Shaughnessy to Senator D. MacInnes, 23 April 1896; Willison Papers, vol. 13, J.D. Edgar to Willison, 22 April 1896, "Private" (telegram); CHCD, 1897, 4530, 4536 (Sir Charles Tupper's remarks).

33 D.J. Hall, *Clifford Sifton*, vol. 1, *The Young Napoleon 1861–1900* (Vancouver: University of British Columbia Press, 1981), 150.

34 R.T.G. Clippingdale, "J.S. Willison, Political Journalist: from Liberalism to Independence, 1881–1905" (PH D. thesis, University of Toronto, 1970), 355.

35 Robert M. Stamp, "J.D. Edgar and the Liberal Party: 1867–1896," CHR 45 (1964): 93–115.

36 Willison Papers, vol. 13, J.D. Edgar to Willison, 25 January 1896, "Private."

37 VHLB 50, Van Horne to J.D. Edgar, 22 January 1896; VHLB 51, Van Horne to Edgar, "On train No. 7, Soo Branch", 5 June 1896.

38 Clippingdale, "Willison", 355–8. The quotation is taken from Willison's *Reminiscences*, 221.

39 Laurier himself was appointed president of the Privy Council on 11 July: *Guide to Canadian Ministries Since Confederation* (Ottawa: National Archives of Canada, 1957), 27.

40 James C. Graves and Horace B. Graves, "New Brunswick Political Biography" (unpublished manuscript, University of New Brunswick Archives); Fred Cook, "Giants and Jesters in Public Life: The Father of the Railway Commission" (unpublished manuscript, University of New Brunswick Archives); Stamp, "J.D. Edgar," 115; J.K. Johnson, ed., *The Canadian Directory of Parliament 1867–1967* (Ottawa: National Archives of Canada, 1968), 186–7.

41 LP, vol. 19, T.G. Shaughnessy to Laurier, 12 September 1896, "Personal."

42 SLB 48, Shaughnessy to W. Whyte, 26 August 1896.

43 VHLB 52, Van Horne to Thomas P. Irving, 2 October 1896.

44 Ibid., Van Horne to J.D. Edgar, 2 October 1896. Van Horne stated that the CPR had begun this work in 1891 at the insistence of Sir John A. Macdonald, who was worried that the Crow's Nest Pass might fall under the control of an American company.

45 Ibid., Van Horne to J.D. Edgar, 6 November 1896.

46 PABC, BC Premiers' Papers, vol. 4, James Baker to J.H. Turner (in Vancouver), Victoria, 19 August 1896; LP, reel C-742, J.H. Turner to Wilfrid Laurier, Vancouver, 20 August 1896 (telegram).

47 Roy, "Development of Vancouver," 42–3.

48 Vancouver *News-Advertiser*, 21 October 1896.

49 Ibid., 28 October 1896, editorial.

50 VHLB 52, Van Horne to A.G. Blair, 14 November 1896, with cost estimate prepared by Hugh D. Lumsden. The length of 326.6 miles has been rounded off to 327 miles by the author to simplify calculations. Van Horne's terms would total $8,175,000, and the cash subsidy amount to $1,635,000 (author's calculations).

51 Ibid., Van Horne to Colonel James Baker, 25 November 1896. Another federal minister, Louis H. Davies (Marine and Fisheries) accompanied Blair during his meetings in Vancouver. It is not clear if he travelled with Blair to Vancouver Island. Vancouver *News-Advertiser*, 16 December 1896.

52 Ibid., Van Horne to J.H. Turner, 28 November 1896; BC Premiers' Papers, vol. 405, J.H. Turner to W.C. Van Horne, 18 November 1896, "Confidential"; Morgan 1912. 118.

53 *Victoria Colonist*, 11, 13, 17, 18, 19 December 1896; Vancouver *News-Advertiser*, 23 December 1896.

54 Roy, "Development of Vancouver," 48; Vancouver *News-Advertiser*, 23 December 1896.

55 VHLB 52, Van Horne to J. Heber Haslam, 16 January 1897, "Private"; Hall, *Sifton*, vol. 1, chap. 4&5; NAC, Sir Clifford Sifton Papers, vol. 335, Van Horne to Sifton, 1 January 1897; VHLB 51, Van Horne to J.D. Edgar, 29 June 1896. In June 1896 Van Horne had informed Edgar that Sifton should be in the Cabinet because he was "the only man who can settle the school question."

56 VHLB 52, Van Horne to Colonel James Baker, 21 January 1897, "Confidential."

57 Ibid., Van Horne to A.G. Blair, 4 February 1897.

58 Ibid., Van Horne to Clifford Sifton, 9 February 1897, "Private," Van Horne "Memorandum for Mr. Shaughnessy," 15 February 1897; Willison Papers, vol. 51, Stewart Lyon to Willison, 15 April 1897; LP, vol. 43, Clifford Sifton to Laurier, 19 April 1897, "Personal"; Hall, *Sifton*, vol. 1, 154.

59 VHLB 52, Van Horne to Sifton, 13 February 1897, "Private," Van Horne "Memorandum for Mr. Shaughnessy," 15 February 1897. Van Horne neglected to discuss the BC Southern lands with the executive committee. He expressed his view privately to Shaughnessy.

60 VHLB 52, Van Horne to Sir Donald Smith, 16 February 1897, "Confidential."

61 Winnipeg *Tribune*, 19 February 1897.

62 LP, vol. 38, Laurier to A.T. Wood, 26 February 1897, "Private" (copy).

63 Willison Papers, vol. 51, Stewart Lyon to Willison, Ottawa, 15, 18

April 1897. The four BC members were: Hewitt Bostock, George Maxwell, Aulay Morrison, and W.W.B. McInnes.

64 T.D. Regehr, *The Canadian Northern Railway* (Toronto: Macmillan of Canada, 1976), 62–3.

65 SLB 51, Shaughnessy to Sir Oliver Mowat, 15 April 1897, with attached "Memorandum." The CPR paid no dividend on its common stock in 1894, a 1 $^1/_2$ per cent dividend in 1895, and a 2 per cent dividend in 1896.

66 LP, vol. 43, Clifford Sifton to Laurier, 19 April 1897, "Personal"; Sifton Papers, vol. 11, J.H. Ashdown to Sifton, 2, 13 March 1897; reel c-402, Sifton to Charles N. Bell, 16 February 1897; reel c-403, Sifton to Ashdown, 5 March 1897, "Personal" (copy); vol. 218, Sifton to Ashdown, 17 March 1897 (copy).

67 VHLB 53, Van Horne to J.D. Edgar, 21 April 1897, "Confidential."

68 Roy, "Development of Vancouver," 32, 69; NAC, Crow's Nest Coal and Railway Company Papers, passim; Robert C. Cail, *Land, Man and the Law: The Disposal of Crown Lands in British Columbia, 1871–1913* (Vancouver: University of British Columbia Press, 1974), 159; H. Leslie Brown, "The Pass: Biography of a District, Renewed, and a Town, Long Gone" (unpublished manuscript, 1977), 15–17, 20–2.

69 VHLB 53, Van Horne to Robert Jaffray, "En route to Ottawa," 17 May 1897, "Private," Van Horne to Sir Donald A. Smith, 3 June 1897.

70 *Statutes of Canada*, 1897, c. 36, c.5.

71 Hall, *Sifton*, vol. 1, 154; VHLB 52, Van Horne to Clifford Sifton, 6 February 1897; Gillian Wogin, "The Wealth-Maximizing Behaviour of the Canadian Pacific Railway: Lands, Freight Rates, and the Crow's Nest Pass Agreement" (PH D. thesis, Carleton University, 1983), iii. I am indebted to Ms Wogin for furnishing me a copy of this important study.

72 CHCD, 1897, 4513–19 (18 June).

73 Ibid., 1897, 4522, 4542, 5345, 5348–9 (18, 26 June).

74 Ibid., 1897, 4529–39 (18 June).

75 Ibid., 1897, 4543, 5601 (18 June); Ron Poulton, *The Paper Tyrant: John Ross Robertson of the Toronto Telegram* (Toronto: Clarke Irwin, 1971), 110.

76 CHCD, 1897, 4558–9, 4564–5, 4577 (18 June); *Canadian Directory of Parliament*, 413.

77 CHCD, 1897, 5536; CSD, 1897, 981–8.

78 den Otter, *Civilizing the West*, 221.

79 Wogin, "Crow's Nest Pass Agreement," 38–9. These remarks, made in an open letter to the press, are quoted in J.W. Dafoe, *Clifford Sifton in Relation To His Times* (Toronto: Macmillan of Canada 1931),

146. Sifton's remarks are quoted approvingly by A.W. Currie in his *Economics of Canadian Transportation* (Toronto: University of Toronto Press, 1964). 631.

80 Lamb, *Canadian Pacific*, 210.

CHAPTER THREE

1 G.W. Taylor, *Mining: The History of Mining in British Columbia* (Saanichton, BC: Hancock House, 1978), 161–3.

2 Dorman, 57–8; *Statutes of Canada*, 1897, c. 36, P.C. 2007, 18 August 1898.

3 Morgan, 1912, 670; VHLB 53, Van Horne to Dr George Parkin, 8 June 1897, Van Horne to Clifford Sifton, 23 July 1897; H. Leslie Brown, "The Pass: Biography of a District, Renewed, and a Town Long Gone" (unpublished manuscript, 1977), 46. Lumsden was president of the Canadian Society of Civil Engineers in 1887.

4 Morgan 1912, 496–7; J.L. Rutledge, "Binding the West With Bands of Steel: The Eventful Story of Michael John Haney," *Maclean's Magazine*, 1 April, 15 April, 1 May 1920.

5 Pierre Berton, *The Last Spike* (Toronto: McClelland and Stewart, 1971), 99, 200, 206–8.

6 VHLB 53, Van Horne to Sir Charles Tupper, 17 June 1897.

7 NAC, Clifford Sifton Papers, vol. 32, T.G. Shaughnessy to Sifton, 26 July 1897, "Confidential"; SLB 88, Shaughnessy to H.B. Ledyard, 14 May 1906, "Personal."

8 NAC, Privy Council Records, series 1, vol. 488, P.C. 2249, 21 July 1897; SLB 54, Shaughnessy to Joseph Martin, 7 October 1897; SLB 53, Shaughnessy to W. Whyte, 16 July 1897.

9 Brown, "The Pass," 42–3.

10 Ibid., 48; Canada, Parliament, House of Commons, *Sessional Papers*, 1898, no. 15, Appendix C. All references are to Canadian *Sessional Papers* unless otherwise indicated.

11 Brown, "The Pass," 49; W. Kaye Lamb, *History of the Canadian Pacific Railway* (New York: Macmillan, 1977), 211; *Sessional Papers*, 1898, no. 90a, 3.

12 SLB 60, Shaughnessy to W. Whyte, 6 June 1898.

13 Brown, "The Pass," 73; *Lethbridge News*, 20 October 1898; Lamb, *Canadian Pacific*, 211–12; SLB 62, Shaughnessy to Robert Jaffray, 4 October 1898.

14 Brown, "The Pass," 82; SLB 64, Shaughnessy to M.H. Macleod, 7 December 1898.

15 VHLB 55, Van Horne to Col James Baker, 1 November 1898, Van Horne to W.S. Fielding, 19 September 1898; Vancouver *News-Advertiser*, 5, 26 October 1898.

16 Brown, "The Pass," 72–4; J.L. Mcdougall, *Canadian Pacific: A Brief History* (Montreal: McGill University Press, 1968), 79–80; LP, vol. 569, T.G. Shaughnessy to Laurier, 5 April 1909. This figure represents a subsidy of $11,000 per mile for 309 miles of railway.

17 Fred J. Smyth, *Tales of the Kootenays* (Vancouver: Douglas & McIntyre, 1977), 65–7, 78. This book was first published in 1938.

18 Martin Robin, *The Rush for Spoils: The Company Province 1871–1933* (Toronto: McClelland and Stewart, 1972), 68–9; Smyth, *Tales*, 71–2; Brown, "The Pass," 15–17; VHLB 53, Van Horne to Colonel James Baker, 5 July 1897, "Confidential," Van Horne to C.E.L. Porteous, 5 July 1897; SLB 53, Shaughnessy to M.J. Haney, 27 July 1897; NAC, Crow's Nest Coal and Railway Company Papers, 1A.

19 LP, vol. 52, Hewitt Bostock to Laurier, 20 September 1897; vol. 68, Laurier to T.G. Shaughnessy, 9 March 1898 (copy); vol. 71, T.G. Shaughnessy to Laurier, 28 March 1898; VHLB 55, Van Horne to Col James Baker, 1 November 1898; Smyth, *Tales*, 83; CPR, *Annual Report*, 1913, mileage chart.

20 Donald Avery, *"Dangerous Foreigners": European Immigrant Workers and Labour Radicalism in Canada 1896–1932* (Toronto: McClelland and Stewart, 1979), 32–3; D.J. Hall, *Clifford Sifton*, vol. 1, *The Young Napoleon 1861–1900* (Vancouver: University of British Columbia Press, 1981), 155–6; Sifton Papers, vol. 221, Sifton to D.H. McMillan, 10 July 1897; Privy Council Records, vol. 488, P.C. 2132, 17 July 1897.

21 LP, vol. 49, W.L. Griffith to Laurier, 5 July 1897; SLB 53, M.J. Haney to Shaughnessy, 17 July 1897, Shaughnessy to James A. Smart, 21 July 1897; SLB 55, Shaughnessy to James A. Smart, 27 October 1897; Donald Avery, "Canadian Immigration Policy and the Alien Question, 1896–1919: The Anglo-Canadian Perspective" (PH D. thesis, University of Western Ontario, 1973), 200–2.

22 *Sessional Papers*, 1898, no. 90a, "Report of the Commissioners appointed to inquire into complaints respecting the treatment of labourers on the Crow's Nest Pass Railway, 3, 5–7, 16–17.

23 Ibid., "Report," 21; *Sessional Papers*, 1898, no. 15, "Report of the Commissioner of the North-West Mounted Police Force, 1897," Appendix C, "Annual Report of Superintendent S.B. Steele ..."; NAC, RCMP Records, vol. 1401, Inspector A. Ross Cuthbert to Superintendent Steele, 18 September 1897, Col. James Baker to Major S.B. Steele, 6 November 1897.

24 Ibid., "Report," 8, 11, 15, 21.

25 SLB 55, Shaughnessy to Sir Wilfred Laurier, 20 November 1897, "Personal"; LP, vol. 57, Fred White to Laurier, 20 November 1897.

26 LP, vol. 59, R.W. Jamieson to Laurier, 24 December 1897; Sifton Papers, vol. 10, John Appleton and W. White to Laurier, 21 December 1897; *Sessional Papers*, 1898, no. 90a, "Report," 17–22. The

three commissioners were C.A. Dugas, judge of the territorial court in the Yukon, Frank Pedley, superintendent of the immigration branch of the Interior Department, and John Appleton (Morgan, 1912, 352, 893).

27 SLB 60, Shaughnessy to E.B. Osler, 20 June 1898, to M.J. Haney, 15 June 1898, to W.S. Fielding, 15 July 1898; SLB 68, Shaughnessy to Sir Richard Cartwright, 9 September 1899.

28 Lamb, *Canadian Pacific*, 206; BC *Statutes*, 1896, c. 8, c. 54. The gauge was 3 feet: Omér Lavallée, *Narrow Gauge Railways of Canada* (Montreal: Railfare Enterprises, 1972), 54.

29 The best single source for these developments is Elsie G. Turnbull, *Topping's Trail* (Vancouver: Mitchell Press, 1964). For other sources, see notes to chap. 10.

30 SLB 60, Shaughnessy to F.P. Gutelius, 23, 27 June 1896, to W. Whyte, 27 June 1898, "Personal," 29 June 1898; SLB 61, Shaughnessy to G. Maclaren Brown, 21 July 1898; BC *Statutes*, 1896, c. 8; *Statutes of Canada*, 1898, c. 61; Dorman, 171, citing P.C. 1894, 3 August 1898.

31 Van Horne to Stephen Letterbook, Van Horne to Lord Mount Stephen, 8 February 1898.

32 John Fahey, *Inland Empire: D.C. Corbin and Spokane* (Seattle: University of Washington Press, 1965), 186–7; Patricia Roy, "Railways, Politicians, and the Development of Vancouver as a Metropolitan Centre, 1886–1929" (Master's thesis, University of Toronto, 1963), 50; CHCD, 1898, 744; LP, vol. 64, copy of Bill 26, "An Act to incorporate the Kettle River Valley Railway Company," with attached maps.

33 LP, vol. 68, Hewitt Bostock to Laurier, 11 March 1898, "Private and Confidential"; Johnson, ed., *Canadian Directory of Parliament*, 57–8.

34 LP, vol. 64, E.V. Bodwell to Laurier, 22 February 1898. For information on Bodwell, see Morgan 1912, 115.

35 LP, vol. 62, Duncan Ross to Laurier, 22 January 1898; vol. 64, "Resolution Passed by the Board of Trade of the City of Grand Forks, B.C.," 10 February 1898, "Resolution Passed by the City Council of the City of Grand Forks, B.C.," 10 February 1898; vol. 67, "Resolution Passed by Boundary Creek Mining and Commercial Association," 9 January 1898, Thomas Parker to Laurier, 4 March, 1898 enclosing resolution passed by the Rossland Liberal Association; vol. 68, John A. Turner and Frank Fletcher to House of Commons, 10 March 1898 (telegram); vol. 71, Henry E. Crossdale to Laurier, 25 [March 1898] (telegram).

36 CHCD, 1898, 3015.

37 VHLB 54, Van Horne to F. Elworthy, 22 March 1898, "Private"; Toronto *Globe*, 18 March 1898 (front page report).

38 Ibid., 18 March 1898, editorial, "The Kettle River Railway."

39 Ibid., 21 March 1898, 7; VHLB 54, Van Horne to J.W. Leonard, 19 March 1898 enclosing letter to "the Editor of the *Globe*."

40 LP, vol. 71, J.H. Turner to Laurier, 23 March 1898 (copy), H.S. Wallace to Laurier, 25 March 1898 (telegram); Roy, "Development of Vancouver," 51.

41 VHLB 54, Van Horne to F. Elworthy, 28 March 1898, "Private," to James Crathern, 23, 25 March 1898, "Private," to Elias Rogers, 23 March 1898, "Private," to W.D. Matthews, 25 March 1898, "Private,"; LP, vol. 71, W. Wainwright to Laurier, 28 March 1898 (telegram); Toronto *Globe*, 30 March, 1 April 1898. The petitions from the Montreal, Toronto, and Winnipeg boards of trade were passed by their councils, not by general meetings.

42 Toronto *Globe*, 1 April 1898. The bill was amended to require that a majority of the railway's directors be British subjects. The railway was to be completed in 2 years.

43 LP, vol. 69, Laurier to T.G. Shaughnessy, 21 March 1898 (copy); SLB 63, Shaughnessy to J.C. McLagan, 17 November 1898; CHCD, 5 April 1898, 3352–4. Tupper did not vote on 15 April, but supported the bill strongly in a speech on 4 April (ibid., 3063–71).

44 Ibid., 1898, 3357–60; Laurier L. Lapierre, "Politics, Race, and Religion in French Canada: Joseph Israel Tarte" (PH D. thesis, University of Toronto, 1962), 432–4.

45 CHCD 1898, 3352–4; Fahey, *Inland Empire*, 188; VHLB 55, Van Horne to J. Israel Tarte, 16 April 1898.

46 SLB 59, Shaughnessy to Messrs Mann, Foley & Larsen, 8 June 1898; SLB 60, Shaughnessy to W.F. Tye, 23 June 1898; Turnbull, *Topping's Trail*, 40; NAC, Engineering Institute of Canada Papers, vol. 176, "William Francis Tye."

47 SLB 59, Shaughnessy to Messrs Mann, Foley & Larsen, 8 June 1898; SLB 61, Shaughnessy to W.F. Tye, 9 August 1898; SLB 63, Shaughnessy to J.C. McLagan, 17 November 1898.

48 Turnbull, *Topping's Trail*, 40–2; SLB 60, Shaughnessy to John Haggart, 11 July 1898, "Personal," to W.F. Tye, 11 July 1898; SLB 63, Shaughnessy to W.F. Tye, 16 November 1898, "Personal,"; SLB 64, Shaughnessy to W.F. Tye, 16 December 1898, "Private"; CPR, *Annual Report*, 1898.

49 Turnbull, *Topping's Trail*, 41–2.

50 Meyer, "Railways in the Kootenays," 58; CPR, *Annual Report*, 1903, mileage chart.

51 This is fully documented in the J.J. Hill Papers. See: GC, H.W. Cannon to Hill, 16 June, 5 July 1898, undated, unsigned statement with dates 15 June, 1 July and 9 November 1898; Hill Letterbooks,

vol. P 16, Hill to John S. Kennedy, 17 July 1898, Hill to H.W. Cannon, 17 July, 26 July 1898, Hill to A.R. Ledoux, 28 July 1898, Hill to J. Pierpont Morgan, 2 August 1898, "Personal," Hill to C.S. Mellen, 13 August 1898. Corbin received a special payment of $75,000 (paid by the GN) for facilitating the takeover.

52 *Statutes of Canada*, 1898, c. 80; CHCD, 1898, 3868; VHLB 55, Van Horne to David Mills, 9 May 1898.

53 CSD, 1898, 635–6, 761–7, 770–2, 786. The eleven senators who voted for the motion were: W.J. Almon, J.-F. Armand, Boulton, William J. Macdonald, A.A. Macdonald, Thomas McKay, Samuel Prowse, Alexander Vidal (all Conservatives), John Lovitt, Lawrence Power and Templeman (all Liberals). For biographical material on senators MacInnes, Boulton, Templeman, and Power, see Johnson, ed., *Canadian Directory of Parliament*, 61, 412–13, 472, 564.

CHAPTER FOUR

1 VHLB 54, Van Horne to Harry Moody, 9 November 1897. Emphasis in the original.

2 The best discussion of the CPR in Manitoba in this period is T.D. Regehr, *The Canadian Northern Railway* (Toronto: Macmillan of Canada, 1976), chap. 1.

3 D.J. Hall, *Clifford Sifton*, vol. 1, *The Young Napoleon 1861–1900* (Vancouver: University of British Columbia Press, 1981), 58–9; Joseph A. Hilts, "The Political Career of Thomas Greenway" (PH D. thesis, University of Manitoba, 1974), chap. 3; T.D. Regehr, "The National Policy and Manitoba Railway Legislation 1879–1888" (Master's thesis, Carleton University, 1963), chap. 6; SLB 27, Shaughnessy to Acton Burrows, 30 May 1891, "Private & Confidential," to J.A.M. Aikins, 15 June 1891; GAI, Canadian Railroad Historical Association Archives, Sir William Van Horne Private Correspondence, file 82.5.114, Lord Mount Stephen to Van Horne, 25 June 1892, "Private."

4 Regehr, *Canadian Northern*, chap. 1 to 3; John A. Eagle, "Sir Robert Borden and the Railway Problem in Canada Politics 1911–1920" (PH D. thesis, University of Toronto, 1972), 5–7.

5 Regehr, *Canadian Northern*, 48–9, 60, 74–6; Hall, *Sifton*, vol. 1, 245–6; *Statutes of Canada*, 1899, c. 57. The two companies were the Lake Manitoba Railway and Canal Company and the Winnipeg Great Northern Railway Company.

6 Walter Vaughan, *The Life and Work of Sir William Van Horne* (New York: The Century Company, 1920), 260.

7 VHLB 56, Van Horne to Sir Charles Tupper, "on train," 18 April
   1899, "Private"; VHLB 55, Van Horne to J.A. McMahon, 23 July 1898;
   NAC, Katherine Hughes Papers, vol. 2, "MS. draft biography of
   Van Horne," 258. Hughes here quotes from a long letter from Van
   Horne to Lord Strathcona, 7 February 1899, a letter which is not
   in the Van Horne Letterbooks.

8 Morgan 1912, 123, 789, 864; *CAR*, 1902, 376. Ogden had joined the
   CPR in 1881, Bosworth in 1882.

9 Montreal *Star*, 13 June 1899; CPR, *Annual Report*, 1899.

10 Montreal *Star*, 17 June 1899.

11 SLB 67, Shaughnessy to A. McD. Young, 20 June 1899, "Personal";
   CPR Archives, file 56150, F.N. Finney to Shaughnessy, 15 June 1899.

12 SLB 73, Shaughnessy to W.R. Baker, 26 December 1900.

13 Morgan 1912, 1164; W. Kaye Lamb, *History of the Canadian Pacific
   Railway* (New York: Macmillan, 1977), 101; CPR, *Annual Report*, 1885;
   R.G. MacBeth, "Sir William Whyte: a Builder of the West," *Canadian
   Magazine*, July 1914, 265–9; Sir Augustus Nanton Correspondence
   (in possession of Mr Paul Nanton), Nanton to E.B. Osler, 13 April
   1901. I am indebted to Mr Nanton for permission to cite several
   letters from his collection.

14 SLB 67, Shaughnessy to W. Whyte, 8 July 1899, "Confidential."

15 SLB 67, Shaughnessy to W. Whyte, 13 June 1899, "Personal."

16 SLB 67, Shaughnessy to William Whyte, 27 July 1899, "Personal."
   Later Shaughnessy informed Baker, "I would not tell [premier Hugh
   John] Macdonald, but we did not apply for the Wascada branch
   subsidy." SLB 71, Shaughnessy to W.R. Baker, 12 July 1900, "Personal." Shaughnessy seems to have been suggesting that the offer
   came initially from Greenway. In the Winnipeg South by-election in
   January 1900 the Martin faction revealed that Greenway and J.D.
   Cameron had verbally promised the CPR a subsidy for the Wascada
   extension. David J. Hall, "The Political Career of Clifford Sifton
   1896–1905," (PH D. thesis, University of Toronto, 1973), 505–6.

17 SLB68, Shaughnessy to W. Whyte, 12 August 1899, "Personal"; Hall,
   Sifton, vol. 1, 279–80; Hilts, "Greenway," 331. Hilts uses evidence
   from the Van Horne Letterbooks, but cites none from the Shaughnessy Letterbooks.

18 Henry Guest, "The Old Man's Son: Sir Hugh John Macdonald,"
   Transactions of the Historical and Scientific Society of Manitoba, series 3,
   no. 299, 1972–3; *CAR*, 1901, 184–5; Henry James Guest, "Reluctant
   Politician: A Biography of Sir Hugh John Macdonald," (Master's
   thesis, University of Manitoba, 1973), 93, 99, 236; SLI, file 21970,
   Hugh John Macdonald to Shaughnessy, 18 May 1892, "Private";

SLB 71, Shaughnessy to C.S. Mellen, 21 May 1900, "Confidential." In 1893 the CPR was Macdonald's principal client.

19 NAC, Privy Council Records, vol. 545, P.C. 695, 29 March 1900; CPR, *Annual Report*, 1899, 1900–1.

20 J.W. McCracken, "Yorkton During the Territorial Period, 1882–1905" (Master's thesis, University of Saskatchewan, 1972), 72–3; CPR, *Annual Report*, 1899, 1900–1; SLB 71, Shaughnessy to W.R. Baker, 9 May 1900; Morgan 1912, 54; Dorman, 346. This was a 999-year lease.

21 SLB 69, Shaughnessy to C.S. Mellen, 8 January 1900; SLB 70, Shaughnessy to Mellen, 5 February 1900, "Confidential," to E. Pennington, 17 February 1900, "Private." Shaughnessy was referring to the territories served by the Soo line and the South Shore line, especially North Dakota.

22 SLB 70, Shaughnessy to William Whyte, 10 April 1900, "Personal"; SLB 71, Shaughnessy to J. Stewart Tupper, 25 June 1900, "Private."

23 SLB 71, Shaughnessy to W.R. Baker, "At Sault Ste. Marie," 3 June 1900, "Confidential."

24 SLB 71, Shaughnessy to E.B. Osler, 30 May 1900, "Personal."

25 Regehr, *Canadian Northern*, 89.

26 SLB 72, Shaughnessy to C.S. Mellen, 15 December 1900; SLB 73, Shaughnessy to J.J. Hill, 19 January 1901.

27 NAC, Shaughnessy Papers, vol. 2, Shaughnessy to R.P. Roblin, Winnipeg, 22 January 1901 (copy), 8 February 1901 (copy).

28 Regehr, *Canadian Northern*, 88–92, 104–5.

29 SLB 73, Shaughnessy to W.D. Matthews, 22 February 1901, 13 February 1901, "Confidential," to E.B. Osler, 20 February 1901, "Private," to W.D. Matthews, 20 February 1901, "Private."

30 D.J. Hall, *Clifford Sifton*, vol. 2, *A Lonely Eminence 1901–1929* (Vancouver: University of British Columbia Press, 1985), 19.

31 SLB 73, Shaughnessy to W.D. Matthews, 23 February 1901, "Private," to W.H. Montague, 13 February 1901, "Confidential," to R.L. Richardson, 22 February 1901; Hall, *Sifton*, vol. 2, 19, 372, note 16.

32 Ruben Bellan, *Winnipeg First Century* (Winnipeg: Queenston House, 1978), 111; SLB 74, unsigned, undated memorandum [June 1901], 358–62, "Memorandum for Judge Clark," 1 April 1901; Shaughnessy to E.B. Osler, 5 June 1901, "Personal," with unsigned, undated memorandum; *CAR*, 1903, 422.

33 SLB 73, Shaughnessy to F.L. Govett, 25 February 1901.

34 SLB 74, Statement from the "Office of the President," 1 May 1901.

35 SLB 74, Shaughnessy to Thomas C. Irving, 30 May 1901, to Clifford Sifton, 22 April 1901, to Lord Strathcona, 3 June 1901; SLB 75,

James R. Nelson to T.A. Russell, 1 November 1901, "Special Order," signed by Shaughnessy, 16 September 1901; *CAR*, 1901, 234–72, 376; Morgan 1912, 652.

36 Louis Aubrey Wood, *A History of Farmer's Movements in Canada* (Toronto: University of Toronto Press, 1975), 171–2. This is a reprint of the original 1924 edition.

37 SLB 73, Shaughnessy to H. Moody, 20 March 1901, "Personal"; SLB 75, Shaughnessy to T. Lowry, 24 August 1901, "Personal"; SLB 74, Shaughnessy to L. Zuckermandel, 25 June 1901, to H.P. Timmerman, 22 October 1901; SLB 76, Shaughnessy to G.B. Williamson, 9 November 1901; *CAR*, 1901, 242, 259; J.H. Tuck, "Canadian Railways and the International Brotherhoods: Labour Organization in the Railway Running Trades in Canada 1864–1914" (PH D. thesis, University of Western Ontario, 1975), 191–6.

38 D.J. Hall, "The Manitoba Grain Act: an 'Agrarian Magna Charta'?", *Prairie Forum* 4, no. 1 (1979): 116; SLB 76, Shaughnessy to H.H. Campkin, 2 January 1902. I am indebted to Professor Hall for his comments on Shaughnessy's views on farmers' grain marketing practices.

39 SLB 76, Shaughnessy to W. Whyte, 20 January 1902, "Confidential."

40 *CAR*, 1901, 234–272; SLI, file 64924, Governor-General's Military Secretary to T.G. Shaughnessy, 19 September 1901 (telegram), John Cassils to Shaughnessy, 19 September 1901, S.M. Green to Shaughnessy, 23 September 1901, Israel Tarte to Shaughnessy, 21 September 1901, G.B. Hopkins to Shaughnessy, 20 September 1901 (telegram). For an excellent analysis of the 1901 Royal Tour, see Robert M. Stamp, "Steel of Empire: Royal Tours and the CPR," in Hugh A. Dempsey, ed., *The CPR West* (Vancouver: Douglas & McIntyre, 1984), 277–80.

41 LP, vol. 213, T.G. Shaughnessy to Laurier, 20 November 1901, "Private and Confidential"; vol. 216, T.G. Shaughnessy to Laurier, 17 December 1901, "Private"; vol 215, Laurier to T.G. Shaughnessy, 7 December 1901, "Private and Confidential" (copy); Hall, "Manitoba Grain Act," 116; *CAR*, 1902, 215–16; CPR, *Annual Report*, 1902; SLB 76, Shaughnessy to L. Zuckermandel (in Berlin), 11 February 1902, "Personal."

42 H.S. Patton, *Grain Growers' Cooperation in Western Canada* (Cambridge: Harvard University Press, 1928), 30–5; Wood, *Farmers' Movements in Canada*, 173–7; Hall, "Manitoba Grain Act," 116. The resolution is quoted in Patton, 34.

43 Patton, *Grain Growers'*, 35–6; Wood, *Farmers' Movements*, 180; SLB 79, Shaughnessy to Clifford Sifton, 10 November 1901.

44 *Manitoba Free Press*, 18, 20 December 1902. The total prairie grain crop in 1901 was 108,500,000 bushels, and in 1902, 117,309,000 bushels. *CAR*, 1903, 444.

45 SLB 78, "Memorandum for Mr. McNicoll," "On Line," 3 June 1902.

46 SLB 78, "Memorandum for McNicoll," "On Line, Western Division," 7 June 1902, "Personal," "Memorandum for Mr. McNicoll," "On Line, Vancouver to Seattle," 18 June 1902, "Memorandum for McNicoll," "On Line," 3 June 1902; SLB 81, Shaughnessy to E.D. Smith, 24 June 1903; *CAR*, 1903, 421.

47 SLB 81, Shaughnessy to J.W. Leonard, 2 May 1903, to D. McNicoll, 14, 17 May, 1903; SLB 83, Shaughnessy to W.D. Perley, 23 November 1903; *CAR*, 1903, 422. In October 1905 Leonard was appointed assistant general manager of lines east of Ft William, with an office at Montreal: *CAR*, 1905, 551.

48 SLB 83, Shaughnessy to George R. Harris, 28 October 1903; SLB 82, Shaughnessy to John M. Egan, 27 July 1903; *CAR*, 1903, 427; CHCD, 1903, 4363, 5824; *Statutes of Canada*, 1903, c. 7 (Canadian Northern Railway Bond Guarantee), c. 58 (Railway Act). The Board of Railway Commissioners was established by sections 8 to 50 of the Railway Act; Bellan, *Winnipeg First Century*, 83, footnote 5.

49 G.R. Stevens, *Canadian National Railways*, 2 vols. (Toronto: Clarke Irwin, 1962), 2: 51.

50 SLB 80, Shaughnessy to Ernest Chaplin, 19 February 1903; Sir Augustus Nanton correspondence, Nanton to E.B. Osler, 9 April 1901; Regehr, *Canadian Northern*, 165.

51 SLB 82, Shaughnessy to H. Robertson, 8 July 1903, to I.G. Ogden, 28 July 1903; R.A. Christenson, "The Calgary and Edmonton Railway and the Edmonton *Bulletin*" (Master's thesis, University of Alberta, 1967), 221–5, 244; Privy Council Records, vol. 614, P.C. 2162, 8 January 1904; Regehr, *Canadian Northern*, 165–7. The CPR purchased all the company's stock for $500,000 and between 1905 and 1912 it purchased all its first mortgage bonds.

52 SLI, file 75670, W. Whyte to Shaughnessy, 16 July 1904; file 79485, W. Whyte to Shaughnessy, 11 June 1906 (cipher telegram).

53 Regehr, *Canadian Northern*, 179–83; SLB 84, Shaughnessy to W. Whyte, 31 July 1904; SLB 89, Shaughnessy to E.B. Osler, 7 June 1906.

CHAPTER FIVE

1 *CAR*, 1902, 220; G.R. Stevens, *Canadian National Railways*, 2 vols. (Toronto: Clarke Irwin, 1962) 2: 231–2. In 1900–1 Hays served 11

months as president of the Union Pacific Railroad. He resumed
his duties as Grand Trunk general manager on 8 January 1902.

2 Preceding material taken from John A. Eagle, "Sir Robert Borden
and the Railway Problem in Canadian Politics, 1911–1920" (PH D.
thesis, University of Toronto, 1972), 23–5. See also A.W. Currie, *The
Grand Trunk Railway of Canada* (Toronto: University of Toronto
Press, 1957), 368–71, 392, 433, 453, and Stevens, *Canadian National*,
1: 381–5 and 2: 231–2.

3 Eagle, "Railway Problem," 25–6.

4 Provincial Archives of Ontario, Sir James Whitney Papers, J.L.
Englehart to J.L. Black, 9 February 1911, "Private" (copy); Sifton
Papers, vol. 199, Sifton to J.W. Dafoe, 9 January 1912 (copy); D.J.
Hall, *Clifford Sifton*, vol. 2, *A Lonely Eminence 1901–1929* (Vancouver:
University of British Columbia Press, 1985), 272.

5 Eagle, "Railway Problem," 27.

6 NAC, Charles M. Hays Letterbooks, Hays to Sir Charles Rivers Wilson,
24 October 1902; the formal petition is in Laurier Papers, vol. 243,
Petition of George A. Cox, Charles M. Hays and William Wainwright
to Laurier, 3 November 1902, "Confidential"; *CAR*, 1902, 220–1.

7 NAC, Earl of Minto Papers, vol. 4, "Memorandum of a Conversation
with Mr. Tarte," 17 September 1902, "Secret."

8 Hays Letterbooks, Hays to Sir Charles Rivers Wilson, 9 December
1902.

9 Ibid.

10 Hall, *Sifton*, vol. 2, 102; Hays Letterbooks, Hays to Sir Charles Rivers
Wilson, 14 February, 27 March 1903; T.D. Regehr, *The Canadian
Northern Railway* (Toronto: Macmillan of Canada, 1976), 123–5.

11 Hays Letterbooks, Hays to Sir Charles Rivers Wilson, 9 December
1902; R.M. Coutts, "The Railway Policy of Sir Wilfrid Laurier: The
Grand Trunk Pacific-National Transcontinental" (Master's thesis,
University of Toronto, 1968), 84; LP, vol. 272, A.G. Blair to Laurier,
10, 13 July 1903; CHCD, 1903, 6736–48.

12 Coutts, "Railway Policy of ... Laurier," 70–1.

13 Hays Letterbooks, Hays to Sir Charles Rivers Wilson, 16 March 1903;
CAR, 1903, 49–50.

14 Hays Letterbooks, "Proceedings of the Railways and Canals Standing
Committee," 7 May 1903, 117–48; Paul Stevens, "Laurier and the
Liberal Party in Ontario 1887–1911" (PH D. thesis, University of To-
ronto, 1966), 245; Public Archives of Nova Scotia, W.S. Fielding
Papers, vol. 444, Fielding to Sir W. Laurier, 29 July 1903,
"Confidential."

15 The formal title of the bill was The Grand Trunk Pacific Subsidy

Bill, but the statute is usually referred to as the National Transcontinental Railway Act. See *Statutes of Canada*, 1903, 3 Edward VII, c. 71. The contract is the "Schedule" attached to the act.

16 *CAR*, 1903, 36–45; CHCD, 1903, 12777.

17 *Statutes of Canada*, 1904, 4 Edward VII, c. 24, "Schedule."

18 Stevens, *Canadian National*, vol. 2, 151–2; *CAR*, 1904, 68–82; CHCD, 1904, 710–25 (Laurier), 3717 (third reading).

19 Norman Penlington, *The Alaska Boundary Dispute: A Critical Reappraisal* (Toronto: McGraw-Hill Ryerson, 1972), 103–4.

20 For purposes of clarity, the term "National Transcontinental Railway" (NTR) has been used to designate the line from Winnipeg to Moncton. Technically, the whole line from Moncton to Prince Rupert was the NTR, the line from Winnipeg to Moncton was its Eastern Division and the GTPR line from Winnipeg to Prince Rupert was its Western Division.

21 *CAR*, 1902, 221; Hays Letterbooks, Sir Charles Rivers to Wilson Hays, 26 November 1902.

22 SLB 79, Shaughnessy to E. Pennington, 25 November 1902, to W.D. Matthews, 25 November 1902, "Personal," to Harry Moody, 1 December 1902, "Private."

23 *CAR*, 1903, 48; Hays Letterbooks, Hays to Sir Charles Rivers Wilson, 26 January 1903.

24 SLB 81, Shaughnessy to Sir Richard Cartwright, 8 May 1903, "Private."

25 LP, vol. 266, T.G. Shaughnessy to Laurier, "At Broadview, Assa.," 24 May 1903, Laurier to Shaughnessy, 2 June 1903 (copy).

26 CHCD, 1903, 8329; CSD, 1903, 951.

27 SLB 82, Shaughnessy to E.B. Osler, 22 July 1903.

28 Eagle, "Railway Problem," 65–6. The four were John F. Stairs, leader of the Nova Scotia Conservative Party, Joseph Flavelle, a prominent Toronto businessman, Hugh Graham, publisher of the Montreal *Star*, and Sanford Evans, editor-in-chief of the Winnipeg *Telegram*. For Shaughnessy's proposals, see NAC, Sir Robert Laird Borden Papers, vol. 404, "Memorandum," unsigned and undated with notation in Borden's handwriting, "From Shaughnessy 1903," 5744.

29 CHCD, 1903, 8961–9006.

30 Ibid., 1903, 9768–9.

31 Hays Letterbooks, Hays to Sir Charles Rivers Wilson, 4 September 1903; CHCD, 1903, 9281–9305, 10186–90, 10497–502, 10506.

32 Hays Letterbooks, Hays to Sir Charles Rivers Wilson, 31 July, 4 September 1903; SLB 82, Shaughnessy to E.B. Osler, 22 July 1903; CSD, 1903, 1384, 1594–5, 1688.

33   SLB 83, Shaughnessy to E.B. Osler, 22 December 1903, "Confiden-
      tial"; SLB 84, Shaughnessy to E.F. Clarke, 28 April 1904; CHCD, 1904,
      2008–55; *CAR*, 1904, 90.
34   *CAR*, 1904, 201.
35   SLB 85, Shaughnessy to H.P. Timmerman, 31 October 1904, "Pri-
      vate." See also Shaughnessy to J.C. McCorkill, 7 November 1904.
36   LP, vol. 357, T.G. Shaughnessy to Laurier, 25 February 1905, "Pri-
      vate," Laurier to Shaughnessy, 27 February 1905 (copy); Regehr,
      Canadian Northern, 148–9.
37   SLB 85, Shaughnessy to W.H. Montague, 10 November 1904, "Pri-
      vate"; J.M. Beck, *Pendulum of Power* (Scarborough, Ontario: Prentice-
      Hall of Canada, 1968), 104, 106.
38   G.R. Stevens, *Canadian National*, vol. 2, 224.
39   *Manitoba Free Press*, 12 September 1905; *CAR*, 1905, 555; Hays
      Letterbooks, Hays to Sir Charles Rivers Wilson, 22 September 1905.
40   *CAR*, 1905, 553.
41   Ibid., 1905, 555.
42   LP, vol. 377, T.G. Shaughnessy to Laurier, 9 August 1905, Laurier to
      Shaughnessy, 21 August 1905; SLB 87, Shaughnessy to C. Hyman
      (Public Works), R.W. Scott (Secretary of State), Charles Fitzpatrick
      (Justice), all dated 12 August 1905 and marked "Private," Shaugh-
      nessy to R. Cartwright (Trade and Commerce), 16 August 1905.
43   SLB 87, Shaughnessy to William Whyte, no date (*circa* September
      1905); *CAR*, 1905, 555.
44   SLB 88, Shaughnessy to F.T. Griffin, 19 November 1905; Shaughnessy
      to W. Whyte, 9 November 1905.
45   Lewis H. Thomas, "Saskatoon, 1883–1920: The Formative Years," in
      Alan F.J. Artibise, ed., *Town and City* (Regina: Canadian Plains
      Research Center, 1981), 254.
46   John Gilpin, "Failed Metropolis: The City of Strathcona, 1891–
      1912," in Artibuse, ed., *Town and City*, 278–9.
47   Hays Letterbooks, Hays to Sir Charles Rivers Wilson, 18 January
      1906; *Statutes of Canada*, 3 Edward VII, c. 71.
48   Gilpin, "Strathcona," 280–1; Stevens, *Canadian National*, vol. 2, 199–
      200.
49   CHCD, 3 April 1906, 999; Hays Letterbooks, Hays to Sir Charles
      Rivers Wilson, 11 June 1906.
50   CHCD, 1906, 5460, 5469–73 (Pringle), 5480–1 (Emmerson), 5485–6
      (Borden), 5955–7 (Henderson), 6609–14 (Lancaster motion), 6706;
      CSD, 1906, 1026–7.
51   CPR, *Annual Report*, 1905.
52   Ibid., 1906; *CAR*, 128, 132.

53 *CAR*, 1907, 131; CPR, *Annual Report*, 1907; Don Kerr and Stan Hanson, *Saskatoon: The First Half-Century* (Edmonton: NeWest Press, 1982), 72–4.

54 *CAR*, 1908, 567–8; CPR, *Annual Report*, 1908; *Manitoba Free Press*, 27 January 1908.

55 SLB 92, Shaughnessy to W. Whyte, 13 June 1908, "Personal."

56 SLB 92, Shaughnessy to G.P. Graham, 1 June 1908; NAC, George P. Graham Papers, vol. 59, Shaughnessy to Graham, 22 June 1908.

57 SLB 94, Shaughnessy to W. Whyte, 21 November 1908, "Personal."

58 CPR., *Annual Report*, 1904, 1905; *CAR*, 1904, 489, 1905, 547; LP, vol. 322, T.G. Shaughnessy to Laurier, 7 June 1904, "Confidential"; vol. 323, Laurier to Shaughnessy, 14 June 1904 (copy), Shaughnessy to Laurier, 14 June 1904.

59 *CAR*, 1909, 596; SLB 103, Shaughnessy to Grant Hall, "Personal," 3 March 1913; *Canadian Railway and Marine World*, February 1912, 73, February 1913, 76; December 1914, 543; W. Kaye Lamb, *History of the Canadian Pacific Railway* (New York: Macmillan, 1977), 264–5. Lamb gives a figure of 850 miles for total double-track. The author has used the figures from *CRMW*.

60 *CAR*, 1908, 573, 1909, 598, 1911, 637–8; Morgan 1912, 179–80; *CRMW*, March 1907, 185; SLB 84, Shaughnessy to G.J. Bury, 4 July 1904; *Who's Who in Canada* (1922), 831; SLB 100, N.J. Power to George Bury, 5 October 1911, Shaughnessy to A.M. Nanton, 12 October 1911, "Personal"; T. Murray Hunter, "Sir George Bury and the Russian Revolution," Canadian Historical Association, *Annual Report*, 1965, 60–1.

61 *CRMW*, February 1913, 76; *CAR*, 1912, 673.

62 *CAR*, 1910, 597–9; SLB 97, Shaughnessy to A. Price, undated [1910], to W. Whyte, 30 May 1910.

63 *Manitoba Free Press*, 23 January 1911; CPR, *Annual Report*, 1911.

64 SLB 100, Shaughnessy to R.L. Borden, 20 December 1911, and to George E. Foster, 4 January 1912.

65 *CAR*, 1912, 636, and 1913, 690; SLB 102, Shaughnessy to George E. Foster, 11 December 1912.

66 *CRMW*, October 1913, 469; SLB 92, Shaughnessy to George Bury, 24 March 1908, "Private."

67 SLB 100, Shaughnessy to Walter Scott, 24 October 1911 and to George Bury, 24 October 1911, "Personal."

68 *CRMW*, February 1912, 73; CPR, *Annual Report*, 1912.

69 *CRMW*, February 1913, 76; CPR, *Annual Report*, 1913; SLB 105, Shaughnessy to George Bury, 28 July 1913. The author calculates that about 224 miles were constructed in Alberta.

70 *CRMW*, February 1914, 17.

71 CPR, *Annual Report*, 1896, 1914, mileage charts. These calculations have been made by the author. The figure includes the AR&C CO's line from Dunmore to Lethbridge which was leased by the CPR until it was purchased in 1897. Some of the Saskatchewan division mileage in 1914 was located in eastern Alberta, but it is not possible to calculate the amount from the CPR mileage chart.

72 CPR, *Annual Report*, 1902; Paul André Linteau, "Le développement du port de Montréal au début du 20e siècle," Canadian Historical Association, *Historical Papers*, 1972, 181–205.

CHAPTER SIX

1 VHLB 53, W.C. Van Horne to Richard Marpole, 14 June 1897; Morgan 1912, 731; SLB 44, Shaughnessy to W. Whyte, 25 November 1895; SLB 48, J. Osborne to R. Marpole, 28 September 1896; SLB 97, Shaughnessy to W. Whyte, 11 May 1910, "Personal"; Vancouver *World*, 6 May, 19 June 1897. Marpole was succeeded by F.F. Busteed who served in the position until 1911 when F.W. Peters was appointed general superintendent. Morgan 1912, 180; CPR, *Annual Reports*, 1907, 1911.

2 James J. Hill Reference Library, James J. Hill Papers, Hill Letterbook P-16, Hill to John S. Kennedy, 30 July 1898.

3 Ibid., Hill Letterbook P-16, Hill to D.S. Lamont, 17 July 1898, to Lord Mount Stephen, 2 August 1898, to Lord Strathcona, 19 August 1898, to W.C. Van Horne, 27 November 1898.

4 Ibid., Hill Letterbook P-17, Hill to Gaspard Farrer, 2 October, 16 October 1899.

5 GC, T.G. Shaughnessy to Hill, 13 June 1899 (telegram), 16 June 1899, "Personal."

6 Hill Papers, Hill Letterbook P-17, Hill to T.G. Shaughnessy, 24 June 1899, "Personal"; GC, Hill to T.G. Shaughnessy, 2 October 1899 (copy); SLB 69, Shaughnessy to J.J. Hill, 28 September 1899.

7 SLB 69, Shaughnessy to J.J. Hill, 9 November 1899, "Private," 29 December 1899; SLB 70, Shaughnessy to James N. Hill, 4 February 1900, 28 March, 9 April 1900, to J.J. Hill, 21 February 1900, to W.F. Tye, 30 April 1900; SLB 71, Shaughnessy to James N. Hill, 28 May, 13 June 1900, to W.F. Tye, 6 August 1900; CPR Archives, file 55203, James N. Hill to Shaughnessy, 30 March 1900.

8 GC, Hill to T.G. Shaughnessy, 10 January 1901, "Confidential" (copy); SLB 72, Shaughnessy to Gaspard Farrer, 10 December 1900, "Private"; SLB 73, Shaughnessy to J.J. Hill, 9 January 1901.

9 Patricia E. Roy, "Railways, Politicians, and the Development of Vancouver as a Metropolitan Centre, 1886–1929" (Master's thesis, University of Toronto, 1963), 57.
10 Ibid., 47–8; Dorman, 618.
11 Roy, "Development of Vancouver," 49–50; T.D. Regehr, *The Canadian Northern Railway* (Toronto: Macmillan of Canada, 1976), 63–4.
12 Margaret Ormsby, *British Columbia: A History* (Toronto: Macmillan of Canada, 1964), 320–4; Roy, "Development of Vancouver," 54–7.
13 Regehr, *Canadian Northern*, 64–5; CPR, *Annual Report*, 1897, 1898; Roy, "Development of Vancouver," 46, 58; Dorman, 618; GC, D.D. Mann to Hill, 11 March 1902, "Private and Confidential"; SLB 73, Shaughnessy to J. Israel Tarte, 3 April 1901, "Confidential."
14 SLB 74, Shaughnessy to J.J. Hill, 10 July 1901; Barrie Sanford, *McCulloch's Wonder* (West Vancouver: Whitecap Books, 1977), 52–3.
15 Hill Papers, Hill Letterbook P-17, Hill to T.G. Shaughnessy, 3 August 1901, "Personal."
16 SLB 75, Shaughnessy to F. Carter-Cotton, 10 September 1901, "Confidential"; Morgan 1912, 206–7.
17 Roy, "Development of Vancouver," 59–60.
18 SLB 73, Shaughnessy to W.F. Tye, 22 February, 8 March 1901; *CAR*, 1901, 109.
19 Roy, "Development of Vancouver," 52–3; Sanford, *McCulloch's Wonder*, 60–2; Dorman, 296. The other four promoters of the KRVR were: Holland's brother Frederick, the Ontario manager of the Dominion Permanent Loan Company; James Stratton, the provincial treasurer of Ontario; Thomas Coffee, manager of the Toronto-based Trusts and Guarantee Company; and George H. Cowan, a Vancouver lawyer.
20 Sanford, *McCulloch's Wonder*, 63–6.
21 SLB 77, Shaughnessy to James N. Hill, 1 March 1902, "Personal"; Sanford, *McCulloch's Wonder*, 62.
22 Ibid., 66–8.
23 NAC, Crow's Nest Coal and Railway Company Papers; *CAR*, 1901, 381; Morgan 1912, 21–2 (Ames), 270 (Cox), 573–4 (Jaffray), 894 (Pellatt), 962–3 (Rogers), 1182 (Wood); Michael Bliss, *A Canadian Millionaire: The Life and Business Times of Sir Joseph Flavelle, Bart., 1858–1939* (Toronto: Macmillan of Canada, 1978).
24 GAI, CPR Papers, vol. 218, file 2119, Agreement (copy) between The British Columbia Southern Railway Company, the Canadian Pacific Railway Company, and the Kootenay Coal Company, 30 July 1897; LP, vol. 184, T.G. Shaughnessy to Laurier, 14 January 1901, "Private" with attached memorandum; H. Leslie Brown, "The Pass: Biography of a District, Renewed, and a Town Long Gone" (unpublished manuscript, 1977), 31–2, 37–41.

25 G.W. Taylor, *Mining: The History of Mining in British Columbia* (Saanichton, B.C.: Hancock House, 1978), 114.

26 *CAR*, 1901, 380–4; SLB 73, Shaughnessy to C.A. Dansereau, 14 February 1901, to F.W. Lewis, 13 February 1901; LP, vol. 184, T.G. Shaughnessy to Laurier, 14 January 1901, "Private," with attached memorandum.

27 *CAR*, 1901, 381; LP, vol. 184, T.G. Shaughnessy to Laurier, 14 January 1901, "Private," with attached memorandum; SLB 73, Shaughnessy to James McMullen, 15 January 1901, "Personal," to John Crerar, 11 February 1901, "Confidential."

28 SLB 73, Shaughnessy to J.J. Hill, 6 February 1901, "Personal," to G.M. Clark, 19 March 1901, to Senator George A. Cox, 22 March 1901.

29 LP, vol. 184, T.G. Shaughnessy to Laurier, 14 January 1901, "Private"; vol. 192, Elias Rogers to Laurier, 3 April 1901, "Private and Confidential"; vol. 193, Shaughnessy to Laurier, 6 April 1901, "Personal"; SLB 73, Shaughnessy to Elias Rogers, 4 March 1901.

30 *CAR*, 1901, 384; LP, vol. 193, T.G. Shaughnessy to Laurier, 8 April 1901 (telegram).

31 SLB 74, Shaughnessy to A.C. Flummerfelt, 15 April 1901; SLB 77, Shaughnessy to Major J.M. Walsh, 24 February 1902.

32 SLB 71, James R. Nelson to James A. Twohey, 11 February 1901, "Personal"; *CAR*, 1902, 309. In 1901 the company delivered to Canadian smelters 71,684 tons of coal and 137,782 tons of coke. The AR&I CO's line to Great Falls was the Great Falls and Montana Railroad, built in 1890.

33 Dorman, 178; W. Kaye Lamb, *History of the Canadian Pacific Railway* (New York: Macmillan, 1977), 236; Hill Papers, Hill Letterbook P-18, Hill to Robert Jaffray, 19 August 1901, to Elias Rogers, 3 October 1902; W.J. Wilgus, *The Railway Interrelations of the United States and Canada* (New Haven: Yale University Press, 1937), 131; Taylor, *Mining in British Columbia*, 113.

34 *CAR*, 1904, 508; Brown, "The Pass," 35, 39; SLB 84, Shaughnessy to W. Whyte, 1 June 1904, 20 June 1904, "Private."

35 Brown, "The Pass," 40–1, 254; SLB 78, Shaughnessy to W. Whyte, 7 July 1902. The Order-in-Council was P.C. 664.

36 Hill Papers, Hill Letterbook P-18, Hill to Elias Rogers, 3 October 1902, to Senator George A. Cox, 10 October 1902; Hill Letterbook P-19, Hill to E.T. Nichols, 7 May 1906, to George A. Cox, 14 January, 16 March 1907, to Jay P. Graves, 21 May 1907; GC, E.T. Nichols to Hill, 2, 3 May, 6 July 1906; *CAR*, 1903, 462, 1907, 55.

37 Taylor, *Mining in British Columbia*, 161–5. For biographical data on Miner see Morgan 1912, 810.

38 Taylor, *Mining in British Columbia*, 163–4; Hal Riegger, *The Kettle*

Valley and its Railways (Edmonds, Washington: Pacific Fast Mail Publications, 1981), 100; Harold A. Innis, *Settlement and the Mining Frontier*, (Toronto: Macmillan of Canada, 1936), vol. 9, part 2, *Canadian Frontiers of Settlement Series*, 9 vols., eds. W.A. Mackintosh and W.G.L. Joerg, 283–4.

39 Roy, "Development of Vancouver," 111; *CAR*, 1904, 508; Riegger, *Kettle Valley*, 101; Hill Letterbrook P-18, Hill to Jay P. Graves, 22 January 1904, to George C. Clark, 21 February 1905, P-19, Hill to Jay P. Graves, 21 May 1907; F.W. Howay, W.N. Sage and H.F. Angus, *British Columbia and the United States* (New York: Russell & Russell, 1970), 257–8; Sanford, *McCulloch's Wonder*, 105–6.

40 SLB 82, Shaughnessy to D. McNicoll, "At St. Andrews," 13 July 1903.

41 SLB 81, Shaughnessy to P.H. Ashworth, 18 April 1903.

42 SLB 85, Shaughnessy to F.W. Peters, 20 October 1904, "Private."

43 SLB 81, Shaughnessy to Sir Charles Hibbert Tupper, 10 June 1903, "Personal."

44 SLB 77, Shaughnessy to W.D. Matthews, 24 April 1902; SLB 78, Shaughnessy to W.C. Nichol, 8 July 1902, "Private"; Robert D. Turner, *West of the Great Divide* (Victoria: Sono Nis Press, 1967), 46.

45 SLB 77, Shaughnessy to Cecil Ward, 9 May 1902; SLB 78, Shaughnessy to Richard Marpole, 14 July 1902, "Private"; SLB 85, Shaughnessy to B.W. Geer, "On Okanagan Lake," 22 September 1904; SLB 94, Shaughnessy to Richard McBride, 1 January 1908 [1909]; SLB 97, Shaughnessy to Elliot S. Rowe, 25 April 1910; BC Premiers' Papers, vol. 95, Richard McBride to Sir Thomas Shaughnessy, 12 January 1909, "Personal" (copy); PABC, J.M. Robinson Papers, vol. 9, "Memorandum of Agreement," 6 July 1903; David R.B. Dendy, "One Huge Orchard: Okanagan Land and Development Companies Before the Great War" (unpublished Honours History Essay, University of Victoria, 1976), chap. 2. I am grateful to Professor Patricia Roy for bringing the Dendy study to my attention.

46 SLB 81, Shaughnessy to F.H. Hale, 4 June 1903.

47 SLB 80, Shaughnessy to W. Whyte, 11 February 1903; SLB 79, Shaughnessy to W.H. Aldridge, 30 December 1902.

48 SLB 82, "Circular letter, Office of the President, 4 July 1903," Shaughnessy to W.H. Aldridge, 4 July 1903; SLB 80, Shaughnessy to W.H. Aldridge, 11 February 1903, "Private"; SLB 79, Shaughnessy to W.H. Aldridge, 30 December 1902.

49 CPR, *Annual Report*, 1905; John Murray Gibbon, *Steel of Empire* (New York: Bobbs-Merrill, 1935), 360; SLB 84, Shaughnessy to Senator J.N. Kirchhoffer, 22 July 1904.

50 SLB 83, Shaughnessy to William H. Merritt, 15 April 1903, "Private"; SLB 20, Shaughnessy to W. Hamilton Merritt, 25 February 1890;

SLB 82, Shaughnessy to F. Carter-Cotton, 28 July 1903, "Confidential"; SLB 83, Shaughnessy to W.H. Aldridge, 27 November 1903, 22 January 1904, "Personal"; Dorman, 420–1; Sanford, *McCulloch's Wonder*, 97–8; *BC Statutes*, 1891, c. 47, 1903, c. 38; *Statutes of Canada*, 1903, c. 57, sec. 2, item 26. No reference to the report has been found in the SLB. The railway also had authority to build from Nicola Lake to Kamloops.

51 SLB 85, Shaughnessy to W. Whyte, 2 December 1904, "Personal," 19, 21 December 1904, "Private"; SLB 86, Shaughnessy to W. Whyte, 27 March 1905, "Private," to F. Carter-Cotton, 16 May 1905; Morgan 1912, 206–7, 799; Patricia E. Roy, "Progress, Prosperity and Politics: The Railway Policies of Richard McBride," *BC Studies*, No. 47 (Autumn 1980), 5–6; GAI, CPR Papers, vol 224, file 2180, J.S. Dennis to W. Whyte, 25 November 1904, "Private," 12, 13 December 1904, "Private," 28 December 1904 (copies), W. Whyte to J.S. Dennis, 23, 24 December 1904, "Confidential"; J.K. Johnson, ed., *The Canadian Directory of Parliament 1867–1967* (Ottawa: National Archives of Canada, 1968), 244; *Who's Who and Why* (Canada), 1917–18, 1106. Carter-Cotton was appointed to Cabinet in June 1904.

52 BC Premiers' Papers, vol. 158, file 11, "Confidential Memorandum," signed by McBride and J.S. Dennis, Victoria, 6 March 1905, J.S. Dennis to Richard McBride, "At Victoria, B.C.," 5 March 1905, "At Victoria, B.C.," 27 March 1905, "At Victoria," 8 April 1905, McBride to J.S. Dennis, Victoria, 8 April 1905.

53 SLB 86, Shaughnessy to W. Whyte, 27 March 1905, "Private," to R. Marpole, 27 March 1905, "Private," to W. Whyte, 19 May 1905.

54 SLB 85, Shaughnessy to Senator J.K. Kerr, 18 October 1904; SLB 86, Shaughnessy to W. Whyte, 19 December 1904; Sanford, *McCulloch's Wonder*, 99–102; CPR, *Annual Report*, 1905; Dorman, 421; *CAR*, 1909, 573.

55 Sanford, *McCulloch's Wonder*, 105–6; Roy, "Development of Vancouver," 110–11; *CAR*, 1903, 422; SLB 81, Shaughnessy to Richard Cartwright, 22 June 1903.

56 Sanford, *McCulloch's Wonder*, 106–7; *CAR*, 1905, 547–8, 559–60; Roy, "Development of Vancouver," 112–14; LP, vol. 370, T.G. Shaughnessy to Laurier, 19 June 1905, "Personal," 23 June 1905, "Private," Laurier to Shaughnessy, 22 June 1905 (copy).

57 *CAR*, 1905, 548; *Statutes of Canada*, 1905, c. 172; CHCD, 1905, 8315–7, 8640–1, 8819–25, 9042–6, 9049; CSD, 1905, 517, 542–6, 555.

58 Sanford, *McCulloch's Wonder*, 108.

59 Ibid., 108–12; Roy, "Development of Vancouver," 116. Sanford's account of the conflict is an excellent one.

60 Ibid., 112–5.

61 Ibid., 117–9; Morgan 1912, 1146; GAI, CPR Papers, vol. 224, file 2181, J.S. Dennis to George H. Cowan, 5 March 1906, "Private" (copy).

62 SLB 89, Shaughnessy to J.J. Warren, 22 June 1906, 4 July 1906; SLB 92, Shaughnessy to J.J. Warren, 10 December 1907, "Private"; *Statutes of Canada*, 1903, c. 57, item 67, 1906, c. 43, item 39, 1908, c. 63, item 1; Sanford, *McCulloch's Wonder*, 68–70; GAI, CPR Papers, vol. 224, file 2181, J.S. Dennis to W. Whyte, 1 December 1906, "Confidential" (copy); Roy, "Development of Vancouver," 115–6. The federal subsidy, granted in 1905, was revoted in 1906 and 1908.

63 Sanford, *McCulloch's Wonder*, 119–24; Public Archives of Manitoba, Doupe Family Papers, file 11, J.G. Sullivan to A. McCulloch, 2 March 1937 (copy). Sanford's source is an interview with Charles Gordon, who accompanied Shaughnessy on this trip as his private secretary.

64 SLB 87, Shaughnessy to W. Whyte, 30 October 1905.

65 Sanford, *McCulloch's Wonder*, 124–5; Brian R.D. Smith, "Sir Richard McBride: A Study in the Conservative Party of British Columbia, 1903–1916" (Master's thesis, Queen's University, 1959), 118. Roy, "Railway Policies of ... McBride," 8–10; BC Premiers' Papers, vol. 97, Richard McBride to G.H. Barnard, 17 May 1909 (copy).

66 Roy, "Railway Policies of ... McBride," 10; *BC Statutes*, 1910, c. 26; BC Premiers' Papers, vol. 154, "Agreement" (copy), signed by McBride and J.J. Warren in Victoria, 20 October 1909. The CPR appears to have acquired the Midway and Vernon Railway in 1904; SLB 84, Shaughnessy to T.A. Gillespie, 30 June 1904, to W. Whyte, 4 July 1904; SLB 85, Shaughnessy to T.A. Gillespie, 5 August 1904.

67 Roy, "Railway Policies of ... McBride," 10 –14; Peter R. Hunt, "The Political Career of Sir Richard McBride" (Master's thesis, University of British Columbia, 1953), 144; Regehr, *Canadian Northern*, 297–8; *BC Statutes*, 1910, c. 26. The agreement with the KRVR was dated 28 February 1910.

68 *Statutes of Canada*, 1910, c. 51, item 42; Sanford, *McCulloch's Wonder*, 126–7.

69 Ibid., 127–9; SLB 97, Shaughnessy to W. Whyte, 4 June 1910, "Personal." Warren signed the agreement with McBride in October 1909 as KRVR president.

70 Sanford, *McCulloch's Wonder*, 129.

71 Ibid., 134–40, 186; *Statutes of Canada*, 1911, c. 101, 1913, c. 140; BC Premiers' Papers, vol. 154, J.J. Warren to McBride, 1 July 1910; Privy Council Records, vol. 817, P.C. 1978, 2 August 1913; CPR, *Annual Report*, 1912. The KVR agreement was sanctioned by federal Order-in-Council on 2 August 1913.

72 Sanford, *McCulloch's Wonder*, 138; BC Premiers' Papers, vol. 154, J.J.

Warren to Martin Burrell, 27 October 1913, "Personal" (copy); Johnson, ed., *Canadian Directory of Parliament*, 84–5.

73 *CAR*, 1912, 607; Smith, "Sir Richard McBride," 196, 216; *BC Statutes*, 1912, c. 35, c. 48, sec. 3, item 4, 1913, c. 46, sec. 2, item 13; Sanford, *McCulloch's Wonder*, 143–4; Donald H. Avery, "Canadian Immigration Policy and the Alien Question, 1896–1919: the Anglo-Canadian Perspective" (PH D. thesis, University of Western Ontario, 1973), 216.

74 Sanford, *McCulloch's Wonder*, 147, 153; BC Premiers' Papers, vol. 95, letterhead of The Southern Okanagan Land Company, Penticton, BC; vol. 154, J.J. Warren to McBride, Vancouver, 9 December 1911, 21 December 1911, "Personal," Victoria, 27 February 1912; Turner, *Great Divide*, 139, A.W.T. Shatford was the other managing director of the land company.

75 Sanford, *McCulloch's Wonder*, 150–2.

76 Ibid., 155–60, 177–80; BC Premiers' Papers, vol. 154, J.J. Warren to McBride, 18 March 1913.

77 Sanford, *McCulloch's Wonder*, 181–90; SLB 106, Shaughnessy to J.J. Warren, 23 July 1914, "Personal"; Public Archives of Manitoba, Doupe Family Papers, file 11, J.G. Sullivan to H.W. McLeod, 2 March 1937 (copy).

78 John Fahey, *Inland Empire* (Seattle: University of Washington Press, 1965), 209–10; SLB 81, Shaughnessy to Senator George Turner, 21 April 1903, "Private."

79 Fahey, *Inland Empire*, 212–14; SLB 86, Shaughnessy to E. Pennington, 24 January 1905, "Personal," to D.C. Corbin, 1 February 1905, to Charles Fitzpatrick, 7 February 1905; SLB 88, Shaughnessy to D.C. Corbin, 24 February 1906. The bond issue was later increased by $200,000, of which the CPR purchased $25,000.

80 Sanford, *McCulloch's Wonder*, 106; Fahey, *Inland Empire*, 214–6; SLB 86, "Memorandum For Mr. W.R. Baker," 18 May 1905, Shaughnessy to C.D. Simpson, 27 June 1906; CPR, *Annual Report*, 1905.

81 Sanford, *McCulloch's Wonder*, 113; SLB 86, Shaughnessy to E. Pennington, 15 February 1905, "Private"; SLB 89, Shaughnessy to E.H. Harriman, 2 August 1906, "Personal," to E. Pennington, 29 August 1906, "Personal"; SLB 91, Shaughnessy to W. Whyte, 8 June 1907.

82 *BC Statutes*, 1884, c. 14; Howay *et al.*, *British Columbia and the United States*, 243–6; Robert D. Turner, *Vancouver Island Railroads* (San Marino, California: Golden West Books, 1973), 40–51. The three American railway magnates were Charles Crocker and Leland Stanford, of San Francisco, and Collis P. Huntington of New York, who controlled the Central Pacific Railroad.

83 BC Premiers' Papers, vol. 159, file 7, James Dunsmuir to McBride, 28 December 1903, 26 January 1904, McBride to James Dunmuir, 23

January 1904, "Confidential" (copy); Smith, "Sir Richard McBride," 46.

84 Turner, *Island Railroads*, 53; Donald F. MacLachlan, *The Esquimalt & Nanaimo Railway* (Victoria: BC Railway Historical Association, 1986), 140–1; *Statutes of Canada*, 1905, c. 90; *CAR*, 1905, 547; CPR, *Annual Report*, 1905; SLB 86, Shaughnessy to W. Whyte, 6 January 1905; SLB 89, Shaughnessy to Lord Grey, 31 October 1906.

85 SLB 81, Shaughnessy to W. Whyte, 29 October 1907, "Private"; SLB 97, Shaughnessy to R. Marpole, 20 July 1910, "Confidential"; SLB 98, Shaughnessy to R. Marpole, 25 August 1901, "Private"; *CAR*, 1908, 572.

86 SLB 86, Shaughnessy to W. Whyte, 6 January 1905; SLB 91, Shaughnessy to W. Whyte, 29 October 1907, "Private"; SLB 92, Shaughnessy to I.G. Ogden, 16 December 1907, to W. Whyte, 26 December 1907, "Private," to I.G. Ogden, 10 June 1908; SLB 93, Shaughnessy to R. Marpole, 25 August 1908; GAI, CPR Papers, file 1973, "Agreement" between the CPR and the Wellington Coal Company, 20 February 1908 (copy), R. Marpole to W.H. Aldridge, 24 February 1910 (copy); CPR, *Annual Report*, 1907; *CAR*, 1907, 136, 139, 1908, 572, 1911, 597; *Statutes of Canada*, 1907, c. 40, item 20; *Victoria Colonist*, 23 October 1908. The CPR estimate was based on a 58-mile line.

87 SLB 98, Shaughnessy to Richard McBride, 2 November 1910, "Private"; SLB 101, Shaughnessy to Richard Marpole, 9 March 1912, "Confidential"; Smith, "Sir Richard McBride," 194–5; *BC Statutes*, 1912, c. 32.

88 Privy Council Records, vol. 795, P.C. 2457; *BC Statutes*, 1912, c. 33, with Schedule containing an agreement between the BC government and the E&N, dated 7 February 1912.

89 CPR, *Annual Report*, 1910, 1914; James C. Bonar, compiler, "Canadian Pacific Railway Company and Its Contributions Towards the Early Development and to the Continued Progress of Canada" (Montreal: CPR in house, 1950), vol. 7, 16; *Statutes of Canada*, 1901, c. 71, 1903, c. 57, item 66, 1906, c. 43, item 31, 1910, c. 51, item 43, 1912, c. 48, item 17; *BC Statutes*, 1901, c. 79; Privy Council Records, vol. 754, P.C. 2656; SLB 85, Shaughnessy to I.G. Ogden, 24 October 1904, to W.A. Macdonald, 9 November 1904; SLB 86, "Memorandum for Mr. Tye," 28 January 1905; SLB 87, Shaughnessy to Hugh Watt, 5 July 1905; SLB 90, Shaughnessy to W. Whyte, 7 January 1907, "Private and Confidential"; SLB 91, Shaughnessy to W. Whyte, 10 August 1907; SLB 97, Shaughnessy to A. Price, 2 April 1910; GAI, CPR Papers, vol. 244, file 2356, J.S. Schwitzer to J.S. Dennis, 13 May 1910, W. Whyte to J.S. Dennis, 30 January 1911 (copy). The

CPR acquired the charter from C. Hungerford Pollen, who was president of the company. Dr Hugh Watt of Fort Steele owned some stock in the company; he was president of the company in 1901. SLB 75, Shaughnessy to Hugh Watt, 21 October 1901.

90 John S. Marsh, "The Spiral and Connaught Tunnels," in Hugh A. Dempsey, ed., *The CPR West* (Vancouver: Douglas & McIntyre, 1984), 173; SLB 90, Shaughnessy to W. Whyte, 15 April 1907.

91 *CAR*, 1907, 139; Marsh, "Spiral and Connaught Tunnels," 174–6.

92 Ibid., 177–78; *The Canadian Encyclopedia* 3 vols. (Edmonton: Hurtig 1985), "Rogers Pass," 3: 1596.

93 Marsh, "Spiral and Connaught Tunnels," 177–8; Gary G. Backler, "The C.P.R.'s Capacity and Investment Strategy in Rogers Pass, B.C., 1882–1916" (Master's thesis, University of British Columbia, 1981), 395–6; Gary G. Backler and Trevor D. Heaver, "The Timing of a Major Investment in Railway Capacity: CPR's 1913 Connaught Tunnel Decision," *Business History* 24 (1982) : 300–14.

94 SLB 103, Shaughnessy to George Bury, 24 March 1913; Marsh, "Spiral and Connaught Tunnels," 180–3; Backler, "Rogers Pass," 345, 399; Turner, *Great Divide*, 88.

95 *CAR*, 1912, 635–6; CPR, *Annual Report*, 1913; SLB 102, Shaughnessy to George Bury, 27 July 1912; NAC, Borden Papers, OC series, OC 84a, T.G. Shaughnessy to R.L. Borden, 13 August 1912.

96 SLB 103, Shaughnessy to Grant Hall, 3 March 1913, "Personal," to George Bury, 31 March 1913; SLB 104, Shaughnessy to Bury, 16 July 1913; SLB 105, Shaughnessy to Bury, 11 January 1914; *CRMW*, December 1914, 543.

CHAPTER SEVEN

1 E.J. Hart, *The Selling of Canada: The CPR and the Beginnings of Canadian Tourism* (Banff: Altitude Publishing, 1983), 12.

2 SLB 17, Shaughnessy to W. Wainwright, 26 December 1888; CPR, *Annual Reports*, 1885, 1887, 1899; Morgan 1912, 609.

3 Hart, *Selling of Canada*, 12.

4 Ibid., 12–3.

5 Walter Vaughan, *The Life and Work of Sir William Van Horne* (New York: Century Company, 1920), 141–2; SLB 20, Shaughnessy to H.H. Smith, 23 December 1889.

6 Cited in Hart, *Selling of Canada*, 13.

7 Ibid., 14; Anthony A. Barrett and Rhodri W. Liscombe, *Francis Rattenbury and British Columbia: Architecture and Challenge in the Imperial Age* (Vancouver: University of British Columbia Press, 1983), 2.

8 Vaughan, *Van Horne*, 151.

9   Hart, *Selling of Canada*, 14.

10   Vaughan, *Van Horne*, 151.

11   Hart, *Selling of Canada*, 16–7.

12   Harold D. Kalman, *The Railway Hotels and the Development of the Château Style in Canada* (University of Victoria, 1968), 10. My father, Dr. E.D. Eagle, has seen the Trossachs Hotel near Aberfoyle, Scotland, and thinks it resembles the Banff Springs Hotel.

13   Ibid., 9; Hart, *Selling of Canada*, 17–9.

14   Kalman, *Railway Hotels*, 11.

15   Barrett and Liscombe, *Rattenbury*, 92, 351, note 5; Hart, *Selling of Canada*, 16; Robert D. Turner, *The Pacific Empresses* (Victoria: Sono Nis Press, 1981), 23; Patricia E. Roy, *Vancouver: An Illustrated History* (Toronto: James Lorimer, 1980), 29; Norbert MacDonald, "The Canadian Pacific Railway and Vancouver's Development to 1900," in W. Peter Ward and Robert A.J. McDonald, eds., *British Columbia: Historical Readings* (Vancouver: University of British Columbia Press, 1981), 403.

16   SLB 68, Shaughnessy to J.H. Latham, 9 August 1899.

17   Robert A.J. McDonald, "Victoria, Vancouver, and the Economic Development of British Columbia, 1886–1914," in Ward and McDonald, eds., *British Columbia*, 377. In 1901 Victoria's population was 20,919, Vancouver's 27,010.

18   *Vancouver Province*, 2, 11 October 1900.

19   Barrett and Liscombe, *Rattenbury*, 17–8, 21, 31–3, 92, 94; Terry Reksten, *Rattenbury* (Victoria: Sono Nis Press, 1978), xiii.

20   Barrett and Liscombe, 92–4.

21   Ibid., 97, 118.

22   *Vancouver Province*, 11 October 1900. The old hotel had 120 rooms, the reconstructed hotel about 250.

23   Barrett and Liscombe, *Rattenbury*, 117–18; Hart, *Selling of Canada*, 88.

24   Kalman, *Railway Hotels*, 117–8; SLB 98, Shaughnessy to R. Marpole, 19 September 1910, "Personal"; Banff *Craig and Canyon*, 27 February 1957; Archives of the Canadian Rockies, Painter Family Papers, "Professional Biography." Some preliminary work had been done on the new hotel in 1910–11.

25   SLB 67, Shaughnessy to W. Whyte, 13 June 1899, "Personal."

26   SLB 79, Shaughnessy to W. Whyte, 22 December 1902, "Private."

27   *Manitoba Free Press*, 14, 16 September 1903; City of Winnipeg Archives, Winnipeg City Council, *Minutes*, 7, 28 December 1903, 5, 13, 15 January 1904, "By-Laws of the City of Winnipeg Passed By the Council During the Year 1904," By-Law No. 2790, which contains the full text of the agreement of 5 December 1903.

28 *Manitoba Statutes*, 1904, c. 64, sec. 16.

29 *Manitoba Free Press*, 15, 16, 19 September 1903.

30 *The Canadian Encyclopedia*, 3 vols. (Edmonton: Hurtig, 1985), "Edward Maxwell," "William Sutherland Maxwell," 2: 1101; Morgan 1912, 354, 744–5; Barrett and Liscombe, *Rattenbury*, 95 and figure 4.3. Edward, born in 1867, had studied with the successful Montreal architect, Alfred F. Dunlop and then apprenticed with the Boston firm of Shepley, Rutan, and Coolidge. William Sutherland, born in 1868, studied architecture in Boston and then at the Ecole des beaux-arts in Paris.

31 SLB 83, Shaughnessy to W. Whyte, 15 February 1904.

32 SLB 84, Shaughnessy to W. Whyte, 29 April 1904, 1 June 1904, "Personal"; Morgan 1912, 670 (Lyall); C.W. Parker, ed., *Who's Who and Why, 1913*, (Vancouver: International Press, 1913), 639 (O'Leary).

33 GAI, Van Horne Private Correspondence, file 82.5.479, W. Whyte to Van Horne, 27 April 1905, "Personal"; *Manitoba Free Press*, 1 June 1906, 8; SLB 88, Shaughnessy to W. Whyte, 14 February 1906, "Private," 13 March 1906.

34 SLB 85, Shaughnessy to W. Whyte, 23 August 1904.

35 *CRMW*, May 1906, 269, June 1906, 305, 307; Kalman, *Railway Hotels*, 21; *The Canadian Encyclopedia*, "William Sutherland Maxwell," 2:1101.

36 SLB 86, Notice from "Office of the President," 1 January 1905.

37 SLB, 87, Shaughnessy to Hayter Reed, 25 July 1905.

38 *CRMW*, March 1912, 129, August 1913, 388.

39 Norman R. Hacking and W. Kaye Lamb, *The Princess Story* (Vancouver: Mitchell Press, 1974), 184–5.

40 Ibid., 187; Norbert MacDonald, "Seattle, Vancouver and the Klondike," *CHR* 49 (1968), 244.

41 SLB 73, Shaughnessy to R. Marpole, 19 January 1901, "Personal," to C. Chipman, 2 February 1901; Hacking and Lamb, *Princess Story*, 187–8; SLB 72, Shaughnessy to Frederick Buscombe, 16 November 1900, "Personal"; MacDonald, "Seattle ... and the Klondike," 244–5. Buscombe was president of the Vancouver Board of Trade.

42 Hacking and Lamb, *Princess Story*, 188. The new directors were Captain Troup, Richard Marpole, George McLaren Brown, James Thomson, and F.W. Vincent.

43 Ibid., 185–6.

44 Ibid., 188, 193–4; W. Kaye Lamb, *History of the Canadian Pacific Railway*, (New York: Macmillan, 1977), 243. This is Troup's account of the meeting as recalled years later by Mrs Troup.

45 Hacking and Lamb, *Princess Story*, 198, 200, 342–3. These were: *Ena* (1907), *Charlotte* (1908), *Adelaide* (1910), *Alice* (1911), *Sophia* (1911), *Maquinna* (1913), *Mary* (1914), *Margaret* (1914) and *Irene* (1914).

46 McDonald, "Victoria, Vancouver ... 1886–1914," 388.

47 Harry Gregson, *A History of Victoria 1842–1970* (Victoria: Observer Publishing, 1970), 177–8; Barrett and Liscombe, *Rattenbury*, 150; Morgan 1912, 61.

48 J.K. Johnson, ed., *Canadian Directory of Parliament 1867–1967* (Ottawa: National Archives of Canada, 1968), 350 (Mara); Hacking and Lamb, *Princess Story*, 186; Gregson, *Victoria*, 115, 118, 145.

49 *Victoria Colonist*, 23 May 1903; Reksten, *Rattenbury*, 78, 81.

50 Ibid,; Barrett and Liscombe, *Rattenbury*, 124; SLB 79, Shaughnessy to L.G. McQuade and F. Elworthy, 29 October 1902.

51 *Victoria Colonist*, 23 May 1903.

52 Ibid.

53 Ibid.

54 *Victoria Colonist*, 9 June 1903.

55 SLB 81, Shaughnessy to the mayor of Victoria, J.A. Mara, D.R. Ker and Herbert Cuthbert, 8 June 1903. In this letter Shaughnessy quotes his telegram of 8 June to the mayor.

56 *Victoria Colonist*, 9 June 1903, editorial, "The New Hotel."

57 City of Victoria Archives, Victoria City Council, *Minutes*, 24 August 1903, and "By-Laws of the City of Victoria, 1901–1903," By-Law No. 417; Barrett and Liscombe, *Rattenbury*, 150; Derek Pethick, *Summer of Promise: Victoria 1864–1914* (Victoria: Sono Nis Press, 1980), 153.

58 Cited in Barrett and Liscombe, *Rattenbury*, 152–3.

59 Ibid., 163; E. Brian Titley, "Hayter Reed and Indian Administration in the West," unpublished paper delivered at the Western Canadian Studies Conference, November 1985; information from Professor Titley; SLB 70, Shaughnessy to Lucius Tuttle, 23 January 1900, to Hayter Reed, 21 February 1900.

60 Titley, "Hayter Reed"; Henry James Morgan, ed., *Morgan's Types of Canadian Women* (Toronto: William Briggs, 1903), 280; *Beaverton Express* (Ontario), 29 June 1894. I am indebted to Mr R.B. Fleming who supplied Professor Titley with the newspaper reference.

61 Barrett and Liscombe, *Rattenbury*, 153–6.

62 SLB 84, Shaughnessy to Hayter Reed, 16 May 1904.

63 Barrett and Liscombe, *Rattenbury*, 156; SLB 84, Shaughnessy to F. Rattenbury, 26 May 1904, to Hayter Reed, 26 May 1904. Reed's memorandum is included in Shaughnessy's letter to Rattenbury.

64 Barrett and Liscombe, *Rattenbury*, 156–9.

65 Ibid., 159, 177; Gregson, *Victoria*, 177; Godfrey Holloway, *The Empress of Victoria* (Victoria: Pacifica Productions, 1968), 5; Victoria City Council, *Minutes*, 14 July 1904; Reksten, *Rattenbury*, 84. The vote, held 7 July 1904, was 1205 for, 46 against.

66 SLB 86, Shaughnessy to W. Whyte, 31 December 1904, to Thomas Kelly, 20 March 1905.

67 Barrett and Liscombe, *Rattenbury*, 163; *Henderson's City of Victoria and Suburban Directory*, 1908, 413; Holloway, *Empress*, 6; SLB 86, Shaughnessy to R. Marpole, 2 March 1905; SLB 89, Shaughnessy to R. Marpole, 25 October 1906, "Personal"; SLB 91, Shaughnessy to R. Marpole, 25 July 1907, "Personal." W.S. Painter made the cost estimate for the foundations after inspecting the hotel in July 1907.

68 SLB 86, Shaughnessy to R. Marpole, 2 March 1905.

69 Reksten, *Rattenbury*, 84; SLB 88, Shaughnessy to W. Whyte, 18 November 1905, to R. Marpole, 13 December 1905.

70 SLB 89, Shaughnessy to R. Marpole, 1 June 1906.

71 SLB 89, Shaughnessy to R. Marpole, 20 October 1906, "Personal."

72 Reksten, *Rattenbury*, 88; Barrett and Liscombe, *Rattenbury*, 178; Hart, *Selling of Canada*, 87.

73 Barrett and Liscombe, *Rattenbury*, 178–9, 300.

74 *Victoria Colonist*, 21 January, 23 October 1908; Morgan 1912, 491 (Ham), 742 (Matson).

75 Barrett and Liscombe, *Rattenbury*, 300; Kalman, *Railway Hotels*, 19–20; Painter Family Papers, "Professional Biography."

76 *The Canadian Encyclopedia*, "Calgary," 1: 255–7; SLB 90, Shaughnessy to W. Whyte, 2 May 1907; *CRMW*, June 1907, 411, July 1907, 481; Max Foran, *Calgary, An Illustrated History* (Toronto: James Lorimer, 1978), 73.

77 SLB 97, Shaughnessy to W. Whyte, 26 May 1910; SLB 98, Shaughnessy to J.S. Dennis, 14 November 1910, "Private," to W. Whyte, 19 November 1910, "Personal"; Max Foran, "The CPR and the Urban West, 1881–1930," in Hugh Dempsey, ed., *The CPR West* (Vancouver: Douglas & McIntyre, 1984), 101.

78 *CRMW*, March 1912, 129, April 1914, 173; B.S. White, ed., *The Story of Calgary-Alberta-Canada* (n.p., 1914), 27 (copy in GAI Library); Calgary *Herald*, 1 April 1984, article by Betinna Liverant; Linda Collier, "Historical Hotels: Palliser Hotel," *Prairie Hotelman*, January 1979, 12–5; Abraham Rogatnick, "Canadian Castles: Pheonomenon of the Railway Hotel, *Architectural Review*, vol. 141 (May 1967), 364–72; Max and Heather Foran, *Calgary: Canada's Frontier Metropolis* (Calgary: Windsor Publications, 1982), 77. Ellingwood was a member of the New York firm of McKim, Mead, and White. His then most recent work had been the supervision of the Pennsylvania Railroad's new station in New York City; SLB 98, Shaughnessy to F.L. Ellingwood, 4 November 1910.

79 Barrett and Liscombe, *Rattenbury*, 98, 297, 299; Hart, *Selling of Canada*, 87–8.

80 Bart Robinson, *Banff Springs: The Story of a Hotel* (Banff: Summerthought, 1973), 37–8.

81 Ibid., 38–9, 41–3.

82 Ibid., 46, 48, 53–4.

83 Ibid., 53; Hart, *Selling of Canada*, 87.

84 Barrett and Liscombe, *Rattenbury*, 299; SLB 62, Shaughnessy to E. Maxwell, 9 September 1898; Hart, *Selling of Canada*, 75; Robert D. Turner, *West of the Great Divide* (Victoria: Sono Nis Press, 1987), 43–4. A CPR hotel was also built at Balfour, BC, overlooking Kootenay Lake. It was advertised by the CPR in Morgan 1912.

CHAPTER EIGHT

1 Chester Martin, *"Dominion Lands" Policy*, ed. Lewis H. Thomas (Toronto: McClelland and Stewart, 1973), 36; James B. Hedges, *Building the Canadian West* (New York: Macmillan, 1939), 14–16.

2 W. Kaye Lamb, *History of the Canadian Pacific Railway* (New York: Macmillan, 1977), 215.

3 Lewis G. Thomas, general ed., *The Prairie West To 1905: A Canadian Sourcebook* (Toronto: Oxford University Press, 1975), 331–2.

4 Hedges, *Building*, 33–4; J.L. Mcdougall, *Canadian Pacific* (Montreal: McGill University Press, 1968), 128.

5 Ibid.

6 Lamb, *Canadian Pacific*, 215.

7 Ibid.; Hedges, *Building*, 15; Thomas, ed., *Prairie West*, 331.

8 Lamb, *Canadian Pacific*, 215–16.

9 Martin, *"Dominion Lands,"* 35.

10 Cited in Lamb, *Canadian Pacific*, 216. Emphasis in original.

11 Morgan 1912, 577, 495; CPR, *Annual Report*, 1887; Hedges, *Building*, 66–8; Public Archives of Manitoba, Doupe Family Papers, folder 11, biography of Jacob Lonsdale Doupe.

12 Mcdougall, *Canadian Pacific*, 129-30.

13 Charles S. Lee, ed., *Land To Energy 1882–1982* (Calgary: Canada Northwest Energy Limited, n.d. [1983]), 76–7.

14 Ibid., 80–1; Mcdougall, *Canadian Pacific*, 103; VHLB 54, Van Horne to W.F. Munro, 27 November 1897.

15 Lee, ed., *Land To Energy*, 76–9.

16 Hedges, *Building*, 71–2; André N. Lalonde, "Settlement in the North-West Territories by Colonization Companies, 1881–1891," (Doctorat d'Université, Laval University, 1969).

17 Hedges, *Building*, 74, 88–9. Hedges gives a figure of 637,000 acres sold to colonization companies. However, he omits the 171,200 acres that were transferred from a colonization company to Canada North-West Land Co. in 1883 to make up its grant of 2.2 million acres.

18 Ibid., 73–4; Lee, ed., *Land To Energy*, 12.

19 Ibid., 13, 36, 38; Hedges, *Building*, 74–6.

20 Mcdougall, *Canadian Pacific*, 130. This figure is not entirely accurate since it does not include actual sales of CPR lands by colonization companies.

21 Martin, *"Dominion Lands,"* 96.

22 Mcdougall, *Canadian Pacific*, 178; Hedges, *Building*, 47–8; James B. Hedges, *The Federal Railway Land Subsidy Policy of Canada* (Cambridge: Harvard University Press, 1934), 49–52; *Statutes of Canada*, 1890, c. 4, 1891, c. 10, 1894, c. 6; CPR, *Annual Reports*, 1892, 1893.

23 A subsidy for 215 miles would amount to 1,376,000 acres. It appears the company built a 3-mile branch line to earn the additional 20,800 acres.

24 Lamb, *Canadian Pacific*, 158; Mcdougall, *Canadian Pacific*, 175; Hedges, *Building*, 59; Dorman, 352; *Statutes of Canada*, 1879, c. 66, 1884, c. 54, c. 73, 1885, c. 60, 1891, c. 10.

25 Mcdougall, *Canadian Pacific*, 173–4; Dorman, 246–7, 344–6, 553; Hedges, *Building*, 60.

26 Raymond A. Christenson, "The Calgary and Edmonton Railway and the Edmonton *Bulletin*" (Master's thesis, University of Alberta, 1967), 225, 236–7, 244; Kirk N. Lambrecht, "The Land Grant for the Calgary and Edmonton Railway." Paper presented to Amisk Waskahegan Chapter, Historical Society of Alberta, 4 December 1985.

27 A.A. den Otter, *Civilizing the West* (Edmonton: University of Alberta Press, 1982), 306–8; Hedges, *Building*, 60, 310; Dorman, 21.

28 R.C. Brown, "For the Purposes of the Dominion: Background Paper on the History of Federal Public Lands Policy to 1930," in J.C. Nelson, R.C. Scace, and R. Kouri, eds., *Canadian Public Land Use in Perspective* (Ottawa: Social Science Research Council, 1974), 9; D.J. Hall, "Clifford Sifton: Immigration and Settlement Policy, 1896–1905," in H. Palmer, ed., *The Settlement of the West* (Calgary: University of Calgary Press, 1977), 63.

29 VHLB 52, Van Horne to Clifford Sifton, 9 February 1897; D.J. Hall, *Clifford Sifton*, Vol. 1, *The Young Napoleon 1861–1900* (Vancouver: University of British Columbia Press, 1981), 154.

30 Hedges, *Building*, 36, 56.

31 Ibid., 38, 56, citing P.C. 2099, 24 October 1882.

32 Ibid., 39, 56, citing P.C. 2152, 3 November 1888 and P.C. 110, 25 January 1883. This did not apply to lands owned by the Metis and white settlers nor to lands granted to colonization companies, notably the Manitoba and South Western Colonization Company.

33 Ibid., 39.

34 Ibid., citing P.C. 414, 18 February 1895. Technically the lands were

located in a belt 24 miles on each side of a projected line into the district west of Lake Dauphin.

35 Ibid., 40, citing P.C. 3613, 18 December 1895.

36 Ibid., 57–8; University of Alberta Archives, William Pearce Papers, series 7, 3–16, copy of P.C. 1434, 22 August 1903; SLB 82, Shaughnessy to Clifford Sifton, 28 July 1903; D.J. Hall, *Clifford Sifton*, vol. 2, *A Lonely Eminence 1901–1929* (Vancouver: University of British Columbia Press, 1985), 58–9.

37 F.H. Leacy, ed., *Historical Statistics of Canada*, 2nd edition (Ottawa: Statistics Canada, 1985). series A350.

38 Hedges, *Building*, 164–5, 391.

39 Ibid., 161–2.

40 Ibid., 162–3.

41 Ibid., 163. Hedges compiled these figures from CPR land records in the Department of National Resources in Calgary.

42 Ibid., 163–5. The figures on land sales 1897–1906 were compiled by William Pearce in 1921 from CPR land records in the Department of Natural Resources in Calgary.

43 Ibid., 244–7.

44 Ibid., 58.

45 Morgan 1912, 892; E. Alyn Mitchner, "William Pearce and Federal Government Activities in Western Canada, 1882–1904" (PH D. thesis, University of Alberta, 1971), vii–x, 17–21.

46 Ibid., 16, 29–31.

47 Ibid., 14–16, 109–11, chaps. 2, 3, and 4.

48 Ibid., 206–8; A. Mitchner, "The Bow River Scheme: CPR's Irrigation Block," in Hugh A. Dempsey, ed., *The CPR West* (Vancouver: Douglas & McIntyre, 1984), 260.

49 Mitchner, "Bow River Scheme," 260; Sifton Papers, vol. 10, W.C. Van Horne to Sifton, 27 December 1896.

50 Ibid., 260., Mitchner, "William Pearce," 279–83.

51 Pearce Papers, series 7, 3–11, Pearce to L.A. Hamilton, 21 August 1894 (copy), to W. Whyte, 21 August 1894 (copy); Mitchner, "William Pearce," 283–4.

52 Mitchner, "William Pearce," 284–7.

53 Pearce Papers, W.C. Van Horne to Pearce, 1 July 1895 (copy); Mitchner, "William Pearce," 287–8.

54 Ibid., 288–9.

55 Pearce Papers, series 7, 3–11, W.C. Van Horne to Pearce, 16 December 1895 with copy of Peterson's estimates, Pearce to Van Horne, 23 December 1895. Pearce used a figure of 10 cents per cubic yard in his calculations.

56 Mitchner, "William Pearce," 292–8; Mitchner, "Bow River Scheme," 262.

57 Pearce Papers, series 7, 3–11, Pearce to Sir William Van Horne, 6 December 1897 (copy), W.C. Van Horne to Pearce, 26 December 1897, L.A. Hamilton to Pearce, 15 December 1897; Mitchner, "William Pearce," 298–300; Hedges, *Building*, 172–3.

58 Ibid., 300–1; Mitchner, "Bow River Scheme," 262.

59 Mitchner, "William Pearce," 301–2; SLB 75, Shaughnessy to H. Moody, 15 October 1901.

60 Mitchner, "William Pearce," 302; SLB 77, Shaughnessy to W. Whyte, 6 May 1902; Pearce Papers, series 7, 3–14, Pearce to W. Whyte, 5 May 1902 (copy).

61 Pearce Papers, series 7, 3–14, J.S. Dennis to Pearce, 21 May 1902, "Private," Pearce to W. Whyte, Montreal, 17/5/02 (copy); Thomas, ed., *Prairie West*, 332.

62 Pearce Papers, series 7, 3–14, J.S. Dennis to Pearce, 24 May 1902, Pearce to J.S. Dennis, Calgary, 26 May 1902, "Private" (copy), W. Whyte to Pearce, 16 June 1902, "Personal."

63 Mitchner, "William Pearce," 306–7; Pearce Papers, series 7, 3–14, Pearce to W. Whyte, Calgary, 13 June 1902. Mitchner incorrectly dates the trip in 1901 instead of 1902.

64 Pearce Papers, series 7, 3–14, W. Whyte to Pearce, Winnipeg, 16 June 1902, "Personal." Pearce came to Winnipeg and had discussions with Whyte and Shaughnessy before the president's party left for Calgary.

65 CPR, *Annual Reports*, 1898–1902. The company had paid a 4 per cent dividend on common stock in 1898.

66 Pearce Papers, series 7, 3–12, Pearce to W. Whyte, 1 October, 2 October 1902 (copies), 20 October 1902, "Private" (copy).

67 SLB 80, Shaughnessy to F.T. Griffin, 6 January 1903, to W. Whyte, 2 February, 7 April 1903, to Sir Wilfrid Laurier, 10 February 1903; SLB 82, Shaughnessy to Clifford Sifton, 28 July 1903; Pearce Papers, series 7, 3–16, printed copy of P.C. 1434, 22 August 1903; Hall, *Sifton*, vol. 2, 58–9.

68 Mitchner, "William Pearce," 303–4; Pearce Papers, series 7, 3–14, J.S. Dennis to L.A. Hamilton, 26 October 1901, "Personal," to Charles Drinkwater, 28 October 1901, to William Pearce, 5 November 1901, "Personal."

69 Mitchner, "William Pearce," 304; NAC, Engineering Institute of Canada Papers, vol. 68, J.S. Dennis file; Pearce Papers, series 7, 3–12, copy of CPR circular appointing Dennis Superintendent of Irrigation and British Columbia Land Commissioner; Colin F. Read, "John

Stoughton Dennis [Sr]," in Frances G. Halpenny and Jean Hamelin, eds., *Dictionary of Canadian Biography*, vol. 11, *1881 To 1890* (Toronto: University of Toronto Press, 1982), 244–6.

70 Hedges, *Building*, 175; Renie Gross and Lea Nicoll Kramer, *Tapping the Bow* (Brooks, Alberta: Eastern Irrigation District, 1985), 137–8.

71 SLB 86, Shaughnessy to Elwood Mead, 17 May 1905; CPR, *Annual Reports*, 1905, 1909; Gross and Kramer, *Tapping the Bow*, 138; Hedges, *Building*, 175.

72 SLB 85, "Memorandum For Mr. Whyte," 22 September 1904; SLB 87, Shaughnessy to Thomas Skinner, 2 October 1905; SLB 90, Shaughnessy to W. Whyte, 15 May 1907, "Personal."

73 SLB 87, Shaughnessy to Lord Strathcona, 9 October 1905; SLB 90, Shaughnessy to Lord Strathcona, 11 March 1907, "Private," to W. Whyte, 15 March 1907, "Personal"; SLB 92, Shaughnessy to C.C. Chipman, 6 January 1908.

74 SLB 84, Shaughnessy to W. Whyte, 22 April 1904; SLB 87, Shaughnessy to W. Whyte, 30 June 1905.

75 Hedges, *Building*, 180–2; SLB 87, Shaughnessy to W. Whyte, 1 July 1905, "Private."

76 Hedges, *Building*, 182–93. Beiseker and Davidson were also to receive $2 an acre for all land sold by the CPR in 1908.

77 Ibid., 185; Morgan 1912, 900.

78 Hedges, *Building*, 193–8, 210–11.

79 Ibid.

80 CPR, *Annual Reports*, 1909, 1910; SLB 96, Shaughnessy to F.T. Griffin, 1 December 1909.

81 SLB 95, Shaughnessy to W. Whyte, 18 May 1909, 23 August 1909, "Private," 31 August 1909; SLB 96, Shaughnessy to F.T. Griffin, 1 December 1909, 6 December 1909, "Personal," to Lord Strathcona, 7 March 1910, to J.S. Dennis, 7 March 1910; SLB 98, Shaughnessy to J.S. Dennis, 23 November 1910; CPR, *Annual Report*, 1911.

82 Gross and Kramer, *Tapping the Bow*, 6–8, 15, 138–9; Hedges, *Building*, 296–7; Calgary *Herald*, 27 April 1914.

83 den Otter, *Civilizing the West*, 305–7; CPR, *Annual Reports*, 1908, 1911; NAC, Privy Council Records, vol. 777, *P.C.* 2976, 28 December 1911; SLB 97, Shaughnessy to W. Whyte, 2 May 1910, 17 May 1910, "Personal."

84 Hedges, *Building*, 244; SLB 96, Shaughnessy to F.T. Griffin, 1 December 1909, 6 December 1909, "Personal."

85 den Otter, *Civilizing the West*, 230–1, 307–8; Hedges, *Building*, 256–8.

86 Ibid., 257–8.

87 GAI, Canadian Pacific Railway Papers, section 1, P.L. Naismith to

T. Heeney, 26 December 1912; Hedges, *Building*, 233. There were 178,000 acres of irrigable and non-irrigable lands in the Western section in 1911.

88 GAI, CPR papers, section 1, P.L. Naismith to J.S. Dennis, 19 July 1912.

89 Hedges, *Building*, 296–7.

90 Ibid., 212–14.

91 Ibid., 214–16.

92 Ibid., 216–18, 317–18.

93 Ibid., 218–27.

94 On this subject, see Paul L. Voisey, "Forging the Western Tradition: Pioneer Approaches to Settlement and Agriculture in Southern Alberta Communities" (PH D. thesis, University of Toronto, 1982), chap. 3.

95 Ibid., 227; SLB 83, Shaughnessy to W. Whyte, 2 February 1904; SLB 84, Shaughnessy to F.T. Griffin, 22 March 1904, 3 May 1904.

96 Hedges, *Building*, 227–9.

97 Ibid., 236–9, 293, 295–7, 403. The total was calculated by this author.

98 Ibid., 260–3, 403. Calculation of total by this author.

99 Ibid., 293.

100 Ibid., 398–400; Voisey, "Forging the Western Tradition," chap. 3.

101 Hedges, *Building*, 320.

102 Ibid., 322.

103 Ibid., 323–4.

104 Ibid., 325–9; David C. Jones, *Empire of Dust: Settling and Abandoning the Prairie Dry Belt* (Edmonton: University of Alberta Press, 1987).

105 Hedges, *Building*, 329–31.

106 Ibid., 332–36; Morgan 1912, 985.

107 Ibid., 401–2.

108 SLB 89, Shaughnessy to E.B. Osler, 10 July 1906, "Private."

109 SLB 105, Shaughnessy to W.T. White, 13 January 1914; CPR, *Annual Reports*, 1912–1914. It is not clear if Shaughnessy is referring here to sales of the main-line grant, although the context suggests that he was referring to sales of prairie lands and townsites.

110 Lloyd J. Mercer, *Railroads and Land Grant Policy* (New York: Academic Press, 1982), 143. Mercer studied the CPR and six American land-grant railroads. He generally takes issue with Peter George's findings which stress that subsidies given to the CPR were excessive. See Lloyd J. Mercer, "Rates of Return and Government Subsidization of the Canadian Pacific Railway: An Alternate View," *Canadian Journal of Economics* 6, no. 3 (August 1973): 428–37.

111 Hedges, *Building*, 390.

CHAPTER NINE

1 This chapter has been greatly influenced by the views of Max Foran in his excellent article, "The CPR and the Urban West, 1881–1930," in Hugh Dempsey, ed., *The CPR West* (Vancouver: Douglas & McIntyre, 1984), 89–105.
2 Patricia E. Roy, *Vancouver: An Illustrated History* (Toronto: James Lorimer & Company, 1980), 12.
3 Norbert MacDonald, "The Canadian Pacific Railway and Vancouver's Development to 1900," in W. Peter Ward and Robert A.J. McDonald, eds., *British Columbia: Historical Readings* (Vancouver: Douglas & McIntyre, 1981), 399; Robert D. Turner, *West of the Great Divide* (Victoria: Sono Nis Press, 1987), 27.
4 MacDonald, "Canadian Pacific and Vancouver," 400–2.
5 Roy, *Vancouver*, 14–16; Margaret A. Ormsby, *British Columbia: A History* (Vancouver: Macmillan of Canada, 1964), 296–7.
6 MacDonald, "Canadian Pacific and Vancouver," 402–3.
7 Roy, *Vancouver*, 29; SLB 96, T.G. Shaughnessy to Simon Leiser, 13 October 1909. The CPR sold the opera house to private interests in 1909.
8 Robert A.J. McDonald, "City-Building in the Canadian West: A Case Study of Economic Growth in Early Vancouver, 1886–1893," *BC Studies* 43 (Autumn 1979): 9–14.
9 Ruben C. Bellan, *Winnipeg First Century* (Winnipeg: Queenston House, 1978), 15–16; Allan F.J. Artibise, *Winnipeg: A Social History of Urban Growth* (Montreal: McGill-Queen's University Press, 1975), 63–8.
10 Artibise, *Winnipeg*, 68–70.
11 Ibid., 70–3; Bellan, *Winnipeg*, 18–22. Author's emphasis in the quotation. The CPR also received from the city a $200,000 subsidy to build a branch line from Winnipeg into southwestern Manitoba. It was to have gone to the rival Manitoba and South Western Railway.
12 Bellan, *Winnipeg*, 36–9.
13 Donald Kerr, "Wholesale Trade on the Canadian Plains in the Late Nineteenth Century: Winnipeg and its Competition," in Howard Palmer, ed., *The Settlement of the West* (Calgary: Comprint Publishing, 1977), 133, 151.
14 Bellan, *Winnipeg*, 49.
15 Ibid., 53.
16 Ibid., 49–53.
17 Foran, "CPR and the Urban West," 93; Elizabeth Arthur, "Inter-

urban Rivalry in Port Arthur and Fort William, 1870–1907," in Anthony W. Rasporich, ed., *Western Canada Past and Present* (Calgary: McClelland and Stewart West, 1975), 58–62.

18 John A. Eagle, "The Development of Transportation and Communications, 1870–1905," in L.G. Thomas, ed., *The Prairie West to 1905* (Toronto: Oxford University Press, 1975), 310–12; Foran, "CPR and the Urban West," 92.

19 Foran, "CPR and the Urban West," 92, 94–5; Paul Voisey, "The Urbanization of the Canadian Prairies, 1871–1916," *Histoire sociale/Social History* 8, no. 15 (Mai-May 1975): 80–1.

20 V.C. Fowke, *The National Policy and the Wheat Economy* (Toronto: University of Toronto Press, 1957), 75; *CAR*, 1901, 10–13, 67, 1902, 270, 1914, 699; Robert A.J. McDonald, "Victoria, Vancouver and the Economic Development of British Columbia, 1886–1914," in Ward and McDonald, eds., *British Columbia*, 371.

21 Bellan, *Winnipeg*, 73, 113; SLB 67, T.G. Shaughnessy to W. Whyte, 13 June 1899, "Personal."

22 Bellan, *Winnipeg*, 73–5.

23 Voisey, "Urbanization," 85; Bellan, *Winnipeg*, 110–11.

24 Bellan, *Winnipeg*, 111–13; W.T. Jackman, *Economic Principles of Transportation* (Toronto: University of Toronto Press, 1935), 376–8.

25 Max Foran, "Land Development Patterns in Calgary, 1884–1945," in Alan F.J. Artibise and G.A. Stelter, eds., *The Usable Urban Past* (Toronto: Macmillan of Canada, 1979), 293–96.

26 SLB 99, Shaughnessy to W. Whyte, 7 June 1911, "Personal."

27 SLB 99, Shaughnessy to W. Whyte, 7 June 1911, "Personal," 26 July 1911, to R.B. Bennett, 19 June 1911; SLB 100, Shaughnessy to George Bury, 24 November 1911; P.J. Smith, "Change in a Youthful City: The Case of Calgary, Alberta," *Geography* 56, part I (January 1971): 9–10; Max and Heather Foran, *Calgary: Canada's Frontier Metropolis* (Calgary: Windsor Publications, 1982), 76–7; Voisey, "Urbanization," 85; Bryan P. Melnyk, *Calgary Builds* (Edmonton and Calgary: Alberta Culture/Canadian Plains Research Center, 1985), 23.

28 SLB 90, Shaughnessy to W. Whyte, 2 May 1907; Foran, "The Urban West," 104. The rest of the material in this paragraph is taken from chap. 7.

29 John Gilpin, "Failed Metropolis: The City of Strathcona, 1891–1912," in Alan F.J. Artibise, ed., *Town and City* (Regina: Canadian Plains Research Center, 1981), 273, 285; Voisey, "Urbanization," 85.

30 T.D. Regehr, *The Canadian Northern Railway* (Toronto: Macmillan of Canada, 1976), 165–7; Eric J. Holmgren, "Edmonton's Remarkable High Level Bridge," *Alberta History* 26, no. 1 (Winter 1978): 1.

31 Holmgren, "High Level Bridge," 3.

32 John F. Gilpin, "The City of Strathcona 1891–1912" (Master's thesis, University of Alberta, 1978), 122–9.

33 Holmgren, "High Level Bridge," 4.

34 SLB 89, Shaughnessy to W. Whyte, 9 November 1906.

35 CPR Archives, file 82477, W. Whyte to Shaughnessy, cipher telegram, 15 December 1906; SLB 92, Shaughnessy to W. Whyte, 11 December 1907, "Personal."

36 CRMW, December 1907, 909, 911; Holmgren, "High Level Bridge," 4.

37 SLB 94, Shaughnessy to W. Whyte, 31 March 1909, "Private"; Holmgren, "High Level Bridge," 5–6.

38 Holmgren, "High Level Bridge," 6–8; CRMW, August 1913, 386.

39 Mary Balf, Kamloops: A History of the District up to 1914 (Kamloops: Kamloops Museum Association, 1981), 110, 112; Elsie G. Turnbull, Trail Between Two Wars (Victoria: the author, 1980), 19; Turner, Great Divide, 26.

40 Foran, "The Urban West," 98; Norman Gidney, "From Coal to Forest Products: The Changing Resource Base of Nanaimo, B.C.," Urban History Review 1–78: 32.

41 SLB 72, Shaughnessy to Frederick Buscombe, 16 November 1900, "Personal." Material on Victoria taken from chap. 7.

42 Norbert Macdonald, "Canadian Pacific and Vancouver," 421; Robert McDonald, "Victoria, Vancouver, and ... Economic Development," 377.

43 SLB 71, Shaughnessy to George McLaren Brown, 27 June 1900, "Personal."

44 Robert McDonald, "Victoria, Vancouver, and ... Economic Development," 386.

45 SLB 88, Shaughnessy to W. Whyte, 26 December 1905, "Confidential."

46 Patricia E. Roy, "Railways, Politicians and the Development of the City of Vancouver as a Metropolitan Centre, 1886–1929," (Master's thesis, University of Toronto, 1963), 106–7.

47 Ibid., 126–8, 161.

48 Ibid., 143–5, 161; Turner, Great Divide, 94.

49 Ibid., 93–4; CRMW, June 1914, 252–3.

50 See chap. 7. Material on the 1916 hotel taken from Turner, Great Divide, 94.

51 Ibid., 94.

52 Roy, Vancouver, 68–9, 72; Vancouver City Archives, "Shaughnessy," an unpublished article by Betty Walsh; Kerry Banks, "The Right Side of the Tracks," Western Living (December 1973): 24.

CHAPTER TEN

1 H.A. Innis, *Settlement and the Mining Frontier* (Toronto: Macmillan of Canada, 1936), vol. 9, part 2, *Canadian Frontier of Settlement Series*, 9 vols., eds. W.A. Mackintosh and W.G.L. Joerg, 276; G.W. Taylor, *Mining: The History of Mining in British Columbia* (Saanichton, BC: Hancock House, 1978), 130; John S. Church, "Mining Companies in the West Kootenay and Boundary Regions of British Columbia, 1890–1900" (Master's thesis, University of British Columbia, 1961), 63–4.

2 Elsie G. Turnbull, *Topping's Trail* (Vancouver: Mitchell Press, 1964), 8–16.

3 John Fahey, *Inland Empire: D.C. Corbin and Spokane* (Seattle: University of Washington Press, 1965), 130–1; *CAR*, 1901, 57. The subsidy had been passed by Parliament in 1895.

4 Dorman, 170; Church, "Mining Companies," 154; Ronald H. Meyer, "The Evolution of Railways in the Kootenays" (Master's thesis, University of British Columbia, 1970), 57; Robert E. Cail, *Land, Man, and the Law* (Vancouver: University of British Columbia Press, 1974), 160; Turnbull, *Topping's Trail*, 17–18, 29; *BC Statutes*, 1896, c. 8. If Heinze built a narrow-gauge line the subsidy would have been reduced to 10,240 acres per mile.

5 Fahey, *Inland Empire*, 172.

6 Ibid., 174–6.

7 Ibid., 157–63. The BC line was the Red Mountain Railway; the Washington State line was the Columbia and Red Mountain Railway.

8 Ibid., 176–7; Cail, *Land*, 151, note 3; LP, vol. 55, Petition of F. Augustus Heinze to Governor-in-Council re Columbia and Western Railway, 1 November 1897.

9 VHLB 54, Van Horne Letterbooks, Van Horne to A.G. Blair, 11 November 1897; LP, vol. 57; T.G. Blackstock to Sir Richard Cartwright, 26 November 1897 (copy).

10 VHLB 54, Van Horne to A.S. Dwight, 5 November 1897; Lance H. Whittaker, ed., *Rossland, The Golden City* (Rossland, n.p., 1949), 53; Morgan 1912, 11; Turnbull, *Topping's Trail*, 37. The refinery was the one that had employed J.H. Susman, whom the CPR had hired in 1895.

11 LP, vol. 57, T.G. Blackstock to Sir Richard Cartwright, 2 December 1897 (copy). Blackstock did not specifically mention Aldridge as the source of the CPR estimate, but it seems most likely that he was.

12 Ibid., T.G. Blackstock to Sir Richard Cartwright, 2 December 1897 (copy); Church, "Mining Companies," 116–17.

13 Ibid., T.G. Blackstock to Sir Richard Cartwright, 2 December 1897
(copy); vol. 55, Petition of F. Augustus Heinze to Governor-in-
Council re Columbia and Western Railway, 1 November 1897.

14 Ibid., vol. 57, T.G. Blackstock to Sir Richard Cartwright, 10 December 1897 (copy), to A.G. Blair, 28 December 1897 (copy).

15 Turnbull, *Topping's Trail*, 37–8.

16 LP, vol. 57, T.G. Blackstock to A.G. Blair, 14 December 1897 (copy),
to Sir Richard Cartwright, 4 January 1898; vol. 61, T.G. Blackstock
to Laurier, 7 January 1898; VHLB 54, Van Horne to Lord Strathcona,
28 January 1898, "Personal"; NAC Van Horne to Stephen Letterbook
1894–8, Van Horne to Mount Stephen, 8 February 1898; SLB 60,
Shaughnessy to "General Manager, Bank of Montreal, Montreal," 13
July 1898. The sale agreement was signed on 11 February. The
CPR paid $200,000 for the smelter and $600,000 for the two railway
lines. Heinze also retained his interest in the Trail and Robson
townsites. See Fahey, *Inland Empire*, 181–2; Turnbull, *Topping's Trail*,
32.

17 Van Horne to Stephen Letterbook 1894–1898, Van Horne to Lord
Mount Stephen, 8 February 1898.

18 Dorman, 171; CHCD, 1898, 3554; *Statutes of Canada*, 1898, c. 61.
Hewitt Bostock, the Liberal MP for the BC riding of Yale-Cariboo,
was the sponsor of the bill. The Order-in-Council was P.C. 1894.

19 W. Kaye Lamb, *History of the Canadian Pacific Railway* (New York:
Macmillan, 1977). 207. J. Lorne Mcdougall, *Canadian Pacific: A Brief
History* (Montreal: McGill University Press, 1968), 144, asserts that
the CPR in 1898 "had a smelter, as much by accident as by design,"
while Robert Chodos, *The CPR: A Century of Corporate Welfare* (Toronto: James Lewis & Samuel, 1973), 64, remarks that the CPR's
entry into the mining field "was handed to it on a silver, or rather a
copper, platter."

20 SLB 52, Shaughnessy to Charles H. Lugrin, 16 June 1897.

21 SLB 54, Shaughnessy to Sir Richard Cartwright, 5 October 1897.
The Rossland mine owners suggested that their total output could be
increased to between 1200 and 1500 tons per day. See also SLB 54,
Shaughnessy to T.G. Blackstock, 9 September 1897.

22 VHLB 54, Van Horne to T.G. Shaughnessy, "On train, Kamloops
Section," 19 October 1897, "At Vancouver," 19 October 1897.

23 Lamb, *Canadian Pacific*, 207; Turnbull, *Topping's Trail*, 42; SLB 60,
Shaughnessy to W.H. Aldridge, 23 June 1898, 8 July 1898.

24 Turnbull, *Topping's Trail*, 38–9; SLB 59, Shaughnessy to W.H. Aldridge, 14 May 1898, 26 May 1898, Shaughnessy to Messrs Mann
Foley Brothers & Larsen, "Trail," 8 June 1898; SLB 60, Shaughnessy
to W.H. Aldridge, 13 July 1898, to "General Manager, Bank of

Montreal, Montreal," 13 July 1898; SLB 61, Shaughnessy to John McDougald, 30 July 1898.

25 Turnbull, *Topping's Trail*, 38; SLB 61, Shaughnessy to W.H. Aldridge, 8 August 1898; CPR Archives, file 49723, W.H. Aldridge to Shaughnessy, 2 August 1898.

26 Turnbull, *Topping's Trail*, 39; SLB 60, Shaughnessy to W.H. Aldridge, 13 July 1898; SLB 61, Shaughnessy to W.H. Aldridge, 17 August 1898, "Private"; SLB 64, Shaughnessy to W.H. Aldridge, 6 December 1898, "Personal"; Van Horne to Stephen Letterbook 1894–8, Van Horne to Lord Mount Stephen, 28 October 1898.

27 CPR Archives, file 51059, W.H. Aldridge to Shaughnessy, 3 October 1898; file 55711, W.H. Aldridge to Shaughnessy, 3 May 1899.

28 SLB 64, Shaughnessy to W.H. Aldridge, 6 December 1898, "Personal"; SLB 67, Shaughnessy to W.H. Aldridge, 16 May 1899, "Personal."

29 G.W. Taylor, *Mining*, 147, 165.

30 Church, "Mining Companies," 180–2; SLB 73, Shaughnessy to T.G. Blackstock, 7 February 1901; CPR Archives, file 60627, W.H. Aldridge to Shaughnessy, Toronto, 10 July 1900, North Bay, 11 July 1900. No details of the offer are set forth in Shaughnessy's letter.

31 SLB 74, Shaughnessy to W.H. Aldridge, 19 June 1901; *CAR*, 1901, 56–7.

32 SLB 71, Shaughnessy to Warner Miller, 18 May 1900; SLB 73, Shaughnessy to T.G. Blackstock, 7 February 1901; SLB 74, Shaughnessy to W.H. Aldridge, 19 June 1901; SLB 75, Shaughnessy to Oliver Wethered, 1 October 1901; SLB 76, Shaughnessy to Sir Richard Cartwright, 18 December 1901, "Personal"; Taylor, *Mining*, 147.

33 SLB 76, Shaughnessy to Sir Richard Cartwright, 24 December 1901; McDougall, *Canadian Pacific*, 144–5; Taylor, *Mining*, 147–8. The Aldridge quotation is from Taylor. Taylor's date of 1902 for Betts' commission is incorrect.

34 Taylor, *Mining*, 148; SLB 83, Shaughnessy to W.H. Aldridge, 24 November 1903, 23 February 1904; SLB 85, Shaughnessy to W.H. Aldridge, 12 October 1904, "Confidential," 1 November 1904, to F.H. Brydges, 24 October 1904; SLB 86, Shaughnessy to W.H. Aldridge, 19 December 1904, "Personal"; Elsie G. Turnbull, *Trail Between Two Wars* (Victoria: by the author, 1980), 14. Aldridge's letter to Shaughnessy is quoted in Taylor.

35 SLB 86, Shaughnessy to Thomas Skinner, 20 January 1905.

36 *Monetary Times* (Toronto), 30 June 1905, "Important Mining Sale," 1758; Consolidated Mining and Smelting Company of Canada, *Directors' Annual Report*, 1906; Lamb, *Canadian Pacific*, 260; SLB 86, Shaughnessy to T.G. Blackstock, 15 March 1905, "Private"; SLB 91, "Memorandum For the Third Vice-President," 19 September

1907; McDougall, *Canadian Pacific*, 145–6; "George Gooderham," in W. Stewart Wallace, ed., *The Macmillan Dictionary of Canadian Biography*, 3rd edition (Toronto: Macmillan, 1963), 270.

37 Morgan 1912, 743; Consolidated Mining and Smelting Company of Canada, *Directors' Annual Report*, 1919; NAC, Shaughnessy Papers, vol. 2, "Memoranda re Canadian Railway Problems," which has a list of CPR directors from 1881 to 1923.

38 SLB 86, Shaughnessy to R.R. Jamieson, 23 March 1905; SLB 88, Shaughnessy to E.S. Clouston, 27 November 1905, to W.D. Matthews, 30 November 1905, "Private"; *CAR*, 1905, 548–9.

39 SLB 86, Shaughnessy to H. Robertson, 14 February 1905, "Personal," to R. Marpole, 21 February 1905, "Private"; SLB 89, Shaughnessy to R. Marpole, 10 October 1906, "Personal," to H. Robertson, 20 October 1906; Lamb, *Canadian Pacific*, 260.

40 McDougall, *Canadian Pacific*, 146; Lamb, *Canadian Pacific*, 260; Consolidated Mining and Smelting Company of Canada, *Directors' Annual Report*, 1914; Turnbull, *Trail*, 15; SLB 99, Shaughnessy to W.D. Matthews, 26 May, 31 May 1911; PABC, Premiers' Papers, vol. 98, file 5, W.H. Aldridge to Richard McBride, Trail, 30 September 1909, "Private"; GAI, CPR Papers, vol. 198, file 1954, W.H. Aldridge to J.M. Mackie, 25 June 1910 (copy).

41 Lamb, *Canadian Pacific*, 260; McDougall, *Canadian Pacific*, 146–7; *Who's Who in Canada*, 1921, 259; Turnbull, *Trail*, chap. 1.

42 A.A. den Otter, "Bondage of Steam: The CPR and Western Canadian Coal," in Hugh A. Dempsey, ed., *The CPR West* (Vancouver: Douglas & McIntyre, 1984), 192–3.

43 den Otter, "Bondage of Steam," 193; A.A. den Otter, *Civilizing the West* (Edmonton: University of Alberta Press, 1982), 122.

44 den Otter, "Bondage of Steam," 194.

45 SLB 80, Shaughnessy to W. Whyte, 11 February 1903; SLB 86, Shaughnessy to W. Whyte, 10 February 1905.

46 SLB 82, Shaughnessy to W. Whyte, 4 July 1903, Circular letter, Office of the President, 4 July 1903.

47 SLB 81, Shaughnessy to A.H. Reeder, 4 June 1903, to W. Whyte, 8 June 1903; SLB 82, Shaughnessy to James W. Ellsworth, 11 September 1903, to W.H. Aldridge, 6 October 1903, "Personal," 11 October 1903, "Personal."

48 den Otter, "Bondage of Steam," 198–9; SLB 85, Shaughnessy to W.H. Aldridge, 30 August 1904, "Personal"; SLB 88, Shaughnessy to Aldridge, 21 May 1906, "Private"; SLB 92, Shaughnessy to Aldridge, 12 June 1908, "Private"; SLB 93, Shaughnessy to Aldridge, 6 July 1908, "Personal"; SLB 94, Shaughnessy to Aldridge, 6 March 1909, "Private"; John Murray Gibbon, *Steel of Empire* (New York: Bobbs-Merrill, 1935), 360.

49 H. Leslie Brown, "The Pass: Biography of a District, Renewed, and a Town Long Gone" (unpublished manuscript, 1977), 41, 254. The Order-in-Council was P.C. 664. The government chose 5,000 acres just south of Michel and 45,000 acres in the Second Government Reserve.

50 den Otter, "Bondage of Steam," 199; Lamb, *Canadian Pacific*, 259; SLB 92, Shaughnessy to W.H. Aldridge, 22 March 1908; SLB 93, Shaughnessy to D.R. Wilkie, 1 July 1908, "Personal"; SLB 96, Shaughnessy to W.D. Matthews, 27 August 1909, "Private."

51 den Otter, "Bondage of Steam," 19.

52 Chester Martin, *"Dominion Lands" Policy*, ed. Lewis H. Thomas (Toronto: McClelland and Stewart, 1973), 64; David H. Breen, "The CPR and Western Petroleum, 1904–24," in Dempsey, ed., *The CPR West*, 229.

53 Ibid., 230–1; SLB 87, Shaughnessy to Alex M. Hay, 22 July 1905, to W. Whyte, 24 August 1905; SLB 97, Shaughnessy to W. Whyte, 30 June 1910.

54 Breen, "Western Petroleum," 230–1; Morgan 1912, 260.

55 Breen, "Western Petroleum," 231.

56 Ibid., 232; SLB 96, Shaughnessy to W. Whyte, 22 November 1909.

57 SLB 98, Shaughnessy to W. Whyte, 19 September 1910; Norman R. Hacking and W. Kaye Lamb, *The Princess Story* (Vancouver: Mitchell Press, 1974), 227–8.

58 Breen, "Western Petroleum," 233–4.

59 Ibid., 234.

60 Cail, *Land*, 137–8, 150–1.

61 Ibid., 159; Dorman, 58; SLB 75, Shaughnessy to George McLaren Brown, 8 October 1901; *BC Statutes*, 1890, c. 41; 1893, c. 36; 1896, c. 8.

62 Lamb, *Canadian Pacific*, 257; Cail, *Land*, 106. The Columbia and Western grant does not include 543,312 acres that were earned by F.A. Heinze building the lines from Rossland to Trail and Trail to Robson. See GAI, CPR Papers, vol. 231, file 2248, J.S. Dennis to W. Whyte, 26 November 1903 (copy).

63 The Columbia and Western is discussed in chap. 2, the VV&E in chap. 6. See also: Martin Robin, *The Rush for Spoils: The Company Province 1871–1933* (Toronto: McClelland and Stewart, 1972), 96–7.

64 *CAR*, 1906, 490; GAI, CPR Papers, vol. 224, file 2181, J.S. Dennis to Sir Thomas Shaughnessy, 13, 16 January 1906, "Private & Confidential" (copies); J.S. Dennis to "The President, Montreal," 19 January 1906, telegram (copy).

65 *CAR*, 1906, 489–92; Brian R.D. Smith, "Sir Richard McBride: A Study in the Conservative Party of British Columbia" (Master's thesis, Queen's University, 1959), 47; *BC Statutes*, 1906, c. 9; GAI, CPR

Papers, vol. 224, file 2181, J.S. Dennis to Sir Thomas Shaughnessy, 19 January 1906, "Private," 9 March 1906, "Private" (copies), to W. Whyte, 3 February, 20 March 1906, "Private & Confidential" (copies).

66 SLB 80, Shaughnessy to W.H. Aldridge, 11 February 1903, "Private"; SLB 94, Shaughnessy to R. Marpole, 23 December 1908, "Private"; Pearce Papers, series 7, file 3–12, circular, CPR Land Department, dated 29 December 1902 and signed by F.T. Griffin and W. Whyte; SLB 95, Shaughnessy to J.S. Dennis, 30 April 1909, "Personal"; James B. Hedges, *Building the Canadian West* (New York: Macmillan, 1939), 257.

67 GAI, CPR Papers, vol. 231, file 2248, J.S. Dennis to W. Whyte, 4 November 1903 (copy), W. Whyte to R. McBride, 17 November 1903 (copy), Extract from Board Minutes of British Columbia Southern Railway, 7 January 1904, W.S. Gore to J.S. Dennis, 28 April 1904, T.G. Shaughnessy to J.S. Dennis, 8 May 1907, "Personal."

68 Lamb, *Canadian Pacific*, 258; SLB 95, Shaughnessy to J.S. Dennis, 30 April 1909, "Personal"; SLB 97, Shaughnessy to R. Marpole, 17 May 1910, "Private," to J.S. Dennis, 17 May 1910, "Private"; CPR, *Annual Report*, 1912; Cail, *Land*, 106.

69 Lamb, *Canadian Pacific*, 258; SLB 87, Shaughnessy to J.S. Dennis, 21 June 1905, "Private," to W. Whyte, 23 August 1905.

70 SLB 88, Shaughnessy to W. Whyte, 17 November 1905, "Confidential"; SLB 89, Shaughnessy to Lord Grey, 31 October 1906; Victoria *Colonist*, 8 July 1905, "Plans of the C.P.R."

71 SLB 89, Shaughnessy to J.S. Dennis, 2 November 1906; SLB 90, Shaughnessy to Dennis, 5 December 1906, "Personal"; Lamb, *Canadian Pacific*, 258.

72 *BC Statutes*, 1912, c. 33.

CHAPTER ELEVEN

1 Max Foran, "The CPR and the Urban West, 1881–1930," in Hugh Dempsey, ed., *The CPR West* (Vancouver: Douglas & McIntyre, 1984), 90.

2 John S. Galbraith, "Land Policies of the Hudson's Bay Company, 1870–1913," CHR 32 (1951), 21.

3 Renie Gross and Lea Nicoll Kramer, *Tapping the Bow* (Brooks, Alberta: Eastern Irrigation District, 1985), 15.

4 The title of Dempsey's work cited in footnote 1.

Index

Abbott, Harry, 25, 29, 108, 214
Abbott, Sir John, 17
Aikins, J.A.M., 83, 154
Alberta and Great Waterways Railways scandal, 227
Alberta and Saskatchewan Colonization Company, 186
Alberta Central Land Corporation, 186
Alberta Irrigation Company, 191–2
Alberta Railway and Coal Company (AR&C CO), 27, 34, 48
Alberta Railway and Irrigation Company (AR&I CO), 118, 181, 192, 195, 198, 202–3, 209, 248–9
Aldridge, Walter H., 119, 123, 234–5, 237–44, 246–8, 263
Alien Labour Act (1897), 56
American Smelting and Refining Company, 240
Ames, A.E., 115
Anderson, George G., 192, 195
Anglo-Persian Oil Company, 249
Angus, Richard B., 9, 18, 19, 20, 53, 158, 178

AR&C CO. *See* Alberta Railway and Coal Company
AR&I CO. *See* Alberta Railway and Irrigation Company
Arrowhead Branch (CPR), 29, 37
Ashdown, James H., 43, 218
Aylesworth, A.B., 100

Baker, Archer, 14
Baker, James, 34, 44, 54–5
Baker, Walter R., 21, 22, 74, 76, 77, 80, 244
Bank of Montreal, 18, 19
Bannatyne, A.G.B., 218
Barnard, Harry, 159–60
Barney and Smith Company, 149
Barrott, Blackader and Webster, 230
Bassano Dam, 201–2
Bassett, W.I., 131
"Battle of Midway," 129
Battleford, 220
Bedlington and Nelson Railway Company, 67
Beiseker, T.L., 198, 199–200
Beisker, Davidson, and Martin, land purchase by, 185–6
Bennett, R.B., 205

Benoit, A.V., 83
Betts, A.G., 241
Betts patent, 241
Betts process, 263
Bill to Amend the VV&E Charter (Bill 139, 1905), 127–8
Blackstock, T.G., 235, 240, 242
Blackstone, Timothy, 6
Blair, Andrew G., 33–4, 36, 37–8, 39, 41, 42, 44, 46, 52, 65, 90–1, 98, 117–8, 234, 235
Blake, Edward, 32
Blaylock, Selwyn G., 244–5
Board of Railway Commissioners, 86, 99, 137, 223, 226, 229
Bodwell, Ernest V., 63
Borden, Robert L., 94–5, 96, 97, 100, 104, 146
Bostock, Hewitt, 35, 55, 62–3
Bosworth, George M., 72
Boulton, Charles A., 67
Boundary Creek district (Boundary district), 39, 50, 61, 62, 64, 65, 66, 109, 112, 114, 116, 120, 127, 130, 137, 229, 233, 239, 244, 259, 260, 263
Boundary Creek Mining and Commercial Association, 63

Bowell, Sir MacKenzie,
18, 31–2, 96
Bow River Scheme,
189–94. *See also* Irriga-
tion block
Branch lines in the prai-
rie West (CPR), 74–5,
101–12, 103–6, 179–80,
260
Brandon, 220–1
Bray, Edward, 44
Breen, James, 233
British Columbia Copper
Company, 240
British Columbia Devel-
opment Company, 256
British Columbia Land
and Timber Agent, CPR,
(Vancouver), 254
British Columbia Lumber
Company, 255
British Columbia South-
ern Railway, 40, 43–5,
48, 50, 115–16, 252
Browning, J.B., 215–16
Burgess, A.M., 190
Bury, George J., 103,
104–5, 145, 202, 260

Calgary, 168, 202, 221,
224–5, 262
Calgary and Edmonton
Land Company, 180
Calgary and Edmonton
Railway (C&E), 86, 95,
180, 225
Calgary Natural Gas
Company, 250, 251
Calgary Petroleum Prod-
ucts Company, 252
Calgary Power Company,
224
Cambie, H.J., 126, 214
Cameron, John, 32
Campbell, Hardy W., 210
Canada Central Railway,
21
Canada North-West Land
Company, 177–8, 186,
220
Canadian-American Land
Company, 186

Canadian National Rail-
ways, 229
Canadian Northern
Agreement. *See* Mani-
toba Agreement (1901)
Canadian Northern
Pacific, 137, 142
Canadian Northern Rail-
way, 71, 77, 78, 79,
85–6, 87, 90, 98, 120,
132, 134, 141, 224, 226,
258–9, 260
Canadian Pacific Irriga-
tion Company (CPIC),
198–200
Canadian Pacific Naviga-
tion Company (CPN),
156–9, 227–8
C&E. *See* Calgary and Ed-
monton Railway
Caron, Sir Adolphe, 65
Carter-Cotton, Francis,
113–14, 124, 126, 130,
254
Cartwright, Sir Richard,
46–7, 65, 93, 237
Carry, Henry, 131
Cassils, John, 81
Castle, C.C., 83
Château Laurier
(Ottawa), 168
Chicago and Alton Rail-
road, 6, 7, 11
Chicago, Milwaukee and
St Paul Railway. *See* Mil-
waukee Road
Chipman, Clarence, 157,
197, 201
Clark, George M., 190,
195, 237
Clarke, E.F., 96
CM&S. *See* Consolidated
Mining and Smelting
Company of Canada
Coast Cities Case, 229
Coal mining, 245, 263;
in Alberta, 123, 202,
245–6, 246–9, 263; in
BC, 43, 48, 55, 115–20,
123, 126–7, 136, 140,
239, 246–8, 259; in
Manitoba 70; in

Saskatchewan 106.
See also Mining
Cochran, Annie. *See*
Osler, Annie
Columbia and Kootenay
Railway and Navigation
Company (Columbia
and Kootenay), 25, 29,
31, 37, 158, 160, 236,
252
Columbia and Red
Mountain Railway, 62,
67, 234
Columbia and Western
Railway, 61, 62, 65, 66,
109, 120–1, 124, 161,
233, 234, 235, 236,
252–4, 259
Columbia and Western
Railway Bill (1898), 236
Columbia and Western
Railway Land Grant Bill
(1906), 253–4
Connaught (Rogers Pass)
Tunnel, 144–6, 260–1
Consolidated Mining and
Smelting Company of
Canada (CM&S), 243–5
Coquitlam freight yards,
230
Corbin, Daniel C., 24, 25,
50, 61–2, 63, 67, 130,
138–40, 233–4, 236
Coste, Eugene, 249–51
Cox, George A., 42, 115,
117
CPIC. *See* Canadian Pacific
Irrigation Company
CPN. *See* Canadian Pacific
Navigation Company
Cranbrook, 54–5
Creelman, A.R., 21, 119,
141, 193
"Crop payment plan,"
205–6
Crow's Nest and
Kootenay Lake Railway
Company, 43–5
Crow's Nest Pass
Agreement (1897),
xi, 44–9, 116, 211,
229, 258

Crow's Nest Pass Coal
Company, 48, 111,
115–20, 140, 239, 246,
259
Crow's Nest Pass Railway,
23, 27, 31–45, chap. 3,
passim, 69, 191, 224,
235, 239, 258–9
Crow's Nest Southern
Railway, 116–9
Curties, G.D., 167
Cuthbert, A. Ross, 58–9
Cuthbert, Herbert, 161

Davick, M., 230
Davidson, C.H., 198,
199–200
Davies, Louis, 41
Dawson, A.S., 201
Dayman, Peter, 82, 83
Deane, R. Burton, 59
de Lotbinière, Sir Henri
Joly, 65
Demonstration farms,
210–11
Dennis, John Stoughton,
Jr, 123–4, 126, 130, 141,
191, 193–4, 195–6,
198–200, 202–3, 204,
205, 207, 210, 246, 250,
253, 254–6, 256–7, 262
Dennis, John Stoughton,
Sr, 187, 195
Department of Natural
Resources, CPR, (Cal-
gary), 203–4, 210–11,
249, 254, 262
Dewdney, Edgar, 221
Dingman, A.W., 250
Dobell, Richard, 65
Doupe, Jacob L., 190
Driard House (Victoria),
161
Drinkwater, Charles, 20,
21, 79, 98, 177, 183,
190, 195
Drummond, George A.,
15
Dry farming, 209–10
Duke of Connaught, 145
Dunsmuir, Alexander,
140

Dunsmuir, James,
111–12, 114, 140, 141,
142, 254
Dunsmuir, Robert, 140
Dupont, Charles, 62
Dwight, Arthur, 234

E&N. *See* Esquimalt and
Nanaimo Railway
East Kootenays, 34, 36,
42, 44, 48, 54–5, 119,
120, 127, 138, 239, 244,
259
Easton, Jason, 7, 8
Eberts, D.M., 114
Edgar, James D., 32–4
Edmonton, 86, 98, 220,
225–7, 262
Edmonton Board of
Trade, 226
Edmonton City Council,
226
Edmonton, Yukon and
Pacific Railway, 86, 225
Election campaign (1912),
135
Elections (federal):
(1981), 15–17; (1986),
33, 75; (1904), 96–7;
(1911), 16–17
Elections (provincial): BC,
(1907), 132; (1909),
132–3; (1912), 135;
Manitoba, (1886), 70;
(1892), 70; (1899), 75
Ellingwood, F.L., 169
Elliott, W.J., 210–11
Emmerson, H.R., 101
Empress of Japan, 17
Englehart, J.L., 89
Esquimalt and Nanaimo
Railway (E&N), 112,
140–3, 227, 252, 254–5;
aid from federal govern-
ment, 142

Federal Mining and
Smelting, 244
Fernie, William, 44
Fielding, W.S., 21, 65, 91,
240
Fitzpatrick, Charles, 65,

82
Flavelle, J.W., 115
Fleming, Sandford, 216,
220
Foley Bros., Welch and
Stewart, 145
Foley, Timothy, 135
Fort Garry Hotel (Winni-
peg), 168
Fort Macleod, 27, 44, 53,
86
Fort Steele, 54–6
Fort William, 3, 97,
106–7, 219–20, 260
Foster, Sir George, 104,
128
Fraser, J.S.C., 236
Freight rates, 33, 35, 37,
39–45, 64, 69–70, 71,
74, 75, 77–9, 86, 97,
112, 116, 120, 139,
218–9, 222–4, 229, 235,
237, 258–9. *See also*
Crow's Nest Pass Agree-
ment, Manitoba
Agreement
Fulton, F.J., 132–3

Galt, Sir Alexander, 27,
245
Galt, Elliot, 27, 195, 198
Gilman, L.C., 137
GN. *See* Great Northern
Railroad
Gooderham, George, 235,
242
Gordon, Stewart, 167
Gordon, Mrs Stewart, 167
Government ownership
of railways, 75–6, 79, 96,
97
Grain blockade: (1901),
80–1; (1911), 104
Graham, George P., 102
Grain elevators (CPR)
106–7, 229
Granby Consolidated
Mining and Smelting
Company, 120, 239–40
Grand Forks Board of
Trade, 63
Grand Trunk Pacific

Branch Lines Company Incorporation Bill (1906), 100–1
Grand Trunk Pacific Railway (GTPR), 85–6, 87, 88–94, 97, 98, 120, 134, 224, 258, 260
Grand Trunk Pacific Railway Incorporation Bill (1903), 94
Grand Trunk Railway of Canada (GTR), 5, 14, 20, 88–9, 92, 93
Graves, J.P., 120
Great Northern Railroad (GN), 20, 27, 28–9, 37, 66, 67, chap. 6, *passim*, 112, 139, 246, 258, 259; links with Crow's Nest Pass Coal Company, 116–19; links with Granby Consolidated Mining and Smelting Company, 120
Great North West Central Railway, 76, 180, 184
Great Northern Railway (Great Britain), 20
Great West Land Company, 186
Green, R.F., 124, 254
Green, S.M., 81
Greenway, Thomas, 70, 74–5
Griffin, Frederick T., 99, 175, 185, 193, 197, 201, 203, 206
GTPR. *See* Grand Trunk Pacific Railway
GTR. *See* Grand Trunk Railway of Canada
Gutelius, Frederick P., 61, 62, 66, 84, 144

Haggart, John, 31–2
Hall, Grant, 146, 103
Hall brothers, 23
Ham, George, 167
Hamilton, Lauchlan A., 175, 191, 214, 215
Hammond, H.C., 19
Haney, Michael J., 51–2,

55, 57, 59
Haslam, J. Heber, 186
Hays, Charles Melville, 89–90, 91, 93, 95, 100
Hayward, Charles, 160
HBC. *See* Hudson's Bay Company
Heinze, F. Augustus, 50, 61–2, 232–6
Henderson, David, 47, 101, 128
Herchmer, Lawrence W., 59
High Level Bridge (Edmonton), 226–7, 262
Hill, James J., 7, 8, 18, 19, 50, 67, 85, 137, 246, 259–60; relations with Shaughnessy and the CPR, chap. 6, *passim*; Vancouver speech (1905), 129. *See also* Great Northern Railroad, James N. Hill, Louis W. Hill
Hill, James N., 115
Hill, Louis W., 127
Holland, Tracy, 114
Holt, Herbert, 20
Hopkins, G.B., 82
Hosmer, Charles R., 243
Hotels, 153, 159, 160, 168
Hotels (CPR), chap. 7, *passim*, 261; Banff Springs Hotel, 150–1, 170–1, 261; Château Frontenac (Quebec City), 152, 153, 163, 164, 165; Château Lake Louise, 151, 169–71, 261; Empress Hotel (Victoria), 141, 159–68, 228, 261; Fraser Canyon House, 149; Glacier House, 149, 150, 170–1, 261; Hotel Sicamous, 171; Hotel Vancouver, 151, 152, 153, 159, 215, 261; Mount Stephen House (Field, BC), 149, 150, 170–1, 261; Palliser Hotel (Calgary), 152,

168–9, 225, 261; Place Viger Hotel (Montreal), 165; Revelstoke Hotel, 171; Royal Alexandra Hotel (Winnipeg), 74–5, 152, 153–6, 166, 222
Hudson's Bay Company (HBC), 18, 156–7, 217, 220, 262
Humphreys, J.W., 44
H.W. McNeill and Company, 245–6

Illinois Central Railway, 5
Intercolonial Railway (ICR), 90, 94–5
Irrigation block (CPR), 187, 194–8, 196–202, 204, 205–7, 210–11, 224, 262. *See also* Bow River Scheme
Irving, John, 158

Jaffray, Robert, 115, 117
Jamieson, R.W., 59
Japan, 229
J.P. Morgan and Company, 67

Kamloops, 227
Kansas City Smelting and Refining Company, 30
Kaslo and Slocan Railway, 29, 66, 67, 109
Ker, David R., 160–2
Kerr, James, 126
Kettle River Valley Railway (KRVR), 62, 114–15, 130, 259; aid from Laurier government, 133; aid from McBride government, 132–3; change of name (1911), 134; construction, 134
Kettle River Valley Railway Bill (1898), 62–5
Kettle Valley Railway (KVR), 134, 259–60; aid from BC government, 135; aid from federal government, 135; conflict with VV&E, 136–7;

construction, 134–6, 137–8
Kingston Locomotive Works, 84
Kittson, Norman, 7, 18
Knight, Jesse, 209
Knight Sugar Factory, 209
Kootenay Central Railway, 56, 143
Kootenay district, 23, 24, 25, 27, 29, 30, 33, 35, 36, 38, 137, 228–9, 240, 258, 260, 263. See also East Kootenays and West Kootenays
KRVR. See Kettle River Valley Railway
KVR. See Kettle Valley Railway

Labour, 14, 56–7, 80–1, 215, 219, 222, 225, 227; shortage of construction workers in BC, 134–5; treatment of, on construction of Crow's Nest Pass Railway, 57–61
Lancaster, E.A., 101
Land and Colonization Department, CPR, (Calgary), 199, 202–3
Land Department, CPR, (Winnipeg), 175–6, 178, 180, 187, 203, 212, 262
Land grants (CPR), 40, 43, 44, 45, 173–4, 178, 214, 224, 252–7
Land grants (HBC), 174, 189, 193; in Irrigation block, 196–8
Land grants cancelled (CPR), 208–9
Land policies (CPR), chap. 8, passim, 211–12, 262
Land sales (CPR), 177, 178, 184, 198–201, 204, 205–6, 208, 211–12, 216, 255–7, 262
La Presse affair, 96
Lash, Zebulon A., 71
Laurier, Sir Wilfrid, xi,

15, 33–4, 41, 44, 55, 64–5, 72, 82, 87, 89, 90–1, 94, 97, 98–9, 100, 117–18, 128
Leach, W.F., 248
Lead pipe manufacturing, 241–2, 263
Lead refinery (Trail), 240–1, 263
Leonard, James W., 64, 80, 84–5
Le Roi Mining Company, 61, 233, 242, 243
Le Roi Mining and Smelting Company, 233–4
Lethbridge, 31, 245
Lethbridge Collieries, 249
Lindsey, George, 119
Lister, James, 47
"Loan farm," 207, 262
Loss, C.E., 124, 126
Lumsden, Hugh, 51, 52, 53
Luse Land Company of St Paul, 186
Lyall, Peter. See Peter Lyall and Sons
Lynch, F.B., 186
Lyon, Stewart, 41

McBride, Richard, 121, 122, 124, 126, 130, 131–3, 136, 137, 140–1, 142, 143, 253–4
McCandless, Alexander C., 161–3
McCulloch, Andrew, 133
Macdonald, Hugh John, 75–6, 77
McDonald, McMillan and Company, 98
Macdonald, Sir John A., 13, 17, 20, 25–6, 31
Macdonald Hotel (Edmonton), 168
MacFarlane. See Ross and MacFarlane
McHenry (chief engineer, CPR), 85
MacInnes, Donald, 67
McInnes, W.W.B., 35, 47–8, 63

McIntyre, Duncan, 9
Mackenzie, Alexander, 216
Mackenzie, William, 41, 71, 79–80, 86, 90, 111, 112, 142, 225. See also Donald Mann
Mackenzie Mann and Company, 71
McLean brothers, 111
MacLean, M.A., 214
Macleod. See Fort Macleod
Macleod, Malcolm, 53
McNicoll, David, 20, 21, 72, 84–5, 148, 152, 160
Macpherson, T.H., 67
McRae, A.D., 231
McTavish, J.H., 175
Magrath, Charles, 195
Mallory, James A., 12
Manitoba Agreement (with the Canadian Northern Railway, 1901), 78–9, 222–3
Manitoba and North Western Railway Company of Canada, 21, 74, 76, 180, 184
Manitoba Grain Act (1900), 82–3; (1902), 83, 85
Manitoba Land and Immigration Agent, CPR, (Winnipeg), 203
Manitoba Road (St Paul, Minneapolis and Manitoba Railroad), 7, 18, 19
Manitoba Southwestern Railway, 184
Manitoba South Western Colonization Railway, 176, 179
Mann, Donald, 41, 71, 79–80, 86, 90, 111, 112, 135, 142, 225. See also William Mackenzie
Mann, Foley and Larsen, 65
Mara, John A., 160–1
Marpole, Richard, 22,

108, 141, 142, 160, 166, 230, 244, 254
Marquis of Lorne, 21
Matson, J.S.H., 167
Matthews, Wilmot D., 78, 193–4, 242–3
Maxwell, Edward, 154, 155, 156
Maxwell, William Sutherland, 154, 155, 156, 169
Mead, Elwood, 196
Medicine Hat, 224, 249–50
Mellen, C.S., 75, 77
Merrill, S.S., 7
Merritt, William Hamilton, 124
Michigan Central Railway, 6
Midway and Vernon Railway, 132
Mills, David, 65
Milwaukee, 9, 10, 11
Milwaukee Road (also known as Chicago, Milwaukee and St Paul Railway), 5, 7, 10, 11, 12
Miner, S.H.C., 120
Mineral rights on CPR lands, 249–52
Mines, 23. See also coal mining
Mining: in BC, 23–5, 29, 30–1, 36, 37, 42, 46, 50, 61–2, 66, 109, 114, 116–17, 120, 232, 236–7, 239, 242–5, 244–5, 258–9, 263; in US, 24, 46, 109–10, 112
Minto, Lord, 90
Mitchell, Alexander, 10
Mitchell, John J., 6
Montreal Board of Trade, 64
Moody, Harry, 69
Moose Jaw, 221, 223
Moose Jaw Board of Trade, 223
Morse, Frank W., 97, 99–100
Motherwell, W.R., 82, 83
Mount Stephen, Lord. See George Stephen
Mowat, Sir Oliver, 41, 42
Muckleston, B., 201–2
Mulock, William, 41, 95

Nagle, Elizabeth Bridget. See Elizabeth Bridget Shaughnessy
Naismith, P.L., 202–3, 249
Nakusp and Slocan Railway, 29, 37, 67, 228
Nakusp and Slocan Railway Company Bill (1898), 67–8
Nanaimo, 227, 246
Nanton, Augustus, 74, 86
National Transcontinental Railway (NTR), 88, 92
National Transcontinental Railway Bill (1903), 91–2, 94–6
National Transcontinental Railway Amendment Bill (1904), 91–2
Natural gas, 249–52
Nelson and Fort Sheppard Railway, 25, 37, 67, 110
New Westminster Southern Railway, 127
Nicola Branch (CPR), 126–7
Nicola, Kamloops and Similkameen Coal and Railway Company (NK&S), 123–4, 126, 247–8
Nicola Valley Coal and Coke Company, 127, 248
Nicola Valley Lumber Company, 127
NK&S. See Nicola, Kamloops and Similkameen Coal and Railway Company
Norquay, John, 69–70
North Western Coal and Navigation Company, 245
Northern Pacific and

Manitoba Railway, 70, 77–8, 79
Northern Pacific Railroad (NP), 12, 24, 25, 67, 69, 70, 75, 76, 77, 78, 110, 139, 173, 205
Northwest Colonization Company, 186
North-West Irrigation Act (1894), 190
North-West Mounted Police, 58
NP. See Northern Pacific Railroad

Ogden, Isaac G., 72, 225
Ogden Shops (Calgary), 202, 224–5
Ogilvie, W.W., 53
Okanagan district, 112, 122
O'Leary, Frederick J., 155, 166
Oliver, Frank, 41, 47–8, 192–3
Onderdonk, Andrew, 51
Ontario and Quebec Railway, 19, 74
Ontario and Saskatchewan Land Corporation, 186
Oregon Railway and Navigation Company, 139, 158
Osler, Annie, 19
Osler, Edmund Boyd, 19, 20, 53, 86, 95, 177, 178, 193–4, 242–3

Pacific Great Eastern Railway, 135
Painter, Walter S., 153, 166, 168, 170–1
Panama Canal, 229, 261
Parkinson, Percy, 167
Partridge, H.O., 83
Passenger rates, 112
Passenger service (CPR), 148, 159, 171–2
Paterson, William, 65
Pearce, John, 165
Pearce, William, 187–95,

248, 262
Pellatt, Henry M., 19, 115
Pembina Branch, 217
Peter Lyall and Sons
    (contractors), 155, 165,
    169
Peterson, Charles,
    199–200
Peterson, P.A., 66, 191
Peterson, W., 53
Petroleum, 249–52
Port Arthur, 219–20
Port Moody, 3, 24,
    214–15
Portage la Prairie, 223
Power, Lawrence, 67
Prairie Fuel Gas Com-
    pany, 251
Price, Bruce, 150, 152
Prince Albert, 220
Pringle, R.A., 100–1
Pullman Palace Car Com-
    pany, 149

Qu'Appelle, Long Lake
    and Saskatchewan Rail-
    way, 86–7, 95

Rattenbury, Francis Maw-
    son, 152, 153, 160–7,
    169–71
Ready-made farm policy,
    206–7, 262
Red Mountain Railway,
    67
Reed, Hayter, 163–8
Reed, Kate, 156, 163–4,
    166–7, 171
Reeder, A.H., 247
Regina, 86, 220–1, 223
Regina Board of Trade,
    223
Regina Board of Trade
    Case, 223
Republic and Kettle River
    Railway, 114–15
Revelstoke, 24, 25, 29, 37
Richards, Mary, 5
Richardson, Robert L., 79
Robertson, John Ross, 47
Robertson, O.A., 186
Robinson, John Moore,

122
Roblin, Rodmond P.,
    77–8
Rogers, Elias, 115,
    117–18
Rogers, Robert, 135
Ross, Duncan, 128
Ross and MacFarlane
    (architects), 168
Rossland Liberal Asso-
    ciation, 63
Royal Commission on the
    Treatment of Labourers
    on the Crow's Nest Rail-
    way, 60
Royal Tour (1901), 80, 81
Russell, David, 96
Russell, Lindsay, 188
Rutherford, Alexander
    C., 226–7
Rutherford, John G., 211

St Louis, Kansas City and
    Northern Railroad, 6
St Paul and Pacific Rail-
    road, 173–4
St Paul, Minneapolis and
    Manitoba Railroad. See
    Manitoba Road
Salvation Army, 206
Saskatoon, 86, 99, 100,
    101
Sayre, A.J., 198
Scarth, William B., 177
Schwitzer, J.E., 133, 144
Scott, R.W., 48
Scott, Walter, 95, 104–5
Selkirk, 216, 218
Semlin, Charles, 111
SF&N. See Spokane Falls
    and Northern Railroad
Shatford, L.W., 136
Shaughnessy, Alice
    (daughter of Thomas
    George and Elizabeth
    Bridget), 11
Shaughnessy, Elizabeth
    Bridget (wife of Thomas
    George Shaughnessy),
    11, 13, 81
"Shaughnessy Heights"
    (Vancouver), 230–1

Shaughnessy, Lord. See
    Thomas George
    Shaughnessy
Shaughnessy, Marguerite
    (daughter of Thomas
    George and Elizabeth
    Bridget), 17
Shaughnessy, Mary
    (mother of Thomas
    George), 9
Shaughnessy Settlement
    Act (1914), 231
Shaughnessy, Sir
    Thomas. See Thomas
    George Shaughnessy
Shaughnessy, Thomas, Sr
    (father of Thomas
    George), 9, 10
Shaughnessy, Thomas
    George (later Lord
    Shaughnessy), xi, 4, 5,
    12, 13, 14, 15, 17, 18,
    19, 20, 21, 22, 27, 29–
    31, 52, 55, 65, 66, 69,
    73, 76, 77–80, 80–1, 82,
    83, 84–5, 86, 87, 95,
    102, 104, 108, 121, 127,
    128, 132, 144, 151, 152,
    153, 154, 155, 157, 178,
    184, 202, 205, 206, 211,
    222, 224, 226, 228, 229,
    231, 234–5, 243–4, 254,
    256–7; alliance with
    D.C. Corbin, 138–40;
    and 1891 federal elec-
    tion, 15–16; and 1904
    federal election, 96–8;
    and 1911 federal elec-
    tion, 16, 17; appointed
    president of CPR, 72–3;
    Bow River Scheme, 192–
    5; BC agriculture, 122–3,
    126, 256; BC lumber in-
    dustry, 123; career in
    Milwaukee politics, 10–
    11; coal for CPR opera-
    tions, 123–4, 126–7,
    246–8; conflict with
    GTPR, 92–6, 98–9; CPR
    career 1882–96, 14, 15,
    17, 18; CPR hotels, chap.
    7, passim, 261; CPR

steamship service on Pacific coast, 156–9; Crow's Nest Pass Railway negotiations, 31–44; double-tracking program, 102, 121, 146, 260; early life, 9–10; favours acquisition of Trail smelter, 236–7; government ownership of railways, 76, 97; Irrigation block (CPR), 195–202; knighthood, 81–2; marriage, 11; mineral rights on prairie lands, 249–52; negotiations for Empress Hotel, 160–3; oil as fuel for CPR Pacific coastal steamers, 249, 251; prairie branch-line construction, 74–5, 103, 104–6, 121, 260; railway career in US, 10, 11; relations with Crow's Nest Pass Coal Company, 117–19; relations with J.J. Hill and the GN, chap. 6, passim; support for KRVR, 130–1, 133; support for KVR, 138; takeover of E&N, 140–1, 143; Trail smelter policies, 237–43, 263; treatment of construction workers on Crow's Nest Pass Railway, 57, 59, 60–1; views on Kootenay Central Railway, 142–3

Shipping (CPR), 148, 151, 156, 213–14, 215, 228, 229–30, 262. See also Canadian Pacific Navigation Company (CPN)

Shuswap and Okanagan Railway, 122, 134, 171

Sifton, Arthur L., 227

Sifton, Sir Clifford, 38–41, 42–3, 48, 56, 65, 80, 82, 89, 90, 96, 117–18, 119, 182, 183–4, 191, 193, 194–5, 221, 235, 248

Similkameen district, 126

Skene, J.L., 166

Skinner, Sir Thomas, 178

Slocan district, 23

Smart, James, 57, 194

Smelting: in BC, 29, 36, 67, 114–15, 117–18, 120, 130, 138, 232, 237, 239–40, 259. See also Trail smelter. In US, 23–5, 30–1, 36, 42, 62, 64, 67, 114, 116, 117–18, 138, 232, 235, 246, 259

Smith, Sir Donald A. (later Lord Strathcona), 3, 7, 8, 18, 20, 178, 197, 201, 216, 217, 220, 249

Smith, Frank, 14

Soo line, 70, 76, 101, 106, 138

Sorby, Thomas, 149, 151

Souris Branch (CPR), 179

Southern Alberta Irrigation Company, 20

Southern Okanagan Land Company, 136

South Kootenay Board of Trade, 63

Southern Minnesota Railroad, 6, 7

South Shore line (CPR), 76, 95

Spencer, Robert C., 10

Spiral Tunnels (CPR), 133, 144, 260–1

Spokane, 23, 24, 25, 64, 139, 140

Spokane and Kootenai Railway, 138–9

Spokane Falls. See Spokane

Spokane Falls and Northern Railroad (SF&N), 24–5, 46, 67, 108, 115, 138, 233

Spokane International Railway, 139–40, 260

Steele, Sir Samuel B., 53, 54, 58, 59

Stephen, George, 4, 7, 8, 9, 15, 18, 19, 174, 177, 216, 217

Stewart, Robert H., 244

Strathcona, 86, 99, 100, 225–7

Strathcona City Council, 226

Strathcona, Lord. See Sir Donald A. Smith

Stratton, James, 130

Sullivan, J.G., 138, 145

Summerland Development Company, 122

Susman, J.H., 30

Sutherland, Hugh, 112

Sutherland, James, 64

Swales, Francis S., 153

Tarte, Joseph Israel, 65, 82, 90, 117–18

Tatlow, R.G., 124, 132–3

Taylor, Charles, 138

Taylor, E.F., 248

Temiskaming and Northern Ontario Railway, 89

Templeman, William, 67

Territorial Grain Growers' Association, 82–3

Thomas Robertson and Company, 242

Thompson, Sir John, 27–8

Timber on CPR lands, 252–7

Timmerman, H.P., 96

Todd, Frederick, 230

Toronto Board of Trade, 64

Toronto, Grey and Bruce Railway, 20

Trail smelter, 61, 109, 118, 121–2, 227, 232–43, 246, 263

Troup, J.W., 141, 157–8

Trusts and Guarantee Company, 130

Tupper, Sir Charles, 32, 47, 51–2, 65, 217

Turner, George, 138

Turner, John H., 34–5, 37

Tuttle, Lucius, 148

Tye, William F., 65–6, 114, 131, 138

Union Pacific Railroad, 174

Union Trust Company of Toronto, 186

Urban policies (CPR), chap. 9, *passim*, 261–2. *See also* names of major Western cities

Vancouver, 3, 111, 127, 129, 138, 151, 152, 157, 159, 204, 213–16, 228–30, 262

Vancouver and Coast Kootenay Railway, 128

Vancouver Board of Trade, 35, 38, 64, 128, 229

Vancouver City Council, 38, 215

Vancouver, Victoria and Eastern Railway (VV&E), 38, 110–12, 114, 115, 120, 126, 127–9, 136, 253, 259–60; alliance with Canadian Northern Railway, 137; conflict with KVR, 136–7

Van Horne, Adeline (daughter of William Cornelius and Lucy Adeline), 6

Van Horne, Cornelius (father of William Cornelius), 5

Van Horne, Lucy Adeline (wife of William Cornelius), 6

Van Horne, Mary. *See* Mary Richards

Van Horne, Richard Benedict (son of William Cornelius and Lucy Adeline), 6

Van Horne, William Cornelius (later Sir William), xi, 3, 4, 7, 11, 12, 13,

20, 24, 26, 27–8, 29, 62, 67, 69, 71, 109, 148, 149, 150, 160–2, 171, 178, 182, 214–15, 216, 234–5, 236, 237, 238, 263; and 1891 election, 15, 16, 17; and 1911 election, 16; and KRVR Bill, 63–5; becomes president of CPR, 9; Bow River Scheme, 189–91; CPR career 1882–8, 8–9; construction of Crow's Nest Pass Railway, chap. 3, *passim*; Crow's Nest Pass Railway negotiations, 31–44; early life, 5; railway career in US, 5–8; retirement as president of CPR, 72–3

Van Horne, William (son of William Cornelius), 6

Van Horne, Sir William. *See* William Cornelius Van Horne

Victoria, 111, 138, 157, 159, 214, 227–8, 262

Victoria Board of Trade, 64, 127, 128, 157, 160, 168, 256

Victoria City Council, 160

Victoria Tourist Association, 160–1

VV&E. *See* Vancouver, Victoria and Eastern Railway

Wainwright, William, 64, 89

Wallace, N. Clarke, 30

War Eagle Consolidated Mining and Development Company, 235

Warren, James John, 130–1, 132, 133, 135, 136, 137, 138

Washington and Great

Northern Railway, 112, 115

Washington State, 138

Waterlow, George S., 243

Wedekind, E.H., 233

Wellington Colliery Company, 142

Western Canada Land Company, 186

West Kootenay Mining Protective Association, 63

West Kootenay Power and Light Company, 238, 243–4

West Kootenays, 30, 38, 50, 111, 116, 138, 232, 236, 237, 238, 259

Westinghouse, Church, Kerr and Co., 230

Westminster, 127

Weston Shops (Winnipeg), 222, 224

White, Frederick, 59

Whyte, William (later Sir William), 14, 22, 53, 74, 80, 84, 85, 87, 101–4, 119, 124, 140, 154, 155, 184, 194, 197, 198–9, 226, 250, 255–6, 260; CPR career, 1884–97, 74; early life, 74; joins CPR, 74; retirement, 102–3

Willison, Sir John S., 32, 33

Wilson, Charles, 254

Wilson, Sir Charles Rivers, 89, 90, 91, 93

Winnipeg, 7, 85, 153–6, 216–19, 222–4, 228–9, 261–2

Winnipeg Board of Trade, 43, 64, 84, 216, 218–19, 223

Winnipeg City Council, 216–18

Winnipeg Trades and Labour Council, 59–60

Wood, E.R., 115

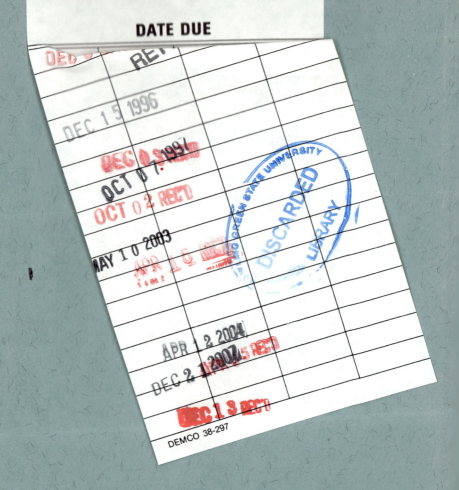